THE THEODORE ROOSEVELT TREASURY

Theodore Roosevelt

The
Theodore Roosevelt
Treasury

A SELF-PORTRAIT FROM HIS WRITINGS

COMPILED AND WITH AN INTRODUCTION BY

Hermann Hagedorn

G. P. Putnam's Sons   New York

Library of Congress Catalog Card Number: 57-11713

The selections from Theodore Roosevelt's writings pre-sented in this book are taken mainly from the National Edition of his Collected Works *published by Charles Scrib-ner's Sons (referred to as "Works"), from his* Collected Letters, *published by the Harvard University Press (referred to as "Letters"), and from the* Letters from Theodore Roose-velt to Anna Roosevelt Cowles (referred to as "Cowles").

Note

The editor is indebted to the generous co-operation of Mr. James A. Garfield, son of President Roosevelt's Secretary of the Interior, in the preparation of this book, and welcomes the opportunity to record his appreciation of his discriminating understanding of Mr. Roosevelt's writings and personality.

The editor's indebtedness extends further to Miss Helen MacLachlan, who recorded, page by page, the sources of the selections; and to his wife, who bore with him in the periods of inhuman concentration which, in the midst of days already crowded, the work demanded.

H.H.

Contents

CONTENTS

CONTENTS

President

Father of a Family

Man of Letters

Adventurer in the Wide Waste Spaces

Friend of Cowboys and Kings

Preacher

Fighter for Social Justice

Defender of the Faith

Introduction

IN his maturity, Theodore Roosevelt had so clear a sense of direction that even those who knew him best might have assumed that politics had been his youth's imperative choice of a profession. In his *Autobiography*, written when he was in his middle fifties, Mr. Roosevelt himself dealt with that assumption. He had originally planned to be a field naturalist, he revealed. He recalled how he had briefly studied law and, before he left college, had made a considerable foray into the realm of historical writing. He enjoyed political life but was convinced, into his middle thirties— or, at least, thought he was convinced—that he could take it or leave it with no inner upheaval either way. We know the lure that the life of a ranchman exercised upon him during the years following the death of his first wife. He was for a time, in the 1880's, a supposedly "silent partner" in a New York publishing house, though evidently not silent enough to permit the partnership to prosper or endure.

With all his activity in these divers fields, he never, in his twenties, kept his eye for long off what appears to have been his major ambition. He wanted to be a writer. He did, in fact, write many books in the course of his crowded life, all of them vigorous and entertaining even to subsequent generations, some of them substantial contributions to history or science. But any ambition to write such books was not the wolf that, in his youth, gnawed at his vitals. He was not thinking then of being an agreeable narrator of hunting adventures, or the journeyman whose capacity to express himself with his pen was a useful and rather rare adjunct of the equipment of the American politician. He wanted to be an artist whose work would gain recognition not for what he said but for what he left unsaid and not only for the *what* of it but for the *how*. His college clubmate, Owen Wister, he noted, had a way with him in his writings that Roosevelt longed to have, and despaired of ever acquiring. He was thinking, it is safe to assume, though he did not say so, of the magic of the creative imagination.

15

At rare moments in his life—brief moments when he was shaken by the enchantment of a mockingbird's song, the memory of a personal experience of the majesty and awe of some remnant of primeval wilderness, the inspiration of a great vision of social and political progress, or the stab of a sorrow for which there seemed to be no solace, short of the grave—he actually became the magician in words he ever longed to be. But a handful of laurel leaves will not suffice for a wreath, though you may cherish the handful and speculate on what it might imply.

Even when he was in his thirties, before the effects of a charge up a Cuban hillside, or high public office, had laid their claims upon him, Roosevelt lamented to a correspondent about the pressures that modern life exerted upon the writer who took his work seriously. There were so many people asking you to address this group or that—for a fee that steak at twenty-five cents a pound, and rising, made essential in the eking out of a meager government salary. There were so many editors and publishers dangling urgently needed dollars before your eyes and imploring you to write casual articles or brief condensations, in book form, of the serious works with which you were associated in the public mind. What Roosevelt was saying, in effect, was that if you had a large and happily hungry family, you became a hack, and the artist you longed to be retired to the Never-neverland.

When, actually, fame plummeted out of the blue like an eagle and lit first on one and then on the other of the eagles that adorned the new national hero's shoulders, the pressures became irresistible. There were the politicians arranging for his nomination for the governorship. There was the dear public, writing letters deposited by the bushel-basket in the Gun Room on the top floor of Sagamore Hill; there were editors and more editors offering what Roosevelt himself recognized as "ridiculous" sums, that promised a respite at last from the perennial pursuit of financial solvency. Under those circumstances you did not write; you dictated, striding up and down, assembling out of your capacious memory the biography of Oliver Cromwell, or adjuring your countrymen to be good in order that they might be useful.

If a gubernatorial candidate had no time to be an artist, a Governor and a President obviously had less. The wonder is not that the hunting books and the occasional essays or reviews or introductions to other men's books, that Roosevelt wrote as President, lack the precisely fashioned or imaginative phrase that lifts narrative or argument into the domain of literature. The thing that is surprising is that these products of such leisure as is granted any President, are as good reporting, as carefully considered criticism as they are. After a half century, they make good reading still. If his Presidency had fallen in a more troubled time that might have stirred

16

his emotions as the primeval wilderness or the death of his son Quentin stirred them, his inaugural address and Thanksgiving proclamations might conceivably have achieved poetic power comparable to the passages these other occasions inspired. But that *if* belongs in the domain of the seraphim.

2

Roosevelt, in his narrative writings, was essentially the reporter, observing closely and accurately, and recounting his observations in a lively style with what might be called high entertainment value. This is true of his hunting stories, which abound in descriptions of the species he was at the moment pursuing—its appearance, its habits and its environment. It is true also of his accounts of ranch life in the Dakotas in the middle 1880's and of the hunters and other frontiersmen whom he met and studied with admiration mixed with amused wonder at the revelation of values startlingly new to his experience. It is true furthermore of his early studies of the political animal as he encountered it in the New York Assembly, and in his efforts, in New York and Washington, to clean up the running ulcers of the Spoils System.

There are charming passages in his early hunting books and in his accounts of his ranching life, pictures of fantastic scenes, of storms in the mountains and on the prairie, of sunrises and sunsets, in which, in a few lines, he fixes a mood. There are memories of lovely birdsong, lovingly dwelt on. He recalls them not as a naturalist or an ornithologist but as a poet. It is a case of "emotion, recollected in tranquillity." He has been stirred and, as he remembers the experience, he puts it into words that, seemingly without effort, convey the mood to the reader. These passages, brief though they be, are, I contend, literature of a high order.[1]

Roosevelt's accounts of the Santiago campaign and the story of his grueling exploration of the River of Doubt in Brazil differ markedly from his earlier narratives of adventures in the wilds, on which he reported when he had leisure to dwell upon details and re-experience a mood. The book that Roosevelt called *The Rough Riders* and Finley Peter Dunne

[1] They also raise a question. Roosevelt had an exceptionally acute ear for birdsong and the capacity to remember the songs of numberless different species over a period of a quarter-century. Walking in England's New Forest in 1910 with the British foreign minister, Sir Edward Grey, he was able to identify every bird that he heard, though he had last heard English birds singing a quarter-century before. The feat seems sufficiently remarkable by itself, but it must be linked to Roosevelt's almost total lack of ear for music played on instruments or produced by human vocal chords, his almost complete inability to distinguish one tune from another. He could tell "America" from the "Star-Spangled Banner," he boasted, but that was as far as his musical discrimination went. It is a nice problem for speculation by musically minded psychologists.

(the beloved "Mr. Dooley") called *Alone in Cubia,* was dictated between visits of politicians and interviews with newspapermen. The story is bare and, in view of the extraordinarily varied character of the regiment's personnel and Roosevelt's perennial delight in frontier types, curiously lacking in color. The River of Doubt story was literally "on the spot reporting," written from day to day by Roosevelt, sitting on a camp stool with his head swathed in mosquito netting and his heart never free long enough from the dread of imminent disaster to the expedition to find that tranquillity in which emotion becomes sublimated in poetry.

3

The fact is that writing came hard to Roosevelt. He had to struggle for what he got. He wrote and revised, rewrote and revised again, as some of his manuscripts and typescripts bear witness. Speeches on political themes, articles on moral issues, he could throw off with zest and little difficulty, but pieces that required careful phrasing took more time and leisure than he was generally able to give them. The magnificent conclusion of his address as president of the American Historical Association which he called "History as Literature"—rich in images, color and rhythmic movement, as it is—was made possible only by the political defeat that preceded its composition.

In the Bull Moose campaign of 1912 Roosevelt had fought to raise American political life to levels which the defenders of the *status quo* had desperately and successfully resisted. He was in the social and political doghouse, shunned by old friends because he had defied the Party that had made him President and, member of the social élite that he was, had "turned against his class." No one pressed him to make speeches or write articles, that bleak December of 1912. Few of his North Shore neighbors even called. For the first time in his life he was lonely, desperately lonely, seeing himself, at fifty-four, at the end of his career; at the end, perhaps, even of his pubic usefulness. To "hear grate on the coast of Britain the keels of the Low Dutch sea-thieves" was a life-saver for him; to "see as living men the hard-faced archers of Agincourt and the warworn spearsmen who followed Alexander down beyond the rim of the known world" was balm to his bruised spirit. More poignantly to him than to the assembled scholars who would hear him speak the words, "the warhorns of King Olaf wailed across the flood."

In defeat and isolation Roosevelt achieved what popular acclaim and political triumph never let him achieve—a passage of enduring literature.

4

A reasonable case might be made out for Roosevelt as a frustrated poet, whose promising career in literature was blighted in the bud by a citizen's dismay at political corruption and the conviction that he was obligated to do something about it and call his countrymen to repentance; blighted too perhaps by an itch to make the big and lesser wheels of the nation's political life turn at his will and by the love of the smoke and dust of battle in his nostrils.

But the "frustrated poet" who, only at long intervals, found sufficient leisure to write as well as he could write, is not the whole story. Some of Roosevelt's best writing is in his letters and most of them—and, among them, the most notable—were dictated, coming hot off his heart and mind and seldom revised except for a word, here and there. They are none of them poetry as certain passages noted above are poetry, but some of them are close to it. The account of the banquet in Butte, Montana, in Roosevelt's long narrative letter to John Hay, written in 1903, paints an episode of the epic struggle for power in American industry with a kind of Homeric vividness. Few of Roosevelt's formal writings have the ease, the charm or the force of his letters to the British historian, George Otto Trevelyan. The secret is not in the dictation; the books he dictated have none of the ease, the charm or the force of his letters; it is in the fact that the books were composed for the public but the letters for a single individual. A man is talking to a friend—or, occasionally, to an ex-friend, as in this immortal bit:

> SIR: When I spoke of the Progressive Party as having a lunatic fringe, I specifically had you in mind. On the supposition that you are of entire sound mind, I should be obliged to say that you are absolutely dishonorable and untruthful. I prefer to accept the former alternative. YOURS TRULY. . . .

5

No critic will presumably be called upon to appraise Roosevelt's exhortations to his countrymen as literature. He never intended them to be such. Being a public leader with an instinctive and imaginative understanding of the hearts and minds he was trying to reach, he recognized that, in his public addresses, imaginative utterance was out of place, and eloquence might benumb rather than enlighten. There were things that he wanted to say and nothing mattered except his saying them so clearly that his hearers would understand, and so vigorously that they might realize that it was important they *should* understand.

He had that aim when he entered political life at the age of twenty-three; he still had it when death withdrew him from the field thirty-seven years later. His purpose impelled him to use simple words that were within the confines of any man's vocabulary and to arrange them in sentences that said what he meant and left no one in doubt what that might be. In his style, he hit his stride early, and he maintained it, for good or ill, unchanged, throughout his life, so that the beginning of a statement—made, say, in 1886—may be linked without a jar to the conclusion of a similar statement, made in 1916. What he said in his efforts to instruct his fellow citizens in the way that they should go was never profound in the sense that its comprehension required concentrated thought or a background of knowledge or philosophic reasoning. It was profound only in that it had a way, sooner or later, of recalling the law that underlies all law, those all-too-familiar Ten Commandments, whose contemporary application he pinpointed so disturbingly. Platitudes? Can it be said that a word, however ancient and time-worn, is a platitude if it stings a slumbering conscience awake? What the President said made a great many people squirm and want to be different: rich people as well as poor people. It hit them where they lived, and made them want to live on a level higher than that on which they actually did live.

"Words with me are instruments," he once explained to a foreign editor who lamented what he called the President's "platitudes." "I am not trying to be subtle or original; I am trying to make the plain everyday citizen here in America stand for the things which I regard as essential to good government." Perhaps the cultivated and slightly supercilious people who jeered at the President's platitudes—and the impression he gave of being "the first that ever burst into that silent sea" laid him open to jeers—read or heard the words only. The ordinary, hard-working men and women, struggling to make ends meet, and not always succeeding too well for the reason that certain men had more power than was good for the majority or even for themselves, these people were conscious of more than words. The farmers and mechanics, the housewives and schoolteachers, and—with these, curiously enough, a not inconsiderable number of capitalists and industrial executives—whom he adjured, scolded, uplifted, inspired and occasionally made into new men—read or heard his words, interwoven, as it were, with action; carefully directed, continuous and determined action. They were seeing a President who was trying to adjust a balance in American life that had somehow got askew, a President—who seemed also a personal friend—trying to build a better future for them and their children, and, at the same time, to hold on to the best of the past.

What they heard when he spoke were not words; they were a life, speaking to *their* lives; and no life, nobly lived, is a platitude. It was, in

20

the case of this man, energy, ambition, zest, love, fire, struggle, aspiration, tenderness, sacrifice, courage, resolution; all these, disciplined and distilled.

To the Greeks, absorbed in the delights of philosophical discussion, certain words, we are told, were "foolishness." To the humble of heart, suffering hunger and thirst, those same words were bread and wine, hope and rebirth.

It was by simple, direct words, dealing with everyday human relations; words, repeated, *ad infinitum,* and, to some, *ad nauseam;* adjurations, dramatized in action and occasionally embellished with gestures in the direction of prison gates, ominously opening, that Theodore Roosevelt, in seven and a half brief years, focussed and galvanized the aspirations of a whole generation and visibly raised the level of American political, financial and industrial life.

In these adjurations, the practical leader of men, speaking to his fellow citizens in the common tongue of ten thousand Main Streets, once or twice yielded the platform to the frustrated poet within; never more persuasively than in the passage of a political speech that brought even his enemies to their feet:

> We, here in America, hold in our hands the hope of the world, the fate of the coming years; and shame and disgrace will be ours if in our eyes the light of high resolve is dimmed, if we trail in the dust the golden hopes of men.

The passage tells something of the reason why a President, who was also a kind of Old Testament prophet, did not allow himself the leisure to become the great writer he might have been.

6

It tells something else. This man of action, this extrovert (as he seemed to many) had a fire inside him that sought and found expression in individual, authentic rhythms. The theme of the passage—even many of the words—were not new in his addresses. He had used them partially and ineffectually before, as William Jennings Bryan had used the concluding passage of his Cross of Gold speech all over the West, in tentative form, before he clinched the Democratic nomination for the Presidency with it in 1896. What gave Roosevelt's words their imperishable quality was his recognition that, at the meeting he was to address in New York in March, 1912, he would be making a final appeal to the Republican leaders to face what he regarded as the "fundamental issue" of the approaching campaign: Were the American people fit to govern themselves?

The man on fire is the final aspect of the many-faceted individual who paints his own portrait in these pages. It is a portrait made from a thousand sketches, drawn in action and in repose, with no thought of a self-portrait, or of the sketch itself as anything of significance beyond its immediate use. For certain aspects of his subject, moreover, the painter made no sketches, and there are questions, therefore, to which the portrait offers no answers. With such inevitable blanks, and recognizing fully his limitations as the assembler of a vast jigsaw puzzle, the editor dares go beyond the obvious "This is the writer," to say, with assurance, "This is the man."

HERMANN HAGEDORN

Ranchman

Mr. Roosevelt went to the Bad Lands of what was then Dakota Territory, briefly in the fall of 1883, to hunt buffalo. He became enchanted with the wild country, the fantastic landscape and the people he met and, when his wife, Alice, died in childbirth, established a cattle ranch on the Little Missouri River and made it his headquarters until a call to run for Mayor of New York in 1886 brought him back East.

1. It Was Still the Wild West

It was still the Wild West in those days, the far West, the West of Owen Wister's stories and Frederic Remington's drawings, the West of the Indian and the buffalo-hunter, the soldier and the cow-puncher. That land of the West has gone now, "gone, gone with lost Atlantis," gone to the isle of ghosts and of strange dead memories. It was a land of vast silent spaces, of lonely rivers, and of plains where the wild game stared at the passing horseman. It was a land of scattered ranches, of herds of long-horned cattle, and of reckless riders who unmoved looked in the eyes of life or of death. In that land we led a free and hardy life, with horse and with rifle. We worked under the scorching midsummer sun, when the wide plains shimmered and wavered in the heat; and we knew the freezing misery of riding night guard round the cattle in the late fall round-up. In the soft springtime the stars were glorious in our eyes each night before we fell asleep; and in the winter we rode through blinding blizzards, when the driven snow-dust burned our faces. There were monotonous days, as we guided the trail cattle or the beef herds, hour after hour, at the slowest of walks; and minutes or hours teeming with excitement as we stopped stampedes or swam the herds across rivers treacherous with quicksands or brimmed with running ice. We knew toil and hardship and hunger and thirst; and we saw men die violent deaths as they worked among the horses

23

and cattle, or fought in evil feuds with one another; but we felt the beat of hardy life in our veins, and ours was the glory of work and the joy of living.[1]

2. *The Home Ranch*

My home-ranch lies on both sides of the Little Missouri, the nearest ranchman above me being about twelve, and the nearest below me about ten, miles distant. . . .

We breakfast early—before dawn when the nights have grown long, and rarely later than sunrise, even in midsummer. Perhaps before this meal, certainly the instant it is over, the man whose duty it is rides off to hunt up and drive in the saddle band. Each of us has his own string of horses, eight or ten in number, and the whole band usually splits up into two or three companies. In addition to the scattered groups of the saddle band, our six or eight mares, with their colts, keep by themselves, and are rarely bothered by us, as no cowboy ever rides anything but horses, because mares give great trouble where all the animals have to be herded together. Once every two or three days somebody rides round and finds out where each of these smaller bands is, but the man who goes out in the morning merely gathers one bunch. He drives these into the corral, the other men . . . coming out with their ropes as soon as they hear the patter of the unshod hoofs and the shouts of the cowboy driver. Going into the corral, and standing near the centre, each of us picks out some one of his own string from among the animals that are trotting and running in a compact mass round the circle; and after one or more trials, according to his skill, ropes it and leads it out. When all have caught their horses the rest are again turned loose, together with those that have been kept up overnight. . . .

Once saddled, the men ride off on their different tasks; for almost everything is done in the saddle. . . .

If any horses have strayed, one or two of the men will be sent off to look for them; for hunting lost horses is one of the commonest and most irksome of our duties. . . .

If the men do not go horse-hunting, they may ride off over the range; for there is generally some work to be done among the cattle, such as driving in and branding calves that have been overlooked by the round-up, or getting some animal out of a bog-hole. . . .

The long forenoon's work, with its attendant mishaps to man and beast, being over, the men who have been out among the horses and cattle come riding in, to be joined by their fellows—if any there be—who have

[1] Autobiography (1913). *Works XX,* pp. 96–7.

been hunting or haying or chopping wood. The midday dinner is variable as to time, for it comes when the men have returned from their work; but, whatever be the hour, it is the most substantial meal of the day, and we feel that we have little fault to find with a table on the clean cloth of which are spread platters of smoked elk meat, loaves of good bread, jugs and bowls of milk, saddles of venison or broiled antelope-steaks, perhaps roast and fried prairie-chickens with eggs, butter, wild plums, and tea or coffee.

The afternoon's tasks are usually much the same as the morning's, but this time is often spent in doing the odds and ends; as, for instance, it may be devoted to breaking in a new horse. Large outfits generally hire a bronco-buster to do this; but we ourselves almost always break our own horses, two or three of my men being pretty good riders, although none of them can claim to be anything out of the common. . . .

A ranchman's work is, of course, free from much of the sameness attendant upon that of a mere cowboy. One day he will ride out with his men among the cattle, or after strayed horses; the next he may hunt, so as to keep the ranch in meat; then he can make the tour of his outlying camps; or, again, may join one of the round-ups for a week or two, perhaps keeping with it the entire time it is working. On occasions he will have a good deal of spare time on his hands, which, if he chooses, he can spend in reading or writing. If he cares for books, there will be many a worn volume in the primitive little sitting-room, with its log walls and huge fireplace; but after a hard day's work a man will not read much, but will rock to and fro in the flickering firelight, talking sleepily over his success in the day's chase and the difficulty he has had with the cattle; or else may simply lie stretched at full length on the elkhides and wolfskins in front of the hearthstone, listening in drowsy silence to the roar and crackle of the blazing logs and to the moaning of the wind outside. . . .

The early rides in the spring mornings have a charm all their own, for they are taken when, for the one and only time during the year, the same brown landscape of these high plains turns to a vivid green, as the new grass sprouts and the trees and bushes thrust forth the young leaves; and at dawn, with the dew glittering everywhere, all things show at their best and freshest. The flowers are out and a man may gallop for miles at a stretch with his horse's hoofs sinking at every stride into the carpet of prairie-roses, whose short stalks lift the beautiful blossoms but a few inches from the ground. Even in the waste places the cactuses are blooming; and one kind in particular, a dwarfish, globular plant, with its mass of splendid crimson flowers, glows against the sides of the gray buttes like a splash of flame. . . .

In the hot noontide hours of midsummer the broad ranch veranda, always in the shade, is almost the only spot where a man can be comfortable;

but here he can sit for hours at a time, leaning back in his rocking-chair, as he reads or smokes, or with half-closed, dreamy eyes gazes across the shallow, nearly dry river-bed to the wooded bottoms opposite, and to the plateaus lying back of them. Against the sheer white faces of the cliffs, that come down without a break, the dark-green tree-tops stand out in bold relief. In the hot, lifeless air all objects that are not near by seem to sway and waver. There are few sounds to break the stillness. From the upper branches of the cottonwood-trees overhead—whose shimmering, tremulous leaves are hardly ever quiet, but if the wind stirs at all, rustle and quiver and sigh all day long—comes every now and then the soft, melancholy cooing of the mourning-dove, whose voice always seems far away and expresses more than any other sound in nature the sadness of gentle, hopeless, never-ending grief. The other birds are still; and very few animals move about. Now and then the black shadow of a wheeling vulture falls on the sun-scorched ground. The cattle, that have strung down in long files from the hills, lie quietly on the sand-bars, except that some of the bulls keep travelling up and down, bellowing and routing or giving vent to long, surly grumblings as they paw the sand and toss it up with their horns. At times the horses, too, will come down to drink, and to splash and roll in the water. . . .

In making a journey over ground we know, during the hot weather we often prefer to ride by moonlight. The moon shines very brightly through the dry, clear night air, turning the gray buttes into glimmering silver; and the horses travel far more readily and easily than under the glaring noonday sun. The road between my upper and lower ranch-houses is about forty miles long, sometimes following the river-bed, and then again branching off inland, crossing the great plateaus and winding through the ravines of the broken country. It is a five hours' fair ride; and so, in a hot spell, we like to take it during the cool of the night, starting at sunset. After nightfall the face of the country seems to alter marvellously, and the clear moonlight only intensifies the change. The river gleams like running quicksilver, and the moonbeams play over the grassy stretches of the plateaus and glance off the wind-rippled blades as they would from water. The Bad Lands seem to be stranger and wilder than ever, the silvery rays turning the country into a kind of grim fairy-land. The grotesque, fantastic outlines of the higher cliffs stand out with startling clearness, while the lower buttes have become formless, misshapen masses, and the deep gorges are in black shadow; in the darkness there will be no sound but the rhythmic echo of the hoof-beats of the horses, and the steady, metallic clank of the steel bridle-chains.[2]

[2] "Hunting Trips of a Ranchman" (1885). *Works I*, pp. 294–311.

3. A Trip on the Prairie

I started in the very earliest morning, when the intense brilliancy of the stars had just begun to pale before the first streak of dawn. By the time I left the river-bottom and struck off up the valley of a winding creek, which led through the Bad Lands, the eastern sky was growing rosy; and soon the buttes and cliffs were lit up by the level rays of the cloudless summer sun. The air was fresh and sweet, and odorous with the sweet scents of the springtime that was but barely passed; the dew lay heavy, in glittering drops, on the leaves and the blades of grass, whose vivid green, at this season, for a short time brightens the desolate and sterile-looking wastes of the lonely Western plains. The rose-bushes were all in bloom, and their pink blossoms clustered in every point and bend of the stream; and the sweet, sad songs of the hermit-thrushes rose from the thickets, while the meadow-larks perched boldly in sight as they uttered their louder and more cheerful music. The round-up had passed by our ranch, and all the cattle with our brands—the Maltese cross and cut dewlap, or the elk-horn and triangle—had been turned loose; they had not yet worked away from the river, and I rode by long strings of them, walking in single file off to the hills, or standing in groups to look at me as I passed.

Leaving the creek, I struck off among a region of scoria buttes, the ground rising into rounded hills, through whose grassy covering the red volcanic rock showed in places, while boulder-like fragments of it were scattered all through the valleys between. There were a few clumps of bushes here and there, and near one of them were two magpies, who lit on an old buffalo skull, bleached white by sun and snow. . . .

After passing the last line of low, rounded scoria buttes, the horse stepped out on the border of the great, seemingly endless stretches of rolling or nearly level prairie, over which I had planned to travel and hunt for the next two or three days. . . . Nowhere, not even at sea, does a man feel more lonely than when riding over the far-reaching, seemingly never-ending plains; and after a man has lived a little while on or near them, their very vastness and loneliness and their melancholy monotony have a strong fascination for him. The landscape seems always the same, and after the traveller has plodded on for miles and miles he gets to feel as if the distance was indeed boundless. As far as the eye can see there is no break; either the prairie stretches out into perfectly level flats, or else there are gentle, rolling slopes, whose crests mark the divides between the drainage systems of the different creeks; and when one of these is ascended, immediately another precisely like it takes its place in the distance, and so

27

roll succeeds roll in a succession as interminable as that of the waves of the ocean. Nowhere else does one seem so far off from all mankind; the plains stretch out in deathlike and measureless expanse, and as he journeys over them they will for many miles be lacking in all signs of life. Although he can see so far, yet all objects on the outermost verge of the horizon, even though within the ken of his vision, look unreal and strange; for there is no shade to take away from the bright glare, and at a little distance things seem to shimmer and dance in the hot rays of the sun. The ground is scorched to a dull brown, and against its monotonous expanse any objects stand out with a prominence that makes it difficult to judge of the distance at which they are. A mile off one can see, through the strange shimmering haze, the shadowy white outlines of something which looms vaguely up till it looks as large as the canvas top of a prairie wagon; but as the horseman comes nearer it shrinks and dwindles and takes clearer form, until at last it changes into the ghastly staring skull of some mighty buffalo, long dead and gone to join the rest of his vanished race. . . .

The sun was just setting when we crossed the final ridge and came in sight of as singular a bit of country as I have ever seen. The cowboys, as we afterward found, had christened the place "Medicine Buttes." In plains dialect, I may explain, "Medicine" has been adopted from the Indians, among whom it means anything supernatural or very unusual. It is used in the sense of "magic," or "out of the common."

Over an irregular tract of gently rolling sandy hills, perhaps about three-quarters of a mile square, were scattered several hundred detached and isolated buttes or cliffs of sandstone, each butte from fifteen to fifty feet high, and from thirty to a couple of hundred feet across. Some of them rose as sharp peaks or ridges, or as connected chains, but much the greater number had flat tops like little table-lands. The sides were perfectly perpendicular, and were cut and channelled by the weather into most extraordinary forms: caves, columns, battlements, spires, and flying buttresses were mingled in the strangest confusion. Many of the caves were worn clear through the buttes, and they were at every height in the sides, while ledges ran across the faces, and shoulders and columns jutted out from the corners. On the tops and at the bases of most of the cliffs grew pine-trees, some of considerable height, and the sand gave everything a clean, white look.

Altogether, it was as fantastically beautiful a place as I have ever seen; it seemed impossible that the hand of man should not have had something to do with its formation. There was a spring of clear cold water a few hundred yards off, with good feed for the horses round it; and we made our camp at the foot of one of the largest buttes, building a roaring pine-log fire in an angle in the face of the cliff, while our beds were under the pine-trees. It was the time of the full moon, and the early part of the night was clear. The flame of the fire leaped up the side of the cliff, the red light bringing out into lurid and ghastly relief the bold corners and strange-looking escarpments of the rock, while against it the stiff limbs of the pines stood out like rigid bars of iron. Walking off out of sight of the circle of firelight, among the tall crags, the place seemed almost as unreal as if we had been in fairyland. The flood of clear moonlight turned the white faces of the cliffs and the grounds between them into shining silver, against which the pines showed dark and sombre, while the intensely black shadows of the buttes took on forms that were grimly fantastic. Every cave or cranny in the crags looked so black that it seemed almost to be thrown out from the surface, and when the branches of the trees moved, the bright moonlight danced on the ground as if it were a sheet of molten metal. Neither in shape nor in color did our surroundings seem to belong to the dull gray world through which we had been travelling all day.[3]

4. "A Boyish Ambition of Mine"

To Anna Roosevelt[4]

Little Missouri
June 23d/84

For the last week I have been fulfilling a boyish ambition of mine—that is, I have been playing at frontier hunter in good earnest, having been off entirely alone, with my horse and rifle on the prairie. I wanted to see if I could not do perfectly well without a guide, and I succeeded beyond my expectations. I shot a couple of antelope and a deer, and missed a great many more. I felt as absolutely free as a man could feel; as you know I do not mind loneliness; and I enjoyed the trip to the utmost. The only disagreeable incident was one day when it rained. Otherwise the weather was lovely, and every night I would lie wrapped up in my blanket looking at the stars till I fell asleep, in the cool air. The country has widely different aspects in different places; one day I would canter hour after hour over the level green grass, or through miles of wild rose thickets, all in bloom; on the next I would be amidst the savage desolation of the Bad Lands, with their dreary plateaus, fantastically shaped buttes and deep, winding canyons. I enjoyed the trip greatly and have never been in better health.[5]

[3] "Hunting Trips of a Ranchman." *Works I*, pp. 150–66.
[4] Theodore Roosevelt's elder sister, later Mrs. William S. Cowles.
[5] *Cowles*, p. 59.

Chimney Butte Ranche
Aug. 17th, 1884

We have been delayed nearly a week by being forced to get some extra ponies; however I was rather glad of it, as I wished to look thoroughly through the cattle before going. Tomorrow morning early we start out. Merrifield and I go on horseback, each taking a spare pony, which will be led behind the wagon, a light "prairie schooner" drawn by two stout horses, and driven by an old French halfbreed. I wear a sombrero, silk neckerchief, fringed buckskin shirt, sealskin chaparajos or riding trowsers; alligator hide boots; and with my pearl-hilted revolver and beautifully finished Winchester rifle, I shall feel able to face anything. How long I will be gone I can not say; we will go in all nearly a thousand miles. If game is plenty and my success is good, I may return in six weeks; more probably I shall be out a couple of months; and if game is so scarce that we have to travel very far to get to it, or if our horses give out or run away, or we get caught by the snow, we may be out very much longer—till towards Xmas; though I will try to be back to vote.

Yesterday I rode 72 miles between dawn and darkness; I have a superb roan pony, or rather horse; he looks well, with his beautifully carved saddle, plated bridle, and silver inlaid bit, and seems to be absolutely tireless.

I grow very fond of this place, and it certainly has a desolate, grim beauty of its own, that has a curious fascination for me. The grassy, scantily wooded bottoms through which the winding river flows are bounded by bare, jagged buttes; their fantastic shapes and sharp, steep edges throw the most curious shadows, under the cloudless, glaring sky; and at evening I love to sit out in front of the hut and see their hard, gray outlines gradually grow soft and purple as the flaming sunset by degrees softens and dies away; while my days I spend generally alone, riding through the lonely rolling prairie and broken lands.[6]

Dickenson, Dakota
April 12th/86

My trip down the river after the three thieves was a grand success, as far as catching the men we were after goes. I took Sewall and Dow along (both of whom were as determined allies as any man could wish) as there was the chance of a fight. But there was no difficulty whatever. We came upon their camp by surprise and, covering them with our cocked

[6] *Ibid.,* pp. 62–3.

rifles "held them up" and disarmed them in the most approved Western fashion. Then we got caught in an ice jam, however, and had the pleasure of their company for eight days, of course having to watch them like hawks all the time. Then my patience gave out and I sent Sewall and Dow on in the boats, while I took the three captives out on a two days' overland trip to here, where I gave them up to the Sheriff, and was heartily glad to get rid of them, too.

This winter has certainly been a marvellously good one for cattle. My loss has been so trifling as hardly to be worth taking into account; although there may be a number strayed off. I think my own expenses out here this summer will be very light indeed, and then we will be able to start all square with the beginning of the new year.

I took "Anna Karenina" along on the thief catching trip and read it through with much more interest than I have any other novel for I do not know how long. Tolstoi is a great writer. His curious habit of never commenting on any of the actions or thoughts of his characters, whether in the way of praise or blame, gives his writings a singularly unmoral (not immoral) aspect. Anna had a character so contradictory, unbalanced, melancholy and fiercely passionate that she can hardly be conceived as being other than partially insane. Ubronsky's faithfulness to and love for her make one forget his wrong doings; Striva, Dolly's husband, is to me the most repulsive character in the book; he is to me a complete proof of my theory that it is criminal folly for a woman to forgive her husband's infidelity and go on living with him; it comes from weakness or wrongheadedness. I do not think it can possibly be other than harmful, certainly not beneficial, to the children. Levine's and Kitty's story was very attractive.

I was struck by the way in which Russians evidently regard themselves out of the European world; perhaps this was the reason that the book seemed to me to show something curiously American in some of the sides of life it showed—much more than a German or French work would have.[7]

5. Winter Weather

When the days have dwindled to their shortest, and the nights seem never-ending, then all the great northern plains are changed into an abode of iron desolation. Sometimes furious gales blow out of the north, driving before them the clouds of blinding snow-dust, wrapping the mantle of death round every unsheltered being that faces their unshackled anger. They roar in a thunderous bass as they sweep across the prairie or whirl through the naked canyons; they shiver the great brittle cottonwoods, and beneath their rough touch the icy limbs of the pines that cluster in the

[7] *Ibid.,* pp. 73–5.

gorges sing like the chords of an Æolian harp. Again, in the coldest midwinter weather, not a breath of wind may stir; and then the still, merciless, terrible cold that broods over the earth like the shadow of silent death seems even more dreadful in its gloomy rigor than is the lawless madness of the storms. All the land is like granite; the great rivers stand still in their beds, as if turned to frosted steel. In the long nights there is no sound to break the lifeless silence. Under the ceaseless, shifting play of the Northern Lights, or lighted only by the wintry brilliance of the stars, the snow-clad plains stretch out into dead and endless wastes of glimmering white.

Then the great fireplace of the ranch-house is choked with blazing logs, and at night we have to sleep under so many blankets that the weight is fairly oppressive. Outside, the shaggy ponies huddle together in the corral, while long icicles hang from their lips, and the hoarfrost whitens the hollow backs of the cattle. For the ranchman the winter is occasionally a pleasant holiday, but more often an irksome period of enforced rest and gloomy foreboding. . . .[8]

The truth is, ours is a primitive industry, and we suffer the reverses as well as enjoy the successes only known to primitive peoples. A hard winter is to us in the north what a dry summer is to Texas or Australia—what seasons of famine once were to all peoples. We still live in an iron age that the old civilized world has long passed by. The men of the border reckon upon stern and unending struggles with their iron-bound surroundings; against the grim harshness of their existence they set the strength and the abounding vitality that come with it. They run risks to life and limb that are unknown to the dwellers in cities; and what the men freely brave, the beasts that they own must also sometimes suffer. . . .[9]

The morning we broke camp was so mild that I did not put on my heaviest winter clothing, starting off in the same that I had worn during the past few days' still-hunting among the hills. Before we had been gone an hour, however, the sky grew overcast and the wind began to blow from the north with constantly increasing vigor. The sky grew steadily more gloomy and lowering, the gusts came ever harder and harder, and by noon the winter day had darkened and a furious gale was driving against us. The blasts almost swept me from my saddle and the teamster from his seat, while we were glad to wrap ourselves in our huge fur coats to keep out the growing cold. Soon after midday the wagon suddenly broke down while we were yet in mid-prairie. It was evident that we were on the eve of a furious snow-blizzard, which might last a few hours, or else, perhaps, as many days. We were miles from any shelter that would permit us to light a fire in the face of such a storm; so we left the wagon as it was, hast-

---

[8] "Ranch Life and the Hunting Trail" (1888). *Works I*, p. 341.
[9] *Ibid.*, p. 348.

ily unharnessed the team horses, and, with the driver riding one and leading the other, struck off homeward at a steady gallop. Once fairly caught
by the blizzard in a country that we only partly knew, it would have been
hopeless to do more than to try for some ravine in which to cower till it
was over; so we pushed our horses to their utmost pace. Our object was to
reach the head coulées of a creek leading down to the river but a few miles
from the ranch. Could we get into these before the snow struck us we felt
we would be all right, for we could then find our way home, even in pitch-
darkness, with the wind in the quarter from which it was coming. So, with
the storm on our backs, we rode at full speed through the gathering gloom,
across the desolate reaches of prairie. The tough little horses, instead of
faltering, went stronger mile by mile. At last the weird rows of hills loomed
vaguely up in our front, and we plunged into the deep ravines for which
we had been heading just as the whirling white wreaths struck us—not the
soft, feathery flakes of a seaboard snow-storm, but fine ice-dust, driven
level by the wind, choking us, blinding our eyes, and cutting our faces if
we turned toward it. The roar of the blizzard drowned our voices when
we were but six feet apart; had it not been on our backs we could not
have gone a hundred yards, for we could no more face it than we could
face a frozen sand-blast. In an instant the strange, wild outlines of the high
buttes between which we were riding were shrouded from our sight. We
had to grope our way through a kind of shimmering dusk; and when once
or twice we were obliged by some impassable cliff or canyon to retrace
our steps, it was all that we could do to urge the horses even a few paces
against the wind-blown snow-grains which stung like steel filings.

But this extreme violence only lasted about four hours. The moon was
full, and its beams struggled through scudding clouds and snow-drift, so
that we reached the ranch without difficulty, and when we got there the
wind had already begun to lull. The snow still fell thick and fast; but before we went to bed this also showed signs of stopping. Accordingly we
determined that we would leave the wagon where it was for a day or two,
and start early next morning for a range of high hills some ten miles off,
much haunted by sheep; for we did not wish to let pass the chance of
tracking the game offered by the first good snow of the season.

Next morning we started by starlight. The snow lay several inches deep
on the ground; the whole land was a dazzling white. It was very cold.
Within the ranch everything was frozen solid in spite of the thick log walls;
but the air was so still and clear that we did not realize how low the tem-
perature was. Accordingly, as the fresh horse I had to take was young and
wild, I did not attempt to wear my fur coat. I soon felt my mistake. The
windless cold ate into my marrow; and when, shortly after the cloudless
winter sunrise, we reached our hunting-grounds and picketed out the

horses, I was already slightly frost-bitten. But the toil of hunting over the snow-covered crags soon made me warm.

All day we walked and climbed through a white wonderland. On every side the snowy hills, piled one on another, stretched away, chain after chain, as far as sight could reach. The stern and iron-bound land had been changed to a frozen sea of billowy, glittering peaks and ridges. At last, late in the afternoon, three great bighorn suddenly sprang up to our right and crossed the table-land in front of and below us at a strong, stretching gallop. The lengthening sunbeams glinted on their mighty horns; their great supple brown bodies were thrown out in bold relief against the white landscape; as they ploughed with long strides through the powdery snow, their hoofs tossed it up in masses of white spray. On the left of the plateau was a ridge, and as they went up this I twice fired at the leading ram, my bullets striking under him. On the summit he stopped and stood for a moment looking back three hundred and fifty yards off, and my third shot went fairly through his lungs. He ran over the hill as if unharmed, but lay down a couple of hundred yards on, and was dead when we reached him.

It was after nightfall when we got back to the horses, and we rode home by moonlight. To gallop in such weather insures freezing; so the ponies shambled along at a single-foot trot, their dark bodies white with hoarfrost, and the long icicles hanging from their lips. The cold had increased steadily; the spirit thermometer at the ranch showed 26° Fahrenheit below zero. We had worked all day without food or rest, and were very tired. On the ride home I got benumbed before I knew it and froze my face, one foot, and both knees. Even my companion, who had a greatcoat, froze his nose and cheeks. Never was a sight more welcome than the gleam of the firelit ranch windows to us that night.[10]

6. Frontier Types

The old race of Rocky Mountain hunters and trappers, of reckless, dauntless Indian fighters, is now fast dying out. Yet here and there these restless wanderers of the untrodden wilderness still linger, in wooded fastnesses so inaccessible that the miners have not yet explored them, in mountain valleys so far off that no ranchman has yet driven his herds thither. To this day many of them wear the fringed tunic or hunting-shirt, made of buckskin or homespun, and belted in at the waist—the most picturesque and distinctively national dress ever worn in America. . . . Many a time I have hunted with them, spent the night in their smoky cabins, or had them as guests at my ranch. But in a couple of years after the

[10] *Ibid.*, pp. 441–3.

inrush of the cattlemen the last herds of the buffalo were destroyed, and the beaver were trapped out of all the plains' streams. Then the hunters vanished likewise, save that here and there one or two still remain in some nook or out-of-the-way corner. The others wandered off restlessly over the land—some to join their brethren in the Cœur d'Alêne or the northern Rockies, others to the coast ranges or to far-away Alaska. Moreover, their ranks were soon thinned by death, and the places of the dead were no longer taken by new recruits. They led hard lives, and the unending strain of their toilsome and dangerous existence shattered even such iron frames as theirs. They were killed in drunken brawls, or in nameless fights with roving Indians; they died by one of the thousand accidents incident to the business of their lives—by flood or quicksand, by cold or starvation, by the stumble of a horse or a foot slip on the edge of a cliff; they perished by diseases brought on by terrible privation, and aggravated by the savage orgies with which it was varied.

Yet there was not only much that was attractive in their wild, free, reckless lives, but there was also very much good about the men themselves. They were—and such of them as are left still are—frank, bold, and self-reliant to a degree. They fear neither man, brute, nor element. They are generous and hospitable; they stand loyally by their friends, and pursue their enemies with bitter and vindictive hatred. For the rest, they differ among themselves in their good and bad points even more markedly than do men in civilized life, for out on the border virtue and wickedness alike take on very pronounced colors. A man who in civilization would be merely a backbiter becomes a murderer on the frontier; and, on the other hand, he who in the city would do nothing more than bid you a cheery good morning, shares his last bit of sun-jerked venison with you when threatened by starvation in the wilderness. . . .

On one of my trips of the mountains I happened to come across several old-style hunters at the same time. Two were on their way out of the woods, after having been all winter and spring without seeing a white face. They had been lucky, and their battered pack-saddles carried bales of valuable furs—fisher, sable, otter, mink, beaver. The two men, though fast friends and allies for many years, contrasted oddly. One was a short, square-built, good-humored Kanuck, always laughing and talking, who interlarded his conversation with a singularly original mixture of the most villainous French and English profanity. His partner was an American, gray-eyed, tall and straight as a young pine, with a saturnine, rather haughty face, and proud bearing. He spoke very little, and then in low tones, never using an oath; but he showed now and then a most unexpected sense of dry humor. Both were images of bronzed and rugged strength. Neither had the slightest touch of the bully in his nature; they

35

treated others with the respect that they also exacted for themselves. They bore an excellent reputation as being not only highly skilled in woodcraft and the use of the rifle, but also men of tried courage and strict integrity whose word could be always implicitly trusted.

I had with me at the time a hunter who, though their equal as marksman or woodsman, was their exact opposite morally. He was a pleasant companion and useful assistant, being very hard-working and possessing a temper that never was ruffled by anything. He was also a good-looking fellow, with honest brown eyes; but he no more knew the difference between right and wrong than Adam did before the fall. Had he been at all conscious of his wickedness, or had he possessed the least sense of shame, he would have been unbearable as a companion; but he was so perfectly pleasant and easy, so good-humoredly tolerant of virtue in others, and he so wholly lacked even a glimmering suspicion that murder, theft, and adultery were matters of anything more than individual taste, that I actually grew to be rather fond of him. . . .[11] He was a man of much shrewdness and of great courage and resolution. Moreover, he possessed what only a few men do possess, the capacity to tell the truth. He saw facts as they were, and could tell them as they were, and he never told an untruth unless for very weighty reasons. He was pre-eminently a philosopher, of a happy, sceptical turn of mind. He had no prejudices. He never looked down, as so many hard characters do, upon a person possessing a different code of ethics. His attitude was one of broad, genial tolerance. He saw nothing out of the way in the fact that he had himself been a road-agent, a professional gambler, and a desperado at different stages of his career. On the other hand, he did not in the least hold it against any one that he had always acted within the law. At the time that I knew him he had become a man of some substance, and naturally a stanch upholder of the existing order of things. But while he never boasted of his past deeds, he never apologized for them, and evidently would have been quite as incapable of understanding that they needed an apology as he would have been incapable of being guilty of mere vulgar boastfulness. He did not often allude to his past career at all. When he did, he recited its incidents perfectly naturally and simply, as events, without any reference to or regard for their ethical significance. It was this quality which made him at times a specially pleasant companion, and always an agreeable narrator. The point of his story, or what seemed to him the point, was rarely that which struck me. It was the incidental side-lights the story threw upon his own nature and the somewhat lurid surroundings amid which he had moved.

On one occasion when we were out together we killed a bear and,

[11] *Ibid.*, pp. 349–53.

after skinning it, took a bath in a lake. I noticed he had a scar on the side of his foot and asked him how he got it, to which he responded, with indifference:

"Oh, that? Why, a man shootin' at me to make me dance, that was all."

I expressed some curiosity in the matter, and he went on:

"Well, the way of it was this: It was when I was keeping a saloon in New Mexico, and there was a man there by the name of Fowler, and there was a reward on him of three thousand dollars——"

"Put on him by the State?"

"No, put on by his wife," said my friend; "and there was this——"

"Hold on," I interrupted; "put on by his wife, did you say?"

"Yes, by his wife. Him and her had been keepin' a faro-bank, you see, and they quarrelled about it, so she just put a reward on him, and so——"

"Excuse me," I said, "but do you mean to say that this reward was put on publicly?" to which my friend answered, with an air of gentlemanly boredom at being interrupted to gratify my thirst for irrelevant detail:

"Oh, no, not publicly. She just mentioned it to six or eight intimate personal friends."

"Go on," I responded, somewhat overcome by this instance of the primitive simplicity with which New Mexican matrimonial disputes were managed, and he continued:

"Well, two men come ridin' in to see me to borrow my guns. My guns was Colt's self-cockers. It was a new thing then, and they was the only ones in town. These come to me, and 'Simpson,' says they, 'we want to borrow your guns; we are goin' to kill Fowler.'

" 'Hold on for a moment,' said I, 'I am willin' to lend you them guns, but I ain't goin' to know what you'r' goin' to do with them—no, sir; but of course you can have the guns.' " Here my friend's face lightened pleasantly, and he continued:

"Well, you may easily believe I felt surprised next day when Fowler come ridin' in, and, says he, 'Simpson, here's your guns.' He had shot them two men! 'Well, Fowler,' says I, 'if I had known them men was after you, I'd never have let them have them guns nohow,' says I. That wasn't true, for I did know it, but there was no cause to tell him that." I murmured my approval of such prudence, and Simpson continued, his eyes gradually brightening with the light of agreeable reminiscence:

"Well, they up and they took Fowler before the justice of the peace. The justice of the peace was a Turk."

"Now, Simpson, what do you mean by that?" I interrupted.

"Well, he come from Turkey," said Simpson, and I again sank back, wondering briefly what particular variety of Mediterranean outcast had drifted down to Mexico to be made a justice of the peace. Simpson laughed and continued: "That Fowler was a funny fellow. The Turk, he committed Fowler, and Fowler, he riz up and knocked him down and tromped all over him and made him let him go!"

"That was an appeal to a higher law," I observed. Simpson assented cheerily, and continued:

"Well, that Turk, he got nervous for fear Fowler he was goin' to kill him, and so he comes to me and offers me twenty-five dollars a day to protect him from Fowler; and I went to Fowler, and 'Fowler,' says I, 'that Turk's offered me twenty-five dollars a day to protect him from you. Now, I ain't goin' to get shot for no twenty-five dollars a day, and if you are goin' to kill the Turk, just say so and go and do it; but if you ain't goin' to kill the Turk, there's no reason why I shouldn't earn that twenty-five dollars a day!' and Fowler, says he, 'I ain't goin' to touch the Turk; you just go right ahead and protect him.' "

So Simpson "protected" the Turk from the imaginary danger of Fowler, for about a week, at twenty-five dollars a day. Then one evening he happened to go out and met Fowler, "and," said he, "the moment I saw him I know he felt mean, for he begun to shoot at my feet," which certainly did seem to offer presumptive evidence of meanness. Simpson continued:

"I didn't have no gun, so I just had to stand there and take it until something distracted his attention, and I went off home to get my gun and kill him, but I wanted to do it perfectly lawful; so I went up to the mayor (he was playin' poker with one of the judges), and says I to him, 'Mr. Mayor,' says I, 'I am goin' to shoot Fowler.' And the mayor he riz out of his chair and he took me by the hand, and says he, 'Mr. Simpson, if you do I will stand by you'; and the judge, he says, 'I'll go on your bond.' "

Fortified by this cordial approval of the executive and judicial branches of the government, Mr. Simpson started on his quest. Meanwhile, however, Fowler had cut up another prominent citizen, and they already had him in jail. The friends of law and order, feeling some little distrust as to the permanency of their own zeal for righteousness, thought it best to settle the matter before there was time for cooling, and accordingly, headed by Simpson, the mayor, the judge, the Turk, and other prominent citizens of the town, they broke into the jail and hanged Fowler. The point in the hanging which especially tickled my friend's fancy as he lingered over the reminiscence, was one that was rather too ghastly to appeal to our own sense of humor. In the Turk's mind there still rankled the memory of Fowler's very unprofessional conduct while figuring before him as a criminal. Said Simpson, with a merry twinkle of the eye: "Do you know, that Turk he was a right funny fellow too after all. Just as the boys were going to string up Fowler, says he, 'Boys, stop; one moment, gentlemen—Mr. Fowler, good-by,' and he blew a kiss to him!" . . .[12]

Though in some ways a true backwoods Donatello . . . my friend . . . never related any of his past deeds of wickedness as matters either for boastfulness or for regret; they were simply repeated incidentally in the course of conversation. Thus, once in speaking of the profits of his different enterprises, he casually mentioned making a good deal of money as a government scout in the Southwest by buying cartridges from some negro troops at a cent apiece and selling them to the hostile Apaches for a dollar each. His conduct was not due to sympathy with the Indians, for it appeared that later on he had taken part in massacring some of these same Apaches when they were prisoners. He brushed aside as irrelevant one or two questions which I put to him: matters of sentiment were not to be mixed up with a purely mercantile speculation. Another time we were talking of the curious angles bullets sometimes fly off at when they ricochet. To illustrate the matter he related an experience which I shall try to give in his own words. "One time, when I was keeping a saloon down in New Mexico, there was a man owed me a grudge. Well, he took sick of the smallpox, and the doctor told him he'd sure die, and he said if that was so he reckoned he'd kill me first. So he come a-riding in with his gun . . . and begun shooting; but I hit him first, and away he rode. I started to get on my horse to follow him; but there was a little Irishman there who said he'd never killed a man, and he begged hard for me to give him my gun and let him go after the other man and finish him. So I let him go; and when he caught up, blamed if the little cuss didn't get so nervous that he fired off into the ground, and the darned bullet struck a crowbar, and glanced up, and hit the other man square in the head and killed him! Now, that *was* a funny shot, wasn't it?" [13]

The cowboys form a class by themselves, and are now quite as typical representatives of the wilder side of Western life as were a few years ago the skin-clad hunters and trappers. They are mostly of native birth, and although there are among them wild spirits from every land, yet the latter soon become undistinguishable from their American companions, for

[12] "The Wilderness Hunter" (1893). *Works II,* pp. 330–4.
[13] "Hunting Trips of a Ranchman" (1885). *Works I,* pp. 353–4.

these plainsmen are far from being so heterogeneous as is commonly supposed. On the contrary, all have a curious similarity to each other; existence in the West seems to put the same stamp upon each and every one of them. Sinewy, hardy, self-reliant, their life forces them to be both daring and adventurous, and the passing over their heads of a few years leaves printed on their faces certain lines which tell of dangers quietly fronted and hardships uncomplainingly endured. . . .[14] They are as hardy and self-reliant as any men who ever breathed—with bronzed, set faces, and keen eyes that look all the world straight in the face without flinching as they flash out from under the broad-brimmed hats. Peril and hardship, and years of long toil broken by weeks of brutal dissipation, draw haggard lines across their eager faces, but never dim their reckless eyes nor break their bearing of defiant self-confidence. They do not walk well, partly because they so rarely do any work out of the saddle, partly because their *chaparejos* or leather overalls hamper them when on the ground; but their appearance is striking for all that, and picturesque too, with their jingling spurs, the big revolvers stuck in their belts, and bright silk handkerchiefs knotted loosely round their necks over the open collars of the flannel shirts. When drunk on the villainous whiskey of the frontier towns, they cut mad antics, riding their horses into the saloons, firing their pistols right and left, from boisterous light-heartedness rather than from any viciousness, and indulging too often in deadly shooting affrays, brought on either by the accidental contact of the moment or on account of some long-standing grudge, or perhaps because of bad blood between two ranches or localities; but except while on such sprees they are quiet, rather self-contained men, perfectly frank and simple, and on their own ground treat a stranger with the most whole-souled hospitality, doing all in their power for him and scorning to take any reward in return. Although prompt to resent an injury, they are not at all apt to be rude to outsiders, treating them with what can almost be called a grave courtesy. . . .[15]

Of course if these men were asked outright as to their stories they would have refused to tell them or else would have lied about them; but when they had grown to regard a man as a friend and companion they would often recount various incidents of their past lives with perfect frankness, and as they combined in a very curious degree both a decided sense of humor and a failure to appreciate that there was anything especially remarkable in what they related, their tales were always entertaining.

[14] *Ibid.*, p. 7.
[15] "Ranch Life and the Hunting Trail." *Works I*, pp. 227–8.

Early one spring, now nearly ten years ago, I was out hunting some lost horses. They had strayed from the range three months before, and we had in a round-about way heard that they were ranging near some broken country, where a man named Brophy had a ranch, nearly fifty miles from my own. When I started thither the weather was warm, but the second day out it grew colder and a heavy snow-storm came on. Fortunately I was able to reach the ranch all right, finding there one of the sons of a Little Beaver ranchman, and a young cow-puncher belonging to a Texas outfit, whom I knew very well. After putting my horse into the corral and throwing him down some hay I strode into the low hut, made partly of turf and partly of cottonwood logs, and speedily warmed myself before the fire. We had a good warm supper, of bread, potatoes, fried venison, and tea. My two companions grew very sociable and began to talk freely over their pipes. There were two bunks one above the other. I climbed into the upper, leaving my friends, who occupied the lower, sitting together on a bench recounting different incidents in the careers of themselves and their cronies during the winter that had just passed. Soon one of them asked the other what had become of a certain horse, a noted cutting pony, which I had myself noticed the preceding fall. The question aroused the other to the memory of a wrong which still rankled, and he began (I alter one or two of the proper names):

"Why, that was the pony that got stole. I had been workin' him on rough ground when I was out with the Three Bar outfit and he went tender forward, so I turned him loose by the Lazy B ranch, and when I came back to git him there wasn't anybody at the ranch and I couldn't find him. The sheep-man who lives about two miles west, under Red Clay butte, told me he seen a fellow in a wolfskin coat, ridin' a pinto bronco with white eyes, leadin' that pony of mine just two days before; and I hunted round till I hit his trail and then I followed to where I'd reckoned he was headin' for—the Short Pine Hills. When I got there a rancher told me he had seen the man pass on towards Cedartown, and sure enough when I struck Cedartown I found he lived there in a 'dobe house, just outside the town. There was a boom on the town and it looked pretty slick. There was two hotels and I went into the first, and I says, 'Where's the justice of the peace?' says I to the bartender.

" 'There ain't no justice of the peace,' says he, 'the justice of the peace got shot.'

" 'Well, where's the constable?' says I.

" 'Why, it was him that shot the justice of the peace,' says he; 'he's skipped the country with a bunch of horses.'

" 'Well, ain't there no officer of the law left in this town?' says I.

41

" 'Why, of course,' says he, 'there's a probate judge; he is over tendin' bar at the Last Chance Hotel.'

"So I went over to the Last Chance Hotel and I walked in there. 'Mornin,' says I.

" 'Mornin,' says he.

" 'You're the probate judge?' says I.

" 'That's what I am,' says he. 'What do you want?' says he.

" 'I want justice,' says I.

" 'What kind of justice do you want?' says he. 'What's it for?'

" 'It's for stealin' a horse,' says I.

" 'Then by God you'll git it,' says he. 'Who stole the horse?' says he.

" 'It is a man that lives in a 'dobe house, just outside the town there,' says I.

" 'Well, where do you come from yourself?' said he.

" 'From Medory,' said I.

"With that he lost interest and settled kind o' back, and says he, 'There won't no Cedartown jury hang a Cedartown man for stealin' a Medory man's horse,' said he.

" 'Well, what am I to do about my horse?' says I.

" 'Do?' says he; 'well, you know where the man lives, don't you?' says he; 'then sit up outside his house tonight and shoot him when he comes in,' says he, 'and skip out with the horse.'

" 'All right,' says I, 'that is what I'll do,' and I walked off.

"So I went off to his house and I laid down behind some sage-bushes to wait for him. He was not at home, but I could see his wife movin' about inside now and then, and I waited and waited, and it growed darker, and I begun to say to myself, 'Now here you are lyin' out to shoot this man when he comes home; and it's gettin' dark, and you don't know him, and if you do shoot the next man that comes into that house, like as not it won't be the fellow you're after at all, but some perfectly innocent man a-comin' there after the other man's wife!'

"So I up and saddled the bronc' and lit out for home," concluded the narrator with the air of one justly proud of his own self-abnegating virtue.

The "town" where the judge above mentioned dwelt was one of those squalid, pretentiously named little clusters of makeshift dwellings which on the edge of the wild country spring up with the rapid growth of mushrooms, and are often no longer-lived. In their earlier stages these towns are frequently built entirely of canvas, and are subject to grotesque calamities. . . . The riders of a huge trail outfit from Texas, to their glad surprise, discovered such a town and abandoned themselves to a night of roaring and lethal carousal. Next morning the city authorities were lamenting, with oaths of bitter rage, that "them hell-and-twenty Flying

42

A cow-punchers had cut the court-house up into pants." It was true. The cowboys were in need of chaps and, with an admirable mixture of adventurousness, frugality, and ready adaptability to circumstances, had made substitutes therefor in the shape of canvas overalls, cut from the roof and walls of the shaky temple of justice.[16]

[16] "The Wilderness Hunter." *Works II*, pp. 327–30.

Hunter Naturalist

*Mr. Roosevelt's interest in natural history began in his boy-
hood and persisted throughout his life.*

1. Hunting in Lonely Lands

No one, but he who has partaken thereof, can understand the keen
delight of hunting in lonely lands. For him is the joy of the horse well
ridden and the rifle well held; for him the long days of toil and hardship,
resolutely endured, and crowned at the end with triumph. In after-years
there shall come forever to his mind the memory of endless prairies shimmering in the bright sun; of vast snow-clad wastes lying desolate under
gray skies; of the melancholy marshes; of the rush of mighty rivers; of
the breath of the evergreen forest in summer; of the crooning of ice-
armored pines at the touch of the winds of winter; of cataracts roaring
between hoary mountain masses; of all the innumerable sights and sounds
of the wilderness; of its immensity and mystery; and of the silences that
brood in its still depths. . . .[1]

The chase of any animal has in it two chief elements of attraction.
The first is the chance given to be in the wilderness; to see the sights and
hear the sounds of wild nature. The second is the demand made by the
particular kind of chase upon the qualities of manliness and hardihood.
As regards the first, some kinds of game, of course, lead the hunter into
particularly remote and wild localities; and the farther one gets into the
wilderness, the greater is the attraction of its lonely freedom. Yet to camp
out at all implies some measure of this delight. The keen, fresh air, the
breath of the pine forests, the glassy stillness of the lake at sunset, the
glory of sunrise among the mountains, the shimmer of the endless prairies, the ceaseless rustle of the cottonwood-leaves where the wagon is
drawn up on the low bluff of the shrunken river—all these appeal in-

[1] "The Wilderness Hunter." *Works II,* p. XXIX.

45

tensely to any man, no matter what may be the game he happens to be following. But there is a wide variation, and indeed contrast, in the qualities called for in the chase itself, according as one quarry or another is sought.[2]

2. *Antelope*

From April to August antelope are the game we chiefly follow, killing only the bucks; after that season, blacktail and whitetail deer. Now and then we get a chance at mountain-sheep, and more rarely at larger game still. As a rule, I never shoot anything but bucks. But in the rutting season, when the bucks' flesh is poor, or when we need to lay in a good stock of meat for the winter, this rule of course must be broken. . . .

Antelope gather together in great bands in the fall, and either travel south, leaving the country altogether, or else go to some out-of-the-way place where they are not likely to be disturbed. Antelope are queer, freaky beasts, and it is hard to explain why, when most of these great bands go off south, one or two always stay in the Bad Lands. Such a band having chosen its wintering ground, which is usually in a valley or on a range of wide plateaus, will leave it only with great reluctance, and if it is discovered by hunters most of its members will surely be butchered before the survivors are willing to abandon the place and seek new quarters.

In April the prong-horned herds come back, but now all broken up into straggling parties. They have regular passes, through which they go every year: there is one such not far from my ranch, where they are certain to cross the Little Missouri in great numbers each spring on their return march. In the fall, when they are travelling in dense crowds, hunters posted in these passes sometimes butcher enormous numbers. . . .

No antelope are found, except rarely, immediately round my ranch-house, where the ground is much too broken to suit them; but on the great prairies, ten or fifteen miles off, they are plentiful, though far from as abundant as they were a few years ago when the cattle were first driven into the land. By plainsmen they are called either pronghorn or antelope, but are most often known by the latter and much less descriptive title. Where they are found they are always very conspicuous figures in the landscape; for, far from attempting to conceal itself, an antelope really seems anxious to take up a prominent position, caring only to be able itself to see its foes.

It is the smallest in size of the plains game, even smaller than a white-tail deer; and its hide is valueless, being thin and porous, and making

[2] "Outdoor Pastimes of an American Hunter" (1905). *Works III,* p. 21.

very poor buckskin. In its whole appearance and structure it is a most singular creature. Unlike all other hollow-horned animals, it sheds its horns annually, exactly as the deer shed their solid antlers; but the shedding process in the pronghorn occupies but a very few days—so short a time, indeed, that many hunters stoutly deny that it takes place at all. The hair is of a remarkable texture, very long, coarse, and brittle; in the spring it comes off in handfuls. In strong contrast to the reddish yellow of the other parts of the body, the rump is pure white, and when alarmed or irritated every hair in the white patch bristles up on end, greatly increasing the apparent area of the color. The flesh, unlike that of any other plains animal, is equally good all through the year. In the fall it is hardly so juicy as deer venison, but in the spring, when no other kind of game is worth eating, it is perfectly good; and at that time of the year, if we have to get fresh meat, we would rather kill antelope than anything else; and as the bucks are always to be instantly distinguished from the does by their large horns, we confine ourselves to them, and so work no harm to the species.

The antelope is a queer-looking rather than a beautiful animal. The curious pronged horns, great bulging eyes, and strange bridle-like marks and bands on the face and throat are more striking, but less handsome, than the delicate head and branching antlers of a deer; and it entirely lacks the latter animal's grace of movement. In its form and look, when standing still, it is rather angular and goat-like, and its movements merely have the charm that comes from lightness, speed, and agility. Its gait is singularly regular and even, without any of the bounding, rolling movement of a deer; and it is, consequently, very easy to hit running, compared with other kinds of game.

Antelope possess a most morbid curiosity. The appearance of anything out of the way or to which they are not accustomed, often seems to drive them nearly beside themselves with mingled fright and desire to know what it is, a combination of feelings that throws them into a perfect panic during whose continuance they will at times seem utterly unable to take care of themselves. . . .

The pronghorn is pre-eminently a gregarious animal. It is found in bands almost all the year through. During the two or three days after he has shed his horns, and while the new ones are growing, the buck retires to some out-of-the-way spot, and while bringing forth her fawns the doe stays by herself. But as soon as possible each again rejoins the band; and the fawns become members of it at a remarkably early age. In the late fall, when the bitter cold has begun, a large number of these bands collect together and immense herds are formed which last throughout the winter. Thus at this season a man may travel for days through regions where antelope are most plentiful during the hot months and never see one; but if he does come across any they will be apt to be in great numbers, most probably along the edge of the Bad Lands, where the ground is rolling rather than broken, but where there is some shelter from the furious winter gales. Often they will even come down to the river-bottom or find their way up to some plateau. They now always hang closely about the places they have chosen for their winter haunts, and seem very reluctant to leave them. They go in dense herds, and when starved and weak with cold are less shy; and can often be killed in great numbers by any one who has found out where they are—though a true sportsman will not molest them at this season. . . .

A pronghorn is by far the fleetest animal on the plains; one can outrun and outlast a deer with the greatest ease. Very swift greyhounds can overtake them, if hunted in leashes or couples; but only a remarkably good dog can run one down single-handed. Besides, pronghorn are most plucky little creatures, and will make a most resolute fight against a dog or wolf, striking with their forefeet and punching with their not very formidable horns, and are so quick and wiry as to be really rather hard to master.[3]

3. The Grizzly

The country was for the most part fairly open, as I kept near the foothills where glades and little prairies broke the pine forest . . . and as dusk was coming on I halted and camped in a little open spot by the side of a small, noisy brook, with crystal water. The place was carpeted with soft, wet, green moss, dotted red with the kinnikinic-berries, and at its edge, under the trees where the ground was dry, I threw down the buffalo bed on the mat of sweet-smelling pine-needles. Making camp took but a moment. I opened the pack, tossed the bedding on a smooth spot, knee-haltered the little mare, dragged up a few dry logs, and then strolled off, rifle on shoulder, through the frosty gloaming, to see if I could pick up a grouse for supper.

For half a mile I walked quickly and silently over the pine-needles, across a succession of slight ridges separated by narrow, shallow valleys. The forest here was composed of lodge-pole pines, which on the ridges grew close together, with tall slender trunks, while in the valleys the growth was more open. Though the sun was behind the mountains there was yet plenty of light by which to shoot, but it was fading rapidly.

At last, as I was thinking of turning toward camp, I stole up to the crest of one of the ridges, and looked over into the valley some sixty

[3] "Hunting Trips of a Ranchman." *Works I,* pp. 138–43.

yards off. Immediately I caught the loom of some large, dark object; and another glance showed me a big grizzly walking slowly off with his head down. He was quartering to me, and I fired into his flank, the bullet, as I afterward found, ranging forward and piercing one lung. At the shot he uttered a loud, moaning grunt, and plunged forward at a heavy gallop, while I raced obliquely down the hill to cut him off. After going a few hundred feet he reached a laurel thicket, some thirty yards broad, and two or three times as long, which he did not leave. I ran up to the edge and there halted, not liking to venture into the mass of twisted, close-growing stems and glossy foliage. Moreover, as I halted, I heard him utter a peculiar, savage kind of whine from the heart of the brush. Accordingly, I began to skirt the edge, standing on tiptoe and gazing earnestly to see if I could not catch a glimpse of his hide. When I was at the narrowest part of the thicket, he suddenly left it directly opposite, and then wheeled and stood broadside to me on the hillside, a little above. He turned his head stiffly toward me; scarlet strings of froth hung from his lips; his eyes burned like embers in the gloom.

I held true, aiming behind the shoulder, and my bullet shattered the point or lower end of his heart, taking out a big nick. Instantly the great bear turned with a harsh roar of fury and challenge, blowing the bloody foam from his mouth, so that I saw the gleam of his white fangs; and then he charged straight at me, crashing and bounding through the laurel bushes, so that it was hard to aim. I waited till he came to a fallen tree, raking him as he topped it with a ball, which entered his chest and went through the cavity of his body, but he neither swerved nor flinched, and at the moment I did not know that I had struck him. He came steadily on, and in another second was almost upon me. I fired for his forehead, but my bullet went low, entering his open mouth, smashing his lower jaw and going into the neck. I leaped to one side almost as I pulled the trigger; and through the hanging smoke the first thing I saw was his paw as he made a vicious side blow at me. The rush of his charge carried him past. As he struck he lurched forward, leaving a pool of bright blood where his muzzle hit the ground; but he recovered himself and made two or three jumps onward, while I hurriedly jammed a couple of cartridges into the magazine, my rifle holding only four, all of which I had fired. Then he tried to pull up, but as he did so his muscles seemed suddenly to give way, his head drooped, and he rolled over and over like a shot rabbit.[4]

[4] "The Wilderness Hunter." *Works II,* pp. 240–2.

49

4. Twilight of the Bears

To John Burroughs[5]

Washington, D. C.
August 12, 1904

I think that nothing is more amusing and interesting than the development of the changes made in wild beast character by the wholly unprecedented course of things in the Yellowstone Park. I have just had a letter from Buffalo Jones, describing his experiences in trying to get tin cans off the feet of the bears in the Yellowstone Park. There are lots of tin cans in the garbage heaps which the bears muss over, and it has now become fairly common for a bear to get his paw so caught in a tin can that he cannot get it off, and of course great pain and injury follow. Buffalo Jones was sent with another scout to capture, tie up and cure these bears. He roped two and got the can off one, but the other tore himself loose, can and all, and escaped, owing, as Jones bitterly insists, to the failure of duty on the part of one of his brother scouts, whom he sneers at as "a foreigner." Think of the grizzly bear of the early Rocky Mountain hunters and explorers, and then think of the fact that part of the recognized duties of the scouts in the Yellowstone Park at this moment is to catch this same grizzly bear and remove tin cans from the bear's paws in the bear's interest! [6]

5. The Prairie Singers

The sun had not risen, and the air had the peculiar chill it always takes on toward morning, while little wreaths of light mist rose from the pools. Getting up and loosing Manitou to let him feed round where he wished and slake his thirst, I took the rifle, strolled up the creek-valley a short distance, and turned off out on the prairie. Nothing was in sight in the way of game; but overhead a skylark was singing, soaring up above me so high that I could not make out his form in the gray morning light. I listened for some time, and the music never ceased for a moment, coming down clear, sweet, and tender from the air above. Soon the strains of another answered from a little distance off, and the two kept soaring and singing as long as I stayed to listen; and when I walked away I could still hear their notes behind me. In some ways the skylark is the sweetest

[5] Naturalist and poet; author of "Camping and Tramping With Roosevelt."
[6] *Letters IV*, p. 290.

singer we have; only certain of the thrushes rival it, but though the songs of the latter have perhaps even more melody, they are far from being as uninterrupted and well sustained, being rather a succession of broken bursts of music. . . .[7]

In the spring mornings the rider on the plains will hear bird songs unknown in the East. The Missouri skylark sings while soaring above the great plateaus so high in the air that it is impossible to see the bird; and this habit of singing while soaring it shares with some sparrow-like birds that are often found in company with it. The white-shouldered larkbunting, in its livery of black, has rich, full notes, and as it sings on the wing it reminds one of the bobolink; and the sweet-voiced lark-finch also utters its song in the air. These birds and most of the sparrows of the plains are characteristic of this region.

But many of our birds, especially those found in the wooded riverbottoms, answer to those of the East; only almost each one has some marked point of difference from its Eastern representative. The bluebird out West is very much of a blue bird indeed, for it has no "earth tinge" on its breast at all; while the indigo-bird, on the contrary, has gained the ruddy markings that the other has lost. The flicker has the shafts of its wing and tail quills colored orange instead of yellow. The towhee has lost all title to its name, for its only cry is a mew like that of a catbird; while, most wonderful of all, the meadow-lark has found a rich, strong voice, and is one of the sweetest and most incessant singers we have.

Throughout June the thickets and groves about the ranch-house are loud with bird music from before dawn till long after sunrise. The thrashers have sung all the night through from among the thorn-bushes if there has been a moon, or even if there has been bright starlight; and before the first glimmer of gray the bell-like, silvery songs of the shy woodland thrushes chime in; while meadow-lark, robin, bluebird, and song-sparrow, together with many rarer singers, like the grosbeak, join in swelling the chorus. There are some would-be singers whose intention is better than their execution. Blackbirds of several kinds are plenty round the house and stables, walking about with a knowing air, like so many dwarf crows; and now and then a flock of yellowheads will mix for a few days with their purple or rusty-colored brethren. The males of these yellow-headed grackles are really handsome, their orange and yellow heads contrasting finely with the black of the rest of their plumage; but their voices are discordant to a degree. When a flock has done feeding it will often light in straggling order among the trees in front of the veranda, and then the males will begin to sing, or rather to utter the most extraordinary collection of broken sounds—creakings, gurglings, hisses, twitters, and every

[7] "Hunting Trips of a Ranchman." *Works I,* pp. 161–2.

now and then a liquid note or two. It is like an accentuated representation of the noise made by a flock of common blackbirds. At nightfall the poorwills begin to utter their boding call from the wooded ravines back in the hills; not "whippoorwill," as in the East, but with two syllables only. They often come round the ranch-house. Late one evening I had been sitting motionless on the veranda, looking out across the water and watching the green and brown of the hilltops change to purple and umber and then fade off into shadowy gray as the sombre darkness deepened. Suddenly a poorwill lit on the floor beside me and stayed some little time; now and then uttering its mournful cries, then ceasing for a few moments as it flitted round after insects, and again returning to the same place to begin anew. The little owls, too, call to each other with tremulous, quavering voices throughout the livelong night, as they sit in the creaking trees that overhang the roof.[8]

6. Larks, and Others

I spoke above of the sweet singing of the Western meadow-lark and plains skylark; neither of them kin to the true skylark, by the way, one being a cousin of the grackles and hangbirds, and the other a kind of pipit. To me both of these birds are among the most attractive singers to which I have ever listened; but with all bird music much must be allowed for the surroundings and much for the mood and the keenness of sense of the listener. The lilt of the little plains skylark is neither very powerful nor very melodious; but it is sweet, pure, long-sustained, with a ring of courage befitting a song uttered in highest air.

The meadow-lark is a singer of a higher order, deserving to rank with the best. Its song has length, variety, power, and rich melody; and there is in it sometimes a cadence of wild sadness, inexpressibly touching. Yet I cannot say that either song would appeal to others as it appeals to me; for to me it comes forever laden with a hundred memories and associations; with the sight of dim hills reddening in the dawn, with the breath of cool morning winds blowing across lonely plains, with the scent of flowers on the sunlit prairie, with the motion of fiery horses, with all the strong thrill of eager and buoyant life. I doubt if any man can judge dispassionately the bird songs of his own country; he cannot disassociate them from the sights and sounds of the land that is so dear to him.

This is not a feeling to regret, but it must be taken into account in accepting any estimate of bird music—even in considering the reputation of the European skylark and nightingale. To both of these birds I have often listened in their own homes; always with pleasure and admiration,

[8] *Ibid.*, pp. 307–9.

but always with a growing belief that relatively to some other birds they were ranked too high. They are pre-eminently birds with literary associations; most people take their opinions of them at second hand, from the poets.

No one can help liking the lark; it is such a brave, honest, cheery bird, and, moreover, its song is uttered in the air, and is very long-sustained. But it is by no means a musician of the first rank. The nightingale is a performer of a very different and far higher order; yet, though it is indeed a notable and admirable singer, it is an exaggeration to call it unequalled. In melody, and above all in that finer, higher melody where the chords vibrate with the touch of eternal sorrow, it cannot rank with such singers as the wood-thrush and hermit-thrush. The serene, ethereal beauty of the hermit's song, rising and falling through the still evening under the archways of hoary mountain forests that have endured from time everlasting; the golden, leisurely chiming of the wood-thrush, sounding on June afternoons, stanza by stanza, through sun-flecked groves of tall hickories, oaks, and chestnuts—with these there is nothing in the nightingale's song to compare. But in volume and continuity; in tuneful, voluble, rapid outpouring and ardor; above all, in skilful and intricate variation of theme, its song far surpasses that of either of the thrushes. In all these respects it is more just to compare it with the mocking-bird's, which, as a rule, likewise falls short precisely on those points where the songs of the two thrushes excel.

The mocking-bird is a singer that has suffered much in reputation from its powers of mimicry. On ordinary occasions, and especially in the daytime, it insists on playing the harlequin. But when free in its own favorite haunts at night in the love season it has a song, or rather songs, which are not only purely original but are also more beautiful than any other bird music whatsoever. Once I listened to a mocking-bird singing the livelong spring night, under the full moon, in the magnolia tree; and I do not think I shall ever forget its song.

It was on the plantation of Major Campbell Brown, near Nashville, in the beautiful, fertile mid-Tennessee country. The mocking-birds were prime favorites on the place; and were given full scope for the development not only of their bold friendliness toward mankind but also of that marked individuality and originality of character in which they so far surpass every other bird as to become the most interesting of all feathered folk. One of the mockers, which lived in the hedge bordering the garden, was constantly engaged in an amusing feud with an honest old setter dog, the point of attack being the tip of the dog's tail. For some reason the bird seemed to regard any hoisting of the setter's tail as a challenge and insult. It would flutter near the dog as he walked; the old setter

53

would become interested in something and raise his tail. The bird would promptly fly at it and peck the tip; whereupon down went the tail until in a couple of minutes the old fellow would forget himself, and the scene would be repeated. The dog usually bore the assaults with a comic resignation; and the mocker easily avoided any momentary outburst of clumsy resentment.

On the evening in question the moon was full. My host kindly assigned me a room of which the windows opened on a great magnolia tree, where, I was told, a mocking-bird sang every night and all night long. I went to my room about ten. The moonlight was shining in through the open window, and the mocking-bird was already in the magnolia. The great tree was bathed in a flood of shining silver; I could see each twig, and mark every action of the singer, who was pouring forth such a rapture of ringing melody as I have never listened to before or since. Sometimes he would perch motionless for many minutes, his body quivering and thrilling with the outpour of music. Then he would drop softly from twig to twig, until the lowest limb was reached, when he would rise, fluttering and leaping through the branches, his song never ceasing for an instant, until he reached the summit of the tree and launched into the warm, scent-laden air, floating in spirals, with outspread wings, until, as if spent, he sank gently back into the tree and down through the branches, while his song rose to an ecstasy of ardor and passion. His voice rang like a clarionet, in rich, full tones, and his execution covered the widest possible compass; theme followed theme, a torrent of music, a swelling tide of harmony, in which scarcely any two bars were alike. I stayed till midnight listening to him; he was singing when I went to sleep; he was still singing when I woke a couple of hours later; he sang through the livelong night.[9]

[9] "The Wilderness Hunter." *Works II*, pp. 52–55.

Emerging Hercules

―――――――――――――――――――――――――――――――

Mr. Roosevelt entered politics shortly after his graduation from Harvard. As a member of the New York Assembly, he sprang almost instantly into leadership, had a state-wide reputation by the middle of his first term, and by the end of his third was a national figure and a power in the Republican Party.

―――――――――――――――――――――――――――――――

1. A Silkstocking Elected

To the Voters of the Twenty-first Assembly District:

New York, November 1, 1881

DEAR SIR, Having been nominated as a candidate for member of Assembly for this District, I would esteem it a compliment if you honor me with your vote and personal influence on Election day.

To Joseph H. Choate[1]

New York, November 10, 1881

As I feel that I owe both my nomination and election more to you than to any other one man, I wish to tell you how I have appreciated both your kind sympathy and the support you have given me.

I have taken a somewhat heavy burden of responsibility upon my shoulders, and I regret that I have, of necessity, had so little experience, but at least I shall endeavor to do my work honestly.

―――――

[1] Lawyer and diplomat; ambassador to Great Britain (1899–1905).

To Charles G. Washburn[2]

New York, November 10, 1881

Too True! Too True! I have become a "political hack."

Finding it would not interfere much with my law I accepted the nomination to the assembly, and was elected by 1500 majority, heading the ticket by 600 votes. But don't think I am going into politics after this year, for I am not.[3]

2. A Private, Personal Resolve

To Josephine Shaw Lowell [4]

Albany, February 24, 1882

. . . I honestly mean to act up here on all questions as nearly as possible as I think Father would have done, if he had lived. I thoroughly believe in the Republican party, *when it acts up to its principles*—but if I can prevent it I never shall let party zeal obscure my sense of right and decency. What my success as a politician may be I do not care an atom; but I do wish to be able to end my work here with an entirely light heart and clear conscience.[5]

3. Phases of State Legislation

Few persons realize the magnitude of the interests affected by State legislation in New York. It is no mere figure of speech to call New York the Empire State; and many of the laws most directly and immediately affecting the interests of its citizens are passed at Albany, and not at Washington. In fact, there is at Albany a little home rule parliament which presides over the destinies of a commonwealth more populous than any one of two thirds of the kingdoms of Europe, and one which, in point of wealth, material prosperity, variety of interests, extent of territory, and capacity for expansion, can fairly be said to rank next to the powers of the first class. This little parliament, composed of one hundred and twenty-eight members in the Assembly and thirty-two in the Senate, is, in the fullest sense of the term, a *representative* body; there is hardly one of the many and widely diversified interests of the State that has not a mouthpiece at Albany, and hardly a single class of its citizens—not

[2] Classmate of Roosevelt; lawyer and member of Congress (1906–1911).
[3] *Letters I*, p. 55.
[4] Prominent in charitable and reform activities in New York.
[5] *Letters VIII*, p. 1425.

even excepting, I regret to say, the criminal class—which lacks its representative among the legislators. In the three Legislatures of which I have been a member, I have sat with bankers and bricklayers, with merchants and mechanics, with lawyers, farmers, day-laborers, saloon-keepers, clergymen, and prizefighters. Among my colleagues there were many very good men; there was a still more numerous class of men who were neither very good nor very bad, but went one way or the other, according to the strength of the various conflicting influences acting around, behind, and upon them; and, finally, there were many very bad men. Still, the New York Legislature, taken as a whole, is by no means as bad a body as we would be led to believe if our judgment was based purely on what we read in the great metropolitan papers; for the custom of the latter is to portray things as either very much better or very much worse than they are. Where a number of men, many of them poor, some of them unscrupulous, and others elected by constituents too ignorant to hold them to a proper accountability for their actions, are put into a position of great temporary power, where they are called to take action upon questions affecting the welfare of large corporations and wealthy private individuals, the chances for corruption are always great; and that there is much viciousness and political dishonesty, much moral cowardice, and a good deal of actual bribe-taking in Albany, no one who has had any practical experience of legislation can doubt; but, at the same time, I think that the good members generally outnumber the bad, and that there is not often doubt as to the result when a naked question of right or wrong can be placed clearly and in its true light before the Legislature. The trouble is that on many questions the Legislature never does have the right and wrong clearly shown it. Either some bold, clever parliamentary tactician snaps the measure through before the members are aware of its nature, or else the obnoxious features are so combined with good ones as to procure the support of a certain proportion of that large class of men whose intentions are excellent, but whose intellects are foggy. Or else the necessary party organization, which we call the "machine," uses its great power for some definite evil aim.

The representatives from different sections of the State differ widely in character. Those from the country districts are generally very good men. They are usually well-to-do farmers, small lawyers, or prosperous storekeepers, and are shrewd, quiet, and honest. They are often narrow-minded and slow to receive an idea; but, on the other hand, when they get a good one, they cling to it with the utmost tenacity. They form very much the most valuable class of legislators. For the most part they are native Americans, and those who are not are men who have become completely Americanized in all their ways and habits of thought. . . .

It is from the . . . great cities that the worst legislators come. . . . They are usually foreigners, of little or no education, with exceedingly misty ideas as to morality, and possessed of an ignorance so profound that it could only be called comic, were it not for the fact that it has at times such serious effects upon our laws. It is their ignorance, quite as much as actual viciousness, which makes it so difficult to procure the passage of good laws or prevent the passage of bad ones; and it is the most irritating of the many elements with which we have to contend in the fight for good government.

Mention has been made above of the bribe-taking which undoubtedly at times occurs in the New York Legislature. . . .

It is almost impossible to actually convict a legislator of bribe-taking; but at the same time, the character of a legislator, if bad, soon becomes a matter of common notoriety, and no dishonest legislator can long keep his reputation good with honest men. If the constituents wish to know the character of their member, they can easily find it out, and no member will be dishonest if he thinks his constituents are looking at him; he presumes upon their ignorance or indifference. I do not see how bribe-taking among legislators can be stopped until the public conscience becomes awake to the matter. Then it will stop fast enough; for just as soon as politicians realize that the people are in earnest in wanting a thing done, they make haste to do it. The trouble is always in rousing the people sufficiently to make them take an *effective* interest,—that is, in making them sufficiently in earnest to be willing to give a little of their time to the accomplishment of the object they have in view. . . .

A member from a large city can often count upon the educated and intelligent men of his district showing the most gross ignorance and stupidity in political affairs. . . .

It is this . . . ignorance of the simplest political matters among really good citizens, combined with their timidity, which is so apt to characterize a wealthy *bourgeoisie,* and with their short-sighted selfishness in being unwilling to take the smallest portion of time away from their business or pleasure to devote to public affairs, which renders it so easy for corrupt men from the city to keep their places in the Legislature. . . .

The people of means in all great cities have in times past shamefully neglected their political duties, and have been contemptuously disregarded by the professional politicians in consequence. A number of them will get together in a large hall, will vociferously demand "reform," as if it were some concrete substance which could be handed out to them in slices, and will then disband with a feeling of the most serene self-satisfaction, and the belief that they have done their entire duty as citizens and members of the community. It is an actual fact that four out of five of our wealthy and educated men, of those who occupy what is called good social position, are really ignorant of the nature of a caucus or a primary meeting, and never attend either. Now, under our form of government, no man can accomplish anything by himself; he must work in combination with others; and the men of whom we are speaking will never carry their proper weight in the political affairs of the country until they have formed themselves into some organization, or else, which would be better, have joined some of the organizations already existing. But there seems often to be a certain lack of the robuster virtues in our educated men, which makes them shrink from the struggle and the inevitable contact with rough politicians (who must often be rudely handled before they can be forced to behave); while their lack of familiarity with their surroundings causes them to lack discrimination between the politicians who are decent, and those who are not; for in their eyes the two classes, both equally unfamiliar, are indistinguishable.[6]

4. First Step into the Augean Stables

MR. SPEAKER:[7] I have introduced these resolutions fully aware that it was an exceedingly important and serious task I was undertaking, and fully aware it would need proofs to substantiate before I would have a right to ask the gentlemen of this House to pass these resolutions. I do not make them on such general statements made in the newspapers. I make them on specific charges against the gentlemen named in the resolution.

These suits were brought as you all know against a fraudulent company—the Manhattan Elevated Railroad. That was a company that had a nominal stock of two million dollars—really of one hundred thousand dollars—that is, it possessed but five per cent of its nominal wealth. An agreement was concluded by that company with two other bona-fide companies by which they purchased the right to run their own roads—I am quoting from the opinion of the present attorney-general—Russell— they purchased the franchise of running their own roads; that is, they purchased nothing. This whole transaction was stigmatized by the Honorable Judge James Emott, of New York, in August of 1880, as a fraud pure and simple. The men who were mainly concerned in this fraud are known throughout New York as men whose financial dishonesty is a matter of common notoriety. I make that statement deliberately; that the

[6] "American Ideals" (1897). *Works XIII*, pp. 47–62.
[7] Speech in the New York Assembly Chamber, Albany, April 6, 1882, on his own resolution calling for the investigation of Judge Westbrook. *New York Times*, April 7, 1882.

three or four wealthy stock-gamblers who are interested in those roads were men who would barely be trusted in financial operations by any reputable business man.

Under such circumstances, almost confessed fraud having been perpetrated on a number of the stockholders by these three or four directors, it would have behooved the judiciary and the gentlemen who held the highest office in the gift of the people of this State to have handled it with peculiar care. A suit was brought in May last, I think, by the attorney-general against the Manhattan corporation. Mr. Burton Harrison was employed to investigate the affair. His report was absolute and conclusive that it was a fraudulent corporation, that it had no legal existence. It could have none when only five per cent of its stock had been paid in, and for a corporation that had only five per cent of its stock paid in to assume an additional debt of thirteen million dollars and to shift that on the community at large, was an absolute fraud. Under such circumstances the attorney-general acted properly in bringing a suit declaring the corporation to be illegal. Without any reason he suddenly discontinued this suit, and after two days brings another admitting the legality of the corporation and merely declaring that it was insolvent, an objection that he knew would be much easier overcome than the one first raised. The reason for discontinuing that suit has never been explained. It never ought to have been discontinued. It was a gigantic fraud and ought to have been stopped. It was an absolute wrong against the interests of the people for the attorney-general to change his suit and at the same time to allow any set of wealthy swindlers to escape the consequences of their misdeeds. One of the men employed by the attorney-general was also employed by the very man he was looking after, I believe, by Jay Gould.

Judge Westbrook's share in the transaction did not come in until about June 13, when the suit was brought before him. He then expressed in his opinion strongly and emphatically that it was a swindle from the beginning. These are all matters of record; they are no newspaper charges; you can see them from the recorded proceedings of the court. Then there was a petition to have receivers appointed. Four men were named by the president of the Manhattan Company, the very company whose issue was in existence, to be receivers. After twenty-four hours' delay—practically after only three or four hours delay—the judge appointed as receivers two men, one of whom was the vice-president of the Wabash Railroad, of which Jay Gould was president, and who was reputed to be Mr. Gould's clerk; the other was one of Gould's lawyers: a man who had, early in the season, procured an injunction against the city to prohibit it from collecting taxes from these railroads. . . .

At the same time the receivers petitioned for leave to issue certificates of indebtedness. The judge granted that petition in Gould's office; while holding court in the office of one of the men whom common repute holds, and as I think holds correctly, was nothing but a wealthy shark, especially in the attitude he had taken toward the people about these very suits. Those certificates were issued on such terms as to make it impossible they could be taken up. The Manhattan stock at that time was only eighty-six per cent. The judge allowed these certificates, to the extent of one million dollars, to be issued, but all should be taken at six per cent or none be taken; all be taken at par or none be taken. It was an absolute impossibility they should be taken up. The issue of the order was simply ridiculous.

The affair went on, and on the 21st of October the judge declared, in a speech, that the corporation was a swindle—declared it emphatically, without any reserve. Four days after, he does not write, but telegraphs, an order allowing the road to go out of the hands of the receivers back into the hands of the Manhattan Company, which by that time had become synonymous with getting into the hands of Jay Gould, Cyrus W. Field, and Russell Sage. That is, four days after he said it was a swindle, he puts the whole road in the hands of the swindlers. That is an absolute fact, and can be verified by matters of record. Finally a court is held, when the final decision is rendered—not in public, not where you would expect a case like this, affecting fourteen million dollars, and which the attorney-general and the judge knew well was a mere swindle upon a large number of innocent stockholders; the court was held, not in a public court-room; but either in Attorney-General Ward's office, as he says, or, as other witnesses say, in Attorney-General Ward's private bedroom in the Delavan House. . . .

In addition to this, it must be remembered that the committee that is now investigating receiverships has published some facts which reflect the reverse of credit upon Judge Westbrook. We have a right to demand that our judiciary should be kept beyond reproach, and we have a right to demand that, if we find men against whom there is not only suspicion, but almost a certainty that they have had collusion with men whose interest was in conflict with those of the public, they shall at least be required to bring positive facts with which to prove there has not been such collusion, and they ought themselves to have been the first to demand such an investigation. It was a matter of great astonishment to me that during the three months that have elapsed such an investigation has not been asked. I was aware it ought to have been done by a man of more experience than myself, but as nobody else chose to demand it I certainly would in the interest of the Commonwealth of New York. I shall move to amend my resolution by allowing the committee to employ a stenographer and summon witnesses before them at a sitting held in New York. This is a most important investigation, and it should be treated with due weight. I hope my resolution will prevail.[8]

5. "A rare set of scoundrels . . ."

To William T. O'Neil [9]

New York, November 12, 1882

All Hail, fellow survivor of the late Democratic Deluge! I see you ran way ahead of your ticket. Down here such voting was never seen before. I carried my Assembly district by 2200 majority, the Republican Congressman by 700, and the Democratic Governor carried it by 1800 the other way! Sprague, in his district, got but 16 majority, and may be counted out. Robb, in the strongest Republican District in the city, was defeated by but 69 votes.

As far as I can judge the next House will contain a rare set of scoundrels, and we Republicans will be in such a hopeless minority that I do not see very clearly what we can accomplish, even in checking bad legislation. But at least we will do our best.[10]

6. "I accept the nomination . . ."

To Elihu Root,[11] *Chairman, and*
William H. Bellamy,[12]
Secretary, of the Republican County Convention.

New York, Oct. 16, 1886

Gentlemen: I accept the nomination for Mayor tendered me by the Republican Convention. I appreciate the honor and shall endeavor to justify your confidence. If elected I shall do my best to serve the Republican Party by serving the city well.

During three years' service in the State Legislature fully half my time was occupied in dealing with the intricate municipal misgovernment of this city, and it became evident to me that there could be no great or effective change for the better in our City Government except through

[8] *Works XIV,* pp. 7–11.
[9] Member of the New York Assembly and Roosevelt's closest ally there.
[10] *Letters I,* p. 58.
[11] New York lawyer, Secretary of War in McKinley's cabinet, headed Departments of War and State in Roosevelt's cabinet.
[12] Secretary, New York County Committee, 1886.

the unsparing use of the knife wielded by some man who could act unhampered by the political interests which sustain the present abuses, and without fear of either personal or political consequences. It is not enough that the Mayor refrain from making bad appointments or that he play a passively good part; to work a real reform he must devote his whole energy to actively grappling with and rooting out the countless evils and abuses already existing.

The chief reason for the continuance of these evils and abuses lies in the fact that hitherto no man having power has dared to deal with them without reference to the effect upon National and State politics. Many excellent gentlemen have deplored their existence and would have been glad to remedy them; but every effort against the spoilsmen who are eating up the substance of the city has been checked by the consideration that to assail them would affect unfavorably the control of some convention or the success of some election. Our City Government has been made a tender to National and State Party Government; the city is governed for the benefit of parties, instead of parties being governed for the benefit of the city. We are practically blackmailed to the extent of millions of dollars annually by a host of sinecurists whose return is rendered not in service to us but in protection and support to certain political leaders, candidates, and factions. Sooner or later the people of New York will realize that it is not sufficient merely to have at the head of their Government a man of high purpose and character, but that they must have one who shall also be entirely free from political entanglement with the beneficiaries of the present abuses; it is practically impossible for any member of the party now, and for so long past, dominant in our local affairs to work a real reform therein, for, no matter how good his aims, he would find himself at every step trammelled by a thousand personal and political ties.

Thanking you for the honor you have conferred upon me, I am, with great respect, yours very truly,

THEODORE ROOSEVELT [13]

7. "I have had first class fun . . ."

To Henry Cabot Lodge

New York, October 28, 1886

At any rate I have had first class fun out of this canvass. When I went into it it did seem the most hopeless, absolutely losing fight that mortal

[13] *Letters I*, p. 110.

can imagine. I have really enjoyed the matter, because, going in purely at the request of the Republican leaders, I felt that it was not at all a personal canvass, and so fought the whole thing through with a perfectly light heart. Of course where the Democratic majority is so overwhelming and where we have such a peculiarly large idiot vote among the so-called intelligent classes, a republican has awful odds against him and the chances are in favor of Hewitt. Still, there now is a certain small chance, although only a very, very small chance that I will succeed; that is, whereas the odds at the start were 100 to 1 against me, now I should think they are not more than five to one and I will probably make a fair run in any event. The *Post* has been pitching into me with all its malevolent hypocrisy. Before I end the campaign I think I shall indulge myself in the pleasure of a personal allusion to that beef-witted Chadband, Godkin. . . . If it were not for the infernal hypocritical rascality of such dishonest independents . . . I would really stand a first-class chance of success. But they succeed in frightening our weak-kneed voters into a perfect panic over George. . . .[14]

I have had every minute of my time taken up from the moment I first went into the canvass. You have no idea of the amount of work that we have done. All the young fellows downtown have stood up to the punishment like men. I've got the young men with me. It is only the timid, elderly gentlemen that I have to fear.

8. *"Something far more important . . ."*

To Laura D'Oremieulx Roosevelt[15]

New York, November 5, 1886

DEAR COUSIN LAURA, I thank you very much for so kindly thinking of me; I assure you it pleased me very greatly.

Now, for something far more important than the mayoralty. Tomorrow I sail for Europe to marry Miss Edith Carow, and I wish your best wishes.[16]

[14] Henry George, author of *Progress and Poverty*, the candidate of labor and various socialist groups. Abram S. Hewitt was the Democratic nominee.
[15] Cousin of Theodore Roosevelt.
[16] *Letters I*, p. 115.

Historian

Mr. Roosevelt began work in college on his first history, THE NAVAL WAR OF 1812, and published it two years after graduation. He wrote THE WINNING OF THE WEST during such intervals as his work as a member of the United States Civil Service Commission (1889–1895) allowed him.

1. The Backwoodsmen of the Alleghanies

Along the western frontier of the colonies that were so soon to be the United States, among the foot-hills of the Alleghanies, on the slopes of the wooded mountains, and in the long trough-like valleys that lay between the ranges, dwelt a peculiar and characteristically American people.

These frontier folk, the people of the up-country, or back-country, who lived near and among the forest-clad mountains, far away from the long-settled districts of flat coast plain and sluggish tidal river, were known to themselves and to others as backwoodsmen. They all bore a strong likeness to one another in their habits of thought and ways of living, and differed markedly from the people of the older and more civilized communities to the eastward. The western border of our country was then formed by the great barrier-chains of the Alleghanies, which ran north and south from Pennsylvania through Maryland, Virginia, and the Carolinas, the trend of the valleys being parallel to the seacoast, and the mountains rising highest to the southward. It was difficult to cross the ranges from east to west, but it was both easy and natural to follow the valleys between. From Fort Pitt to the high hill-homes of the Cherokees this great tract of wooded and mountainous country possessed nearly the same features and characteristics, differing utterly in physical aspect from the alluvial plains bordering the ocean.

So, likewise, the backwoods mountaineers who dwelt near the great watershed that separates the Atlantic streams from the springs of the

65

Watauga, the Kanawha, and the Monongahela, were all cast in the same mould, and resembled each other much more than any of them did their immediate neighbors of the plains. . . .

The backwoodsmen were Americans by birth and parentage, and of mixed race; but the dominant strain in their blood was that of the Presbyterian Irish—the Scotch-Irish, as they were often called. Full credit has been awarded the Roundhead and the Cavalier for their leadership in our history; nor have we been altogether blind to the deeds of the Hollander and the Huguenot; but it is doubtful if we have wholly realized the importance of the part played by that stern and virile people, the Irish whose preachers taught the creed of Knox and Calvin. These Irish representatives of the Covenanters were in the West almost what the Puritans were in the Northeast, and more than the Cavaliers were in the South. Mingled with the descendants of many other races, they nevertheless formed the kernel of the distinctively and intensely American stock who were the pioneers of our people in their march westward, the vanguard of the army of fighting settlers, who, with axe and rifle, won their way from the Alleghanies to the Rio Grande and the Pacific. . . .

That these Irish Presbyterians were a bold and hardy race is proved by their at once pushing past the settled regions, and plunging into the wilderness as the leaders of the white advance. They were the first and last set of immigrants to do this; all others have merely followed in the wake of their predecessors. But, indeed, they were fitted to be Americans from the very start; they were kinsfolk of the Covenanters; they deemed it a religious duty to interpret their own Bible, and held for a divine right the election of their own clergy. For generations their whole ecclesiastic and scholastic systems had been fundamentally democratic. In the hard life of the frontier they lost much of their religion, and they had but scant opportunity to give their children the schooling in which they believed; but what few meeting-houses and schoolhouses there were on the border were theirs. The numerous families of colonial English who came among them adopted their religion if they adopted any. . . .

These Presbyterian Irish were, however, far from being the only settlers on the border, although more than any others they impressed the stamp of their peculiar character on the pioneer civilization of the West and Southwest. Great numbers of immigrants of English descent came among them from the settled districts on the east; and though these later arrivals soon became indistinguishable from the people among whom they settled, yet they certainly sometimes added a tone of their own to backwoods society, giving it here and there a slight dash of what we are accustomed to consider the distinctively Southern or cavalier spirit. There was likewise a large German admixture, not only from the Germans of Pennsylvania, but also from those of the Carolinas. A good many Huguenots likewise came, and a few Hollanders, and even Swedes, from the banks of the Delaware, or perhaps from farther off still.

A single generation, passed under the hard conditions of life in the wilderness, was enough to weld together into one people the representatives of these numerous and widely different races; and the children of the next generation became indistinguishable from one another. Long before the first Continental Congress assembled, the backwoodsmen, whatever their blood, had become Americans, one in speech, thought, and character, clutching firmly the land in which their fathers and grandfathers had lived before them. They had lost all remembrance of Europe and all sympathy with things European; they had become as emphatically products native to the soil as were the tough and supple hickories out of which they fashioned the handles of their long, light axes. Their grim, harsh, narrow lives were yet strangely fascinating, and full of adventurous toil and danger; none but natures as strong, as freedom-loving, and as full of bold defiance as theirs could have endured existence on the terms which these men found pleasurable. Their iron surroundings made a mould which turned out all alike in the same shape. They resembled one another, and they differed from the rest of the world—even the world of America, and infinitely more, the world of Europe—in dress, in customs, and in mode of life.

Where their lands abutted on the more settled districts to the eastward, the population was of course thickest, and their peculiarities least. Here and there at such points they built small backwoods burgs or towns, rude, straggling, unkempt villages, with a store or two, a tavern—sometimes good, often a "scandalous hog-sty," where travellers were devoured by fleas, and every one slept and ate in one room—a small log schoolhouse, and a little church, presided over by a hard-featured Presbyterian preacher, gloomy, earnest, and zealous, probably bigoted and narrow-minded, but nevertheless a great power for good in the community.

However, the backwoodsmen as a class neither built towns nor loved to dwell therein. They were to be seen at their best in the vast, interminable forests that formed their chosen home. They won and kept their lands by force, and ever lived either at war or in dread of war. Hence they settled always in groups of several families each, all banded together for mutual protection. Their red foes were strong and terrible, cunning in council, dreadful in battle, merciless beyond belief in victory. The men of the border did not overcome and dispossess cowards and weaklings; they marched forth to spoil the stout-hearted and to take for a prey the possessions of the men of might. Every acre, every rood of ground which they claimed had to be cleared by the axe and held with the rifle. Not only was the chopping down of the forests the first preliminary to cultivation, but it was also the surest means of subduing the Indians, to whom the unending stretches of choked woodland were an impenetrable cover behind which to move unseen, a shield in making assaults, and a strong tower of defense in repelling counter-attacks. In the conquest of the West the backwoods axe, shapely, well-poised, with long haft and light head, was a servant hardly standing second even to the rifle; the two were the national weapons of the American backwoodsman, and in their use he has never been excelled.

When a group of families moved out into the wilderness they built themselves a station or stockade fort. . . .

The families only lived in the fort when there was war with the Indians. . . . At other times they all separated out to their own farms, universally called clearings, as they were always made by first cutting off the timber. . . . These clearings lay far apart from one another in the wilderness. Up to the door-sills of the log huts stretched the solemn and mysterious forest. There were no openings to break its continuity; nothing but endless leagues on leagues of shadowy, wolf-haunted woodland. The great trees towered aloft till their separate heads were lost in the mass of foliage above, and the rank underbrush choked the spaces between the trunks. On the higher peaks and ridge crests of the mountains there were straggling birches and pines, hemlocks and balsam firs; elsewhere, oaks, chestnuts, hickories, maples, beeches, walnuts, and great tulip-trees grew side by side with many other kinds. The sunlight could not penetrate the roofed archway of murmuring leaves; through the gray aisles of the forest men walked always in a kind of midday gloaming. Those who had lived in the open plains felt when they came to the backwoods as if their heads were hooded. Save on the border of a lake, from a cliff-top, or on a bald knob—that is, a bare hill-shoulder—they could not anywhere look out for any distance.

All the land was shrouded in one vast forest. It covered the mountains from crest to river-bed, filled the plains, and stretched in sombre and melancholy wastes toward the Mississippi. All that it contained, all that lay hid within it and beyond it, none could tell; men only knew that their boldest hunters, however deeply they had penetrated, had not yet gone through it, that it was the home of the game they followed and the wild beasts that preyed on their flocks, and that deep in its tangled depths lurked their red foes, hawk-eyed and wolf-hearted.

Backwoods society was simple, and the duties and rights of each member of the family were plain and clear. The man was the armed protector and provider, the bread-winner; the woman was the housewife and child-bearer. They married young and their families were large, for they were strong and healthy, and their success in life depended on their own stout arms and willing hearts. . . .

The life of the backwoodsmen was one long struggle. The forest had to be felled; droughts, deep snows, freshets, cloudbursts, forest-fires, and all the other dangers of a wilderness life faced. Swarms of deer-flies, mosquitoes, and midges rendered life a torment in the weeks of hot weather. Rattlesnakes and copperheads were very plentiful, and, the former especially, constant sources of danger and death. Wolves and bears were incessant and inveterate foes of the live stock, and the cougar, or panther, occasionally attacked man as well. More terrible still, the wolves sometimes went mad, and the men who then encountered them were almost certain to be bitten and to die of hydrophobia.

Every true backwoodsman was a hunter. . . . The hunter's ordinary game was the deer, and after that the bear; the elk was already growing uncommon. . . . The successful still-hunter of necessity possessed skill in hiding and in creeping noiselessly upon the wary quarry, as well as in imitating the notes and calls of the different beasts and birds; skill in the use of the rifle and in throwing the tomahawk he already had; and he perforce acquired keenness of eye, thorough acquaintance with woodcraft, and the power of standing the severest strains of fatigue, hardship, and exposure. He lived out in the woods for many months with no food but meat, and no shelter whatever, unless he made a lean-to of brush or crawled into a hollow sycamore.

Such training stood the frontier folk in good stead when they were pitted against the Indians; without it they could not even have held their own, and the white advance would have been absolutely checked. Our frontiers were pushed westward by the warlike skill and adventurous personal prowess of the individual settlers; regular armies by themselves could have done little. . . . The West would never have been settled save for the fierce courage and the eager desire to brave danger so characteristic of the stalwart backwoodsmen.

These armed hunters, wood-choppers, and farmers were their own soldiers. They built and manned their own forts; they did their own fighting under their own commanders. There were no regiments of regular troops along the frontier. In the event of an Indian inroad each borderer had to defend himself until there was time for them all to gather together to repel or avenge it. . . . A backwoods levy was formidable because of the high average courage and prowess of the individuals composing it; it was on its own ground much more effective than a like force of regular soldiers, but of course it could not be trusted on a long campaign. The backwoodsmen used their rifles better than the Indians, and also stood punishment better, but they never matched them in surprises nor in skill in taking advantage of cover, and very rarely equalled their discipline in the battle itself. . . .

The frontier, in spite of the outward uniformity of means and manners, is pre-eminently the place of sharp contrasts. The two extremes of society —the strongest, best, and most adventurous, and the weakest, most shiftless, and vicious—are those which seem naturally to drift to the border. Most of the men who came to the backwoods to hew out homes and rear families were stern, manly, and honest; but there was also a large influx of people drawn from the worst immigrants that perhaps ever were brought to America—the mass of convict servants, redemptioners, and the like, who formed such an excessively undesirable substratum to the otherwise excellent population of the tidewater regions in Virginia and the Carolinas. . . .

Moreover, the influence of heredity was no more plainly perceptible than was the extent of individual variation. If a member of a bad family wished to reform, he had every opportunity to do so; if a member of a good family had vicious propensities, there was nothing to check them. All qualities, good and bad, are intensified and accentuated in the life of the wilderness. The man who in civilization is merely sullen and bad-tempered becomes a murderous, treacherous ruffian when transplanted to the wilds; while, on the other hand, his cheery, quiet neighbor develops into a hero, ready uncomplainingly to lay down his life for his friend. One who in an Eastern city is merely a backbiter and slanderer, in the Western woods lies in wait for his foe with a rifle; sharp practice in the East becomes highway robbery in the West; but at the same time negative good-nature becomes active self-sacrifice, and a general belief in virtue is translated into a prompt and determined war upon vice. The ne'er-do-well of a family who in one place has his debts paid a couple of times and is then forced to resign from his clubs and lead a cloudy but innocuous existence on a small pension, in the other abruptly finishes his career by being hung for horse-stealing. . . .

They were superstitious, of course, believing in witchcraft and signs and omens; and it may be noted that their superstition showed a singular mixture of Old World survivals and of practices borrowed from the savages or evolved by the very force of their strange surroundings. At the bottom they were deeply religious in their tendencies; and although ministers and meeting-houses were rare, yet the backwoods cabins often contained Bibles, and the mothers used to instill into the minds of their children reverence for Sunday, while many even of the hunters refused to hunt on that day. Those of them who knew the right honestly tried to live up to it, in spite of the manifold temptations to backsliding offered by their lives of hard and fierce contention. . . .

Thus the backwoodsmen lived on the clearings they had hewed out of the everlasting forest; a grim, stern people, strong and simple, powerful for good and evil, swayed by gusts of stormy passion, the love of freedom rooted in their very hearts' core. Their lives were harsh and narrow, they gained their bread by their blood and sweat, in the unending struggle with the wild ruggedness of nature. They suffered terrible injuries at the hands of the red men, and on their foes they waged a terrible warfare in return. They were relentless, revengeful, suspicious, knowing neither ruth nor pity; they were also upright, resolute, and fearless, loyal to their friends, and devoted to their country. In spite of their many failings, they were of all men the best fitted to conquer the wilderness and hold it against all comers.[1]

2. King's Mountain

During the Revolutionary War the men of the West for the most part took no share in the actual campaigning against the British and Hessians. Their duty was to conquer and hold the wooded wilderness that stretched westward to the Mississippi; and to lay therein the foundations of many future commonwealths. Yet at a crisis in the great struggle for liberty, at one of the darkest hours for the patriot cause, it was given to a band of Western men to come to the relief of their brethren of the seaboard and to strike a telling and decisive blow for all America. When the three Southern provinces lay crushed and helpless at the feet of Cornwallis, the Holston backwoodsmen suddenly gathered to assail the triumphant conqueror. Crossing the mountains that divided them from the beaten and despairing people of the tide-water region, they killed the ablest lieutenant of the British commander, and at a single stroke undid all that he had done. . . .

Ferguson had pushed his victories to the foot of the Smoky and the Yellow mountains. Here he learned, perhaps for the first time, that there were a few small settlements beyond the high ranges he saw in his front; and he heard that some of these backwoods mountaineers had already borne arms against him and were now harboring men who had fled from before his advance. By a prisoner whom he had taken he at once sent them warning to cease their hostilities, and threatened that if they did not desist he would march across the mountains, hang their leaders, put their fighting men to the sword, and waste their settlements with fire. . . .

When the Holston men learned that Ferguson had come to the other side of the mountains . . . a flame of passionate anger was kindled in all their hearts. They did not wait for his attack; they sallied from their

[1] "The Winning of the West" (1889–1896). *Works VIII*, pp. 83–108.

strongholds to meet him. Their crops were garnered, their young men were ready for the march; and though the Otari war bands lowered like thunder-clouds on their southern border, they determined to leave only enough men to keep the savages at bay for the moment, and with the rest to overwhelm Ferguson before he could retreat out of their reach. Hitherto, the war with the British had been something afar off; now it had come to their thresholds, and their spirits rose to the danger. . . .

At Sevier's log house there was feasting and merrymaking, for he had given a barbecue, and a great horse-race was to be run, while the backwoods champions tried their skill as marksmen and wrestlers. In the midst of the merry-making Shelby appeared, hot with hard riding, to tell of the British advance, and to urge that the time was ripe for fighting, not feasting. Sevier at once entered heartily into his friend's plan, and agreed to raise his rifle-rangers, and to gather the broken and disorganized refugees who had fled across the mountains under McDowell. . . .

On the 26th they began the march, over a thousand strong, most of them mounted on swift, wiry horses. They were led by leaders they trusted, they were wonted to Indian warfare, they were skilled as horsemen and marksmen, they knew how to face every kind of danger, hardship, and privation. Their fringed and tasselled hunting-shirts were girded in by bead-worked belts, and the trappings of their horses were stained red and yellow. On their heads they wore caps of coonskin or minkskin, with the tails hanging down, or else felt hats, in each of which was thrust a bucktail or a sprig of evergreen. Every man carried a small-bore rifle, a tomahawk, and a scalping-knife. A very few of the officers had swords, and there was not a bayonet nor a tent in the army. Before leaving their camping-ground at the Sycamore Shoals they gathered in an open grove to hear a stern old Presbyterian preacher invoke on the enterprise the blessing of Jehovah. Leaning on their long rifles, they stood in rings round the black-frocked minister, a grim and wild congregation, who listened in silence to his words of burning zeal as he called on them to stand stoutly in the battle and to smite their foes with the sword of the Lord and of Gideon. . . .

At daybreak on the morning of the 6th the picked men set out, about seven hundred and fifty in number. . . . Riding all day they reached the Cowpens when the sun had already set. . . . The tired troops were speedily engaged in skinning beeves for their supper, roasting them by the blazing camp-fires; and fifty acres of corn, belonging to the rich Tory who owned the Cowpens, materially helped the meal. . . . Shortly after nine o'clock . . . nine hundred and ten picked riflemen, well mounted, rode out of the circle of flickering firelight, and began their night journey. A few determined footmen followed, going almost as fast as the horse, and actually reached the battle-field in season to do their share of the fighting. . . .

The stony, half-isolated ridge on which Ferguson camped was some six or seven hundred yards long and half as broad from base to base, or two-thirds that distance on top. The steep sides were clad with a growth of open woods, including both saplings and big timber. Ferguson parked his baggage-wagons along the northeastern part of the mountain. The next day he did not move; he was as near to the army of Cornwallis at Charlotte as to the mountaineers, and he thought it safe to remain where he was. He deemed the position one of great strength—as indeed it would have been, if assailed in the ordinary European fashion—and he was confident that even if the rebels attacked him he could readily beat them back. But, as General Lee, "Light-Horse Harry," afterward remarked, the hill was much easier assaulted with the rifle than defended with the bayonet. . . .

Without halting, Campbell and the other colonels rode forward together, and agreed to surround the hill so that their men might fire upward without risk of hurting one another. It was a bold plan; for they knew their foes probably outnumbered them; but they were very confident of their own prowess and were anxious to strike a crippling blow. . . . When within a mile of the hill a halt was called . . . and the men, who had been marching in loose order, were formed in line of battle.

The foes were now face to face. On the one side were the American backwoodsmen, under their own leaders, armed in their own manner, and fighting after their own fashion, for the freedom and the future of America; on the opposite side were other Americans—the Loyalists, led by British officers, armed and trained in the British fashion, and fighting on behalf of the empire of Britain and the majesty of the monarchy. The Americans numbered, all told, about nine hundred and fifty men. . . . Ferguson had, all told, between nine hundred and a thousand men.

The Americans were discovered by their foes when only a quarter of a mile away. They had formed their forces as they marched. The right centre was composed of Campbell's troops; the left centre of Shelby's. These two bodies separated slightly so as to come up opposite sides of the narrow southwestern spur of the mountain. The right wing was led by Sevier, with his own and McDowell's troops. On the extreme right Major Winston, splitting off from the main body a few minutes before, had led a portion of Cleavland's men by a round-about route to take the mountain in the rear, and cut off all retreat. He and his followers "rode like fox-hunters," as was afterward reported by one of their number who was accustomed to following the buck and the gray fox with horn and hound. They did not dismount until they reached the foot of the mountain, gal-

73

loping at full speed through the rock-strewn woods; and they struck exactly the right place, closing up the only gap by which the enemy could have retreated. . . .

So rapid were the movements of the Americans, and so unexpected the attack, that a Loyalist officer, who had been out reconnoitring, had just brought word to the British commander that there was no sign of danger, when the first shots were heard; and by the time the officer had paraded and posted his men, the assault had begun, his horse had been killed, and he himself wounded.

When Ferguson learned that his foes were on him, he sprang on his horse, his drums beat to arms, and he instantly made ready for the fight. Though surprised by the unexpected approach of the Americans, he exerted himself with such energy that his troops were in battle array when the attack began. The outcrops of slaty rock on the hillsides made ledges which, together with the boulders strewn on top, served as breastworks for the less-disciplined Tories; while he in person led his regulars and such of the Loyalist companies as were furnished with the hunting-knife bayonets. He hoped to be able to repulse his enemies by himself taking the offensive, with a succession of bayonet charges—a form of attack in which his experience with Pulaski and Huger had given him great confidence.

At three o'clock in the afternoon the firing began, as the Americans drove in the British pickets. The brunt of the battle fell on the American centre, composed of Campbell's and Shelby's men, who sustained the whole fight for nearly ten minutes until the two wings had time to get into place and surround the enemy. Campbell began the assault, riding on horseback along the line of his riflemen. He ordered them to raise the Indian war-whoop, which they did with a will, and made the woods ring. They then rushed upward and began to fire, each on his own account; while their war-cries echoed along the hillside. Ferguson's men on the summit resonded with heavy volley-firing, and then charged, cheering lustily. The mountain was covered with smoke and flame, and seemed to thunder. Ferguson's troops advanced steadily, their officers riding at their head, with their swords flashing; and the mountaineers, who had no bayonets, could not withstand the shock. They fled down the hillside, and being sinewy, nimble men, swift of foot, they were not overtaken, save a few of sullen temper, who would not retreat and were bayoneted. . . .

No sooner had the British charge spent itself than Campbell, who was riding midway between the enemy and his own men, called out to the latter in a voice of thunder to rally and return to the fight, and in a minute or two they were all climbing the hill again, going from tree to tree, and

74

shooting at the soldiers on the summit. Campbell's horse, exhausted by the breakneck galloping hither and thither over the slope, gave out; he then led the men on foot, his voice hoarse with shouting, his face blackened with powder; for he was always in the front of the battle and nearest the enemy.

No sooner had Ferguson returned from his charge on Campbell than he found Shelby's men swarming up to attack on the other side. Shelby himself was at their head. He had refused to let his people return the dropping fire of the Tory skirmishers until they were close up. Ferguson promptly charged his new foes and drove them down the hillside; but the instant he stopped, Shelby, who had been in the thick of the fight, closest to the British, brought his marksmen back, and they came up nearer than ever, and with a deadlier fire. While Ferguson's bayonet-men —both regulars and militia—charged to and fro, the rest of the Loyalists kept up a heavy fire from behind the rocks on the hilltop. The battle raged in every part, for the Americans had by this time surrounded their foes, and they advanced rapidly under cover of the woods. They inflicted much more damage than they suffered, for they were scattered out while the royalist troops were close together, and, moreover, were continually taken in flank. Ferguson, conspicuous from his hunting-shirt, rode hither and thither with reckless bravery, his sword in his left hand—for he had never entirely regained the use of his wounded right—while he made his presence known by the shrill, ear-piercing notes of a silver whistle which he always carried.

Whenever the British and Tories charged with the bayonet, under Ferguson, De Peyster, or some of their lieutenants, the mountaineers were forced back down the hill; but the instant the red lines halted and returned to the summit, the stubborn riflemen followed close behind, and from every tree and boulder continued their irregular and destructive fire. The peculiar feature of the battle was the success with which, after every retreat, Campbell, Shelby, Sevier, and Cleavland rallied their followers on the instant; the great point was to prevent the men from becoming panic-stricken when forced to flee. The pealing volleys of musketry at short intervals drowned the incessant clatter of the less noisy but more deadly backwoods rifles. The wild whoops of the mountain-men, the cheering of the Loyalists, the shouts of the officers, and the cries of the wounded mingled with the reports of the firearms, and shrill above the din rose the calling of the silver whistle. Wherever its notes were heard the wavering British line came on, and the Americans were forced back.

Ferguson dashed from point to point, to repel the attacks of his foes, which were made with ever-increasing fury. Two horses were killed under him; but he continued to lead the charging-parties, slashing and hewing

75

with his sword until it was broken off at the hilt. At last, as he rode full speed against a part of Sevier's men, who had almost gained the hill crest, he became a fair mark for the vengeful backwoods riflemen. Several of them fired together and he fell suddenly from his horse, pierced by half a dozen bullets almost at the same instant. The gallant British leader was dead, while his foot yet hung in the stirrup.

The silver whistle was now silent, but the disheartened Loyalists were rallied by De Peyster, who bravely continued the fight. It is said that he himself led one of the charges which were at this time made on Cleavland's line; the "South Fork" men from the Catawba, under Hambright and Chronicle, being forced back, Chronicle being killed and Hambright wounded. When the Americans fled, they were scarcely a gun's length ahead of their foes; and the instant the latter faced about the former were rallied by their officers, and again went up the hill. . . .

The victory was of far-reaching importance and ranks among the decisive battles of the Revolution. It was the first great success of the Americans in the South, the turning-point in the Southern campaign, and it brought cheer to the patriots throughout the Union.

The British regulars had lost half their number; the remainder had been scattered and exhausted in their successive charges. The bayonet companies of the Loyalist militia were in the same plight; and the North Carolina Tories, the least disciplined, could no longer be held to their work. Sevier's men gained the summit at the same time with Campbell's and part of Shelby's. The three colonels were heading their troops; and as Sevier saw Shelby, he swore, by God, the British had burned off part of his hair; for it was singed on one side of his head.

When the Holston and Watauga men gained the crest the Loyalists broke and fled to the east end of the mountain, among the tents and baggage-wagons, where they again formed. But they were huddled together, while their foes surrounded them on every hand. The fighting had lasted an hour; all hope was gone; and De Peyster hoisted a white flag.[2]

3. The Battle of Lake Champlain

A British army of 11,000 men under Sir George Prevost undertook the invasion of New York by advancing up the western bank of Lake Champlain. This advance was impracticable unless there was a sufficiently strong British naval force to drive back the American squadron at the same time. Accordingly, the British began to construct a frigate, the *Confiance,* to be added to their already existing force, which consisted of a brig, 2 sloops, and 12 or 14 gunboats. The Americans already possessed

[2] *Ibid.,* pp. 467–500.

a heavy corvette, a schooner, a small sloop, and 10 gunboats or row-galleys; they now began to build a large brig, the *Eagle,* which was launched about the 16th of August. Nine days later, on the 25th, the *Confiance* was launched. . . .

The British army advanced slowly toward Plattsburg, which was held by General Macomb with less than 2,000 effective American troops. Captain Thomas Macdonough, the American commodore, took the lake a day or two before his antagonist, and came to anchor in Plattsburg harbor. The British fleet, under Captain George Downie, moved from Isle-aux-Noix, on September 8th, and on the morning of the 11th sailed into Plattsburg harbor. . . .

Macdonough saw that the British would be forced to make the attack in order to get the control of the waters. On this long, narrow lake the winds usually blow pretty nearly north or south, and the set of the current is of course northward; all the vessels, being flat and shallow, could not beat to windward well, so there was little chance of the British making the attack when there was a southerly wind blowing. So late in the season there was danger of sudden and furious gales, which would make it risky for Downie to wait outside the bay till the wind suited him; and inside the bay the wind was pretty sure to be light and baffling. Young Macdonough (then but twenty-eight years of age) calculated all these chances very coolly and decided to await the attack at anchor in Plattsburg Bay, with the head of his line so far to the north that it could hardly be turned, and then proceeded to make all the other preparations with the same foresight. . . .

The morning of September 11th opened with a light breeze from the northeast. Downie's fleet weighed anchor at daylight, and came down the lake with the wind nearly aft, the booms of the two sloops swinging out to starboard. At half past seven, the people in the ships could see their adversaries' upper sails across the narrow strip of land ending in Cumberland Head, before the British doubled the latter. Captain Downie hove to with his four large vessels when he had fairly opened the bay, and waited for his galleys to overtake him. Then his four vessels filled on the starboard tack and headed for the American line, going abreast, the *Chubb* to the north heading well to windward of the *Eagle,* for whose bows the *Linnet* was headed, while the *Confiance* was to be laid athwart the hawse of the *Saratoga;* the *Finch* was to leeward with the twelve gunboats, and was to engage the rear of the American line.

As the English squadron stood bravely in, young Macdonough, who feared his foes not at all, but his God a great deal, knelt for a moment, with his officers, on the quarterdeck; and then ensued a few minutes of perfect quiet, the men waiting with grim expectancy for the opening of

77

the fight. The *Eagle* spoke first with her long 18's, but to no effect, for the shot fell short. Then, as the *Linnet* passed the *Saratoga,* she fired her broadside of long 12's, but her shot also fell short, except one that struck a hen-coop which happened to be aboard the *Saratoga.* There was a game-cock inside, and instead of being frightened at his sudden release, he jumped up on a gun-slide, clapped his wings, and crowed lustily. The men laughed and cheered; and immediately afterward Macdonough himself fired the first shot from one of the long guns. The 24-pound ball struck the *Confiance* near the hawse-hole and ranged the length of her deck, killing and wounding several men. All the American long guns now opened and were replied to by the British galleys.

The *Confiance* stood steadily on without replying. But she was baffled by shifting winds, and was soon so cut up, having both her port bow-anchors shot away, and suffering much loss, that she was obliged to port her helm and come to while still nearly a quarter of a mile distant from the *Saratoga.* Captain Downie came to anchor in grand style—securing everything carefully before he fired a gun, and then opening with a terribly destructive broadside. The *Chubb* and *Linnet* stood further in, and anchored forward of the *Eagle's* beam. Meanwhile the *Finch* got abreast of the *Ticonderoga,* under her sweeps, supported by the gunboats. The main fighting was thus to take place between the vans, where the *Eagle, Saratoga,* and six or seven gunboats were engaged with the *Chubb, Linnet, Confiance,* and two or three gunboats; while in the rear, the *Ticonderoga,* the *Preble,* and the other American galleys engaged the *Finch* and the remaining nine or ten English galleys.

The battle at the foot of the line was fought on the part of the Americans to prevent their flank being turned, and on the part of the British to effect that object. At first the fighting was at long range, but gradually the British galleys closed up, firing very well. The American galleys at this end of the line were chiefly the small ones, armed with one 12-pounder apiece, and they by degrees drew back before the heavy fire of their opponents. About an hour after the discharge of the first gun had been fired the *Finch* closed up toward the *Ticonderoga,* and was completely crippled by a couple of broadsides from the latter. She drifted helplessly down the line and grounded near Crab Island; some of the convalescent patients manned the 6-pounder and fired a shot or two at her, when she struck, nearly half of her crew being killed or wounded. About the same time the British gunboats forced the *Preble* out of line, whereupon she cut her cable and drifted inshore out of the fight. Two or three of the British gunboats had already been sufficiently damaged by some of the shot from the *Ticonderoga's* long guns to make them wary; and the contest at this part of the line narrowed down to one between the Amer-

78

ican schooner and the remaining British gunboats, who combined to make a most determined attack upon her. . . .

Meanwhile the fighting at the head of the line had been even fiercer. The first broadside of the *Confiance,* fired from 16 long 24's, double shotted, coolly sighted, in smooth water, at pointblank range, produced the most terrible effect on the *Saratoga.* Her hull shivered all over with the shock, and when the crash subsided nearly half of her people were seen stretched on deck, for many had been knocked down who were not seriously hurt. . . .

The survivors carried on the fight with undiminished energy. Macdonough himself worked like a common sailor, in pointing and handling a favorite gun. While bending over to sight it a round shot cut in two the spanker-boom, which fell on his head and struck him senseless for two or three minutes; he then leaped to his feet and continued as before, when a shot took off the head of the captain of the gun and drove it in his face with such a force as to knock him to the other side of the deck. . . .

At the extreme head of the line the advantage had been with the British. The *Chubb* and *Linnet* had begun a brisk engagement with the *Eagle* and American gunboats. In a short time the *Chubb* had her cable, bowsprit, and main-boom shot away, drifted within the American lines, and was taken possession of by one of the *Saratoga*'s midshipmen. The *Linnet* paid no attention to the American gunboats, directing her whole fire against the *Eagle,* and the latter was, in addition, exposed to part of the fire of the *Confiance.* . . . The *Linnet* now directed her attention to the American gunboats, which at this end of the line were very well fought, but she soon drove them off, and then sprung her broadside so as to rake the *Saratoga* on her bows.

Macdonough by this time had his hands full, and his fire was slackening; he was bearing the whole brunt of the action, with the frigate on his beam and the brig raking him. Twice his ship had been set on fire by the hot shot of the *Confiance;* one by one his long guns were disabled by shot, and his carronades were either treated the same way or else rendered useless by excessive overcharging. Finally but a single carronade was left in the starboard batteries, and on firing it the naval-bolt broke, the gun flew off the carriage and fell down the main-hatch, leaving the commodore without a single gun to oppose to the few the *Confiance* still presented. The battle would have been lost had not Macdonough's foresight provided the means of retrieving it. The anchor suspended astern of the *Saratoga* was let go, and the men hauled in on the hawser that led to the starboard quarter, bringing the ship's stern up over the kedge. The ship now rode by the kedge and by a line that had been bent to a bight in the stream cable, and she was raked badly by the accurate fire of the *Linnet.* By rousing on the line the ship was at length got so far round that the aftermost gun of the port broadside bore on the *Confiance.* The men had been sent forward to keep as much out of harm's way as possible, and now some were at once called back to man the piece, which then opened with effect. The next gun was treated in the same manner; but the ship now hung and would go no farther round. The hawser leading from the port quarter was then got forward under the bows and passed aft to the starboard quarter, and a minute afterward the ship's whole port battery opened with fatal effect.

The *Confiance* meanwhile had also attempted to round. Her springs, like those of the *Linnet,* were on the starboard side, and so of course could not be shot away as the *Eagle*'s were; but, as she had nothing but springs to rely on, her efforts did little beyond forcing her forward, and she hung with her head to the wind. She had lost over half of her crew, most of her guns on the engaged side were dismounted, and her stout masts had been splintered till they looked like bundles of matches; her sails had been torn to rags, and she was forced to strike, about two hours after she had fired the first broadside.

Without pausing a minute the *Saratoga* again hauled on her starboard hawser till her broadside was sprung to bear on the *Linnet,* and the ship and brig began a brisk fight, which the *Eagle* from her position could take no part in, while the *Ticonderoga* was just finishing up the British galleys. The shattered and disabled state of the *Linnet*'s masts, sails, and yards precluded the most distant hope of Captain Pring's effecting his escape by cutting his cable; but he kept up a most gallant fight with his greatly superior foe, in hopes that some of the gunboats would come and tow him off, and despatched a lieutenant to the *Confiance* to ascertain her state. The lieutenant returned with news of Captain Downie's death, while the British gunboats had been driven half a mile off; and, after having maintained the fight single-handed for fifteen minutes until, from the number of shot between wind and water, the water had risen a foot above her lower deck, the plucky little brig hauled down her colors, and the fight ended, a little over two hours and a half after the first gun had been fired. Not one of the larger vessels had a mast that would bear canvas, and the prizes were in a sinking condition. The British galleys drifted to leeward, none with their colors up; but as the *Saratoga*'s boarding officer passed along the deck of the *Confiance* he accidentally ran against a lock-string of one of her starboard guns, and it went off. This was apparently understood as a signal by the galleys, and they moved slowly off, pulling but a very few sweeps, and not one of them hoisting an ensign.

On both sides the ships had been cut up in the most extraordinary manner; the *Saratoga* had 55 shot-holes in her hull, and the *Confiance* 105 in hers, and the *Eagle* and *Linnet* had suffered in proportion. The number of killed and wounded cannot be exactly stated; it was probably about 200 on the American side, and over 300 on the British. . . .

The effects of the victory were immediate and of the highest importance. Sir George Prevost and his army at once fled in great haste and confusion back to Canada, leaving our northern frontier clear for the remainder of the war; while the victory had a very great effect on the negotiations for peace. . . .

Macdonough in this battle won a higher fame than any other commander of the war, British or American. He had a decidedly superior force to contend against, the officers and men of the two sides being about on a par in every respect; and it was solely owing to his foresight and resource that we won the victory. He forced the British to engage at a disadvantage by his excellent choice of position; and he prepared beforehand for every possible contingency. His personal prowess had already been shown at the cost of the rovers of Tripoli, and in this action he helped fight the guns as ably as the best sailor. His skill, seamanship, quick eye, readiness of resource, and indomitable pluck are beyond all praise.

Down to the time of the Civil War he is the greatest figure in our naval history. A thoroughly religious man, he was as generous and humane as he was skilful and brave; one of the greatest of our sea-captains, he has left a stainless name behind him.[3]

4. *"New Fields for Research"*

To Frederick Jackson Turner[4]

Washington, February 10, 1894

My Dear Sir: I have been greatly interested in your pamphlet on the Frontier. It comes at *the* right time for me, for I intend to make use of it in writing the third volume of my "Winning of the West," of course making full acknowledgment. I think you have struck some first class ideas, and have put into definite shape a good deal of thought which has been floating around rather loosely.[5]

[3] "The Naval War of 1812" (1882). *Works VI,* pp. 309–28.
[4] American historian, at that time professor of American history at the University of Wisconsin.
[5] *Letters I,* p. 363.

Washington, April 10, 1895

It was a great pleasure to me to find that you were my reviewer. I can assure you that I am not at all sensitive to intelligent criticism, and I entirely agree with you as to there being new fields for research in Western history upon which I haven't even touched. Take the two great points to which you are devoting yourself, the reaction of the West upon the East, and the history of institutions; the former of these I scarcely touch upon, and shall scarcely touch upon at all. The latter I shall touch upon but slightly, and hardly at all in the fourth volume. My aim is especially to show what the frontiersmen were and what they did, as they gradually conquered the West. The very interesting question of county as opposed to township government, for instance, I shall hardly more than allude to. Every man has his own limitations and his own special capacities. While I have been a government officer in various positions, ranging from Assemblyman in New York and Civil Service Commissioner in Washington to Deputy Sheriff in North Dakota, I have always been more interested in the men themselves than in the institutions through and under which they worked. Of course I understand entirely that you can't possibly treat one without treating the other more or less, but you can lay particular stress upon one or the other matter. . . .

I don't quite agree with you as to the unity of the West. It was a unit as against the East, and was not split by the North & South division of the East; but there was not a very great cohesion of the parts, as it seems to me.

New York, December 15, 1896

I was delighted to receive your letter. I am more and more inclined to think that you are quite right as to the inadvisability of my taking the tone I did toward Jefferson. The trouble is, that I meet so many understudies of Jefferson in politics and suffer so much from them that I am apt to let my feelings find vent in words! Fundamentally, I doubt if our conceptions, both of him and his Federalist opponents, differ very widely.

5. Francis Parkman's Histories

It is a fortunate thing when some great historic event, or chain of events, is commemorated by a great historian; and it is a matter for no small congratulation that the greatest historian whom the United States has yet produced should have found ready to his hand the all-important and singularly dramatic struggle which decided whether the destiny of

82

the North American continent should be shaped by the French or the English race.

Mr. Parkman has now finished the work to which he has devoted his life. He has portrayed from the beginning the history of the French power in North America, through all its phases, to the time when it went down in the final struggle with England. He has published different volumes under different titles; but now that they are completed they form a connected whole, under the general title of "France and England in North America." In addition, Mr. Parkman has published "The Conspiracy of Pontiac," which in point of time of publication antedates his volumes upon the French and Indian struggles, but which should really come in as the final volume of the series, as it describes the last great Indian war waged by the English on behalf of themselves and the colonists, and fills the gap between the close of the Franco-English struggle and the beginning of the Revolutionary War. In yet another book, the "Oregon Trail," he has recounted his adventures when, fresh from Harvard, he travelled across the great plains to the Rocky Mountains, with parties of wandering trappers and horse Indians. This book is not only interesting because it is one of the best accounts extant of the characteristic life of the American wilderness in the middle of this century, but because it was on this trip that the author largely acquired the comprehension of Indian life and character which give his histories no small portion of their peculiar excellence.

It is hard indeed for the average man to appreciate rightly the relative importance of the different movements going on about him. American historians very often fail signally in this respect. Questions of the tariff or of the currency, and the rise and fall of parties connected therewith absorb their attention. In reality all matters of this sort are of merely minor importance in our history. The conquest of this continent by the white race; which branch of the white race should win for itself the right to make this conquest; the struggle between the different European nationalities, and between all of them and the original red lords of the land; the establishment of national independence; the building of the National Government; the long contest over slavery; the war for the preservation of the Union—these are the really great matters with which American history deals. Mr. Parkman has seen clearly the epochal nature of the long rivalry between France and England in America; and with that eye for the dramatic which no great historian can lack, he has appreciated, and in his writings has made clear, not only the development of the drama through its various stages up to the crowning catastrophe of Wolfe and Montcalm, but also its place in history as one of the most important in the stages of the conquest of the North American continent.

Mr. Parkman would have been quite unequal to his task if he had not appreciated its romance as well as its importance. The effect of the settlement of North America by European races upon civilized mankind has been incalculable, and the movement has abounded with incidents of wild and picturesque adventure. Mr. Parkman has been himself a wilderness hunter and wanderer, and no one can read his writings without seeing that the strange charm of the wilderness and of wilderness life appeals to his very inmost soul. He himself can literally see before his eyes, and so can make his readers in turn see, the interminable wildness of the land —at once forbidding and attractive—as it stretched out before the eyes of the first European adventurers. The endless leagues of frowning forests, the great, lonely rivers, the limitless prairies, the lakes as large as inland seas, and the snow-capped summits of the Rocky Mountains—these he has himself seen, even as they were seen by the daring French explorers who first gazed upon them. . . .

Mr. Parkman has nowhere more clearly shown that combination of sympathy with his heroes, and yet of impartial judgment concerning their actions, than in his treatment of the marvellous career of the early Jesuit fathers in North America. Inspired by a fervent devotion to their church and religion, which was akin both to that of the early Christian martyrs and to that of the most warlike crusaders, these early Jesuits were among the pioneers in the exploration of the New World, and baptized and converted to at least nominal Christianity scores of tribes from the Bay of Fundy to Lake Superior and the mouth of the Mississippi. They suffered every conceivable kind of danger, discomfort, and hardship; they braved toil and peril like knights errant of the Middle Ages, and they met the most terrible deaths with cheerful, resolute composure. At one time it looked as though they might build up a great empire in the interior of this continent, with converted tribes of Indian warriors as its buttresses; and yet the fabric which they so laboriously reared proved unsubstantial and crumbled without in any way fulfilling its promise. Most of the Indians whom they had converted lapsed into heathenism, and most of the remainder remained Christians in little save the name. The lasting services they rendered were less as pioneers of Christianity than as explorers and map-makers.

In no one respect does Mr. Parkman more strikingly show his superiority to the average historian than in his treatment of the Indians. . . .

He knows the Indian character and the character of white frontiersman by personal observation as well as by books; neither knowledge by itself being of much value for a historian. In consequence he writes with a keen and clear understanding of the conditions which led to or influenced any given result. He is as little likely to take the view of the mere sentimentalist concerning the Indian as he is to take the view of the most brutal white borderer. He is not a special pleader for either race. He sets out facts as they are, blind neither to the fickleness, treachery, and inhuman cruelty of the red men, nor to the lawlessness, brutality, and ungovernable greed of the whites; nor yet is he blind to their good qualities. He is not one of those hysterical beings who feel that this continent ought to have been left to the Indians because it was wholly impossible to take it from them without inflicting and suffering a myriad of wrongs. In writing of New England at the time it was an Indian-harried province, he remarks, with quiet humor, that active sympathy for the Indian has never existed save in those who are out of reach of his tomahawk. On the other hand, he is careful to show with equal clearness the brutality so often evinced by the white borderers.

He shows the same sympathetic insight and the same absolute fairness in dealing with the chief actors in the drama of which he recounts the gradual development and ultimate outcome. Impartiality does not mean neutrality. The best historian must of necessity take sides when treating at least of certain conflicts and certain movements. All that is necessary is that the faults and merits of each party should be set forth clearly and fairly. Mr. Parkman never ceases from insisting upon the great central fact in the struggle he portrays. He shows with the utmost clearness that the French stood for the spirit of absolutism in Church and State, and the English for the spirit of religious and political freedom. In other words, the English colonists, whatever their imperfections, embodied the new spirit that was stirring mankind. They stood for the ideas which have gradually come to be called American; and the French, on the other hand, stood for the outworn feudalism and sacerdotalism of mediæval Europe. The real reason for the success of the English over the French lay deeper than the causes which produced defeat or failure in any given campaign or series of campaigns. The French colonists were controlled absolutely by a European government and by a foreign hierarchy. The English colonists, the Americans of that day, the fathers of the more fully developed Americans who won the Revolutionary War, represented— indeed, almost incarnated—the spirit of individualism, the spirit of equal rights and equal duties for all. In consequence, the English colonies flourished while the French did not. The French explorers, who were sometimes fur traders, sometimes officers of the king, sometimes officers of the church, pushed far and wide over the country, and reduced the vast expanse of continent to precarious submission to the French crown. The English colonies covered much less territory. They were more compact and far more densely peopled; and they had in them the spirit of growth, which the French had not. Their people increased, as the French did not;

and they finally broke down their antagonists by the sheer weight of the overflow of their hardy and vigorous population.

Yet while fully showing the necessity of English triumph if America was ever to be more than a geographical expression and while brushing aside with half-contemptuous courtesy the sentimental fabric that has been reared, for instance, over the fate of the Acadians, Mr. Parkman writes in a spirit of the fullest enthusiasm for the brilliant and lofty virtues of the French opponents of his people. He sets forth their mighty deeds as no historian of their own race has ever set them forth, because he is a great historian, and it is given to no nation to produce more than a very few such in a century. He dwells with loving admiration on their many feats, both as explorers and warriors. They were, indeed, a race with whom one can be proud to claim kinship, and proud to come of people who have manfully and successfully opposed them in battle. . . .

Mr. Parkman has done a great work which there is no need of any one trying to do again. He has shown all the qualities of the historian, capacity for wide and deep research, accuracy in details combined with power to subordinate these details to the general effect, a keen perception of the essential underlying causes and results, and the mastery of a singularly clear, pure, and strong style. He has had a great subject, he has considered it philosophically, and has treated it with knowledge, with impartiality, and with enthusiasm. He has now brought to an end the life task he set himself. He has produced a great book, and added to the sum of the successful efforts of his countrymen in a way that is given to but few of them to add.[6]

[6] *Works XII*, pp. 246–9.

Civic Reformer

~~~~~~

*As Civil Service Commissioner (1889–1895) and Presi-
dent of the New York Police Board (1895–1897), Mr.
Roosevelt laid the foundations of that public trust in his
integrity, courage and vision which gave the frothy fame of
his charge up San Juan Hill enduring substance.*

~~~~~~

1. "I hated to take the place . . ."

To Charles Joseph Bonaparte[1]

Washington, May 14, 1889

I hated to take the place; but I hardly thought I ought to refuse. I was
a good deal surprised at the offer, after my attack on Ingalls, and my
strenuous efforts to keep Pearson in. I had been pushing Swift of Indiana
for the place.

Now, we are so hampered that we must get our outside friends to help
us [by] information; do let me know if there is any crookedness, within
the scope of our powers to reduce, going on in Baltimore. I think—no
man can ever be sure—this commission means business.[2]

To Douglas and Corinne Robinson[3]

Washington, July 28, 1889

I have mortally hated being so much away from home this summer;
but I am very glad I took this place, and I have really enjoyed my work.
I feel it incumbent on me to try to amount to something, either in politics

[1] Grandnephew of Napoleon I, civil service reformer, Secretary of the Navy and
Attorney General under Roosevelt.
[2] *Letters I,* p. 161.
[3] Douglas Robinson married Roosevelt's younger sister Corinne.

87

or literature, because I have deliberately given up the hope of going into a money-making business. Of course, however, my political life is but an interlude—it is quite impossible to continue long to do much, between two sets of such kittle-cattle as the spoilsmen and the mugwumps.[4]

2. The Spoils System in Operation

It is mere idle chatter to talk of the merit system as being undemocratic and un-American. The spoils system is emphatically undemocratic, for the spoils system means the establishing and perpetuation of a grasping and ignorant oligarchy. The merit system is essentially democratic and essentially American, and in line with the utterances and deeds of our forefathers of the days of Washington and Madison. If you will pardon me, I will give a personal experience of mine in New York to prove the corruption of the spoils system. Without expressing too much local pride, I doubt if even Baltimore offers more fertile object-lessons of this sort than New York.

I remember when I was first elected to the legislature receiving several applications for appointment on the police force. One applicant said he wished to be a policeman because he unfortunately had the habit of getting drunk and so could not get any other work. Another wrote me, and I have the letter now, that he wanted me to get a friend of his appointed a policeman because the friend had promised him two hundred dollars to get him appointed, and he knew I would rather have that money go to a Republican than to a Democrat. Another instance occurred during the course of an investigation which, as chairman of a legislative committee, I conducted, into the working of some of the departments in New York. I cannot be absolutely certain as to the details of the figures at this distance of time, but what I shall say is in substance correct. We had under examination the county clerk, Mr. Keenan.

He was one of the most delightful witnesses that was ever before a legislative committee. Not having engaged counsel, he held back nothing and told us the literal truth. We asked him what was the amount of his fees in a year. He said eighty-two thousand dollars a year. Now, that is about a quarter of a million dollars for his three years' term. We asked him what he had contributed to the campaign fund of his party. Well, he didn't know. We pressed him, and finally he replied he could not say whether it was over or under fifty thousand dollars. Then came a question which was asked perfunctorily and to which an entirely perfunctory answer was expected. I asked him if he attended to the duties of his office. He rather electrified the committee by saying very promptly that he did

[4] *Ibid.,* p. 175.

not. I said: "Mr. Keenan, I doubt if you have understood the point of what I have asked you; I mean, do you do your official duties?" He answered: "Yes, when they don't interfere with my political duties." "Now," I said, "will you kindly explain to me what you mean by political duties?" That he evidently regarded as a piece of hypocrisy on my part, for he said to me reproachfully: "Mr. Roosevelt, you are a member of a political organization yourself." He then told us, by way of illustration of the pressure of his political duties, that he was unable to come down earlier in the morning than twelve o'clock, as he had to spend a good part of the morning "bailing out his 'constitutents'!"

I use this illustration merely to point out to you what is a spoilsman's theory of duty. He represented, I believe, the better class of spoilsmen, because there is a worse class—the class that steals. We had at that time a prominent member of the board of aldermen who in his leisure hours was a burglar. In his youth he had followed that trade, and though rather an old man, and one who had risen in the world, he would still resume it occasionally for amusement. We had another very prominent politician who was a "fence," a receiver of stolen goods. Mr. Keenan was a perfectly honest man as far as I know. It never occurred to him that that was not the right way to run a public office. He told us another fact which illustrates the wastefulness of the spoils system. I asked Keenan how he did his duties, and he said he paid his deputy extra to do them. This deputy was paid three thousand dollars a year by the city to do his own work as deputy, but Keenan, out of his eighty-two thousand dollars, paid one thousand five hundred dollars more to his deputy to do Keenan's work. So that gives you the exact market value of the work Keenan had to do. This immense sum of eighty-two thousand dollars was regarded partly as a reward for Keenan's political services, and partly as a fund to defray campaign expenses for his party. A state of affairs like that will inevitably produce corruption in the ballot. In New York City I don't believe there is as much actual buying of votes, although there is a good deal, as there is in the country districts, but corruption is generally effected by buying the district leaders or the district organizations. These would be powerless but for the spoils system.

Pardon me one more personal reminiscence. The last time I appeared before my people for office, a gentleman told me that whatever party I belonged to before the election, after the election I belonged to the party of "the extreme left." Possibly this story will explain my misfortune as well as illustrate my point.

I was at our headquarters one day, when a card was brought in from O'Donovan Rossa. I went out to see him, and he was not a prepossessing-looking gentleman. He came down straight and square and instantly to work. He said I was running for mayor and he would like to help me, and would guarantee me his influence in his journal and in his local dynamite societies for the sum of two hundred and fifty dollars. I told him that I was much obliged for his courtesy in thinking of me, but I would not close with his offer. "I see," he said, "you are running this canvass for your health; I thought you wanted to win." Then I told him there were very few people in New York whom I could afford to insult at that time, but he was one of them, and I would thank him to get out.

These are not exceptional cases, but are the habitual, invariable accompaniment and product of the spoils system in great cities.

I think that, of all people who are harmed by the spoils system, the poor suffer most. The rich man who wishes to corrupt a legislature, or the rich company which wishes to buy franchises from a board of aldermen and pay a big price for it, do not suffer so much as the poor from the results of the system. I dare say that in New York we see the system at its worst, but at its best it is thoroughly rotten, and a disgrace to every community enjoying the right of suffrage.[5]

3. Sad Story of a Bright Young Man

To Arthur P. Gorman[6]

Washington, March 1, 1891

Sir: On Feb. 23rd last you commented with some temper upon me for having in a letter to you, and also in public speeches "called you to account very severely" for what you said on the floor of the Senate, a a couple of years ago, in criticising the action of the Civil Service Commission; and you further remarked that you had at the time "sought to correct a great evil" which had arisen owing to our "stupidity"; and that I had "gone beyond the bounds of propriety" and been guilty of "audacity" because as you said, I had found fault with you for having "attempted to correct the defects growing out of [the Commissioner's] want of ability to enforce the Civil Service law in a practical and fair way." You added that you had neither answered nor taken any notice of my letter, deeming my action outrageous and insolent.

Permit me to refresh your memory as to the facts in the case. In a speech in the Senate in 1889 you criticised the alleged extraordinary and impractical questions which the Commission propounded to applicants and gave an account of a [purely imaginary] "outrage" perpetrated by

[5] *Works XIV*, pp. 89–92.
[6] Democratic senator from Maryland.

our local board in Baltimore upon a friend of yours, "a bright young man" who tried to pass the letter carriers' examination. You said "They wanted him to tell them what was the most direct route from Baltimore to Japan, and, as he said, he never intended to go to Japan, he had never looked into that question, and he failed to make the proper answer. They then wanted to know the number of lines of steamers plying between the United States and Liverpool or London. . . . They then branched him off into geometry . . . and passing over everything that looked to his qualifications he was rejected." There is not one word of truth in this statement from beginning to end; each individual assertion is a falsehood. No such questions and none even remotely resembling them have ever been asked in any of our examinations for letter carriers, whether at Baltimore or elsewhere. In these as in all our other examinations the questions asked are practical and are relevant to the duties to be performed in the place sought for.

Later in the same year you substantially reiterated these statements in interviews in the press and they were widely quoted and used as arguments against the Commission. Your high official position, which gave them currency and credence, made it imperative that they should be answered.

As there was not a word of truth in your allegations it was evident either that you were wilfully stating what you knew to be false, or else that you had been grossly deceived by your friend "the bright young man." I acted on the latter supposition, and wrote you a perfectly respectful letter, pointing out that we had never asked any such questions as you alleged, and offering to show all the letter carrier examination papers we had ever used either to you, or if you had not the time, to some one whom you might appoint to examine them at his leisure. You received this letter but never answered it. Be it remembered that my offer to you to examine all our letter carriers' examination papers is still open. Or you can give us the name of the "bright young man," if he has any name, or if you have forgotten his name, you can state to us the time at which he was examined, and we shall send to you or make public any examination papers we then used.

It was then evident, after you refused to answer and failed to retract your statements, that whether you had originally erred through ignorance or not you had no intention of withdrawing the untruths you had uttered. The only course left me was to publish an authoritative and flat contradiction of your statement, with an account of my dealings with you. This was the course I followed. That it should have irritated you I do not wonder. Your position was not a pleasant one, and it is no pleasanter now.[7]

[7] *Letters I,* pp. 239–40.

4. "I am having a hard row to hoe . . ."

To Henry Cabot Lodge

Washington, June 29, 1889

I am having a hard row to hoe. I have made this Commission[8] a living force, and in consequence the outcry among the spoilsmen has become furious; it has evidently frightened both the President and Halford a little. They have shown symptoms of telling me that the law should be rigidly enforced where people will stand it, and gingerly handled elsewhere. But I have answered militantly; that as long as I was responsible the law should be enforced up to the handle *every where;* fearlessly and honestly. I am a great believer in practical politics; but when my duty is to enforce the law, that law is surely going to be enforced, without fear or favor. I am perfectly willing to be turned out—or legislated out—but while in I mean business. As a matter of fact, I believe I have strengthened the administration by showing, in striking contrast to the facts under Cleveland, that there was no humbug in the law now. All the Chicago and Milwaukee papers are backing me up heartily. The Indiana men are very angry—even Browne has gone back on his previous record. It is disheartening to see such folly; but its only effect on me personally is to make me more doggedly resolute than ever to insist on exact and full justice.[9]

5. "There will be a row . . ."

To Henry Cabot Lodge

Washington, June 24, 1889

We had only a week's trip but we stirred things up well; the President has made a great mistake in appointing a well-meaning, weak old fellow in Indianapolis, but I think we have administered a galvanic shock that will reinforce his virtue for the future. Cleveland's postmaster at Milwaukee is about as thorough paced a scoundrel as I ever saw—an oily-Gammon, church-going specimen. We gave him a neat hoist. The Chicago postmaster is a trump; a really good fellow (Republican). At Grand Rapids, the redoubtable Congressman Belknap turned up as meek as a lamb and we fraternized most amicably. The West knows much less

[8] The Civil Service Commission.
[9] *Letters I*, p. 167.

about civil service reform than the East, and there will be a row next winter.

Oyster Bay, July 6, 1889

You blessed but jaundiced sage, Your letters were so very gloomy that they made me quite regain my spirits. Edith thoroughly agrees with you about interviews; so I cry *peccavi* and will assume a statesmanlike reserve of manner whenever reporters come near me. Seriously, I was led into saying so much by the not unnatural desire to hit back at the western politicians who were hitting at me.

6. *"I would like to do my share . . ."*

To Anna Roosevelt

Washington, April 14, 1895

Strong first offered me the position of Police Commissioner through a third party, and I refused. He then offered it to me again, directly. By this time I had received numerous requests to accept; and I have accepted subject to getting decent colleagues; but it is not yet final, for I have not heard in response from the Mayor.

I hated to leave Washington, for I love the life; and I shall have, if I go, much hard work, and I will hardly be able to keep on with my literary matters. Moreover it is a position in which it is absolutely impossible to do what will be expected of me; the conditions will not admit it. I must make up my mind to much criticism and disappointment.

But, on the other hand, I am nearly through what I can do here; and this is a good way of leaving a position which I greatly like but which I do not wish permanently to retain, and I think it a good thing to be definitely identified with my city once more. I would like to do my share in governing the city after our great victory; and so far as may be I would like once more to have my voice in political matters. It was a rather close decision; but on the whole I felt I ought to go, though it is "taking chances." [10]

7. *Administering the New York Police Force*

In New York, in the fall of 1894, Tammany Hall was overthrown by a coalition composed partly of the regular republicans, partly of anti-

[10] *Ibid.,* pp. 441–2.

Tammany democrats, and partly of independents. Under the latter head must be included a great many men who in national politics habitually act with one or the other of the two great parties, but who feel that in municipal politics good citizens should act independently. The tidal wave, which was running high against the democratic party, was undoubtedly very influential in bringing about the anti-Tammany victory; but the chief factor in producing the result was the wide-spread anger and disgust felt by decent citizens at the corruption which, under the sway of Tammany, had honeycombed every department of the city government, but especially the police force. A few well-meaning people have at times tried to show that this corruption was not really so very great. In reality it would be difficult to overestimate the utter rottenness of many branches of the city administration. There were a few honorable and high-minded Tammany officials, and there were a few bureaus which were administered with more or less efficiency, although dishonestly. But the corruption had become so wide-spread as seriously to impair the work of administration, and to bring us back within measurable distance of the days of Tweed.

The chief centre of corruption was the Police Department. No man not intimately acquainted with both the lower and humbler sides of New York life—for there is a wide distinction between the two—can realize how far this corruption extended. Except in rare instances, where prominent politicians made demands which could not be refused, both promotions and appointments toward the close of Tammany rule were made almost solely for money, and the prices were discussed with cynical frankness. There was a well-recognized tariff of charges ranging from two or three hundred dollars for appointment as a patrolman, to twelve or fifteen thousand dollars for promotion to the position of captain. The money was reimbursed to those who paid it by an elaborate system of blackmail. This was chiefly carried on at the expense of gamblers, liquor sellers, and keepers of disorderly houses; but every form of vice and crime contributed more or less, and a great many respectable people who were ignorant or timid were blackmailed under pretence of forbidding or allowing them to violate obscure ordinances and the like. From top to bottom the New York police force was utterly demoralized by the gangrene of such a system, where venality and blackmail went hand in hand with the basest forms of low ward politics, and where the policeman, the ward politician, the liquor seller, and the criminal alternately preyed on one another and helped one another to prey on the general public.

In May, 1895, I was made president of the newly appointed police board, whose duty it was to cut out the chief source of civic corruption in

94

New York by cleansing the police department. The police board consisted of four members. . . .

Certain of the difficulties we had to face were merely those which confronted the entire reform administration in its management of the municipality. Many worthy people expected that this reform administration would work an absolute revolution, not merely in the government, but in the minds of the citizens as a whole; and felt vaguely that they had been cheated because there was not an immediate cleansing of every bad influence in civic or social life. Moreover, the different bodies forming the victorious coalition felt the pressure of conflicting interests and hopes. The mass of effective strength was given by the republican organization, and not only all the enrolled party workers, but a great number of well-meaning republicans who had no personal interest at stake, expected the administration to be used to further the fortunes of their own party. Another great body of the administration's supporters took a diametrically opposite view, and believed that the administration should be administered without the least reference whatever to party. In theory they were quite right, and I cordially sympathized with them; but as a matter of fact the victory could not have been won by the votes of this class of people alone, and it was out of the question to put these theories into complete effect. Like all other men who actually try to do things instead of confining themselves to saying how they should be done, the members of the new city government were obliged to face the facts and to do the best they could in the effort to get some kind of good result out of the conflicting forces. They had to disregard party so far as was possible; and yet they could not afford to disregard all party connections so utterly as to bring the whole administration to grief. . . .

Immediately after the new board was appointed to office the machine got through the Legislature the so-called bi-partisan or Lexow law, under which the department is at present administered; and a more foolish or vicious law was never enacted by any legislative body. . . . It provides for a four-headed board, so that it was difficult to get a majority anyhow; but, lest we should get such a majority, it gave each member power to veto the actions of his colleagues in certain very important matters; and, lest we should do too much when we were unanimous, it provided that the chief, our nominal subordinate, should have entirely independent action in the most important matters, and should be practically irremovable, except for proved corruption; so that he was responsible to nobody. The Mayor was similarly hindered from removing any Police Commissioner, so that when one of our colleagues began obstructing the work of the board, and thwarting its effort to reform the force, the Mayor in

95

vain strove to turn him out. In short, there was a complete divorce of power and responsibility, and it was exceedingly difficult either to do anything, or to place anywhere, the responsibility for not doing it.

If, by any reasonable concessions, if, indeed, by the performance of any act not incompatible with our oaths of office, we could have stood on good terms with the machine, we would certainly have made the effort, even at the cost of sacrificing many of our ideals; and in almost any other department we could probably have avoided a break, but in the police force such a compromise was not possible. What was demanded of us usually took some such form as the refusal to enforce certain laws, or the protection of certain lawbreakers, or the promotion of the least fit men to positions of high power and grave responsibility; and on such points it was not possible to yield. We were obliged to treat all questions that arose purely on their merits, without reference to the desires of the politicians. We went into this course with our eyes open, for we knew the trouble it would cause us personally, and, what was far more important, the way in which our efforts for reform would consequently be hampered. However, there was no alternative, and we had to abide by the result. We had counted the cost before we adopted our course, and we followed it resolutely to the end. . . .

In administering the police force we found, as might be expected, that there was no need of genius, nor indeed of any very unusual qualities. What was needed was exercise of the plain, ordinary virtues, of a rather commonplace type, which all good citizens should be expected to possess. Common sense, common honesty, courage, energy, resolution, readiness to learn, and a desire to be as pleasant with everybody as was compatible with a strict performance of duty—these were the qualities most called for. We soon found that, in spite of the widespread corruption which had obtained in the New York Police Department, the bulk of the men were heartily desirous of being honest. There were some who were incurably dishonest, just as there were some who had remained decent in spite of terrific temptation and pressure; but the great mass came in between. Although not possessing the stamina to war against corruption when the odds seemed well-nigh hopeless, they were nevertheless heartily glad to be decent and to welcome the change to a system under which they were rewarded for doing well, and punished for doing ill.

Our methods for restoring order and discipline were simple, and indeed so were our methods for securing efficiency. We made frequent personal inspections, especially at night, turning up anywhere, at any time. We thus speedily got an idea of whom among our upper subordinates we could trust and whom we could not. We then proceeded to punish those guilty of shortcomings, and to reward those who did well, refusing

96

to pay any heed whatever in either case to anything except the man's own character and record. A very few of these promotions and dismissals sufficed to show our subordinates that at last they were dealing with superiors who meant what they said, and that the days of political "pull" were over while we had the power. The effect was immediate. The decent men took heart, and those who were not decent feared longer to offend. The morale of the entire force improved steadily. . . .

To break up the system of blackmail and corruption was less easy. . . . The criminal who is blackmailed has a direct interest in paying the blackmailer, and it is not easy to get information about it. Nevertheless, we put a complete stop to most of the blackmail by the simple process of rigorously enforcing the laws, not only against crime, but against vice.

It was the enforcement of the liquor law which caused most excitement. In New York we suffer from the altogether too common tendency to make any law which a certain section of the community wants, and then to allow that law to be more or less of a dead-letter if any other section of the community objects to it. The multiplication of laws by the Legislature, and their partial enforcement by the executive authorities, go hand in hand, and offer one of the many serious problems with which we are confronted in striving to better civic conditions. New York State felt that liquor should not be sold on Sunday. The larger part of New York City wished to drink liquor on Sunday. Any man who studies the social condition of the poor knows that liquor works more ruin than any other one cause. He knows also, however, that it is simply impracticable to extirpate the habit entirely, and that to attempt too much often merely results in accomplishing too little; and he knows, moreover, that for a man alone to drink whiskey in a bar-room is one thing, and for men with their families to drink light wines or beer in respectable restaurants is quite a different thing. The average citizen, who doesn't think at all, and the average politician of the baser sort, who only thinks about his own personal advantage, find it easiest to disregard these facts, and to pass a liquor law which will please the temperance people, and then trust to the police department to enforce it with such laxity as to please the intemperate.

The results of this pleasing system were evident in New York when our board came into power. The Sunday liquor law was by no means a dead letter in New York City. On the contrary no less than eight thousand arrests for its violation had been made under the Tammany régime the year before we came in. It was very much alive; but it was only executed against those who either had no political pull, or who refused to pay money. The liquor business does not stand on the same footing with other occupations. It always tends to produce criminality in the population at large, and law-breaking among the saloonkeepers themselves. It is absolutely necessary to supervise it rigidly, and impose restrictions upon the traffic. In large cities the traffic cannot be stopped; but the evils can at least be minimized.

In New York the saloonkeepers have always stood high among professional politicians. Nearly two thirds of the political leaders of Tammany Hall have, at one time or another, been in the liquor business. The saloon is the natural club and meeting place for the ward heelers and leaders, and the bar-room politician is one of the most common and best recognized factors, in local political government. The saloonkeepers are always hand in glove with the professional politicians, and occupy toward them a position such as is not held by any other class of men. The influence they wield in local politics has always been very great, and until our board took office no man ever dared seriously to threaten them for their flagrant violations of the law. The powerful and influential saloonkeeper was glad to see his neighbors closed, for it gave him business. On the other hand, a corrupt police captain, or the corrupt politician who controlled him, could always extort money from a saloonkeeper by threatening to close him and let his neighbor remain open. Gradually the greed of corrupt police officials and of corrupt politicians, grew by what it fed on, until they began to blackmail all but the very most influential liquor sellers; and as liquor sellers were very numerous, and the profits of the liquor business great, the amount collected was enormous.

The reputable saloonkeepers themselves found this condition of blackmail and political favoritism almost intolerable. . . . The law . . . was enforced, but it was corruptly and partially enforced. It was a prominent factor in the Tammany scheme of government. It afforded a most effective means for blackmailing a large portion of the liquor sellers and for the wholesale corruption of the police department. The high Tammany officials and police captains and patrolmen blackmailed and bullied the small liquor sellers without a pull, and turned them into abject slaves of Tammany Hall. On the other hand, the wealthy and politically influential liquor sellers controlled the police, and made or marred captains, sergeants, and patrolmen at their pleasure. In some of the precincts most of the saloons were closed; in others almost all were open. The rich and powerful liquor seller violated the law at will, unless he had fallen under the ban of the police or the ward boss, when he was not allowed to violate it at all.

Under these circumstances the new police board had one of two courses to follow. We could either instruct the police to allow all the saloonkeepers to become law-breakers, or else we could instruct them to allow none to be law-breakers. We followed the latter course, because we had some regard for our oaths of office. For two or three months we had a regular fight, and on Sundays had to employ half the force to enforce the liquor law; for the Tammany legislators had drawn the law so as to make it easy of enforcement for purposes of blackmail, but not easy of enforcement generally, certain provisions being deliberately inserted with the intention to make it difficult of universal execution. However, when once the liquor sellers and their allies understood that we had not the slightest intention of being bullied, threatened or cajoled out of following the course which we had laid down, resistance practically ceased. During the year after we took office the number of arrests for violation of the Sunday liquor law sank to about one half of what they had been during the last year of the Tammany rule; and yet the saloons were practically closed, whereas under Tammany most of them had been open. We adopted no new methods, save in so far as honesty could be called a new method. We did not enforce the law with unusual severity; we merely enforced it against the man with a pull, just as much as against the man without a pull. We refused to discriminate in favor of influential law-breakers. The professional politicians of low type, the liquor sellers, the editors of some German newspapers, and the sensational press generally, attacked us with a ferocity which really verged on insanity. . . .

There was no species of mendacity to which our opponents did not resort in the effort to break us down in our purpose. For weeks they eagerly repeated the tale that the saloons were as wide open as ever. . . . They then took the line that by devoting our attention to enforcing the liquor law we permitted crime to increase. . . . A commentary upon its accuracy was furnished toward the end of our administration; for in February 1897, the Judge who addressed the grand jury of the month was able to congratulate them upon the fact that there was at that time less crime in New York relatively to the population than ever before; and this held true for our two years' service. . . .

There was a striking increase in the honesty of the force, and there was a like increase in its efficiency. When we took office it is not too much to say that the great majority of the citizens of New York were firmly convinced that no police force could be both honest and efficient. They felt it to be part of the necessary order of things that a policeman should be corrupt, and they were convinced that the most efficient way of warring against certain forms of crime—notably crimes against person and property—was by enlisting the service of other criminals, and of purveyors of vice generally, giving them immunity in return for their aid. Before we took power the ordinary purveyor of vice was allowed to ply his or her trade unmolested, partly in consideration of paying blackmail to the police, partly in consideration of giving information about any criminal

99

who belonged to the unprotected classes. We at once broke up this whole business of blackmail and protection, and made war upon all criminals alike, instead of getting the assistance of half in warring on the other half.

Nevertheless, so great was the improvement in the spirit of the force, that, although deprived of their former vicious allies, they actually did better work than ever before against those criminals who threatened life and property. Relatively to the population, fewer crimes of violence occurred during our administration of the Board than in any previous two years of the city's history in recent times; and the total number of arrests of criminals increased, while the number of cases in which no arrest followed the commission of crime decreased. . . .

The result of our labors was of value to the city, for we gave the citizens better protection than they had ever before received, and at the same time cut out the corruption which was eating away civic morality. We showed conclusively that it was possible to combine both honesty and efficiency in handling the police. We were attacked with the most bitter animosity by every sensational newspaper and every politician of the baser sort, not because of our shortcomings, but because of what we did that was good. We enforced the laws as they were on the statute books, we broke up blackmail, we kept down the spirit of disorder, and repressed rascality, and we administered the force with an eye single to the welfare of the city. In doing this we encountered, as we had expected, the venomous opposition of all men whose interest it was that corruption should continue, or who were of such dull morality that they were not willing to see honesty triumph at the cost of strife.[11]

8. "I spent the night in patrolling New York . . ."

To Anna Roosevelt

Sagamore Hill, June 16, 1895

Twice I have spent the night in patrolling New York on my own account, to see exactly what the men were doing. My experiences were interesting, and the trips did good, though each meant my going forty hours at a stretch without any sleep. But in spite of my work I really doubt whether I have often been in better health. It is very interesting; and I feel as though it was so eminently practical; it has not a touch of the academic. Indeed anything more practical it would be hard to imag-

[11] "American Ideals." *Works VIII,* pp. 118–34.

ine. I am dealing with the most important, and yet most elementary, problems of our municipal life. The work has absorbed me.[12]

9. "A Welter of Small Political Intrigue"

To Henry Cabot Lodge

Oyster Bay, December 23, 1895

Here I am living in a welter of small political intrigue of the meanest kind. . . . I find that Whitelaw Reid was given orders that in the *Tribune* I am not to be mentioned save to attack me, unless it is unavoidable; this came to me in a curious fashion, first hand. Mayor Strong has been guilty of flagrant double dealing, and intends to attack us in his message to the Board of Aldermen. The Platt people are planning to legislate me out of office under cover of a necessary amendment to the Greater New York bill; and are getting Morton's help by insisting that I am for Tom Reed, whereas *they* are for Morton—and are trying to impress Reed to the contrary meanwhile. Many of the Brookfield wing, headed by the Mayor, are really hostile to me because they wish either McKinley or Harrison.

Every now and then I feel a momentary discouragement; for it really seems that there *must* be some fearful shortcoming on my side to account for the fact that I have not one N.Y. city newspaper or one N.Y. city politician of note on my side. Don't think that I even for a moment dream of abandoning my fight; I shall continue absolutely unmoved on my present course and shall accept philosophically whatever violent end may be put to my political career.[13]

To Anna Roosevelt Cowles[14]

689 Madison Avenue
Feb. 16th, '96

All day I strive to push matters along; to keep on good terms with the Mayor, while rejecting his advice and refusing to obey his orders; not to be drawn into a personal quarrel with Platt; not to let my colleagues split

---

[12] *Letters I*, p. 462.
[13] *Ibid.*, p. 502.
[14] Anna Roosevelt married W. Sheffield Cowles, captain, U.S.N., in November, 1895.

either among themselves or with me; to work with reformers like Dr. Parkhurst, and yet not let them run away with the Department; to keep weeding out the bad men; to attend to the thousand complaints, well and ill-founded, of citizens; to try to improve discipline, and to build up the detective bureau, and develop leaders; and so on and so on.[15]

Sagamore Hill
June 28, 1896

The work of the Police Board has absorbed all the time and energy I could give to such work at all. There is nothing of the purple in it; it is as grimy as all work for municipal reform over here must be for some decades to come; and it is inconceivably arduous, disheartening and irritating, beyond almost all other work of the kind, because of the special circumstances of the case. I have to contend with the hostility of Tammany, and the almost equal hostility of the Republican machine; I have to contend with the folly of the reformers and the indifference of decent citizens; above all, I have to contend with the singularly foolish law under which we administer the Department. If I were like Waring, a single-headed commission, with absolute power (not to speak of his having an infinitely less difficult problem to solve) I could in a couple of years have accomplished almost all I desire; were I even the member of a three-headed commission, like the Boston Police Department, with absolute power, I could have accomplished very much; but as it is I am one of four commissioners, anyone of whom possesses a veto power in promotions, who can only dismiss after a trial, which is as technical as that in a court of law, and whose immediate subordinate, practically irremoveable, possesses the great bulk of the power, with none of the responsibility. Add to this a hostile legislature, a bitterly antagonistic press, an unscrupulous scoundrel as comptroller, quite shameless if he can only hamper us, and you have a difficult problem to face. However, I have faced it as best I could and I have accomplished something. The work itself is hard, worrying and often very disagreeable. The police deal with vile crime and hideous vice; and it is not work that can be done on a rosewater basis. The actual fighting, with any of my varied foes, I do not much mind; I take it as part of the day's work; but there is that that is painful. But fight after fight is won, and its very memory vanishes.[16]

[15] *Cowles*, p. 172.
[16] *Letters I*, pp. 545–6.

10. *The Law Must Be Enforced*

I do not deal with public sentiment. I deal with the law. How I might act as a legislator or what kind of legislation I should advise has no bearing on my conduct as an executive officer charged with administering the law. I shall try to procure the enforcement of the Sunday Closing Law, not by spurts, but with steadily increasing rigor. If it proves impossible to enforce it, it will only be after the experiment of breaking many a captain of the police in the endeavor to secure the enforcement has first been tried.

With the new magistrates and with the excise board working as it is, I feel that there is a good chance to stop the lawbreaking. In any event the police have got to strain every nerve and to satisfy me beyond the possibility of doubt that everything possible has been done, before I admit that the law cannot be enforced.

Moreover, when I get at it, I am going to see if we cannot break the license forthwith of any saloon-keeper who sells on Sunday. I will try to get at it through the excise board, and whether I succeed or fail with either I shall not let up for one moment in my endeavor to make the police understand that no excuse will be permitted on their part when the law is not observed, and that Sunday by Sunday it is to be enforced more and more rigorously.

This applies just as much to the biggest hotel as to the smallest grog-shop. *The Sun* prophesies success for public sentiment. I am an officer of the law, and I recognize the public sentiment that is embodied in law. Moreover, let me point out one feature upon which *The Sun* has not dwelt. I should enforce the law anyhow because it is the law; but in addition to this I shall insist upon the rigid enforcement of the law as the only way to stop blackmail and corruption.

To allow a lax enforcement of the law means to allow it to be enforced just so far as individual members of the police force are willing to wink at its evasion. It is not necessary to say that this must mean in very many cases that the saloons which pay blackmail, or have political backing, get off free, so that the law will be enforced rigidly in the interest of every honest saloon-keeper, and in the interest of honesty in the management of the police force.

Law-abiding citizens are rarely blackmailed. The chief chance for blackmail, with all its frightful attendant demoralization, arises from having a law which is not strictly enforced, which certain people are allowed to violate with impunity for corrupt reasons, while other offenders who lack their political influence are mercilessly harassed. All our resources

103

will be strained to prevent any such discrimination and to secure the equal punishment of all offenders.

Woe be to the policeman who exposes himself to the taint of corruption.[17]

11. The Anticipatory Jitters

To Frances Theodora Parsons[18]

New York, July 10, 1896

Edith has recently on several different occasions spoken to me about the fact that I betrayed altogether too much nervousness before the different crises that come up in the course of my very harassing work here, notably before the recent hearings by the Mayor. . . .

I have always been nervous before a contest, although I have not a particle of nervousness when once the fight is actually on, and indeed rather enjoy it. In the old days I was always nervous before a boxing match or polo game, or even a hard day with hounds; after killing my first grizzly I recollect the hunter who was with me telling me that from the way I looked just before I went into the thing he would have believed if the bear had happened to get away that I had been afraid of it; and I remember Bob Sedgwick chaffing me about my seeming uneasy before a run with the Meadowbrook hounds, at the end of which I had the satisfaction of showing him the brush, he having utterly failed to keep anywhere in the first flight. It was the same way at Albany and before the Mayor. I have minded this war against one of my colleagues more than any of the fights which we made as a unit against the enemies of law and order. . . . and I felt very nervous before I actually got to grips with my foe. I did not try to control the appearance of this nervousness as much as I should have done, partly because I knew perfectly well that it would disappear the minute I came down to actual fighting, and that then I should be perfectly cool and collected; but I see now that it was a mistake not to try to command myself as much in advance as at the contest; I shall do it hereafter. In the trial before the Mayor I scored a complete victory . . . and had the satisfaction of stating under oath to Parker, who was not six feet distant, all that I thought worst in his moral character.[19]

[17] *Works XIV*, pp. 181–2.
[18] A friend of Roosevelt's childhood.
[19] *Letters VIII*, p. 1438.

12. "Not even the President has had as heavy a task . . ."

To Anna Roosevelt Cowles

300 Mulberry Street
Feb. 25, 1896

Gradually and in spite of great difficulties with two of my colleagues I am getting this force into good shape; but I am quite sincere when I say that I do not believe that any other man in the United States, not even the President, has had as heavy a task as I have had during the past ten months. In itself the work was herculean, even had I been assisted by an honest and active public sentiment and had I received help from the press and the politicians. As a matter of fact, public sentiment is apathetic and likes to talk about virtue in the abstract, but it does not want to obtain the virtue if there is any trouble about it. The papers of the widest circulation have been virulent against me. The Democrats of course oppose me to a man, so far as their public representatives are concerned, and the Republican machine is almost as bitterly hostile. Governor Morton in a feeble way would like to stand by me, but he does not dare to antagonize Platt; he is now so miserable over having to decide whether or not he will veto the bill putting me out that he is almost sick. As yet they are not sure of his consent. They have not yet brought the bill in, but I think that in the end they will bring it in. However, I can afford to look at the result with a good deal of equanimity; they can't put me out much before I have finished my year's term of service; I will then have practically done the great bulk of our work, that is the re-organizing of the Department; we will leave the Force immeasurably improved, compared to the Force we found; and with all the worry and hard work, I have heartily enjoyed it. It has been emphatically a man's work, worth doing from every aspect. I feel I have been a useful citizen, and, though this is a point of very much less importance, I think that in the end decent people will realize that I have done a good deal. I am writing to you with frank egoism. My excuse must be that I have not worked in any way egotistically, for I can conscientiously say that not one single step I have taken has been influenced by any considerations save by those which I have deemed for the public good.[20]

[20] *Letters I*, pp. 516–17.

13. *"The only thing I am afraid of . . ."*

To Anna Roosevelt Cowles

March 9, 1896

I am busy correcting the proof of the fourth volume of "The Winning of The West," and by the middle of May or June, I shall be through the hardest part of my work both literary and official; I shall then have finished a year of as hard work and of as much worry and responsibility as a man could well have; yet, I have enjoyed it extremely, and am in excellent health. I don't mind work; the only thing I am afraid of is that by and by I will have nothing to do; and I should hate to have the children grow up and see me having nothing to do. . . .[21]

[21] *Ibid.*, p. 521.

Teacher of the Ideals and Disciplines of American Freedom

After his death, Mr. Roosevelt was appraised by Mr. Elihu Root, his former Secretary of War and Secretary of State, as the "greatest teacher of the essentials of popular self-government the world has ever known." He taught both by word and action, never more eloquently than in the years as a young political reformer (1882–1897).

1. The Manly Virtues and Practical Politics

To decent, upright citizens it is hardly necessary to preach the doctrine of morality as applied to the affairs of public life. It is an even graver offence to sin against the commonwealth than to sin against an individual. The man who debauches our public life, whether by malversation of funds in office, by the actual bribery of voters or of legislators, or by the corrupt use of the offices as spoils wherewith to reward the unworthy and the vicious for their noxious and interested activity in the baser walks of political life,—this man is a greater foe to our well-being as a nation than is even the defaulting cashier of a bank, or the betrayer of a private trust. No amount of intelligence and no amount of energy will save a nation which is not honest, and no government can ever be a permanent success if administered in accordance with base ideals. The first requisite in the citizen who wishes to share the work of our public life, whether he wishes himself to hold office or merely to do his plain duty as an American by taking part in the management of our political machinery, is that he shall act disinterestedly and with a sincere purpose to serve the whole commonwealth.

But disinterestedness and honesty and unselfish desire to do what is right are not enough in themselves. A man must not only be disinter-

107

ested, but he must be efficient. If he goes into politics he must go into practical politics, in order to make his influence felt. Practical politics must not be construed to mean dirty politics. On the contrary, in the long run the politics of fraud and treachery and foulness are unpractical politics, and the most practical of all politicians is the politician who is clean and decent and upright. But a man who goes into the actual battles of the political world must prepare himself much as he would for the struggle in any other branch of our life. He must be prepared to meet men of far lower ideals than his own, and to face things, not as he would wish them, but as they are. He must not lose his own high ideal, and yet he must face the fact that the majority of the men with whom he must work have lower ideals. He must stand firmly for what he believes, and yet he must realize that political action, to be effective, must be the joint action of many men, and that he must sacrifice somewhat of his own opinions to those of his associates if he ever hopes to see his desires take practical shape.

The prime thing that every man who takes an interest in politics should remember is that he must act, and not merely criticize the actions of others. It is not the man who sits by his fireside reading his evening paper, and saying how bad our politics and politicians are, who will ever do anything to save us; it is the man who goes out into the rough hurly-burly of the caucus, the primary, and the political meeting, and there faces his fellows on equal terms. The real service is rendered, not by the critic who stands aloof from the contest, but by the man who enters into it and bears his part as a man should, undeterred by the blood and the sweat. It is a pleasant but a dangerous thing to associate merely with cultivated, refined men of high ideals and sincere purpose to do right, and to think that one has done all one's duty by discussing politics with such associates. It is a good thing to meet men of this stamp; indeed it is a necessary thing, for we thereby brighten our ideals, and keep in touch with the people who are unselfish in their purposes; but if we associate with such men exclusively we can accomplish nothing. The actual battle must be fought out on other and less pleasant fields. The actual advance must be made in the field of practical politics among the men who represent or guide or control the mass of the voters, the men who are sometimes rough and coarse, who sometimes have lower ideals than they should, but who are capable, masterful, and efficient. It is only by mingling on equal terms with such men, by showing them that one is able to give and to receive heavy punishment without flinching, and that one can master the details of political management as well as they can, that it is possible for a man to establish a standing that will be useful to him in fighting for a great reform.

Every man who wishes well to his country is in honor bound to take an active part in political life. If he does his duty and takes that active part he will be sure occasionally to commit mistakes and to be guilty of shortcomings. For these mistakes and shortcomings he will receive the unmeasured denunciation of the critics who commit neither because they never do anything but criticize. Nevertheless he will have the satisfaction of knowing that the salvation of the country ultimately lies, not in the hands of his critics, but in the hands of those who, however imperfectly, actually do the work of the nation. I would not for one moment be understood as objecting to criticism or failing to appreciate its importance. We need fearless criticism of our public men and public parties; we need unsparing condemnation of all persons and all principles that count for evil in our public life: but it behooves every man to remember that the work of the critic, important though it is, is of altogether secondary importance, and that, in the end, progress is accomplished by the man who does the things, and not by the man who talks about how they ought or ought not to be done.

Therefore the man who wishes to do good in his community must go into active political life. If he is a Republican, let him join his local Republican association; if a Democrat, the Democratic association; if an Independent, then let him put himself in touch with those who think as he does. In any event let him make himself an active force and make his influence felt. Whether he works within or without party lines he can surely find plenty of men who are desirous of good government, and who, if they act together, become at once a power on the side of righteousness. Of course, in a government like ours, a man can accomplish anything only by acting in combination with others, and equally, of course, a number of people can act together only by each sacrificing certain of his beliefs or prejudices. That man is indeed unfortunate who cannot in any given district find some people with whom he can conscientiously act. He may find that he can do best by acting within a party organization; he may find that he can do best by acting, at least for certain purposes, or at certain times, outside of party organizations, in an independent body of some kind; but with some association he must act if he wishes to exert any real influence.

One thing to be always remembered is that neither independence on the one hand nor party fealty on the other can ever be accepted as an excuse for failure to do active work in politics. The party man who offers his allegiance to party as an excuse for blindly following his party, right or wrong, and who fails to try to make that party in any way better, commits a crime against the country; and a crime quite as serious is committed by the independent who makes his independence an excuse for easy self-indulgence, and who thinks that when he says he belongs to neither party he is excused from the duty of taking part in the practical work of party organizations. The party man is bound to do his share in party management. He is bound to attend the caucuses and the primaries, to see that only good men are put up, and to exert his influence as strenuously against the foes of good government within his party, as, through his party machinery, he does against those who are without the party. In the same way the independent, if he cannot take part in the regular organizations, is bound to do just as much active constructive work (not merely the work of criticism) outside; he is bound to try to get up an organization of his own and to try to make that organization felt in some effective manner. Whatever course the man who wishes to do his duty by his country takes in reference to parties or to independence of parties, he is bound to try to put himself in touch with men who think as he does, and to help make their joint influence felt in behalf of the powers that go for decency and good government. He must try to accomplish things; he must not vote in the air unless it is really necessary. Occasionally a man must cast a "conscience vote," when there is no possibility of carrying to victory his principles or his nominees; at times, indeed, this may be his highest duty; but ordinarily this is not the case. As a general rule a man ought to work and vote for something which there is at least a fair chance of putting into effect.

Yet another thing to be remembered by the man who wishes to make his influence felt for good in our politics is that he must act purely as an American. If he is not deeply imbued with the American spirit he cannot succeed. Any organization which tries to work along the line of caste or creed, which fails to treat all American citizens on their merits as men, will fail, and will deserve to fail. Where our political life is healthy, there is and can be no room for any movement organized to help or to antagonize men because they do or do not profess a certain religion, or because they were or were not born here or abroad. We have a right to ask that those with whom we associate, and those for whom we vote, shall be themselves good Americans in heart and spirit, unhampered by adherence to foreign ideals, and acting without regard to the national and religious prejudices of European countries; but if they really are good Americans in spirit and thought and purpose, that is all that we have any right to consider in regard to them. In the same way there must be no discrimination for or against any man because of his social standing. On the one side, there is nothing to be made out of a political organization which draws an exclusive social line, and on the other it must be remembered that it is just as un-American to vote against a man because he is rich as to vote against him because he is poor. The one man has just as much right as the other to claim to be treated purely on his merits as a man. In short, to do good work in politics, the men who organize must organize wholly without regard to whether their associates were born here or abroad, whether they are Protestants or Catholics, Jews or Gentiles, whether they are bankers or butchers, professors or day-laborers. All that can rightly be asked of one's political associates is that they shall be honest men, good Americans, and substantially in accord as regards their political ideas.

Another thing that must not be forgotten by the man desirous of doing good political work is the need of the rougher, manlier virtues, and above all the virtue of personal courage, physical as well as moral. If we wish to do good work for our country we must be unselfish, disinterested, sincerely desirous of the well-being of the commonwealth, and capable of devoted adherence to a lofty ideal; but in addition we must be vigorous in mind and body, able to hold our own in rough conflict with our fellows, able to suffer punishment without flinching, and, at need, to repay it in kind with full interest. A peaceful and commercial civilization is always in danger of suffering the loss of the virile fighting qualities without which no nation, however cultured, however refined, however thrifty and prosperous, can ever amount to anything. Every citizen should be taught, both in public and in private life, that while he must avoid brawling and quarreling, it is his duty to stand up for his rights. He must realize that the only man who is more contemptible than the blusterer and bully is the coward. No man is worth much to the commonwealth if he is not capable of feeling righteous wrath and just indignation, if he is not stirred to hot anger by misdoing, and is not impelled to see justice meted out to the wrongdoers. No man is worth much anywhere if he does not possess both moral and physical courage. A politician who really serves his country well, and deserves his country's gratitude, must usually possess some of the hardy virtues which we admire in the soldier who serves his country well in the field.

An ardent young reformer is very apt to try to begin by reforming too much. He needs always to keep in mind that he has got to serve as a sergeant before he assumes the duties of commander-in-chief. It is right for him from the beginning to take a great interest in national, State, and municipal affairs, and to try to make himself felt in them if the occasion arises; but the best work must be done by the citizen working in his own ward or district. Let him associate himself with men who think as he does, and who, like him, are sincerely devoted to the public good. Then let them try to make themselves felt in the choice of alderman, of councilman, of assemblyman. The politicians will be prompt to recognize their power, and the people will recognize it too, after a while. Let them organize and work,

111

undaunted by any temporary defeat. If they fail at first, and if they fail again, let them merely make up their minds to redouble their efforts, and perhaps alter their methods; but let them keep on working.

It is sheer unmanliness and cowardice to shrink from the contest because at first there is failure, or because the work is difficult or repulsive. No man who is worth his salt has any right to abandon the effort to better our politics merely because he does not find it pleasant, merely because it entails associations which to him happen to be disagreeable. Let him keep right on, taking the buffets he gets good-humoredly, and repaying them with heartiness when the chance arises. Let him make up his mind that he will have to face the violent opposition of the spoils politician, and also, too often, the unfair and ungenerous criticism of those who ought to know better. Let him be careful not to show himself so thin-skinned as to mind either; let him fight his way forward, paying only so much regard to both as is necessary to enable him to win in spite of them. He may not, and indeed probably will not, accomplish nearly as much as he would like to, or as he thinks he ought to: but he will certainly accomplish something; and if he can feel that he has helped to elevate the type of representative sent to the municipal, the State, or the national legislature from his district, or to elevate the standard of duty among the public officials in his own ward, he has a right to be profoundly satisfied with what he has accomplished.[1]

2. "Learning by bitter experience"

To Theodore Roosevelt, Jr.[2]

Washington, October 20, 1903

I think your decision was wise and right. And oh, Ted! I was so much amused and interested with the description of the way you got to feel because you had won the position for yourself in the football field among the older fellows. I never did well enough in athletics while a boy to get such a position, either at school or college; but immediately after leaving college I went to the legislature. I was the youngest man there, and I rose like a rocket. I was re-elected next year by an enormous majority in a time when the Republican party as a whole met with great disaster; and the Republican minority in the house, although I was the youngest member, nominated me for speaker, that is, made me the leader of the minority. I immediately proceeded to lose *my* perspective, also. Unfortunately, I did not recover it as early as you have done in this case, and the result was that I came an

[1] "American Ideals." *Works XIII*, pp. 27–33.
[2] Eldest son of Theodore Roosevelt.

awful cropper and had to pick myself up after learning by bitter experience the lesson that I was not all-important and that I had to take account of many different elements in life. It took me fully a year before I got back the position I had lost, but I hung steadily at it and achieved my purpose.[3]

3. The College Graduate in Public Life

We have in this country an equality of rights. It is the plain duty of every man to see that his rights are respected. That weak good-nature which acquiesces in wrong-doing, whether from laziness, timidity, or indifference, is a very unwholesome quality. It should be second nature with every man to insist that he be given full justice. But if there is an equality of rights, there is an inequality of duties. It is proper to demand more from the man with exceptional advantages than from the man without them. A heavy moral obligation rests upon the man of means and upon the man of education to do their full duty by their country. On no class does this obligation rest more heavily than upon the men with a collegiate education, the men who are graduates of our universities. Their education gives them no right to feel the least superiority over any of their fellow-citizens but it certainly ought to make them feel that they should stand foremost in the honorable effort to serve the whole public by doing their duty as Americans in the body politic. . . . The service may be rendered in many different ways. In a reasonable number of cases, the man may himself rise to high political position. . . . These cases must necessarily, however, form but a small part of the whole. The enormous majority of our educated men have to make their own living, and are obliged to take up careers in which they must work heart and soul to succeed. Nevertheless, the man of business and the man of science, the doctor of divinity and the doctor of law, the architect, the engineer, and the writer, all alike owe a positive duty to the community, the neglect of which they cannot excuse on any plea of their private affairs. They are bound to follow understandingly the course of public events; they are bound to try to estimate and form judgment upon public men; and they are bound to act intelligently and effectively in support of the principles which they deem to be right and for the best interests of the country.

The most important thing for this class of educated men to realize is that they do not really form a class at all. I have used the word in default of another, but I have merely used it roughly to group together people who have had unusual opportunities of a certain kind. A large number of the people to whom these opportunities are offered fail to take advantage of them, and a very much larger number of those to whom they have not

[3] *Letters III*, pp. 634-5.

been offered succeed none the less in making them for themselves. An educated man must not go into politics as such; he must go in simply as an American; and when he is once in, he will speedily realize that he must work very hard indeed, or he will be upset by some other American, with no education at all, but with much natural capacity. His education ought to make him feel particularly ashamed of himself if he acts meanly or dishonorably, or in any way falls short of the ideal of good citizenship, and it ought to make him feel that he must show that he has profited by it; but it should certainly give him no feeling of superiority until by actual work he has shown that superiority. In other words, the educated man must realize that he is living in a democracy and under democratic conditions, and that he is entitled to no more respect and consideration than he can win by actual performance.

This must be steadily kept in mind not only by educated men themselves, but particularly by the men who give the tone to our great educational institutions. These educational institutions, if they are to do their best work, must strain every effort to keep their life in touch with the life of the nation at the present day. This is necessary for the country, but it is very much more necessary for the educated men themselves. It is a misfortune for any land if its people of cultivation take little part in shaping its destiny; but the misfortune is far greater for the people of cultivation. The country has a right to demand the honest and efficient service of every man in it, but especially of every man who has had the advantage of rigid mental and moral training; the country is so much the poorer when any class of honest men fail to do their duty by it; but the loss to the class itself is immeasurable. If our educated men as a whole become incapable of playing their full part in our life, if they cease doing their share of the rough, hard work which must be done, and grow to take a position of mere dilettanteism in our public affairs, they will speedily sink in relation to their fellows who really do the work of governing, until they stand toward them as a cultivated, ineffective man with a taste for bric-a-brac stands toward a great artist. When once a body of citizens becomes thoroughly out of touch and out of temper with the national life, its usefulness is gone, and its power of leaving its mark on the times is gone also.

The first great lesson which the college graduate should learn is the lesson of work rather than of criticism. Criticism is necessary and useful; it is often indispensable; but it can never take the place of action, or be even a poor substitute for it. The function of the mere critic is of very subordinate usefulness. It is the doer of deeds who actually counts in the battle for life, and not the man who looks on and says how the fight ought to be fought, without himself sharing the stress and the danger. . . . Wrongs should be strenuously and fearlessly denounced, evil principles and evil

114

men should be condemned. The politician who cheats or swindles, or the newspaper man who lies in any form, should be made to feel that he is an object of scorn for all honest men. We need fearless criticism; but we need that it should also be intelligent. At present, the man who is most apt to regard himself as an intelligent critic of our political affairs is often the man who knows nothing whatever about them. Criticism which is ignorant or prejudiced is a source of great harm to the nation; and where ignorant or prejudiced critics are themselves educated men, their attitude does real harm also to the class to which they belong. . . . The worst offence that can be committed against the Republic is the offence of the public man who betrays his trust; but second only to it comes the offence of the man who tries to persuade others that an honest and efficient public man is dishonest or unworthy. . . . Good can often be done by criticising sharply and severely the wrong; but excessive indulgence in criticism is never anything but bad, and no amount of criticism can in any way take the place of active and zealous warfare for the right.

Again, there is a certain tendency in college life . . . to make educated men shrink from contact with the rough people who do the world's work, and associate only with one another and with those who think as they do. . . . It is very agreeable to deceive one's self into the belief that one is performing the whole duty of man by sitting at home in ease, doing nothing wrong, and confining one's participation in politics to conversations and meetings with men who have had the same training and look at things in the same way. . . . Those who do nothing else often speak as if in some way they deserved credit for their attitude, and as if they stood above their brethren who plough the rough fields. Moreover, many people whose political work is done more or less after this fashion are very noble and very sincere in their aims and aspirations, and are striving for what is best and most decent in public life.

Nevertheless, this is a snare round which it behooves every young man to walk carefully. Let him beware of associating only with the people of his own caste and of his own little ways of political thought. Let him learn that he must deal with the mass of men; that he must go out and stand shoulder to shoulder with his friends of every rank, and face to face with his foes of every rank, and must bear himself well in the hurly-burly. He must not be frightened by the many unpleasant features of the contest, and he must not expect to have it all his own way, or to accomplish too much. He will meet with checks and will make many mistakes; but if he perseveres, he will achieve a measure of success and will do a measure of good such as is never possible to the refined, cultivated, intellectual men who shrink aside from the actual fray.

Yet again, college men must learn to be as practical in politics as they would be in business or in law. It is surely unnecessary to say that by "practical" I do not mean anything that savors in the least of dishonesty. On the contrary, a college man is peculiarly bound to keep a high ideal and to be true to it; but he must work in practical ways to try to realize this ideal, and must not refuse to do anything because he cannot get everything. . . .

Much of the best work that has been done in the field of political study has been done by men who were not active politicians, though they were careful and painstaking students of the phenomena of politics. . . .

It is a misfortune for any people when the paths of the practical and the theoretical politicians diverge so widely that they have no common standing-ground. When the Greek thinkers began to devote their attention to purely visionary politics of the kind found in Plato's Republic, while the Greek practical politicians simply exploited the quarrelsome little commonwealths in their own interests, then the end of Greek liberty was at hand. No government that cannot command the respectful support of the best thinkers is in an entirely sound condition; but it is well to keep in mind the remark of Frederick the Great, that if he wished to punish a province, he would allow it to be governed by the philosophers. It is a great misfortune for the country when the practical politician and the doctrinaire have no point in common, but the misfortune is, if anything, greatest for the doctrinaire. The ideal to be set before the student of politics and the practical politician alike is the ideal of the *Federalist*. Each man should realize that he cannot do his best, either in the study of politics or in applied politics unless he has a working knowledge of both branches.[4]

4. A Private Lesson for Mr. Platt

To Thomas C. Platt[5]

Oyster Bay, August 20, 1900

I have your letter of the 16th. I wish to see a straight Republican nominated for the governorship. The men whom I have mentioned, such as ex-Judge Andrews and Secretary Root, are as good Republicans as can be found in the state, and I confess I haven't the slightest idea what you mean when you say "If we are to lower the standard and nominate such men as you suggest, we might as well die first as last." To nominate such a man as either of these is to raise the standard; to speak of it as lowering the standard is an utter misuse of words.

You say that we must nominate some Republican who "will carry out

[4] "American Ideals." *Works XIII*, pp. 36–41.
[5] United States senator from New York, boss of the State Republican Party.

the wishes of the organization," and add that "I have not yet made up my mind who that man is." Of one thing I am certain: That, to have it publicly known that the candidate, whoever he may be, "will carry out the wishes of the organization" would insure his defeat; for such a statement implies that he would merely register the decrees of a small body of men inside the Republican party, instead of trying to work for the success of the party as a whole and of good citizenship generally. It is not the business of a governor to "carry out the wishes of the organization" unless these wishes coincide with the good of the party and of the state. If they do, then he ought to have them put into effect; if they do not, then as a matter of course he ought to disregard them. To pursue any other course would be to show servility; and a servile man is always a most undesirable—not to say contemptible—public servant. A governor should, of course, try in good faith to work with the organization; but under no circumstances should he be servile to it, or "carry out its wishes" unless his own best judgment is that they ought to be carried out.

I am a good organization man myself, as I understand the word "organization," but it is in the highest degree foolish to make a fetish of the word "organization" and to treat any man or any small group of men as embodying the organization. The organization should strive to give effective, intelligent and honest leadership to and representation of the Republican party, just as the Republican party strives to give wise and upright government to the state. When what I have said ceases to be true of either organization or party, it means that the organization or party is not performing its duty, and is losing the reason for its existence.[6]

5. The Governor and the People of New York

Would it were in my power to make each of you feel how dependent the public servant is in the way of doing good work upon popular opinion, which you, and the men like you, must shape. A public man can learn to a certain extent, but he has got to keep in touch with the people whom he represents. If he gets too far away from them, so that he is out of touch with them, then his usefulness is almost as much impaired, as if he were too far behind. All that can be done is this: he can get a certain distance away, and he must take care that that certain distance is in the right direction. It is not possible for any man ever to do or to get all that he would like to do, or all that he would like to get in the way of good government and in the way of striving to see his ideals realized.

Mr. President, you have spoken very kindly of the fact that you believed I would be a good governor. Now I intend to try. But the measure of my success is going to largely depend upon the support that I get from

[6] *Letters II*, p. 1387.

117

just such men as I see before me to-night. I am a loyal party man, but I believe very firmly that I can best render aid to my party by doing all that in me lies to make that party responsive to the needs of the State, responsive to the needs of the people, and just so far as I work along those lines I have the right to challenge the support of every decent man, no matter what his party may be. It is not an easy thing, when you come down to the practical realities, to work for the best; it is a good deal easier to sit at home in one's parlor and decide what the best is than to get out in the field and try to win it. When one is in the midst of the strife, with the dust, and the blood and the rough handling, and is receiving blows (and if he is worth anything, is returning them), it is difficult always to see perfectly straight in the direction the right lies. Perhaps we must always advance a little by zigzags; only we must always advance; and the zigzags should go toward the right goal. . . .

I earnestly hope that all of you here will thoroughly appreciate what you now know in the abstract, but what we none of us realize entirely in practice, that here in this government it is not the public officials that really govern, it is the people themselves. It is the people who must make their ideals take tangible shape. You govern just as much if you decline to let your weight be felt for decency, as if you make it felt outright for what is bad. You are just as responsible. You, the leaders of the people, you, the people, are just as responsible for what goes wrong, whether it is because you actively favor the wrong or because you sit supinely by, and let the wrong triumph, without checking it. Appreciating to the full the heavy weight of responsibility that rests upon me, as it does upon every other servant of the Commonwealth, appreciating the weight of responsibility that rests upon the executive officers of the State, a weight only less heavy than that which rests upon the judges, appreciating all that, I ask you in turn to appreciate that an even heavier load of responsibility rests upon each citizen and all the private citizens of this Commonwealth, to see that decency, that honesty, that righteousness, that courage are triumphant in the government of this State.[7]

6. Nomination for Vice President

To Anna Roosevelt Cowles

Oyster Bay, June 25, 1900

DEAR BYE: The thing could not be helped. There were two entirely different forces at work. The first was the desire to get me out of New

[7] Works XIV, pp. 308–10.

York, partly because the machine naturally prefers someone more pliable, but mainly because of the corporations' or rather the big speculative corporations' unhealthy attitude toward me. This desire was absolutely unoperative as regards results for I stood Mr. Platt and the machine on their heads when the trial of strength came and forced the entire New York delegation to declare for someone else. It was the feeling of the great bulk of the Republicans that I would strengthen the National ticket and they wanted me on it at all hazards. Mr. Hanna was quite as much opposed to my going on as Mr. Platt was to my staying off, but both were absolutely and utterly powerless. While, of course, I should have preferred to stay where there was more work I would be both ungrateful and a fool not to be deeply touched by the way in which I was nominated. The vital thing in this election is to re-elect President McKinley and to do this I shall bend all my energies. If we succeed, well and good, and as regards myself I shall try most earnestly, and I most humbly hope not to forfeit the respect and good will of the people who put me in as vice-president. If we are beaten, my own disappointment will not be a drop in the ocean to my bitter regret and alarm for the Nation.[8]

To Henry Cabot Lodge

Oyster Bay, June 25, 1900

. . . Well, old man, I am completely reconciled and I believe it all for the best . . . I should be a conceited fool if I were discontented with the nomination when it came in such a fashion, and according to my lights I shall endeavor to act not only fearlessly and with integrity but with good judgment. Edith is becoming somewhat reconciled. . . .

As for you, old trump, I shall never forget how, as I mounted the platform, you met me with a face of almost agonized anxiety and put your head down on the table as I began to speak, and, as I turned for a glass of water in the middle of my speech, you whispered with a face of delight that I was doing splendidly. It certainly is odd to look back sixteen years when you and I sat in the Blaine convention, on the beaten side, while the mugwumps foretold our utter ruin, and then in this convention, over which you presided, to think how you recognized me to second McKinley's nomination and afterwards declared me myself nominated in the second place on the ticket.[9]

[8] *Letters II*, p. 1339.
[9] *Ibid.*, p. 1340.

To Andrew Dickson White[10]

Albany, December 3, 1900

MY DEAR MR. WHITE: Your letter of November 16th pleased me greatly. But for Heaven's sake do not think of me as a possible Presidential candidate. In the first place, the possibility is merely that of lightning striking; and in the next place, with the examples of Tom Reed and Dewey fresh before me, it seems to me there can be no more awful fate than for a man to get a Presidential bee in his bonnet.

Moreover, when I think of the kind of life I have led, the marvel is that I have gotten as far as I have. I have always expressed my opinions with great freedom, and though I think I have grown fairly judicious now, this was certainly not the case ten or a dozen years ago. There are plenty of printed statements I have made, some of them absolutely true, some of them true from my standpoint, but expressed in such a shape as legitimately to give offense and which would operate against me at any rate among politicians and perhaps among some who are not politicans. While I did not want the Vice-Presidency I am now entirely content to have taken it, for it enabled me to be of considerable use in a great campaign. Now all that there is for me to do is to perform with regularity and dignity the duty of presiding over the Senate, and to remember the fact that the duty not being very important is no excuse for shirking it.[11]

7. American Ideals

Every great nation owes to the men whose lives have formed part of its greatness not merely the material effect of what they did, not merely the laws they placed upon the statute books or the victories they won over armed foes, but also the immense but indefinable moral influence produced by their deeds and words themselves upon the national character. It would be difficult to exaggerate the material effects of the careers of Washington and of Lincoln upon the United States. Without Washington we should probably never have won our independence of the British crown, and we should almost certainly have failed to become a great nation, remaining instead a cluster of jangling little communities, drifting toward the type of government prevalent in Spanish America. Without Lincoln we might perhaps have failed to keep the political unity we had won; and even if, as is possible, we had kept it, both the struggle by which it was kept and the results of this struggle would have been so different that the

[10] First president of Cornell University; later minister to Russia and ambassador to Germany.
[11] *Letters II,* p. 1446.

effect upon our national history could not have failed to be profound. Yet the nation's debt to these men is not confined to what it owes them for its material well-being, incalculable though this debt is. Beyond the fact that we are an independent and united people, with half a continent as our heritage, lies the fact that every American is richer by the heritage of the noble deeds and noble words of Washington and of Lincoln. Each of us who reads the Gettysburg speech or the second inaugural address of the greatest American of the nineteenth century, or who studies the long campaigns and lofty statesmanship of that other American who was even greater, cannot but feel within him that lift toward things higher and nobler which can never be bestowed by the enjoyment of mere material prosperity.

It is not only the country which these men helped to make and helped to save that is ours by inheritance; we inherit also all that is best and highest in their characters and in their lives. We inherit from Lincoln and from the might of Lincoln's generation not merely the freedom of those who once were slaves; for we inherit also the fact of the freeing of them, we inherit the glory and the honor and the wonder of the deed when done. The bells that rang at the passage of the Emancipation Proclamation still ring in Whittier's ode; and as men think over the real nature of the triumph then scored for humankind their hearts shall ever throb as they cannot over the greatest industrial success or over any victory won at a less cost than ours.

The captains and the armies who, after long years of dreary campaigning and bloody, stubborn fighting, brought to a close the Civil War have likewise left us even more than a reunited realm. The material effect of what they did is shown in the fact that the same flag flies from the Great Lakes to the Rio Grande, and all the people of the United States are richer because they are one people and not many, because they belong to one great nation and not to a contemptible knot of struggling nationalities. But besides this, besides the material results of the Civil War, we are all, North and South, incalculably richer for its memories. We are richer for each grim campaign, for each hard-fought battle. We are the richer for valor displayed alike by those who fought so valiantly for the right and by those who, no less valiantly, fought for what they deemed the right. We have in us nobler capacities for what is great and good because of the infinite woe and suffering, and because of the splendid ultimate triumph.

In the same way that we are the better for the deeds of our mighty men who have served the nation well, so we are the worse for the deeds and the words of those who have striven to bring evil on the land. Most fortunately we have been free from the peril of the most dangerous of all examples. We have not had to fight the influence exerted over the minds of eager and ambitious men by the career of the military adventurer who heads some successful revolutionary or separatist movement. No man works such incalculable woe to a free country as he who teaches young men that one of the paths to glory, renown, and temporal success lies along the line of armed resistance to the Government, or its attempted overthrow.

Yet if we are free from the peril of this example, there are other perils from which we are not free. All through our career we have had to war against a tendency to regard, in the individual and the nation alike, as most important, things that are of comparatively little importance. We rightfully value success, but sometimes we overvalue it, for we tend to forget that success may be obtained by means which should make it abhorred and despised by every honorable man. One section of the community deifies as "smartness" the kind of trickery which enables a man without conscience to succeed in the financial or political world. Another section of the community deifies violent homicidal lawlessness. If ever our people as a whole adopt these views, then we shall have proved that we are unworthy of the heritage our forefathers left us; and our country will go down in ruin.

The people that do harm in the end are not the wrongdoers whom all execrate; they are the men who do not do quite as much wrong, but who are applauded instead of being execrated. The career of Benedict Arnold has done us no harm as a nation because of the universal horror it inspired. The men who have done us harm are those who have advocated disunion, but have done it so that they have been enabled to keep their political position; who have advocated repudiation of debts, or other financial dishonesty, but have kept their standing in the community; who preach the doctrines of anarchy, but refrain from the action that will bring them within the pale of the law; for these men lead thousands astray by the fact that they go unpunished or even rewarded for their misdeeds.

It is unhappily true that we inherit the evil as well as the good done by those who have gone before us, and in the one case as in the other the influence extends far beyond the mere material effects. The foes of order harm quite as much by example as by what they actually accomplish. So it is with the equally dangerous criminals of the wealthy classes. The conscienceless stock speculator who acquires wealth by swindling his fellows, by debauching judges and corrupting legislatures, and who ends his days with the reputation of being among the richest men in America, exerts over the minds of the rising generation an influence worse than that of the average murderer or bandit. . . .

There are other members of our mercantile community who, being perfectly honest themselves, nevertheless do almost as much damage as the dishonest. The professional labor agitator, with all his reckless incendiarism of speech, can do no more harm than the narrow, hard, selfish merchant or manufacturer who deliberately sets himself to keep the laborers he employs in a condition of dependence which will render them helpless to combine against him; and every such merchant or manufacturer who rises to sufficient eminence leaves the record of his name and deeds as a legacy of evil to all who come after him. But of course the worst foes of America are the foes to that orderly liberty without which our Republic must speedily perish. The reckless labor agitator who arouses the mob to riot and bloodshed is in the last analysis the most dangerous of the workingman's enemies. . . .

There are, however, plenty of wrong-doers besides those who commit the overt act. Too much cannot be said against the men of wealth who sacrifice everything to getting wealth. There is not in the world a more ignoble character than the mere money-getting American, insensible to every duty, regardless of every principle, bent only on amassing a fortune, and putting his fortune only to the basest uses . . . These men are equally careless of the workingmen, whom they oppress, and of the state, whose existence they imperil. . . .

Another class, merging into this, and only less dangerous, is that of the men whose ideals are purely material. . . . No bandit community of the Middle Ages can have led a more unlovely life than would be the life of men to whom trade and manufactures were everything, and to whom such words as national honor and glory, as courage and daring, and loyalty and unselfishness, had become meaningless. The merely material, the merely commercial ideal, the ideal of the men "whose fatherland is the till," is in its very essence debasing and lowering. It is as true now as ever it was that no man and no nation shall live by bread alone. Thrift and industry are indispensable virtues; but they are not all-sufficient. We must base our appeals for civic and national betterment on nobler grounds than those of mere business expediency.

We have examples enough and to spare that tend to evil; nevertheless, for our good fortune, the men who have most impressed themselves upon the thought of the nation have left behind them careers the influence of which must tell for good. The unscrupulous speculator who rises to enormous wealth by swindling his neighbor; the capitalist who oppresses the workingman; the agitator who wrongs the workingman yet more deeply by trying to teach him to rely not upon himself, but partly upon the charity of individuals or of the state and partly upon mob violence; the man in public life who is a demagogue or corrupt, and the newspaper writer who fails to attack him because of his corruption, or who slanderously assails him when he is honest; the political leader who, cursed by some obliquity of moral or of mental vision, seeks to produce sectional or social strife—all

123

these, though important in their day, have hitherto failed to leave any lasting impress upon the life of the nation. The men who have profoundly influenced the growth of our national character have been in most cases precisely those men whose influence was for the best and was strongly felt as antagonistic to the worst tendency of the age. The great writers, who have written in prose or verse, have done much for us. The great orators whose burning words on behalf of liberty, of union, of honest government, have rung through our legislative halls, have done even more. Most of all has been done by the men who have spoken to us through deeds and not words, or whose words have gathered their especial charm and significance because they came from men who did speak in deeds. A nation's greatness lies in its possibility of achievement in the present, and nothing helps it more than the consciousness of achievement in the past.[12]

8. True Americanism

Patriotism was once defined as "the last refuge of a scoundrel"; and somebody has recently remarked that when Dr. Johnson gave this definition he was ignorant of the infinite possibilities contained in the word "reform." Of course both gibes were quite justifiable, in so far as they were aimed at people who use noble names to cloak base purposes. Equally of course the man shows little wisdom and a low sense of duty who fails to see that love of country is one of the elemental virtues, even though scoundrels play upon it for their own selfish ends; and, inasmuch as abuses continually grow up in civic life as in all other kinds of life, the statesman is indeed a weakling who hesitates to reform these abuses because the word "reform" is often on the lips of men who are silly or dishonest.

What is true of patriotism and reform is true also of Americanism. There are plenty of scoundrels always ready to try to belittle reform movements or to bolster up existing iniquities in the name of Americanism; but this does not alter the fact that the man who can do most in this country is and must be the man whose Americanism is most sincere and intense. Outrageous though it is to use a noble idea as the cloak for evil, it is still worse to assail the noble idea itself because it can thus be used. The men who do iniquity in the name of patriotism, of reform, of Americanism, are merely one small division of the class that has always existed and will always exist,—the class of hypocrites and demagogues, the class that is always prompt to steal the watchwords of righteousness and use them in the interests of evil-doing.

The stoutest and truest Americans are the very men who have the least sympathy with the people who invoke the spirit of Americanism to aid

[12] "American Ideals." *Works XIII*, pp. 3–12.

what is vicious in our government or to throw obstacles in the way of those who strive to reform it. It is contemptible to oppose a movement for good because that movement has already succeeded somewhere else, or to champion an existing abuse because our people have always been wedded to it. . . . But we must never let our contempt for these men blind us to the nobility of the idea which they strive to degrade.

We Americans have many grave problems to solve, many threatening evils to fight, and many deeds to do, if, as we hope and believe, we have the wisdom, the strength, the courage, and the virtue to do them. But we must face facts as they are. We must neither surrender ourselves to a foolish optimism, nor succumb to a timid and ignoble pessimism. Our nation is that one among all the nations of the earth which holds in its hands the fate of the coming years. We enjoy exceptional advantages, and are menaced by exceptional dangers; and all signs indicate that we shall either fail greatly or succeed greatly. I firmly believe that we shall succeed; but we must not foolishly blink the dangers by which we are threatened, for that is the way to fail. On the contrary, we must soberly set to work to find out all we can about the existence and extent of every evil, must acknowledge it to be such, and must then attack it with unyielding resolution. There are many such evils, and each must be fought after a fashion; yet there is one quality which we must bring to the solution of every problem,—that is, an intense and fervid Americanism. We shall never be successful over the dangers that confront us; we shall never achieve true greatness, nor reach the lofty ideal which the founders and preservers of our mighty Federal Republic have set before us, unless we are Americans in heart and soul, in spirit and purpose, keenly alive to the responsibility implied in the very name of American, and proud beyond measure of the glorious privilege of bearing it.

There are two or three sides to the question of Americanism, and two or three senses in which the word "Americanism" can be used to express the antithesis of what is unwholesome and undesirable. In the first place we wish to be broadly American and national, as opposed to being local or sectional. We do not wish, in politics, in literature, or in art, to develop that unwholesome parochial spirit, that over-exaltation of the little community at the expense of the great nation, which produces what has been described as the patriotism of the village, the patriotism of the belfry. . . . The patriotism of the village or the belfry is bad, but the lack of all patriotism is even worse. There are philosophers who assure us that, in the future, patriotism will be regarded not as a virtue at all, but merely as a mental stage in the journey toward a state of feeling when our patriotism will include the whole human race and all the world. This may be so; but the age of which these philosophers speak is still several æons distant. In fact, philosophers of this type are so very advanced that they are of no practical service to the present generation. It may be, that in ages so remote that we cannot now understand any of the feelings of those who will dwell in them, patriotism will no longer be regarded as a virtue, exactly as it may be that in those remote ages people will look down upon and disregard monogamic marriage; but as things now are and have been for two or three thousand years past, and are likely to be for two or three thousand years to come, the words "home" and "country" mean a great deal. Nor do they show any tendency to lose their significance. At present, treason, like adultery, ranks as one of the worst of all possible crimes. . . .

We must Americanize the newcomers to our shores in every way, in speech, in political ideas and principles, and in their way of looking at the relations between Church and State. We welcome the German or the Irishman who becomes an American. We have no use for the German or Irishman who remains such. We do not wish German-Americans and Irish-Americans who figure as such in our social and political life; we want only Americans, and, provided they are such, we do not care whether they are of native or of Irish or of German ancestry. We have no room in any healthy American community for a German-American vote or an Irish-American vote, and it is contemptible demagogy to put planks into any party platform with the purpose of catching such a vote. We have no room for any people who do not act and vote simply as Americans, and as nothing else. . . . We demand that all citizens, Protestant and Catholic, Jew and Gentile, shall have fair treatment in every way; that all alike shall have their rights guaranteed them. The very reasons that make us unqualified in our opposition to State-aided sectarian schools make us equally bent that, in the management of our public schools, the adherents of each creed shall be given exact and equal justice, wholly without regard to their religious affiliations; that trustees, superintendents, teachers, scholars, all alike shall be treated without any reference whatsoever to the creed they profess. We maintain that it is an outrage, in voting for a man for any position, whether State or national, to take into account his religious faith, provided only he is a good American. . . .

The mighty tide of immigration to our shores has brought in its train much of good and much of evil; and whether the good or the evil shall predominate depends mainly on whether these newcomers do or do not throw themselves heartily into our national life, cease to be Europeans, and become Americans like the rest of us. . . . An immense number of them have become completely Americanized, and these stand on exactly the same plane as the descendants of any Puritan, Cavalier, or Knickerbocker among us, and do their full and honorable share of the nation's work. But where immigrants, or the sons of immigrants, do not heartily

126

and in good faith throw in their lot with us, but cling to the speech, the customs, the ways of life, and the habits of thought of the Old World which they have left, they thereby harm both themselves and us. If they remain alien elements, unassimilated, and with interests separate from ours, they are mere obstructions to the current of our national life, and, moreover, can get no good from it themselves. In fact, though we ourselves also suffer from their perversity, it is they who really suffer most. It is an immense benefit to the European immigrant to change him into an American citizen. To bear the name of American is to bear the most honorable titles; and whoever does not so believe has no business to bear the name at all, and, if he comes from Europe, the sooner he goes back there the better. Besides, the man who does not become Americanized nevertheless fails to remain a European, and becomes nothing at all. The immigrant cannot possibly remain what he was, or continue to be a member of the Old-World society. If he tries to retain his old language, in a few generations it becomes a barbarous jargon; if he tries to retain his old customs and ways of life, in a few generations he becomes an uncouth boor. He has cut himself off from the Old World, and cannot retain his connection with it; and if he wishes ever to amount to anything he must throw himself heart and soul, and without reservation, into the new life to which he has come. . . .

From his own standpoint, it is beyond all question the wise thing for the immigrant to become thoroughly Americanized. Moreover, from our standpoint, we have a right to demand it. We freely extend the hand of welcome and of good-fellowship to every man, no matter what his creed or birthplace, who comes here honestly intent on becoming a good United States citizen like the rest of us; but we have a right, and it is our duty, to demand that he shall indeed become so and shall not confuse the issues with which we are struggling by introducing among us Old-World quarrels and prejudices . . . but must merge them into love for our common country, and must take pride in the things which we can all take pride in. He must revere only our flag; not only must it come first, but no other flag should even come second. . . . Above all, the immigrant must learn to talk and think and *be* United States.

Americanism is a question of spirit, conviction, and purpose, not of creed or birthplace. The politician who bids for the Irish or German vote, or the Irishman or German who votes as an Irishman or German, is despicable, for all citizens of this commonwealth should vote solely as Americans; but he is not a whit less despicable than the voter who votes against a good American, merely because that American happens to have been born in Ireland or Germany. . . . It is a base outrage to oppose a man because of his religion or birthplace, and all good citizens will hold any

127

such effort in abhorrence. A Scandinavian, a German, or an Irishman who has really become an American has the right to stand on exactly the same footing as any native-born citizen in the land, and is just as much entitled to the friendship and support, social and political, of his neighbors. . . .

We Americans can only do our allotted task well if we face it steadily and bravely, seeing but not fearing the dangers. Above all we must stand shoulder to shoulder, not asking as to the ancestry or creed of our comrades, but only demanding that they be in very truth Americans, and that we all work together, heart, hand, and head, for the honor and the greatness of our common country.[13]

[13] *Ibid.*, pp. 13–24.

The Soldier

Mr. Roosevelt was a soldier for only four months in 1898, but, as Assistant Secretary of the Navy and as President, he played a substantial part in guiding both the preparations and the consequences of the Spanish War.

1. "If I am to be of any use in politics . . ."

To Alexander Lambert[1]

Washington, April 1, 1898

Indeed I deeply appreciate your letter, old man, and the genuine friendship it shows . . .

I don't think you understand quite what the situation is. I have been a very useful man in this Department (Navy) during the past year; it would be foolish for me to affect a belief that this was not the case. . . . My chief usefulness has arisen from the fact that when I was Acting Secretary I did not hesitate to take responsibilities, and from the further fact that I have continually meddled with what was not my business, because I was willing to jeopardize my position in a way that a naval officer could not. Now, as regards the first, I will of course never be made Acting Secretary in time of war; and as regards the second, in time of war the military advisers will promptly come to the front. Their words will be taken and their advice will be heeded, and the conditions which made it a good thing for me to be in the Department will disappear. . . .

But if I am to be of any use in politics it is because I am supposed to be a man who does not preach what he fears to practice, and who will carry out himself what he advocates others carrying out. I have for some time steadily preached a vigorous foreign policy, and for the last year I have preached war with Spain. I should feel distinctly ashamed, and I

[1] Roosevelt's close friend and personal physician.

129

should feel that my possibilities of usefulness were largely at an end if I now failed to practice what I have preached. I don't think I could do any good work in the future.

I can assure you that I am quite disinterested in this. I am not acting in a spirit of recklessness or levity, or purely for my own selfish enjoyment. I don't want to be shot at any more than anyone else does; still less to die of yellow fever. I am altogether too fond of my wife and children, and enjoy the good things of this life too much to wish lightly to hazard their loss, or to go away from my family; but the above is my duty as I see it. It is very hard to have to act against the wishes and strongly expressed advice of all my best friends—you, Lodge, Sturgis Bigelow and the rest. It may be that I am mistaken, but I can assure you that I am acting conscientiously, after having weighed the matter very carefully in all its bearings.[2]

2. *"The Regiment"*

To Henry Cabot Lodge

San Antonio, May 25, 1898

I really doubt if there ever has been a regiment quite like this. I know you will believe that more than ever I fail to get the relations of this regiment and the universe straight, but I cannot help being a little enthusiastic about it. It is as typical an American regiment as ever marched or fought. I suppose about 95 per cent of the men are of native birth, but we have a few from everywhere, including a score of Indians, and about as many of Mexican origin from New Mexico; then there are some fifty Easterners—almost all graduates of Harvard, Yale, Princeton, etc.,—and almost as many Southerners; the rest are men of the plains and the Rocky Mountains. Three fourths of our men have at one time or another been cowboys or else small stockmen; certainly two thirds have fathers who fought on one side or the other in the civil war. Of course, a regiment cannot be made in a week, but these men are in it because they want to be in it. They are intelligent as well as game, and they study the tactics, talking all the movements over among themselves; in consequence we have made really remarkable progress. You would enjoy seeing the mounted drill, for the way these men have got their wild half-broken horses into order is something marvelous. I am surprised at the orderly manner in which they have behaved; now and then a small squad goes to town and proceeds to paint things red, and then we get hold of them and

[2] *Letters II,* pp. 807–8.

put them into the guardhouse, but the great bulk of the men are as quiet and straight as possible. . . . I have been both astonished and pleased at my own ability in the line of tactics. I thoroughly enjoy handling these men, and I get them on the jump so that they execute their movements at a gallop.[3]

3. Steaming Southward

To Corinne Roosevelt Robinson

June 15th '98—in the Gulf of Mexico.

Today we are steaming southward through a sapphire sea, wind rippled under an almost cloudless sky. There are some forty craft in all, in three columns, the black hulls of the transports setting off the gray hulls of the men of war. Last evening we stood up on the bridge and watched the red sun sink and the lights blaze upon the ships, for miles ahead and astern, while the band played piece after piece—from the Star Spangled Banner, at which we all rose and stood uncovered, to the "Girl I left behind me"— But it is a great historical expedition, and I thrill to feel that I am part of it. If we fail of course we share the fate of all who do fail; but if we are allowed to succeed (for we certainly shall succeed, if allowed) we have scored the first great triumph in what will be a world movement. All the young fellows here dimly feel what this means; though the only articulate soul and imagination among them belong, rather curiously to ex-sheriff Captain "Bucky" O'Neil of Arizona. We have school for the officers and under officers, and we drill the men a couple of hours in the manual, especially for firing. Everyone seems happy now that we are going; though our progress is so slow that we may be a week before we reach Santiago, if we are going there. Thanks to the folly of having kept us a needless six days on board there will probably be some sickness among the men.

Monday, June 20th '98—Troopship nearing Santiago.

We didn't stop anywhere after all, so you'll get this letter with my last one I suppose. Until yesterday we sailed slowly but steadily south of east, against the trade wind that blew all the time in our faces. The weather was always fine. There were vexatious delays, thanks to a schooner which, by an act of utter folly at Washington or here, is being towed, stopping the whole fleet; and by an act of further folly our steamer, which has no tow rope, was sent back to bear it company, and all the rest of the

[3] *Ibid.*, pp. 832–3.

fleet are out of sight ahead. If the Spaniards had any enterprise they would somewhere or other have cut into this straggling convoy, especially when Gen. Shafter left us as stragglers in the rear; but they haven't any, and so we are safe and nearly in sight of Santiago; wondering much whether that city has fallen, in which case our expedition is wasted, or whether it will fight, and if so how hard. All day we have steamed close to the Cuban coast, high barren looking mountains rising abruptly from the shore, and at this distance looking much like those of Montana. We are well within the tropics, and at night the Southern cross shows low above the horizon; it seems strange to see it in the same sky with the friendly Dipper.[4]

4. Landing and First Fight

All next day we rolled and wallowed in the seaway, waiting until a decision was reached as to where we should land. On the morning of June 22d the welcome order for landing came.

We did the landing as we had done everything else—that is, in a scramble, each commander shifting for himself. The port at which we landed was called Daiquiri, a squalid little village where there had been a railway and iron-works. There were no facilities for landing, and the fleet did not have a quarter the number of boats it should have had for the purpose. All we could do was to stand in with the transports as close as possible, and then row ashore in our own few boats and the boats of the war-ships. . . .

There was plenty of excitement to the landing. . . . The surf was high, and the landing difficult; so that the task of getting the men, the ammunition, and provisions ashore was not easy. Each man carried three days' field rations and a hundred rounds of ammunition. . . . Meanwhile, from another transport, our horses were being landed, together with the mules, by the simple process of throwing them overboard and letting them swim ashore, if they could. . . .[5]

It was mid-afternoon and the tropic sun was beating fiercely down when Colonel Wood started our regiment—the First and Tenth Cavalry and some of the infantry regiments having already marched. Colonel Wood himself rode in advance, while I led my squadron, and Major Brodie followed with his. It was a hard march, the hilly jungle trail being so narrow that often we had to go in single file. We marched fast, for Wood was bound to get us ahead of the other regiments, so as to be sure of our place in the body that struck the enemy next morning. If it had

[4] *Ibid.,* pp. 843–4.
[5] "The Rough Riders" (1899). *Works XI,* pp. 46–7.

not been for his energy in pushing forward, we should certainly have missed the fight. As it was, we did not halt until we were at the extreme front.

The men were not in very good shape for marching, and moreover they were really horsemen, the majority being cowboys who had never done much walking. The heat was intense and their burdens very heavy. Yet there was very little straggling. Whenever we halted they instantly took off their packs and threw themselves on their backs. Then at the word to start they would spring into place again. . . .

It was long after nightfall when we tramped through the darkness into the squalid coast hamlet of Siboney. As usual when we made a night camp, we simply drew the men up in column of troops, and then let each man lie down where he was. Black thunder-clouds were gathering. Before they broke the fires were made and the men cooked their coffee and pork, some frying the hardtack with the pork. The officers, of course, fared just as the men did. Hardly had we finished eating when the rain came, a regular tropic downpour. We sat about, sheltering ourselves as best we could, for the hour or two it lasted; then the fires were relighted and we closed around them, the men taking off their wet things to dry them, so far as possible, by the blaze. . . .

We were to start by sunrise toward Santiago, General Young taking four troops of the Tenth and four troops of the First up the road which led through the valley; while Colonel Wood was to lead our eight troops along a hill trail to the left, which joined the valley road about four miles on, at a point where the road went over a spur of the mountain chain and from thence went downhill toward Santiago. The Spaniards had their lines at the junction of the road and the trail. . . .

At six o'clock, the Rough Riders began their advance. . . . Many of the men, footsore and weary from their march of the preceding day, found the pace up this hill too hard, and either dropped their bundles or fell out of line, with the result that we went into action with less than five hundred men—as, in addition to the stragglers, a detachment had been left to guard the baggage on shore. . . .

After reaching the top of the hill the walk was very pleasant. Now and then we came to glades or rounded hill-shoulders, whence we could look off for some distance. The tropical forest was very beautiful, and it was a delight to see the strange trees, the splendid royal palms and a tree which looked like a flat-topped acacia, and which was covered with a mass of brilliant scarlet flowers. We heard many bird-notes, too, the cooing of doves and the call of a great brush cuckoo. Afterward we found that the Spanish guerillas imitated these bird-calls, but the sounds we heard that morning, as we advanced through the tropic forest, were from birds, not guerillas, until we came right up to the Spanish lines. It was very beautiful and very peaceful, and it seemed more as if we were off on some hunting excursion than as if were about to go into a sharp and bloody little fight. . . .

After marching for somewhat over an hour, we suddenly came to a halt, and immediately afterward Colonel Wood sent word down the line that the advance-guard had come upon a Spanish outpost. Then the order was passed to fill the magazines, which was done.

The men were totally unconcerned, and I do not think they realized that any fighting was at hand; at any rate, I could hear the group nearest me discussing in low murmurs, not the Spaniards, but the conduct of a certain cow-puncher in quitting work on a ranch and starting a saloon in some New Mexican town. In another minute, however, Wood sent me orders to deploy three troops to the right of the trail, and to advance when we became engaged; while, at the same time, the other troops, under Major Brodie, were deployed to the left of the trail where the ground was more open than elsewhere—one troop being held in reserve in the centre, besides the reserves on each wing. Later all the reserves were put into the firing-line.

To the right the jungle was quite thick, and we had barely begun to deploy when a crash in front announced that the fight was on. It was evidently very hot, and L Troop had its hands full; so I hurried my men up abreast of them. So thick was the jungle that it was very difficult to keep together. . . .

Meanwhile I had gone forward with Llewellen, Greenway, Kane, and their troopers until we came out on a kind of shoulder, jutting over a ravine, which separated us from a great ridge on our right. It was on this ridge that the Spaniards had some of their intrenchments, and it was just beyond this ridge that the Valley Road led, up which the regulars were at that very time pushing their attack; but, of course, at the moment we knew nothing of this. The effect of the smokeless powder was remarkable. The air seemed full of the rustling sound of the Mauser bullets, for the Spaniards knew the trails by which we were advancing, and opened heavily on our position. Moreover, as we advanced we were, of course, exposed, and they could see us and fire. But they themselves were entirely invisible. The jungle covered everything, and not the faintest trace of smoke was to be seen in any direction to indicate from whence the bullets came. It was some time before the men fired; Llewellen, Kane, and I anxiously studying the ground to see where our opponents were, and utterly unable to find out.

It was Richard Harding Davis who gave us our first opportunity to shoot back with effect. He was behaving precisely like my officers, being on the extreme front of the line, and taking every opportunity to study with his glasses the ground where we thought the Spaniards were. I had tried some volley firing at points where I rather doubtfully believed the Spaniards to be, but had stopped firing and was myself studying the jungle-covered mountain ahead with my glasses, when Davis suddenly said, "There they are, Colonel; look over there; I can see their hats near that glade," pointing across the valley to our right. In a minute I, too, made out the hats, and then pointed them out to three or four of our best shots, giving them my estimate of the range. For a minute or two no result followed, and I kept raising the range, at the same time getting more men on the firing-line. Then, evidently, the shots told, for the Spaniards suddenly sprang out of the cover through which we had seen their hats, and ran to another spot; and we could now make out a large number of them.

I accordingly got all of my men up in line and began quick firing. In a very few minutes our bullets began to do damage, for the Spaniards retreated to the left into the jungle, and we lost sight of them. . . . The trees, of course, furnished no protection from the Mauser bullets. Once I was standing behind a large palm with my head out to one side, very fortunately; for a bullet passed through the palm, filling my left eye and ear with the dust and splinters.

A perfect hail of bullets was sweeping over us as we advanced. Once I got a glimpse of some Spaniards, apparently retreating, far in the front, and to our right, and we fired a couple of rounds after them. . . . I became convinced, after much anxious study, that we were being fired at from some large red-tiled buildings, part of a ranch on our front. . . . It was very hot and the men were getting exhausted, though at this particular time we were not suffering heavily from bullets, the Spanish fire going high. As we advanced, our cover became a little thicker and I lost touch of the main body under Wood; so I halted and we fired industriously at the ranch buildings ahead of us, some five hundred yards off. Then we heard cheering on the right, and I supposed that this meant a charge on the part of Wood's men, so I sprang up and ordered the men to rush the buildings ahead of us. They came forward with a will. There was a moment's heavy firing from the Spaniards, which all went over our heads, and then it ceased entirely. When we arrived at the buildings, panting and out of breath, they contained nothing but heaps of empty cartridge-shells and two dead Spaniards, shot through the head.[6]

[6] *Ibid.*, pp. 50–64.

5. *"We have a lovely camp . . ."*

To Corinne Roosevelt Robinson

June 27th '98. Camp 5 miles from Santiago.

We have a lovely camp here by a beautiful stream, which runs through jungle-lined banks. So far the country is lovely; plenty of grass, and great open woods of palms . . . with mango trees and many others; but most of the land is covered by a dense tropical jungle. This was what made it so hard for us in the fight. It was very trying to stand, or advance slowly, while the men fell dead or wounded, shot down from we knew not whence; for smokeless powder renders it almost impossible to place a hidden foe.

The morning after the fight we buried our dead in a great trench, reading the solemn burial service over them, and all the regiment joining in singing "Rock of Ages." The vultures were wheeling over head by hundreds. They plucked out the eyes and tore the faces and the wounds of the dead Spaniards before we got to them, and even one of our own men who lay in the open. The wounded lay in the path, a ghastly group; there were no supplies for them; our doctors did all they could, but had little with which to do it; a couple died in the night, and the others we took back on improvised litters to the landing place.

One of them, a New Mexican cow puncher, named Rowland, shot through the side, who had returned to the firing line after his wound caused him to fall out, refused to go aboard the hospital ship, and yesterday toiled out here to rejoin us. I really don't see how he ever walked with such a wound. One of the mortally wounded, Heffner, got me to prop him against a tree and give him his water canteen and rifle, and continued firing until we left him as we went forward. The woods are full of land crabs, some of which are almost as big as rabbits; when things grew quiet they slowly gathered in gruesome rings round the fallen.[7]

6. *The San Juan Fight*

As the sun rose the men fell in, and at the same time a battery of field-guns was brought up on the hill crest just beyond, between us and toward Santiago. It was a fine sight to see the great horses straining under the lash as they whirled the guns up the hill and into position. . . .

Wood formed his brigade, with my regiment in front, and gave me

[7] *Letters II*, p. 845.

orders to follow behind the First Brigade, which was just moving off the ground. In column of fours we marched down the trail toward the ford of the San Juan River. . . .

Our orders had been of the vaguest kind, being simply to march to the right and connect with Lawton—with whom, of course, there was no chance of our connecting. No reconnoissance had been made, and the exact position and strength of the Spaniards was not known. A captive balloon was up in the air at this moment, but it was worse than useless. . . .

I was now ordered to cross the ford, march half a mile or so to the right, and then halt and await further orders; and I promptly hurried my men across, for the fire was getting hot, and the captive balloon, to the horror of everybody, was coming down to the ford . . . a special target for the enemy's fire. . . .

As I led my column slowly along, under the intense heat, through the high grass of the open jungle, the First Brigade was to our left, and the firing between it and the Spaniards on the hills grew steadily hotter and hotter. After a while I came to a sunken lane, and as by this time the First Brigade had stopped and was engaged in a stand-up fight, I halted my men and sent back words for orders.

I got the men as well sheltered as I could. Many of them lay close under the bank of the lane, others slipped into the San Juan River and crouched under its hither bank, while the rest lay down behind the patches of bushy jungle in the tall grass. The heat was intense, and many of the men were already showing signs of exhaustion.

While we were lying in reserve we were suffering nearly as much as afterward when we charged. I think that the bulk of the Spanish fire was practically unaimed, or at least not aimed at any particular man, and only occasionally at a particular body of men; but they swept the whole field of battle up to the edge of the river, and man after man in our ranks fell dead or wounded. . . .

I sent messenger after messenger to try to find General Sumner or General Wood and get permission to advance, and was just about making up my mind that in the absence of orders I had better "march toward the guns," when Lieutenant-Colonel Dorst came riding up through the storm of bullets with the welcome command "to move forward and support the regulars in the assault on the hills in front." . . .

The instant I received the order I sprang on my horse and then my "crowded hour" began. . . . I formed my men in column of troops, each troop extended in open skirmishing order, the right resting on the wire fences which bordered the sunken lane. . . .

I started in the rear of the regiment, the position in which the colonel

137

should theoretically stay . . . but I speedily . . . found that I could get that line, behind which I personally was, faster forward than the one immediately in front of it, with the result that the two rearmost lines of the regiment began to crowd together; so I rode through them both, the better to move on the one in front. This happened with every line in succession until I found myself at the head of the regiment. . . .

We [there] ran into the left wing of the Ninth Regulars, and some of the First Regulars, who were lying down; that is, the troopers were lying down, while the officers were walking to and fro. . . .

I spoke to the captain in command of the rear platoons, saying that I had been ordered to support the regulars in the attack upon the hills, and that in my judgment we could not take these hills by firing at them, and that we must rush them. He answered that his orders were to keep his men lying where they were, and that he could not charge without orders. I asked where the colonel was, and as he was not in sight, said, "Then I am the ranking officer here and I give the order to charge"—for I did not want to keep the men longer in the open suffering under a fire which they could not effectively return. Naturally the captain hesitated to obey this order when no word had been received from his own colonel. So I said, "Then let my men through, sir," and rode on through the lines, followed by the grinning Rough Riders, whose attention had been completely taken off the Spanish bullets, partly by my dialogue with the regulars, and partly by the language I had been using to themselves as I got the lines forward, for I had been joking with some and swearing at others, as the exigencies of the case seemed to demand. When we started to go through, however, it proved too much for the regulars, and they jumped up and came along, their officers and troops mingling with mine, all being delighted at the chance. When I got to where the head of the left wing of the Ninth was lying . . . I was enabled to get back into the lane, at the same time waving my hat, and giving the order to charge the hill on our right front. Out of my sight, over on the right, Captains McBlain and Taylor, of the Ninth, made up their minds independently to charge at just about this time; and at almost the same moment Colonels Carroll and Hamilton, who were off, I believe, to my left, where we could see neither them nor their men, gave the order to advance. But of all this I knew nothing at the time. The whole line, tired of waiting, and eager to close with the enemy, was straining to go forward; and it seems that different parts slipped the leash at almost the same moment. The First Cavalry came up the hill just behind, and partly mixed with my regiment and the Ninth. As already said, portions of the Third, Sixth, and Tenth followed, while the rest of the members of these three regiments kept more in touch with the infantry on our left.

By this time we were all in the spirit of the thing and greatly excited by the charge, the men cheering and running forward between shots, while the delighted faces of the foremost officers . . . as they ran at the head of their troops, will always stay in my mind.

Being on horseback I was, of course, able to get ahead of the men on foot, excepting my orderly, Henry Bardshar, who had run ahead very fast in order to get better shots at the Spaniards, who were now running out of the ranch buildings. . . . Some forty yards from the top I ran into a wire fence and jumped off little Texas, turning him loose. He had been scraped by a couple of bullets, one of which nicked my elbow, and I never expected to see him again. As I ran up to the hill, Bardshar stopped to shoot, and two Spaniards fell as he emptied his magazine. These were the only Spaniards I actually saw fall to aimed shots by any one of my men, with the exception of two guerillas in trees.

Almost immediately afterward the hill was covered by the troops, both Rough Riders and the colored troopers of the Ninth, and some men of the First. . . .

No sooner were we on the crest than the Spaniards from the line of hills in our front, where they were strongly intrenched, opened a very heavy fire upon us with their rifles. They also opened upon us with one or two pieces of artillery, using time fuses which burned very accurately, the shells exploding right over our heads. . . .

Suddenly, above the cracking of the carbines, rose a peculiar drumming sound, and some of the men cried: "The Spanish machine-guns!" Listening, I made out that it came from the flat ground to the left, and jumped to my feet, smiting my hand on my thigh, and shouting aloud with exultation: "It's the Gatlings, men, our Gatlings!" Lieutenant Parker was bringing his four Gatlings into action, and shoving them nearer and nearer the front. Now and then the drumming ceased for a moment; then it would resound again, always closer to San Juan hill, which Parker, like ourselves, was hammering to assist the infantry attack. Our men cheered lustily. We saw much of Parker after that, and there was never a more welcome sound than his Gatlings as they opened. It was the only sound which I ever heard my men cheer in battle.

The infantry got nearer and nearer the crest of the hill. At last we could see the Spaniards running from the rifle-pits as the Americans came on in their final rush. Then I stopped my men for fear they should injure their comrades, and called to them to charge the next line of trenches, on the hills in our front, from which we had been undergoing a good deal of punishment. Thinking that the men would all come, I jumped over the wire fence in front of us and started at the double; but, as a matter of fact, the troopers were so excited, what with shooting and being shot, and shouting and cheering, that they did not hear, or did not heed me; and after running about a hundred yards I found I had only five men along with me. Bullets were ripping the grass all around us, and one of the men . . . was mortally wounded; another . . . was shot first in the leg and then through the body. He made not the slightest murmur, only asking me to put his water canteen where he could get at it, which I did; he ultimately recovered. There was no use going on with the remaining three men, and I bade them stay where they were while I went back and brought up the rest of the brigade.

This was a decidedly cool request, for there was really no possible point in letting them stay there while I went back; but at the moment it seemed perfectly natural to me, and apparently so to them, for they cheerfully nodded, and sat down in the grass, firing back at the line of trenches from which the Spaniards were shooting at them. Meanwhile, I ran back, jumped over the wire fence, and went over the crest of the hill, filled with anger against the troopers, and especially those of my own regiment, for not having accompanied me. They, of course, were quite innocent of wrong-doing; and even while I taunted them bitterly for not having followed me, it was all I could do not to smile at the look of injury and surprise that came over their faces, while they cried out: "We didn't hear you, we didn't see you go, Colonel; lead on now, we'll sure follow you." I wanted the other regiments to come too, so I ran down to where General Sumner was and asked him if I might make the charge; and he told me to go and that he would see that the men followed. By this time everybody had his attention attracted, and when I leaped over the fence again, with Major Jenkins beside me, the men of the various regiments which were already on the hill came with a rush, and we started across the wide valley which lay between us and the Spanish intrenchments. . . . The long-legged men like Greenway, Goodrich, Sharp-shooter Proffit, and others, outstripped the rest of us, as we had a considerable distance to go. Long before we got near them the Spaniards ran, save a few here and there, who either surrendered or were shot down. When we reached the trenches we found them filled with dead bodies in the light blue and white uniform of the Spanish regular army. There were very few wounded. Most of the fallen had little holes in their heads from which their brains were oozing; for they were covered from the neck down by the trenches. . . .

In the course of the afternoon the Spaniards in our front made the only offensive movement which I saw them make during the entire campaign; for what were ordinarily called "attacks" upon our lines consisted merely of heavy firing from their trenches and from their skirmishers. In this case they did actually begin to make a forward movement, their cavalry coming up as well as the marines and reserve infantry, while their skirmishers, who were always bold, redoubled their activity. It could not be called a charge, and not only was it not pushed home, but it was stopped almost as soon as it began, our men immediately running forward to the crest of the hill with shouts of delight at seeing their enemies at last come into the open. A few seconds' firing stopped their advance and drove them into the cover of the trenches. . . .

In this fight our regiment had numbered four hundred and ninety men, as, in addition to the killed and wounded of the first fight, some had had to go to the hospital for sickness and some had been left behind with the baggage, or were detailed on other duty. Eighty-nine were killed and wounded: the heaviest loss suffered by any regiment in the cavalry division. The Spaniards made a stiff fight, standing firm until we charged home. They fought much more stubbornly than at Las Guasimas. . . . On this day they showed themselves to be brave foes, worthy of honor for their gallantry.[8]

7. Aftermath

To Edith K. Roosevelt[9]

> *Trenches outside Santiago*
> *July 5th '98*

We have had a truce which ends in two hours . . . and for the first time in six days I have had a few minutes to myself, so I bathed in a bucket and changed my clothes, and now write you by a tree where some of my men are digging a bombproof for me to use when the bombardment begins. Astonishing to say, I am in good health which as the men are falling out steadily with fever and dysentery is a matter for congratulation. A shrapnel grazed my hand breaking the skin but otherwise I haven't a scratch. It has been hard and dangerous work, for though we have been victorious it was only after heavy loss and it looks as if we had still heavier fighting ahead. But how proud I am of the regiment! And I verily believe the men would follow me anywhere. A gamier crowd never got together. The army has fought excellently; but the mismanagement in high quarters has been shameful, and Gen. Shafter has displayed criminal incompetency. Ultimately we shall get Santiago; but we may have some rough times yet.[10]

[8] "The Rough Riders." *Works XI*, pp. 75–100.
[9] Wife of Theodore Roosevelt.
[10] From copy of letter from Mr. Roosevelt sent by Mrs. Roosevelt to her sister, Emily Carow, in Italy. From the Roosevelt Association collection.

To Henry Cabot Lodge

Outside Santiago, July 5, 1898

DEAR CABOT: Not since the campaign of Crassus against the Parthians has there been so criminally incompetent a General as Shafter; and not since the expedition against Walcheren has there been grosser mismanagement than in this. The battle simply fought itself; three of the Brigade Commanders, most of the Colonels, and all the regiments individually did well; and the heroism of some of the regiments could not be surpassed; but Shafter never came within three miles of the line, and never has come; the confusion is incredible. The siege guns have not yet been landed! The mortars have not been started from the landing place. Our artillery has been poorly handled. There is no head; the orders follow one another in rapid succession, and are confused and contradictory to a degree. I have held the extreme front of the fighting line; I shall do all that can be done, whatever comes; but it is bitter to see the misery and suffering, and think that nothing but incompetency in administering the nation's enormous resources caused it.[11]

Trenches before Santiago
July 7th '98

"Château qui parle"—the Spaniards keep sending out flags of truce. They may surrender or they may fight, but at best they have given us a respite during which to try to remedy some of the hideous shortcomings and general mismanagement which caused us such jeopardy. We are getting up the artillery; we are caring for the wounded (and without the Red Cross society I really don't know what we should have done to grapple with the congested misery of the field hospitals, where the wounded died in the tropic sun and tropic rain, without shelter or care or food); we are getting up food at last.

Hitherto the men who all day lay in the trenches, and all night long worked at them, have had only pork and hardtack; by the greatest exertion I have now got them sugar and coffee, and enough beans for one meal apiece. We all share alike. You can hardly imagine the strength a plate of beans puts into a wornout man; or the eagerness with which he devours a can of tomatoes, after being sickened with grease and hardtack. The heat of the sun is terrible, and yet we are drenched half the time. The men are sickening daily with fever and dysentery; but I am myself in astonishingly good health, taking it all in all. I sleep right up

[11] *Letters II*, p. 849.

on the firing line, as we are continually menaced by night attacks. I simply roll up in a blanket and a canvas sheet. The men are perfectly cheerful, and I am deeply touched by their devotion to me. . . . I share their fortune absolutely, whether it be hardship or danger; I care for them as much as I can, and make them feel that I like and respect them, and am bound to them by the strongest ties of comradeship; and yet I will not tolerate the slightest insubordination, and am merciless to any form of cowardice or shirking. I can now command this regiment in the field as well as any man; and Wood is doing equally well with the brigade. The scenery is very beautiful, the crest we hold is marked by groups of the beautiful Royal Palm; and sunrise and moonrise over these mountains are beautiful beyond description. I am also interested in the birds which are new to me.

The guerillas have been very bad, shooting the doctors, the wounded men in litters and the burying parties. I sent out some sharp shooters who killed thirteen, out of trees. My officers have been of great help to me.[12]

To Douglas Robinson

Santiago, July 27, 1898

. . . As for the political effect of my actions; in the first place, I never can get on in politics, and in the second, I would rather have led that charge and earned my colonelcy than served three terms in the United States Senate. It makes me feel as though I could now leave something to my children which will serve as an apology for my having existed.[13]

To Edith K. Roosevelt

Camp near Santiago, July 30th '98.

Today there came a cable from the Secretary, which, if he doesn't change his mind, will mean an absolutely ideal arrangement for me. He says we are to go to Montauk Pt. to camp as soon as we move north, and that we are to go North in some reasonable time. This is really too good to be true. I'll get home continually, and will bring some of the best fellows from time to time to the house; and the children shall come to camp.

There is but litttle to write of now. It is hardly worth while to tell how I put one man under arrest, and make another sergeant because he shows energy in policing the camp; how today we have 87 cases of fever, and the other cavalry regiments even more, proportionately; how Texas has

[12] See note on earlier letters to Mrs. Roosevelt, p. 141.
[13] *Letters II,* p. 860.

grown thin and weak, but can still carry me; how I mete out justice, and keep discipline, and also struggle mightily to see that the Rough Riders get clothes and food—in which I finally succeed—and also tentage—in which I have hitherto failed; how Gievers, who was shot through the loins has actually got back from hospital to work again; how Hull of Harvard, sent back to Tampa after the first fight, has come back here as a stowaway, bound to share the luck of the regiment even if it means yellow fever; how I have enlisted nine new men in the past fortnight, four from Harvard and one from Princeton, who have made their way out with great difficulty, because they wished beyond all things to cast in their lot with ours (one Harvard man, Emerson, a traveller and writer, who has turned out an invaluable addition, arrived in brown silk pajamas with all his baggage, one pair of socks and five of spectacles); how the Red Cross goods delighted the souls of the men, and, funnily enough, the most appreciated of all were the coarse cotton suits of pajamas, all of which were appropriated by the officers, who use them as a kind of undress day uniform; and how the sun beats down, and the rains fall in torrents, and the miasma rises in vapors, and the wagons bog down and overturn, with our sugar, and our mail, and everything. There! I didn't know there was so much to tell, after all.[14]

[14] See note following letter to Mrs. Roosevelt dated July 5, 1898, p. 141.

President

Mr. Roosevelt succeeded to the Presidency on the assassination of President McKinley in September 1901. He was elected President in his own right in 1904 and served until 1909.

1. Accession to the Presidency

To Henry Cabot Lodge

Buffalo, September 9, 1901.

There is no use in telling you of the stunned amazement of the people over the attempted assassination of the President. You know all about it, because you know your own feelings. . . . You and I have lived too long, and have seen human nature from too many different sides to be astounded at ordinary folly or ordinary wickedness, but it did not seem possible that just at this time in just this country, and in the case of this particular President, any human being could be so infamous a scoundrel, so crazy a fool as to attempt to assassinate him. It was in the most naked way an assault not on power, not on wealth, but simply and solely upon free government, government by the common people, because it *was* government, and because, though in the highest sense a free and representative government, it yet stood for order as well as for liberty.

McKinley is a man hardly even of moderate means. He is about as well off, say, as a division superintendent of the New York Central railroad. He lives in a little house at Canton just as such a division superintendent who had retired would live in a little house in Auburn or some other small New York city or big country town. He comes from the typical hard-working farmer stock of our country. In every instinct and feeling he is closely in touch with and the absolute representative of the men who make up the immense bulk of our Nation—the small merchants, clerks,

145

farmers and mechanics who formed the backbone of the patriotic party under Washington in the Revolution; of the Republican Party under Lincoln at the time of the Civil War. His one great anxiety while President has been to keep in touch with this body of people and to give expression to their desires and sentiments. He has been so successful that within a year he has been re-elected by an overwhelming majority, a majority including the bulk of the wage-workers and the very great bulk of the farmers.

He has been to a high degree accessible to everyone. At his home in Canton anyone could see him just as easily as anyone else could be seen. All that was necessary was, if he was engaged, to wait until his engagement was over. More than almost any public man I have ever met, he has avoided exciting personal enmities. I have never heard him denounce or assail any man or any body of men. There is in the country at this time the most widespread confidence in and satisfaction with his policies. The occasion chosen by the assassin was one when the President was meeting great masses of his fellow-citizens in accordance with the old American idea of the relations between the President and the people. That there might be no measure of Judas-like infamy lacking, the dog approached him under pretense of shaking hands.

Under these conditions of national prosperity, of popular content, of democratic simplicity and of the absolutely representative character of the President, it does seem utterly impossible to fathom the mind of the man who would do such a deed. Moreover, the surgeons who have in all probability saved the President's life, have thereby saved the life of his assailant. If he is only indicted for assault with intent to kill, and behaves well while in jail, he will be a free man seven years hence, and this, after having committed a crime against free government, a thousand times worse than any murder of a private individual could be. Of course I feel as I always have felt, that we should war with relentless efficiency not only against anarchists, but against all active and passive sympathizers with anarchists. Moreover, every scoundrel . . . who for whatever purposes appeals to and inflames evil passion, has made himself accessory before the fact to every crime of this nature, and every soft fool who extends a maudlin sympathy to criminals has done likewise.[1]

Washington, September 23, 1901.

. . . It is a dreadful thing to come into the Presidency this way; but it would be a far worse thing to be morbid about it. Here is the task, and I have got to do it to the best of my ability; and that is all there is about

[1] *Letters III*, pp. 141–3.

it. I believe you will approve of what I have done and of the way I have handled myself so far. It is only a beginning, but it is better to make a beginning good than bad.[2]

To Sarah B. Leavitt[3]

Washington, October 7, 1901.

Yes, I have thought of Father all the time, and of how pleased he would be; what would I not give if only he could have lived until now and seen me here in the White House, and all his grandchildren, and everything! Edith is too sweet and pretty and dignified and wise as mistress of the White House, and very happy with it; she will write you soon.

Do you know that at the end of my term here, in 1905, I shall be exactly the age Father was when he died? Unconsciously, I always find I am trying to model myself with my children on the way he was with us.[4]

2. Liberty under the Law

Ours is a government of liberty by, through, and under the law. No man is above it and no man is below it. The crime of cunning, the crime of greed, the crime of violence, are all equally crimes, and against them all alike the law must set its face. This is not and never shall be a government either of a plutocracy or of a mob. It is, it has been, and it will be, a government of the people; including alike the people of great wealth and of moderate wealth, the people who employ others, the people who are employed; the wage-worker, the lawyer, the mechanic, the banker, the farmer; including them all, protecting each and every one if he acts decently and squarely, and discriminating against any one of them, no matter from what class he comes, if he does not act squarely and fairly, if he does not obey the law. While all people are foolish if they violate or rail against the law—wicked as well as foolish, but all foolish—yet the most foolish man in this Republic is the man of wealth who complains because the law is administered with impartial justice against or for him. His folly is greater than the folly of any other man who so complains; for he lives and moves and has his being because the law does in fact protect him and his property.

We have the right to ask every decent American citizen to rally to the support of the law if it is ever broken against the interest of the rich man; and we have the same right to ask that rich man cheerfully and gladly to

---

[2] *Ibid.*, p. 150.
[3] An old family friend of the Roosevelts.
[4] *Letters III*, p. 161.

acquiesce in the enforcement against his seeming interest of the law, if it is the law. Incidentally, whether he acquiesces or not, the law will be enforced, and this whoever he may be, great or small, and at whichever end of the social scale he may be.

I ask that we see to it in our country that the line of division in the deeper matters of our citizenship be drawn, never between section and section, never between creed and creed, never, thrice never, between class and class; but that the line be drawn on the line of conduct, cutting through sections, cutting through creeds, cutting through classes; the line that divides the honest from the dishonest, the line that divides good citizenship from bad citizenship, the line that declares a man a good citizen only if, and always if, he acts in accordance with the immutable law of righteousness, which has been the same from the beginning of history to the present moment, and which will be the same from now until the end of recorded time.[5]

3. The Regulation of Corporations

We are passing through a period of great commercial prosperity, and such a period is as sure as adversity itself to bring mutterings of discontent. At a time when most men prosper somewhat some men always prosper greatly; and it is as true now as when the tower of Siloam fell upon all alike, that good fortune does not come solely to the just, nor bad fortune solely to the unjust. When the weather is good for crops it is good for weeds. Moreover, not only do the wicked flourish when the times are such that most men flourish, but, what is worse, the spirit of envy and jealousy springs up in the breasts of those who, though they may be doing fairly well themselves, see others no more deserving who do better.

Wise laws and fearless and upright administration of the laws can give the opportunity for such prosperity as we see about us. But that is all that they can do. When the conditions have been created which make prosperity possible, then each individual man must achieve it for himself by his own energy and thrift and business intelligence. If when people wax fat they kick, as they have kicked since the days of Jeshurun, they will speedily destroy their own prosperity. If they go into wild speculation and lose their heads they have lost that which no laws can supply. If in a spirit of sullen envy they insist upon pulling down those who have profited most in the years of fatness, they will bury themselves in the crash of the common disaster. It is difficult to make our material condition better by the best laws, but it is easy enough to ruin it by bad laws.

The upshot of all this is that it is peculiarly incumbent upon us in a

[5] *Works XVI,* pp. 18–19.

time of such material well-being, both collectively as a nation and individually as citizens, to show, each on his own account, that we possess the qualities of prudence, self-knowledge, and self-restraint. In our government we need above all things stability, fixity of economic policy; while remembering that this fixity must not be fossilization, that there must not be inability to shift our laws so as to meet our shifting national needs. There are real and great evils in our social and economic life, and these evils stand out in all their ugly baldness in time of prosperity; for the wicked who prosper are never a pleasant sight. There is every need of striving in all possible ways, individually and collectively, by combinations among ourselves and through the recognized governmental agencies, to cut out those evils. All I ask is to be sure that we do not use the knife with an ignorant zeal which would make it more dangerous to the patient than to the disease.

One of the features of the tremendous industrial development of the last generation has been the very great increase in private, and especially in corporate, fortunes. We may like this or not, just as we choose, but it is a fact nevertheless; and as far as we can see it is an inevitable result of the working of the various causes, prominent among them steam and electricity. Urban population has grown in this country, as in all civilized countries, much faster than the population as a whole during the last century. . . . There is evil in these conditions, but you can't destroy it unless you destroy the civilization they have brought about. Where men are gathered together in great masses it inevitably results that they must work far more largely through combinations than where they live scattered and remote from one another. Many of us prefer the old conditions of life, under which the average man lived more to himself and by himself, where the average community was more self-dependent, and where even though the standard of comfort was lower on the average, yet there was less of the glaring inequality in worldly conditions which we now see about us in our great cities. It is not true that the poor have grown poorer; but some of the rich have grown so very much richer that, where multitudes of men are herded together in a limited space, the contrast strikes the onlooker as more violent than formerly. On the whole, our people earn more and live better than ever before, and the progress of which we are so proud could not have taken place had it not been for the upbuilding of industrial centres, such as this in which I am speaking.

But together with the good there has come a measure of evil. Life is not so simple as it was; and surely, both for the individual and the community, the simple life is normally the healthy life. There is not in the great cities the feeling of brotherhood which there is still in country localities; and the lines of social cleavage are far more deeply marked,

149

For some of the evils which have attended upon the good of the changed conditions we can at present see no complete remedy. For others the remedy must come by the action of men themselves in their private capacity, whether merely as individuals or by combination. For yet others some remedy can be found in legislative and executive action—national, State, or municipal. Much of the complaint against combinations is entirely unwarranted. Under present-day conditions it is as necessary to have corporations in the business world as it is to have organizations, unions, among wage-workers. We have a right to ask in each case only this: that good, and not harm, shall follow. Exactly as labor organizations, when managed intelligently and in a spirit of justice and fair play, are of very great service not only to the wage-workers, but to the whole community, as has been shown again and again in the history of many such organizations; so wealth, not merely individual, but corporate, when used aright is not merely beneficial to the community as a whole, but is absolutely essential to the upbuilding of such a series of communities as those whose citizens I am now addressing. This is so obvious that it ought to be too trite to mention, and yet it is necessary to mention it when we see some of the attacks made upon wealth, as such.

Of course a great fortune if used wrongly is a menace to the community. A man of great wealth who does not use that wealth decently is, in a peculiar sense, a menace to the community, and so is the man who does not use his intellect aright. Each talent—the talent for making money, the talent for showing intellect at the bar, or in any other way—if unaccompanied by character, makes the possessor a menace to the community. But such a fact no more warrants us in attacking wealth than it does in attacking intellect. Every man of power, by the very fact of that power, is capable of doing damage to his neighbors; but we cannot afford to discourage the development of such men merely because it is possible they may use their power for wrong ends. If we did so we should leave our history a blank, for we should have no great statesmen, soldiers, merchants, no great men of arts, of letters, of science. Doubtless on the average the most useful citizen to the community as a whole is the man to whom has been granted what the Psalmist asked for—neither poverty nor riches. But the great captain of industry, the man of wealth, who, alone or in combination with his fellows, drives through our great business enterprises, is a factor without whom the civilization that we see roundabout us here could not have been built up. Good, not harm, normally comes from the upbuilding of such wealth. Probably the greatest harm done by vast wealth is the harm that we of moderate means do ourselves when we let the vices of envy and hatred enter deep into our own natures.

But there is other harm; and it is evident that we should try to do

150

away with that. The great corporations which we have grown to speak of rather loosely as trusts are the creatures of the State, and the State not only has the right to control them, but it is in duty bound to control them wherever the need of such control is shown. There is clearly need of supervision—need to possess the power of regulation of these great corporations through the representatives of the public—wherever, as in our own country at the present time, business corporations become so very powerful alike for beneficent work and for work that is not always beneficent. It is idle to say that there is no need for such supervision. There is, and a sufficient warrant for it is to be found in any one of the admitted evils appertaining to them.

We meet a peculiar difficulty under our system of government, because of the division of governmental power between the nation and the States. When the industrial conditions were simple, very little control was needed, and the difficulties of exercising such control under our Constitution were not evident. Now the conditions are complicated and we find it hard to frame national legislation which shall be adequate; while as a matter of practical experience it has been shown that the States either cannot or will not exercise a sufficient control to meet the needs of the case. Some of our States have excellent laws—laws which it would be well indeed to have enacted by the national legislature. But the wide-spread differences in these laws, even between adjacent States, and the uncertainty of the power of enforcement, result practically in altogether insufficient control. I believe that the nation must assume this power of control by legislation; if necessary by constitutional amendment. The immediate necessity in dealing with trusts is to place them under the real, not the nominal, control of some sovereign to which, as its creatures, the trusts shall owe allegiance, and in whose courts the sovereign's orders may be enforced.

This is not the case with the ordinary so-called "trust" to-day; for the trust nowadays is a large State corporation, which generally does business in other States, often with a tendency toward monopoly. Such a trust is an artificial creature not wholly responsible to or controllable by any legislation, either by State or nation, and not subject to the jurisdiction of any one court. Some governmental sovereign must be given full power over these artificial, and very powerful, corporate beings. In my judgment this sovereign must be the National Government. When it has been given full power, then this full power can be used to control any evil influence, exactly as the government is now using the power conferred upon it by the Sherman antitrust law.

Even when the power has been granted it would be most unwise to exercise it too much, to begin by too stringent legislation. The mechan-

151

ism of modern business is as delicate and complicated as it is vast, and nothing would be more productive of evil to all of us, and especially to those least well off in this world's goods, than ignorant meddling with this mechanism—above all, meddling in a spirit of class legislation or hatred or rancor. It is eminently necessary that the power should be had, but it is just as necessary that it should be exercised with wisdom and self-restraint. The first exercise of that power should be the securing of publicity among all great corporations doing an interstate business. The publicity, though non-inquisitorial, should be real and thorough as to all important facts with which the public has concern. Daylight is a powerful discourager of evil. Such publicity would by itself tend to cure the evils of which there is just complaint; it would show us if evils existed, and where the evils are imaginary, and it would show us what next ought to be done.

Above all, let us remember that our success in accomplishing anything depends very much upon our not trying to accomplish everything. Distrust whoever pretends to offer you a patent cure-all for every ill of the body politic, just as you would a man who offers a medicine which would cure every evil of your individual body. A medicine that is recommended to cure both asthma and a broken leg is not good for either. Mankind has moved slowly upward through the ages, sometimes a little faster, sometimes a little slower, but rarely indeed by leaps and bounds. At times a great crisis comes in which a great people, perchance led by a great man, can at white heat strike some mighty blow for the right—make a long stride in advance along the path of justice and of orderly liberty. But normally we must be content if each of us can do something—not all that we wish, but something—for the advancment of those principles of righteousness which underlie all real national greatness, all true civilization and freedom. I see no promise of any immediate and complete solution of all the problems we group together when we speak of the trust question. But we can make a beginning in solving these problems, and a good beginning, if only we approach the subject with a sufficiency of resolution, of honesty, and of that hard common sense which is one of the most valuable, and not always one of the most common, assets in any nation's greatness. The existing laws will be fully enforced as they stand on the statute-books without regard to persons, and I think good has already come from their enforcement. I think, furthermore, that additional legislation should be had and can be had, which will enable us to accomplish much more along the same lines. No man can promise a perfect solution, at least in the immediate future. But something has already been done, and much more can be done if our people temperately and determinedly will that it shall be done.

In conclusion let me add one word. While we are not to be excused if we fail to do whatever is possible through the agency of government, we must keep ever in mind that no action of the government, no action by combination among ourselves, can take the place of the individual qualities to which in the long run every man must owe the success he can make of life. There never has been devised, and there never will be devised, any law which will enable a man to succeed save by the exercise of those qualities which have always been the prerequisites of success—the qualities of hard work, of keen intelligence, of unflinching will. Such action can supplement those qualities but it cannot take their place. No action by the State can do more than supplement the initiative of the individual; and ordinarily the action of the State can do no more than to secure to each individual the chance to show under as favorable conditions as possible the stuff that there is in him.[6]

4. The Coal Strike

To Joseph Bucklin Bishop[7]

Washington, October 5, 1902

The attitude of the operators was such at the meeting as to make it hopeless to expect anything therefrom and I certainly shall not communicate with them again. Mitchell shone so in comparison with them as to make me have a very uncomfortable feeling that they might be far more to blame relatively to the miners than I had supposed. I never knew six men show to less advantage. Some of their number evidently did not even understand that I have no possible authority to send United States troops into the district unless asked to do so by the Pennsylvania authorities because they cannot preserve order, or unless government property is attacked.

I thought Mitchell's proposition eminently fair. I shall now try, although without much hope of success, to get him to have the miners go back to work anyhow, on the understanding that I shall appoint a commission of inquiry who will report in full upon all conditions, and that I shall do whatever I may be able to do to secure action along the line of the report of such commission. . . . Exactly what I can do I am not certain, and I still think it possible that what has been started by my action will result in forcing some kind of agreement. If not, I think there are ugly times ahead.

[6] *Ibid.*, pp. 61–7.
[7] New York newspaperman; secretary, Isthmian Canal Commission; edited *Theodore Roosevelt and His Time As Shown in His Letters.*

After the operators left the other day I explained in the most friendly way to Mitchell and his companions that I most earnestly hoped they would do everything in their power to put a stop to violence. I explained that violence meant that they would inevitably lose; that of course they understood that if I had to interfere, through Pennsylvania's being unable to put down rioting, I would interfere in a way which would put an absolute stop to mob violence within twenty-four hours, and put a stop to it for good and all, too. Mitchell assured me that he had done, and would continue to do, everything possible to prevent all disorder. As I say, I do not know the facts; but certainly the other day Mitchell was more straightforward in his statements than were the operators.[8]

Washington, October 13, 1902

Do you think you are fully alive to the gross blindness of the operators? They fail absolutely to understand that they have any duty toward the public. Most emphatically I shall not compromise with lawlessness. But with a hundred and forty thousand workmen idle there is certain to be some disorder. I have been told, on excellent authority, that this disorder has been very great in the present instance and of a very evil kind. On equally good authority I am told the exact contrary. I shall speedily find out for myself. But in any event what has been done so far in no wise justified a refusal to have some dispassionate body settle the respective rights and wrongs of the two parties. The coal operators and their friends, and their allies of the type of the *Sun,* have been attacking me, just as they attacked me about the trust business. . . . Do they not realize that they are putting a very heavy burden on us who stand against socialism; against anarchic disorder?

A word as to the interference of politicians. Quay and Hanna are Senators; Odell is Governor; I am President. If any one of us interferes in a spirit of mere political trickery, or to gain political ends of an unworthy kind in an unworthy manner, if he threatens or hectors, why he should be condemned without stint. But the heaviest weight of condemnation should be reserved for any one of us who represents the people and who yet fails to do all in his power in the interest of the people to bring to an end a situation fraught with such infinite danger to the whole commonwealth. If during the ensuing week there comes some heavy riot on the East Side of New York, in my judgment the operators, more than the miners, are responsible for it.

Meanwhile I am sure that you know that I shall take no step which I do not think can be justified by the sound common sense of both of us

[8] *Letters III,* pp. 341–2.

six months or a year hence. I shall do whatever I can to meet the present emergency, but I shall not meet it in a way that will invite future disaster.[9]

To Winthrop M. Crane[10]

Washington, October 22, 1902

. . . A most comic incident ensued. For two hours I talked with Bacon and Perkins, both of whom were nearly frenzied. They begged me to make the miners yield, asserting that the operators would not, and freely acceding to my view of the danger of the situation. In fact, they said they believed we would have anarchy and social war; but that under no circumstances would the operators ever consent to have an additional man put upon the commission who was a labor man. During these two hours it never occurred to me that the operators were willing to run all this risk on a mere point of foolish pride; but Bacon finally happened to mention that they would not object at all to my exercising any latitude I chose in appointments under the headings that they had given. I instantly said that I should appoint my labor man as the "eminent sociologist." To my intense relief this utter absurdity was received with delight by Bacon and Perkins, who said they were sure the operators would agree to it! . . . Messrs. Morgan and Baer gave their assent by telephone, and the thing was done.[11]

5. The Strike in the Government Printing Office

To Albert Shaw[12]

Oyster Bay, August 1, 1903

. . . Now as to what you say about my method of taking hold of that Printing Office case. I became convinced that if I tried to do it in any way that would give the appearance of an effort to avoid difficulty on my part, I would simply insure the difficulty's coming. The labor unions were very arrogant and domineering, because they did not believe I would face the music, and it was necessary to give them a good jolt to make them understand at the outset that I would not tolerate anything in the nature of tyranny on their part. I was very sorry to have to go into the matter, because I entirely appreciate the political disadvantages of what

[9] *Ibid.*, p. 349.
[10] U.S. senator from Massachusetts.
[11] *Letters III*, p. 366.
[12] Editor of *American Review of Reviews;* lifelong student of government and friend of Roosevelt.

I did, and I should be a fool if I did not regret having to do anything that I thought would be politically disadvantageous to me; but this was a case where I did not feel that I should be justified in any hesitancy.[13]

6. "Get in touch with the labor people . . ."

To Philander Chase Knox[14]

Washington, November 10, 1904

Now that the fight is over, I want to say one word about general policy. There seems to me to be nothing of better augury for the country than the fact that you and Murray Crane are in the Senate—and especially that you are in the Senate. I shall serve for four years in the White House, if I live. You, I trust, will serve for twenty or thirty years in the Senate; and I feel that with every additional year you will render better service, for the Senate is peculiarly a body in which length of service enables a man to do constantly better work. Now, you have done what no other man of our generation has done in grappling with the great problem of the day—or rather, the multitude of problems connected with the relations of organized labor and organized capital to each other as well as to the general public. . . .

So far as organized capital is concerned, I have not even a suggestion to make to you. You know far too much for any hint of mine to be of any service to you. But I do most earnestly hope that you will make the problem of labor as thoroughly yours as you have made the problem of capital. More and more the labor movement in this country will become a factor of vital importance, not merely in our social but in our political development. If the attitude of the New York *Sun* toward labor, as toward the trust, becomes the attitude of the Republican party, we shall some day go down before a radical and extreme democracy with a crash which will be disastrous to the Nation. We must not only do justice, but be able to show the wageworkers that we are doing justice. We must make it evident that while there is not any weakness in our attitude, while we unflinchingly demand good conduct from them, yet we are equally resolute in the effort to secure them all just and proper consideration.

It would be a dreadful calamity if we saw this country divided into two parties, one containing the bulk of the property owners and conservative people, the other the bulk of the wageworkers and the less prosperous people generally; each party insisting upon demanding much that was wrong, and each party sullen and angered by real and fancied griev-

---

[13] *Letters III,* p. 537.
[14] Attorney General in Roosevelt's cabinet.

ances. The friends of property, of order, of law, must never show weakness in the face of violence or wrong or injustice; but, on the other hand, they must realize that the surest way to provoke an explosion of wrong and injustice is to be shortsighted, narrow-minded, greedy and arrogant, and to fail to show in actual work that here in this republic it is peculiarly incumbent upon the man with whom things have prospered to be in a certain sense the keeper of his brother with whom life has gone hard.

Now, my dear Senator, I hope you won't mind my writing you in this way. I feel that you have definitely put your hand to the plow in political life, and that you neither can nor ought to draw back, and I know that all you care for in political life is to render service; and furthermore, I know that you have to an extraordinary degree not merely the desire to render service but the power to render it. You have the mind and the training; and you have an impatient contempt for the little prizes, and the little, sordid arts, methods and aims of the ordinary politician. Therefore you have the chance to do this great service.

I wish you would get into touch with some of the labor people. After getting in touch with them you might find that you had to go against most of what they wished; but I would like you to know what they desire to— what their real feelings are.

When you and I first came together I found that the aspirations I had half formulated, the policies in which I earnestly believed but to which I could not myself give shape, were exactly those in which you most thoroughly believed; and that you had thought them all out and were able to give them shape in speech and in action in fashion which made them effective. Now I feel that you can do the same thing on an even larger scale during the years to come in the Senate, with reference not only to capital, but to labor. I feel that you can do infinitely more than, under any circumstances, I could have done.

7. *"They have found themselves powerless to control the government"*

To Thomas M. Patterson[15]

Washington, April 8, 1907

The real trouble with ——— and his associates is that they have found themselves absolutely powerless to control any action by the national government. There is no form of mendacity or bribery or corruption that they will not resort to in the effort to take vengeance. The ———

[15] U.S. senator from Colorado; editor, *Rocky Mountain News.*

157

combination and the other owners of predatory wealth hate me far more than do those who make a profession of denouncing them, because they have learned that while I do not attack them in words as reckless as those often used against them, I do try to make my words bear fruit in deeds. They have never before been obliged really to reckon with the federal government. They have never before seen practical legislation such as the rate bill, the beef inspection bill and the like become laws. They have never before had to face the probability of adverse action by the courts and the possibility of being put in stripes. Such being the case, and inasmuch as they have no moral scruple of any kind whatsoever, it is not to be wondered at that they should be willing to go to any length in the effort to reverse the movement against them. By reading the New York *Sun* and similar papers we can get a clear idea of the extent to which they will go in that portion of the press which they control.[16]

To Nicholas Murray Butler[17]

Washington, February 6, 1908

DEAR MURRAY: Your letter of the 4th does not surprise me, for I had heard through Jimmy Speyer how you felt, and of course I have been aware that for the last year or two you have been steadily growing out of sympathy with my purposes and policies.

Really, my dear fellow, there is very little I can answer to your letter. You think that my last message is like Andrew Johnson's speeches and messages. I think you might just as well have said that it is like Jefferson Davis'; but that is a mere difference of opinion. You say that it has left a very painful impression upon the public mind and that everywhere the loyal supporters of my administration, east and west, speak of the message with grief and sorrow, and that only my critics and enemies are delighted.

Of course I may be utterly mistaken, but my experience has been that whereas my critics and enemies have foamed at the mouth over it, and whereas my lukewarm friends and the men who have been preparing to turn, have been upset by it, yet my real supporters—those whose deep convictions I most nearly represent—have hailed it as they have no other speech or action of mine for a long time. In the mail with your letter, for example, comes one from General Horatio C. King, a copy of which I enclose. This is typical of the hundreds of letters I have received, and I have received more from judges, relatively, than from any other body of men. But they have not been the corporation judges, or the judges who,

[16] *Letters V*, p. 643.
[17] President, Columbia University.

tho honest, are susceptible to corporation influences. Of course, as I have said, I am well aware that I may be entirely mistaken, but I will add that the events of the last three months have made me for the first time sincerely regret that this is not my first term, and that I cannot have a showdown with my foes both without and within the party. In my judgment, there would not be even a fight west of the Alleghenies; and if I were a betting man I should like to bet heavily on the fight in New York.

But this feeling represents in me only the old Adam, which is not wholly eradicated from any man, and does not at all represent my deepest feelings. I care not at all that the fight must now be carried on by somebody else, provided only that it is carried on. You regret what I have done. To me your regret is incomprehensible. You blame me for what I have done. To me it seems that I have the right to the fullest and heartiest support of every good man whose eyes are not blinded by unhappy surroundings, and who has in him a single trace of the fervor for righteousness and decency without which goodness tends to be empty sham. If your soul does not rise up against corruption in politics and corruption in business, against the unspeakable degradation and baseness of a community . . . which will tolerate the vileness of the New York *Sun* and kindred newspapers in its family—why, then naturally you are out of sympathy with me.[18]

To Henry Lee Higginson[19]

Washington, March 28, 1907

You ask that real assistance be given to the money market, but you do not say what that assistance should be. I was under the impression that Mr. Cortelyou had rendered all the assistance that it was possible to render at this time. You then say that the fear of investors in railway securities must be dispelled; and you say that the people now have the impression that the greatest business interests (those of railroads) are imperiled. I am inclined to think that this is the case. If so, the responsibility lies primarily and overwhelmingly upon the railway and corporation people—that is, the manipulators of railroad and other corporation stocks —who have been guilty of such scandalous irregularities during the last few years. Secondarily it lies, of course, with the agitators and visionaries to whom the misdeeds of the conscienceless speculators I have named gave the chance to impress the people as a whole. Not one word of mine; not one act, administrative or legislative, of the National Government, is

---

[18] *Letters VI*, pp. 924–5.
[19] Prominent Boston banker; founder, Boston Symphony Orchestra.

responsible, directly or indirectly, in any degree whatsoever for the present situation. I trust I have stated this with sufficient emphasis, for it would be quite impossible to overemphasize it.

Two years ago the railroads were all clamoring against the passage of the rate law—an act of folly on their part and on the part of their friends and abettors which cannot be too harshly stigmatized. The only hope for the honest railroad man, for the honest investor, is in the extension and perfection of the system inaugurated by that law; in the absolute carrying out of the law at present and in its strengthening, if possible, at the next session of the Congress so as to make it even more effective.

I will not deviate one hand's breadth from the course I have marked out, and anything I may say will contain this explicit statement. Moreover, it is an act of sheer folly and shortsightedness on the part of the railway men not to realize that I am best serving their interests in following out precisely this course. I have never seen more foolish and hysterical speeches and acts than those of the so-called industrial leaders during the past few months. At one moment they yell that I am usurping the rights of the States. The next they turn around in literally a panic frenzy and beseech me to make some public utterance forbidding the States to do the very things that they have just asserted the States alone had the power to do.

You are from Massachusetts. I assume that you are familiar with the railway and corporation acts of Massachusetts. If so, you of course realize that I am trying to get the National Government to adopt legislation such as Massachusetts now has on its statute books, such as England now has on its statute books. How any sane man can construe this into an attack on capital I fail to see. As for the suits or other executive actions I have undertaken, I can only say that as yet every individual one of them has been entirely right and proper, and it is of course out of the question to ask me to announce that swindlers will not be prosecuted.[20]

8. Death of Mark Hanna

To Elihu Root

Washington, February 16, 1904

Hanna's death has been very sad. Did I tell you the last letter he wrote was one to me? As soon as he was seriously sick I called at the hotel, as a matter of course. For some inexplicable reason this affected him very

[20] *Letters V*, pp. 633–4.

much, appealing to the generous and large-hearted side of his nature, and he at once sent me a pencil note running as follows:

My dear Mr. President:
  You touched a tender spot, old man, when you called personally to inquire after me this a.m. I may be worse before I can be better, but all the same such "drops" of kindness are good for a fellow.

Sincerely yours,
M. A. Hanna

Friday p.m.

No man had larger traits than Hanna. He was a big man in every way and as forceful a personality as we have seen in public life in our generation. I think that not merely I myself, but the whole party and the whole country have reason to be very grateful to him for the way in which, after I came into office, under circumstances which were very hard for him, he resolutely declined to be drawn into the position which a smaller man of meaner cast would inevitably have taken; that is, the position of antagonizing public policies if I was identified with them. He could have caused the widest disaster to the country and the public if he had attacked and opposed the policies referring to Panama, the Philippines, Cuban reciprocity, army reform, the navy and legislation for regulating corporations. But he stood by them just as loyally as if I had been McKinley.[21]

9. Panama

To Kermit Roosevelt[22]

U.S.S. Louisiana, At Sea, November 20, 1906

It certainly adds to one's pleasure to have read history and to appreciate the picturesque. When on Wednesday we approached the coast and the jungle-covered mountains loomed clearer and clearer until we could see the surf beating on the shores, while there was hardly a sign of human habitation, I kept thinking of the four centuries of wild and bloody romance, mixed with abject squalor and suffering, which made up the history of the Isthmus until three years ago. I could see Balboa crossing at Darien, and the wars between the Spaniards and the Indians, and the settlement and the building of the quaint walled Spanish towns; and the trade,

---

[21] *Letters IV*, p. 730.
[22] Second son of Theodore Roosevelt.

across the seas by galleon, and over land by pack train and river canoe, in gold and silver, in precious stones; and then the advent of the buccaneers, and of the English seamen, of Drake and Frobisher and Morgan, and many, many others, and the wild destruction they wrought. Then I thought of the rebellion against the Spanish dominion, and the uninterrupted and bloody civil wars that followed, the last occurring when I became President; wars, the victorious heroes of which have their pictures frescoed on the quaint rooms of the palace at Panama city, and in similar palaces in all the other capitals of these strange, turbulent little half-caste civilizations. Meanwhile the Panama railroad had been built by Americans over a half century ago, with appalling loss of life, so that it is said, of course with exaggeration, that every sleeper laid represented the death of a man. Then the French canal company started work, and for two or three years did a good deal until it became evident that the task far exceeded its powers; and then to miscalculation and inefficiency was added the hideous greed of adventurers, trying each to save something from the general wreck, and the company closed with infamy and scandal.

Now we have taken hold of the job. We have difficulties with our own people, of course, I haven't a doubt that it will take a little longer and cost a little more than men now appreciate, but I believe that the work is being done with a very high degree both of efficiency and honesty; and I am immensely struck by the character of American employees who are engaged not merely in superintending the work, but in doing all the jobs that need skill and intelligence. The steam shovels, the dirt trains, the machine shops, and the like are all filled with American engineers, conductors, machinists, boilermakers, carpenters. From the top to the bottom these men are so hardy, so efficient, so energetic, that it is a real pleasure to look at them. Stevens, the head engineer, is a big fellow, a man of daring and good sense, and burly power. All of these men are quite as formidable, and would if it were necessary do quite as much in battle as the crews of Drake and Morgan; but as it is they are doing a work of infinitely more lasting consequence. Nothing whatever remains to show what Drake and Morgan did. They produced no real effect down here. But Stevens and his men are changing the face of the continent, are doing the greatest engineering feat of the ages, and the effect of their work will be felt while our civilization lasts.

I went over everything that I could possibly go over in the time at my disposal. I examined the quarters of married men and single men, white men and negroes. I went over the ground of the Gatun and La Boca dams; went through Panama and Colón, and spent a day at Culebra cut, where the great work is being done. There the huge steam shovels are hard at it;

scooping huge masses of rock and gravel and dirt previously loosened by the drillers and dynamite blasters, loading it on trains which take it away to some dump, either in the jungle or where the dams are to be built. They are eating steadily into the mountain cutting it down and down. Little tracks are laid on the side hills, rocks blasted out, and the great ninety-five ton steam shovels work up like mountain howitzers until they come to where they can with advantage begin their work of eating into and destroying the mountainside. With intense energy men and machines do their task, the white men supervising matters and handling the machines, while the tens of thousands of black men do the rough manual labor where it is not worth while to have machines do it. It is an epic feat, and one of immense significance.

The deluge of rain meant that many of the villages were knee-deep in water, while the flooded rivers tore through the tropic forests. It is a real tropic forest, palms and bananas, breadfruit trees, bamboos, lofty ceibas, and gorgeous butterflies and brilliant colored birds fluttering among the orchids. There are beautiful flowers, too. All my old enthusiasm for natural history seemed to revive, and I would have given a good deal to have stayed and tried to collect specimens. It would be good hunting country too; deer and now and then jaguars and tapir, and great birds that they call wild turkeys; there are alligators in the rivers. One of the trained nurses from a hospital went to bathe in a pool last August and an alligator grabbed him by the legs and was making off with him, but was fortunately scared away, leaving the man badly injured.

I tramped everywhere through the mud. Mother did not do this roughest work, and had time to see more of the really picturesque and beautiful side of the life, and really enjoyed herself. . . .

P.S. The Gatun dam will make a lake miles long, and the railroad now goes at what will be the bottom of this lake, and it was curious to think that in a few years great ships will be floating in water 100 feet above where we were.[23]

10. *The Natural Resources—Their Wise Use or Their Waste*

Governors of the several States, and gentlemen:

I welcome you to this conference at the White House. You have come hither at my request so that we may join together to consider the question of the conservation and use of the great fundamental sources of wealth of

[23] *Letters V*, pp. 496–8.

this nation. So vital is this question, that for the first time in our history the chief executive officers of the States separately, and of the States together forming the nation, have met to consider it.

With the governors come men from each State chosen for their special acquaintance with the terms of the problem that is before us. Among them are experts in natural resources and representatives of national organizations concerned in the development and use of these resources; the senators and representatives in Congress; the Supreme Court, the Cabinet, and the Inland Waterways Commission have likewise been invited to the conference, which is therefore national in a peculiar sense.

This conference on the conservation of natural resources is in effect a meeting of the representatives of all the people of the United States called to consider the weightiest problem now before the nation; and the occasion for the meeting lies in the fact that the natural resources of our country are in danger of exhaustion if we permit the old wasteful methods of exploiting them longer to continue.

With the rise of peoples from savagery to civilization, and with the consequent growth in the extent and variety of the needs of the average man, there comes a steadily increasing growth of the amount demanded by this average man from the actual resources of the country. Yet, rather curiously, at the same time the average man is apt to lose his realization of this dependence upon nature.

Every step of the progress of mankind is marked by the discovery and use of natural resources previously unused. Without such progressive knowledge and utilization of natural resources population could not grow, nor industries multiply, nor the hidden wealth of the earth be developed for the benefit of mankind.

When the founders of this nation met at Independence Hall in Philadelphia the conditions of commerce had not fundamentally changed from what they were when the Phœnician keels first furrowed the lonely waters of the Mediterranean. In Washington's time anthracite coal was known only as a useless black stone; and the great fields of bituminous coal were undiscovered. As steam was unknown, the use of coal for power production was undreamed of. Water was practically the only source of power, save the labor of men and animals; and this power was used only in the most primitive fashion. But a few small iron deposits had been found in this country, and the use of iron by our countrymen was very small. Wood was practically the only fuel, and what lumber was sawed was consumed locally, while the forests were regarded chiefly as obstructions to settlement and cultivation.

Such was the degree of progress to which civilized mankind had attained when this nation began its career. It is almost impossible for us in this day to realize how little our Revolutionary ancestors knew of the great store of natural resources whose discovery and use have been such vital factors in the growth and greatness of this nation, and how little they required to take from this store in order to satisfy their needs.

Since then our knowledge and use of the resources of the present territory of the United States have increased a hundredfold. Indeed, the growth of this nation by leaps and bounds makes one of the most striking and important chapters in the history of the world. Its growth has been due to the rapid development, and alas! that it should be said, to the rapid destruction of our natural resources. Nature has supplied to us in the United States, and still supplies to us, more kinds of resources in a more lavish degree than has ever been the case at any other time or with any other people. Our position in the world has been attained by the extent and thoroughness of the control we have achieved over nature; but we are more, and not less, dependent upon what she furnishes than at any previous time of history since the days of primitive man.

Yet our fathers, though they knew so little of the resources of the country, exercised a wise forethought in reference thereto. Washington clearly saw that the perpetuity of the States could only be secured by union, and that the only feasible basis of union was an economic one; in other words, that it must be based on the development and use of their natural resources. Accordingly, he helped to outline a scheme of commercial development, and by his influence an interstate waterways commission was appointed by Virginia and Maryland.

It met near where we are now meeting, in Alexandria, adjourned to Mount Vernon, and took up the consideration of interstate commerce by the only means then available, that of water. Further conferences were arranged, first at Annapolis, and then at Philadelphia. It was in Philadelphia that the representatives of all the States met for what was in its original conception merely a waterways conference; but when they had closed their deliberations the outcome was the Constitution which made the States into a nation.

The Constitution of the United States thus grew in large part out of the necessity for united action in the wise use of one of our natural resources. The wise use of all of our natural resources, which are our national resources as well, is the great material question of to-day. I have asked you to come together now because the enormous consumption of these resources, and the threat of imminent exhaustion of some of them, due to reckless and wasteful use, once more calls for common effort, common action.

Since the days when the Constitution was adopted, steam and electricity have revolutionized the industrial world. Nowhere has the revolu-

165

tion been so great as in our own country. The discovery and utilization of mineral fuels and alloys have given us the lead over all other nations in the production of steel. The discovery and utilization of coal and iron have given us our railways, and have led to such industrial development as has never before been seen. The vast wealth of lumber in our forests, the riches of our soils and mines, the discovery of gold and mineral oils, combined with the efficiency of our transportation, have made the conditions of our life unparalleled in comfort and convenience.

The steadily increasing drain on these natural resources has promoted to an extraordinary degree the complexity of our industrial and social life. Moreover, this unexampled development has had a determining effect upon the character and opinions of our people. The demand for efficiency in the great task has given us vigor, effectiveness, decision, and power, and a capacity for achievement which in its own lines has never yet been matched. So great and so rapid has been our material growth that there has been a tendency to lag behind in spiritual and moral growth; but that is not the subject upon which I speak to you to-day. Disregarding for the moment the question of moral purpose, it is safe to say that the prosperity of our people depends directly on the energy and intelligence with which our natural resources are used. It is equally clear that these resources are the final basis of national power and perpetuity. Finally, it is ominously evident that these resources are in the course of rapid exhaustion.

This nation began with the belief that its landed possessions were illimitable and capable of supporting all the people who might care to make our country their home; but already the limit of unsettled land is in sight, and indeed but little land fitted for agriculture now remains unoccupied save what can be reclaimed by irrigation and drainage. We began with an unapproached heritage of forests; more than half of the timber is gone. We began with coal-fields more extensive than those of any other nation and with iron ores regarded as inexhaustible, and many experts now declare that the end of both iron and coal is in sight.

We have become great because of the lavish use of our resources and we have just reason to be proud of our growth. But the time has come to inquire seriously what will happen when our forests are gone, when the coal, the iron, the oil, and the gas are exhausted, when the soils shall have been still further impoverished and washed into the streams, polluting the rivers, denuding the fields, and obstructing navigation. These questions do not relate only to the next century or to the next generation. It is time for us now as a nation to exercise the same reasonable foresight in dealing with our great natural resources that would be shown by any prudent man in conserving and widely using the property which contains the assurance of well-being for himself and his children.

The natural resources I have enumerated can be divided into two sharply distinguished classes accordingly as they are or are not capable of renewal. Mines if used must necessarily be exhausted. The minerals do not and cannot renew themselves. Therefore in dealing with the coal, the oil, the gas, the iron, the metals generally, all that we can do is to try to see that they are wisely used. The exhaustion is certain to come in time.

The second class of resources consists of those which cannot only be used in such manner as to leave them undiminished for our children, but can actually be improved by wise use. The soil, the forests, the waterways come in this category. In dealing with mineral resources, man is able to improve on nature only by putting the resources to a beneficial use which in the end exhausts them; but in dealing with the soil and its products man can improve on nature by compelling the resources to renew and even reconstruct themselves in such manner as to serve increasingly beneficial uses—while the living waters can be so controlled as to multiply their benefits.

Neither the primitive man nor the pioneer was aware of any duty to posterity in dealing with the renewable resources. When the American settler felled the forests, he felt that there was plenty of forest left for the sons who came after him. When he exhausted the soil of his farm he felt that his son could go West and take up another. So it was with his immediate successors. When the soil wash from the farmer's fields choked the neighboring river he thought only of using the railway rather than boats for moving his produce and supplies.

Now all this is changed. On the average the son of the farmer of to-day must make his living on his father's farm. There is no difficulty in doing this if the father will exercise wisdom. No wise use of a farm exhausts its fertility. So with the forests. We are over the verge of a timber famine in this country, and it is unpardonable for the nation or the States to permit any further cutting of our timber save in accordance with a system which will provide that the next generation shall see the timber increased instead of diminished. Moreover, we can add enormous tracts of the most valuable possible agricultural land to the national domain by irrigation in the arid and semiarid regions and by drainage of great tracts of swampland in the humid regions. We can enormously increase our transportation facilities by the canalization of our rivers so as to complete a great system of waterways on the Pacific, Atlantic, and Gulf coasts and in the Mississippi valley, from the great plains to the Alleghanies and from the northern lakes to the mouth of the mighty Father of Waters. But all these various uses of our natural resources are so closely connected that they should be

167

co-ordinated and should be treated as part of one coherent plan and not in haphazard and piecemeal fashion.[24]

11. Foreign Policy

The steady aim of this nation, as of all enlightened nations, should be to strive to bring ever nearer the day when there shall prevail throughout the world the peace of justice. There are kinds of peace which are highly undesirable, which are in the long run as destructive as any war. Tyrants and oppressors have many times made a wilderness and called it peace. Many times peoples who were slothful or timid or short-sighted, who had been enervated by ease or by luxury, or misled by false teachings, have shrunk in unmanly fashion from doing duty that was stern and that needed self-sacrifice, and have sought to hide from their own minds their shortcomings, their ignoble motives, by calling them love of peace. The peace of tyrannous terror, the peace of craven weakness, the peace of injustice, all these should be shunned as we shun unrighteous war. The goal to set before us as a nation, the goal which should be set before all mankind, is the attainment of the peace of justice, of the peace which comes when each nation is not merely safeguarded in its own rights, but scrupulously recognizes and performs its duty toward others. Generally peace tells for righteousness; but if there is conflict between the two, then our fealty is due first to the cause of righteousness. Unrighteous wars are common, and unrighteous peace is rare; but both should be shunned. The right of freedom and the responsibility for the exercise of that right cannot be divorced. One of our great poets has well and finely said that freedom is not a gift that tarries long in the hands of cowards. Neither does it tarry long in the hands of those too slothful, too dishonest, or too unintelligent to exercise it. The eternal vigilance which is the price of liberty must be exercised, sometimes to guard against outside foes; although of course far more often to guard against our own selfish or thoughtless shortcomings.

If these self-evident truths are kept before us, and only if they are so kept before us, we shall have a clear idea of what our foreign policy in its larger aspects should be. It is our duty to remember that a nation has no more right to do injustice to another nation, strong or weak, than an individual has to do injustice to another individual; that the same moral law applies in one case as in the other. But we must also remember that it is as much the duty of the nation to guard its own rights and its own interests as it is the duty of the individual so to do.

Within the nation the individual has now delegated this right to the State, that is, to the representative of all the individuals, and it is a maxim

[24] *Works XVI*, pp. 119–26.

of the law that for every wrong there is a remedy. But in international law we have not advanced by any means as far as we have advanced in municipal law. There is as yet no judicial way of enforcing a right in international law. When one nation wrongs another or wrongs many others, there is no tribunal before which the wrong-doer can be brought. Either it is necessary supinely to acquiesce in the wrong, and thus put a premium upon brutality and aggression, or else it is necessary for the aggrieved nation valiantly to stand up for its rights. Until some method is devised by which there shall be a degree of international control over offending nations, it would be a wicked thing for the most civilized powers, for those with most sense of international obligations and with keenest and most generous appreciation of the difference between right and wrong, to disarm. If the great civilized nations of the present day should completely disarm, the result would mean an immediate recrudescence of barbarism in one form or another.

Under any circumstances a sufficient armament would have to be kept up to serve the purposes of international police; and until international cohesion and the sense of international duties and rights are far more advanced than at present, a nation desirous both of securing respect for itself and of doing good to others must have a force adequate for the work which it feels is allotted to it as its part of the general world duty. Therefore it follows that a self-respecting, just, and far-seeing nation should on the one hand endeavor by every means to aid in the development of the various movements which tend to provide substitutes for war, which tend to render nations in their actions toward one another, and indeed toward their own peoples, more responsive to the general sentiment of humane and civilized mankind; and on the other hand that it should keep prepared, while scrupulously avoiding wrong-doing itself, to repel any wrong, and in exceptional cases to take action which in a more advanced stage of international relations would come under the head of the exercise of the international peace. A great free people owes it to itself and to all mankind not to sink into helplessness before the powers of evil.[25]

To John Hay[26]

Oyster Bay, July 10, 1902

In the Cabinet room there stands a globe made in London by the map makers for the Admiralty. On this the boundary in question is given as it is on the British admiralty charts of the same period, this boundary being precisely that now claimed by us, which was also the boundary claimed

[25] *Works XV*, pp. 254–6.
[26] Secretary of State in McKinley and Roosevelt cabinets.

or conceded by both the British and Canadian authorities until the last few years. The terms of the original treaty seem to me to be well-nigh impossible of any construction other than that which the Russians and we ourselves have always put upon them, save only as regards the southernmost portion of the boundary. As regards this portion of the boundary there is an evident ambiguity, one well-known channel being *named,* while the *description,* including the fixing of the latitude and longitude and an allusion to a certain island, is seemingly incompatible with this same well-known channel being the one actually meant. If the treaty were now to be construed for the first time, while in my judgment there could be no possible question as to most of the boundary, and while in my judgment we could not be warranted in claiming less or submitting to an award of less than all contained within the boundary as defined in the British admiralty charts for 1884, save along the southernmost boundary; yet there would be room for an honest difference of opinion about this southernmost portion. But even this doubt must necessarily vanish in view of the construction put upon the terms of the treaty for over three-quarters of a century both by the Russians, by us as their successors, and by the British and Canadians alike until within the last few years. The Russian maps and our own maps have always presented the boundary according to our present contention. Almost without an exception the English maps, official and unofficial, have adopted the same construction, and until some fifteen years ago this was likewise true of the Canadian maps, including the great Canadian map which at one time hung in the Parliament House at Ottawa. When Sir George Simpson presented his official map to show the lease by the British fur companies of the strip of then Russian territory in question, he colored this leased strip differently from that of the British-American territory, and his map is conclusive proof that, at that time, as for a generation before and a generation afterwards, the Canadian view of the boundary was precisely the view we now take.

In my judgment it is not possible to compromise such a claim. I think that the Canadian contention is an outrage pure and simple. I do not regard the Canadians as having any more right to the land in question than they have to Aroostook County, Maine, or than we have to New Brunswick. The fact that they have set up such an outrageous and indefensible claim and in consequence are likely to be in hot water with their constituents when they back down, does not seem to me to give us any excuse for paying them in money or territory. To pay them anything where they are entitled to nothing would in a case like this come dangerously near blackmail. I could not submit to any arbitration in the matter. I am entirely willing to appoint three commissioners on our side to meet three commissioners on theirs and try to fix the line, but I should definitely instruct

170

our three commissioners that they were not to yield any territory whatsoever, but were as a matter of course to insist upon our entire claim; their functions being merely to decide the particular line of limitation which this claim would imply.[27]

To Theodore Roosevelt, Jr.

Washington, October 20, 1903

I am very much pleased over what has just been accomplished in the Alaska Boundary award. I hesitated sometime before I would consent to a commission to decide the case and I declined absolutely to allow any arbitration of the matter. Finally I made up my mind I would appoint three men of such ability and such firmness that I could be certain there would be no possible outcome disadvantageous to us as a nation; and would trust to the absolute justice of our case, as well as to a straight-out declaration to certain high British officials that I meant business, and that if this commission did not decide the case at issue, I would decline all further negotiations and would have the line run on my own hook. I think that both factors were of importance in bringing about the result. That is, I think that the British Commissioner who voted with our men was entitled to great credit, and I also think that the clear understanding the British Government had as to what would follow a disagreement was very important and probably decisive.[28]

To Albert Shaw

Washington, June 22, 1903

The Manchurian business is taking an acute stage owing to the well-nigh incredible mendacity of the Russians. I enclose you a statement made by Hay to Cassini and repeated to him again and again. In it you see we disclaim any intent to interfere with the political future of Manchuria. All we ask is that our great and growing trade shall not be interrupted and that Russia shall keep its solemn promises. Russia has not only declined to keep these promises but has declined in that most irritating way—by persistent lying.[29] She tells our Ambassador and through her Ambassador

[27] *Letters III*, pp. 287–8.
[28] *Ibid.*, p. 635.
[29] As early as August 5, 1896, Mr. Roosevelt was writing his friend, Cecil A. Spring-Rice, about the "appalling" nature of the Russian problem:
"All other nations of European blood, if they develop at all, seem inclined to develop on much the same lines; but Russia seems bound to develop her own way, and on lines that run directly counter to what we are accustomed to consider as progress. If she ever does take possession of Northern China and drill the Northern Chinese to serve as her Army, she will indeed be a formidable power. It has always

our State Department that she is delighted to have the ports thrown open to us as we request and is doing nothing to prevent it, and meanwhile, through her agent at Peking, positively forbids China acting as we request and as Russia has solemnly agreed she shall act. I have a strong feeling in favor of Russia, but she is doing everything in her power to make it impossible for us to continue this feeling. She seems to be ingeniously endeavoring to force us, not to take sides with Japan and England, but to acquiesce in their taking sides with us.[30]

To Cecil A. Spring-Rice[31]

Washington, March 19, 1904

There is much about the Russians which I admire, and I believe in the future of the Slavs if they can only take the right turn. But I do not believe in the future of any race *while it is under a crushing despotism*. The Japanese are non-Aryan and non-Christian, but they are under the weight of no such despotism as the Russians; and so, although the Russians are fundamentally nearer to us, or rather would be if a chance were given them, they are not in actual fact nearer to us at the present. People who feel as we do would be happier today living in Japan than living in Russia. . . .

This country as a whole tends to sympathize with Russia . . . I do not think that the country looks forward to, or concerns itself about, the immense possibilities which the war holds for the future. I suppose democracies will always be shortsighted about anything that is not brought roughly home to them. Still, when I feel exasperated by the limitations upon preparedness and forethought which are imposed by democratic conditions, I can comfort myself by the extraordinary example of these very limitations which the autocratic government of Russia has itself furnished in this crisis. . . .

The Slav is a great and growing race. But, if the Japanese win out, not only the Slav, but all of us will have to reckon with a great new force in eastern Asia. The victory will make Japan by itself a formidable power in the Orient, because all the other powers having interests there will have

---

seemed to me that the Germans showed shortsightedness in not making some alliance that will enable them to crush Russia. Even if, in the dim future, Russia should take India and become the preponderant power in Asia, England would merely be injured in one great dependency; but when Russia grows so as to crush Germany, the crushing will be once for all. The growth of the great Russian state in Siberia is portentous; but it is stranger still nowadays to see the rulers of the nation deliberately keeping it under a despotism, deliberately setting their faces against any increase of the share of the people in government. (*Letters I*, p. 555.)

[30] *Letters III*, p. 497.

[31] British diplomat; best man at Roosevelt's wedding in London to Edith Kermit Carow.

divided interests, divided cares, double burdens, whereas Japan will have but one care, one interest, one burden. If, moreover, Japan seriously starts in to organize China, and makes any headway, there will result a shifting of the center of equilibrium as far as the white races are concerned. Personally I believe that Japan will develop herself, and seek to develop China, along paths which will make the first, and possibly the second, great civilized powers; but the civilization must of course be of a different type from our civilizations. I do not mean that the mere race taken by itself would cause such a tremendous difference. I have met Japanese, and even Chinese, educated in our ways, who in all their emotions and ways of thought were well-nigh identical with us. But the weight of their own ancestral civilization will press upon them, and will prevent their ever coming into exactly our mould.

However, all of this is mere speculation. . . . All that any of us can do is to try to make our several nations fit themselves by the handling of their own affairs, external and internal, so as to be ready for whatever the future may hold. If new nations come to power, if old nations grow to greater power, the attitude of us who speak English should be one of ready recognition of the rights of the newcomers, of desire to avoid giving them just offense, and at the same time of preparedness in body and in mind to hold our own if our interests are menaced.

I cannot believe that there will be such a continental coalition against England as that of which you speak. Undoubtedly England is in some immediate, and America in some remote, danger, because each is unmilitary—judged by the standard of continental Europe—and yet both rich and aggressive. Each tends to think itself secure by its own position from the danger of attack at home. We are not so spread out as you are. We are farther away from Europe; therefore, our danger is for the time being less. But we have, to a greater degree than you have, although you have it too, the spirit of mere materialism and shortsighted vanity and folly at work for mischief among us. A society of which a bloated trust magnate is accepted quite simply as the ideal is in a rotten condition; and yet this is exactly the condition of no inconsiderable portion of our society. Many people of property admire such a man; many people of no property envy him; and both the admiration and the envy are tributes to which he is not in the least entitled.[32]

[32] *Letters IV*, pp. 760–1.

To Arthur Hamilton Lee[33]

Washington, October 17, 1908

I have been persistently telling so many Englishmen that I thought their fears of Germany slightly absurd and did not believe that there was need of arming against Germany, I feel that perhaps it is incumbent upon me now to say that I am by no means as confident as I was in this position.

As regards many points I have a real regard for the Emperor. I admire his energy, his ability, his activity, and what I believe to be his sincere purpose to do all that he can for the greatness of his country. He is, however, very jumpy; and more than once in the last seven years I have had to watch him very hard and speak to him, with great politeness, but with equal decision, in order to prevent his doing things that I thought against the interests of this country. Last summer an American newspaperman named Hale, a very honorable fellow whom I know well, got an interview with the Kaiser. The Kaiser spoke to him with astounding frankness. The part of his conversation with which I am now concerned was that relating to England. He displayed great bitterness toward England. He said that England was a traitor to the white race because she had been encouraging the yellow peril by her alliance with Japan, and that Japan certainly intended to have war with the United States in a short time. Without any sense of inconsistency he then added that he was himself trying to give arms and organization to the Mussulmans, especially in Turkey, because they would in time be a bulwark against the yellow peril —a somewhat farfetched conclusion. He stated that he thought England was decadent; that India was seething with revolt which would probably find expression in open war before a year was over, and that the same was true of the Sudan and Egypt. Finally he remarked that he regarded war between England and Germany as inevitable and as likely soon to take place. He spoke very bitterly of the King, saying that he and all those immediately around him were sunk in ignoble greed and looked at life from a purely stock market standpoint, and that he and they hated me virulently because they had money invested in America and attributed the loss of value in their investments to my action (parenthetically I think this was merely said to influence me; and I neither believed it nor, if I had believed it, would I have cared).

Hale wrote this interview down and very honorably showed it both to the American Ambassador, Hill, and to the German Foreign Office. The Foreign Office nearly went thru the roof, and protested most emphatically that the utmost damage would result from its publication. Meanwhile he

[33] British military attaché in Washington, later First Lord, British Admiralty; created Viscount Lee of Fareham.

cabled his interview to the *New York Times,* who sent a representative out to me to ask my advice about printing the matter. I earnestly urged that it be not done, stating that it undoubtedly would create a general panic and would cause extraordinary bitterness between England and Germany; and adding, what I think was a much more effective argument with the *Times,* that while they would gain temporarily by the sensational nature of the interview, yet as the Emperor was absolutely certain to repudiate it and to insist that the correspondent had lied, that in the long run I did not think it would prove of credit to the *Times* itself. Which argument convinced them, or whether they were convinced by something wholly different, I do not know; but at any rate they have not printed the article, and Hale very honorably accepted the amendments of the Foreign Office and if he prints the article will print it viséed by them.

Now, I do not for a moment believe that the utterances of the Emperor indicated a settled purpose; but they did make me feel that he indulged in red dreams of glory now and then, and that if he was indiscreet enough to talk to a strange newspaperman in such fashion it would be barely possible that sometime he would be indiscreet enough to act on impulse in a way that would jeopardize the peace. Therefore, as my advice to England of recent years has been in the direction of saying that there was nothing to apprehend from Germany, and as it is thru you that most of what I have said has been said (altho not all of it) I feel that you ought to know these facts. They should be told to no one save to Balfour and Grey, and to them only on the understanding that they are to go no further. I do not believe that the British Empire has any more intention of acting aggressively than has the United States, and I believe that in one case as in the other a powerful fleet is not only in the interest of the nation itself, but is in the interest of international peace, and therefore to be desired by all who wish to see the peace of the world preserved. I am now striving to have us build up our fleet because I think its mere existence will be the most potent factor in keeping the peace between Japan and ourselves and in preventing any possible outbreak thru disregard of the Monroe Doctrine in America. In exactly the same way I feel that Britain's great navy is a menace to no Power, but on the contrary is a distinct help in keeping the peace of the world, and I hope to see it maintained in full efficiency.[34]

To John Hay

Washington, February 15, 1902

. . . By the way, when we come to go into the state dinner how in the name of heaven will we avoid hurting various Teutonic susceptibilities?

[34] *Letters VI,* pp. 1292–4.

Will the Prince take Mrs. Roosevelt, while I walk in solemn state ahead by myself? How do we do it anyhow? I am quite clear that I ought not to walk in with my wife on one arm and my daughter on the other and the Prince somewhere alongside—but further than this I do not go.[35]

12. The President Blows His Top

To the Department of State

Washington, December 2, 1908

I wish to find out from the Department why it permitted the Chinese Ambassador today twice to use the phrase "Your Excellency" in addressing the President. Not only law but wise custom and propriety demand that the President shall be addressed only as "Mr. President" or as "the President." It is wholly improper to permit the use of a silly title like "Excellency" (and incidentally if titles were to be allowed at all, this title is entirely unworthy of the position of the President). Any title is silly when given the President. This title is rather unusually silly. But it is not only silly but inexcusable for the State Department, which ought, above all other Departments, to be correct in its usage, to permit foreign representatives to fall into the blunder of using this title. I would like an immediate explanation of why the blunder was permitted and a statement in detail as to what has been done by the Department to prevent the commission of any similar blunder in the future.

Now, as to the address itself. I did not deliver it as handed me because it was fatuous and absurd. I have already had to correct the ridiculous telegram that was drafted for me to send to China on the occasion of the death of the Emperor and the Empress Dowager. I do not object to the utter fatuity of the ordinary addresses made to me by, and by me to, the representatives of foreign governments when they come to me to deliver their credentials or to say good-by. The occasion is merely formal and the absurd speeches interchanged are simply rather elaborate ways of saying good morning and good-by. It would of course be better if they were less absurd and if we had a regular form to be used by the Minister and by the President on all such occasions, the form permitting of the slight variations which would be necessary in any particular case. It seems to me that some such form could be devised, just as we use special forms in the absurd and fatuous letters I write to Emperors, Apostolic Kings, Presidents, and the like—those in which I address them as "Great and Good Friend," and sign myself "Your good friend." These letters are

[35] *Letters III,* p. 230.

176

meaningless; but perhaps on the whole not otherwise objectionable, when formally and conventionally announcing that I have sent a minister or ambassador or that I have received one. They strike me as absurd and fatuous only when I congratulate the sovereigns on the birth of babies, with eighteen or twenty names, to people of whose very existence I have never heard; or condole with them on the deaths of unknown individuals. Still if trouble would be caused by abandoning this foolish custom, then it would be far more foolish to cause the trouble than it is to keep to the custom.

But, on a serious occasion, as in the present instance where a statesman of rank has come here on a mission which may possess real importance, then there should be some kind of effort to write a speech that shall be simple, and that shall say something, or, if this is deemed inexpedient, that shall at least not be of a fatuity so great that it is humiliating to read it. It should be reasonably grammatical, and should not be wholly meaningless. In the draft of the letter handed me, for instance, I am made to say of the letter I receive: "I accept it with quite exceptional sentiments as a message of especial friendship." Of course any boy in school who wrote a sentence like that would be severely and properly disciplined. The next sentence goes on: "I receive it with the more profound sentiments in that you bring it now no less from the Emperor." What in Heaven's name did the composer of this epistle mean by "more profound sentiments" and "quite exceptional sentiments"? Cannot he write ordinary English? Continuing, at the end of the same sentence he speaks of the new Government and what he anticipates from it, in terms that would not be out of place in a prophecy about Alexander the Great on the occasion of his accession to the throne of Macedon. Politeness is necessary, but gushing and obviously insincere and untruthful compliments merely make both sides ridiculous; and are underbred in addition.[36]

13. The National Defense

We have met to-day to do honor to the mighty dead. Remember that our words of admiration are but as sounding brass and tinkling cymbals if we do not by steady preparation and by the cultivation of soul and mind and body fit ourselves so that in time of need we shall be prepared to emulate their deeds. Let every midshipman who passes through this institution remember, as he looks upon the tomb of John Paul Jones, that while no courage can atone for the lack of that efficiency which comes only through careful preparation in advance, through careful training of the men, and careful fitting out of the engines of war, yet that none

[36] *Letters VI*, pp. 1405–7.

of these things can avail unless in the moment of crisis the heart rises level with the crisis. The navy whose captains will not surrender is sure in the long run to whip the navy whose captains will surrender, unless the inequality of skill or force is prodigious. The courage which never yields cannot take the place of the possession of good ships and good weapons and the ability skilfully to use these ships and these weapons. . . .

We can afford as a people to differ on the ordinary party questions; but if we are both far-sighted and patriotic we cannot afford to differ on the all-important question of keeping the national defenses as they should be kept; of not alone keeping up, but of going on with building up of, the United States navy, and of keeping our small army at least at its present size and making it the most efficient for its size that there is on the globe.[37]

To William Howard Taft[38]

Washington, March 3, 1909

One closing legacy. Under no circumstances divide the battleship fleet between the Atlantic and Pacific Oceans prior to the finishing of the Panama Canal. Malevolent enemies of the navy . . . timid fools . . . and conscienceless scoundrels . . . will try to lead public opinion in a matter like this without regard to the dreadful harm they may do the country; and good, but entirely ignorant, men may be thus misled. I should obey no direction of Congress and pay heed to no popular sentiment, no matter how strong, if it went wrong in such a vital matter as this. When I sent the fleet around the world there was a wild clamor that some of it should be sent to the Pacific, and an equally mad clamor that some of it should be left in the Atlantic. I disregarded both. At first it seemed as if popular feeling was nearly a unit against me. It is now nearly a unit in favor of what I did.

It is now nearly four years since the close of the Russian-Japanese war. There were various factors that brought about Russia's defeat; but most important by all odds was her having divided her fleet between the Baltic and the Pacific, and, furthermore splitting up her Pacific fleet into three utterly unequal divisions. The entire Japanese force was always used to smash some fraction of the Russian force. The knaves and fools who advise the separation of our fleet nowadays and the honest, misguided creatures who think so little that they are misled by such advice, ought to take into account this striking lesson furnished by actual experience in a great war but four years ago. Keep the battle fleet either in one ocean

[37] *Works XVI,* pp. 246–8.
[38] Secretary of War in Roosevelt's cabinet; later President and Chief Justice.

or the other and have the armed cruisers always in trim, as they are now, so that they can be at once sent to join the battle fleet if the need should arise.[39]

14. Class Hatred

In dealing with both labor and capital, with the questions affecting both corporations and trades-unions, there is one matter more important to remember than aught else, and that is the infinite harm done by preachers of mere discontent. These are the men who seek to excite a violent class hatred against all men of wealth. They seek to turn wise and proper movements for the better control of corporations and for doing away with the abuses connected with wealth, into a campaign of hysterical excitement and falsehood in which the aim is to inflame to madness the brutal passions of mankind. The sinister demagogues and foolish visionaries who are always eager to undertake such a campaign of destruction sometimes seek to associate themselves with those working for a genuine reform in governmental and social methods, and sometimes masquerade as such reformers. In reality they are the worst enemies of the cause they profess to advocate, just as the purveyors of sensational slander in newspaper or magazine are the worst enemies of all men who are engaged in an honest effort to better what is bad in our social and governmental conditions.

To preach hatred of the rich man as such, to carry on a campaign of slander and invective against him, to seek to mislead and inflame to madness honest men whose lives are hard and who have not the kind of mental training which will permit them to appreciate the danger in the doctrines preached—all this is to commit a crime against the body politic and to be false to every worthy principle and tradition of American national life. Moreover, while such preaching and such agitation may give a livelihood and a certain notoriety to some of those who take part in it, and may result in the temporary political success of others, in the long run every such movement will either fail or else will provoke a violent reaction, which will itself result not merely in undoing the mischief wrought by the demagogue and the agitator, but also in undoing the good that the honest reformer, the true upholder of popular rights, has painfully and laboriously achieved.

Corruption is never so rife as in communities where the demagogue and the agitator bear full sway, because in such communities all moral bands become loosened, and hysteria and sensationalism replace the spirit of sound judgment and fair dealing as between man and man. In sheer

[39] *Letters VI*, p. 1543.

revolt against the squalid anarchy thus produced men are sure in the end to turn toward any leader who can restore order, and then their relief at being free from the intolerable burdens of class hatred, violence, and demagogy is such that they cannot for some time be aroused to indignation against misdeeds by men of wealth; so that they permit a new growth of the very abuses which were in part responsible for the original outbreak. . . . There must be a stern refusal to be misled into following either that base creature who appeals and panders to the lowest instincts and passions in order to arouse one set of Americans against their fellows, or that other creature, equally base but no baser, who, in a spirit of greed, or to accumulate or add to an already huge fortune, seeks to exploit his fellow Americans with callous disregard to their welfare of soul and body. The man who debauches others in order to obtain a high office stands on an evil equality of corruption with the man who debauches others for financial profit; and when hatred is sown the crop which springs up can only be evil.

The plain people who think—the mechanics, farmers, merchants, workers with head or hand, the men to whom American traditions are dear, who love their country and try to act decently by their neighbors, owe it to themselves to remember that the most damaging blow that can be given popular government is to elect an unworthy and sinister agitator on a platform of violence and hypocrisy. Whenever such an issue is raised in this country nothing can be gained by flinching from it, for in such case democracy is itself on trial, popular self-government under Republican forms is itself on trial. The triumph of the mob is just as evil a thing as the triumph of the plutocracy, and to have escaped one danger avails nothing whatever if we succumb to the other. In the end the honest man, whether rich or poor, who earns his own living and tries to deal justly by his fellows, has as much to fear from the insincere and unworthy demagogue, promising much and performing nothing or else performing nothing but evil, who would set on the mob to plunder the rich, as from the crafty corruptionist, who, for his own ends, would permit the common people to be exploited by the very wealthy. If we ever let this government fall into the hands of men of either of these two classes, we shall show ourselves false to America's past. Moreover, the demagogue and the corruptionist often work hand in hand. There are at this moment wealthy reactionaries of such obtuse morality that they regard the public servant who prosecutes them when they violate the law, or who seeks to make them bear their proper share of the public burdens, as being even more objectionable than the violent agitator who hounds on the mob to plunder the rich. There is nothing to choose between such a reactionary and such an agitator; fundamentally they are alike in their selfish disregard of the

180

rights of others; and it is natural that they should join in opposition to any movement of which the aim is fearlessly to do exact and even justice to all.[40]

15. Postal Frauds

To Philander C. Knox

Washington, June 22, 1903

As you know, the charges in connection with the Post-Office Department are now being investigated by Fourth Assistant Postmaster General Bristow. . . . As a result of this investigation, a number of indictments have already been had and it is probable that other indictments will hereafter be asked for. There can be no greater offence against the Government than a breach of trust on the part of a public official or the dishonest management of his office, and, of course, every effort must be exerted to bring such offenders to punishment by the utmost rigor of the law. . . .

I suggest, therefore, that if you cannot detail some of your present staff, you appoint special assistants in these post-office cases, not only to take up the cases in which indictments have been found or hereafter may be found, but to examine into all charges that have been made against officials in the postal service, with a view to the removal and prosecution of all guilty men in the service and the prosecution of guilty men whether in the service or not.[41]

16. The Man with the Muck-rake

In Bunyan's "Pilgrim's Progress" you may recall the description of the Man with the Muck-rake, the man who could look no way but downward, with the muck-rake in his hand; who was offered a celestial crown for his muck-rake, but who would neither look up nor regard the crown he was offered, but continued to rake to himself the filth of the floor.

In "Pilgrim's Progress" the Man with the Muck-rake is set forth as the example of him whose vision is fixed on carnal instead of on spiritual things. Yet he also typifies the man who in this life consistently refuses to see aught that is lofty, and fixes his eyes with solemn intentness only on that which is vile and debasing. Now, it is very necessary that we should not flinch from seeing what is vile and debasing. There is filth on the floor, and it must be scraped up with the muck-rake; and there are times and places where this service is the most needed of all the serv-

[40] *Works XV*, pp. 356–8.
[41] *Letters III*, pp. 496–7.

ices that can be performed. But the man who never does anything else, who never thinks or speaks or writes, save of his feats with the muck-rake, speedily becomes, not a help to society, not an incitement to good, but one of the most potent forces for evil.

There are, in the body politic, economic and social, many and grave evils, and there is urgent necessity for the sternest war upon them. There should be relentless exposure of and attack upon every evil man whether politician or business man, every evil practice, whether in politics, in business, or in social life. I hail as a benefactor every writer or speaker, every man who, on the platform, or in book, magazine, or newspaper, with merciless severity makes such attack, provided always that he in his turn remembers that the attack is of use only if it is absolutely truthful. The liar is no whit better than the thief, and if his mendacity takes the form of slander, he may be worse than most thieves. It puts a premium upon knavery untruthfully to attack an honest man, or even with hysterical exaggeration to assail a bad man with untruth. An epidemic of indiscriminate assault upon character does not good, but very great harm. The soul of every scoundrel is gladdened whenever an honest man is assailed, or even when a scoundrel is untruthfully assailed.

Now, it is easy to twist out of shape what I have just said, easy to affect to misunderstand it, and, if it is slurred over in repetition, not difficult really to misunderstand it. Some persons are sincerely incapable of understanding that to denounce mud-slinging does not mean the indorsement of whitewashing; and both the interested individuals who need whitewashing, and those others who practise mud-slinging, like to encourage such confusion of ideas. One of the chief counts against those who make indiscriminate assault upon men in business or men in public life, is that they invite a reaction which is sure to tell powerfully in favor of the unscrupulous scoundrel who really ought to be attacked, who ought to be exposed, who ought, if possible, to be put in the penitentiary. If Aristides is praised overmuch as just, people get tired of hearing it; and overcensure of the unjust finally and from similar reasons results in their favor.

Any excess is almost sure to invite a reaction; and, unfortunately, the reaction, instead of taking the form of punishment of those guilty of the excess, is very apt to take the form either of punishment of the unoffending or of giving immunity, and even strength, to offenders. The effort to make financial or political profit out of the destruction of character can only result in public calamity. Gross and reckless assaults on character, whether on the stump or in newspaper, magazine, or book, create a morbid and vicious public sentiment, and at the same time act as a profound deterrent to able men of normal sensitiveness and tend to prevent them from entering the public service at any price. . . .

At the risk of repetition let me say again that my plea is, not for immunity to but for the most unsparing exposure of the politician who betrays his trust, of the big business man who makes or spends his fortune in illegitimate or corrupt ways. There should be a resolute effort to hunt every such man out of the position he has disgraced. Expose the crime, and hunt down the criminal; but remember that even in the case of crime, if it is attacked in sensational, lurid, and untruthful fashion, the attack may do more damage to the public mind than the crime itself. . . .

The men with the muck-rakes are often indispensable to the well-being of society; but only if they know when to stop raking the muck, and to look upward to the celestial crown above them, to the crown of worthy endeavor. There are beautiful things above and roundabout them; and if they gradually grow to feel that the whole world is nothing but muck, their power of usefulness is gone. If the whole picture is painted black there remains no hue whereby to single out the rascals for distinction from their fellows. Such painting finally induces a kind of moral color-blindness; and people affected by it come to the conclusion that no man is really black, and no man really white, but they are all gray. In other words, they neither believe in the truth of the attack, nor in the honesty of the man who is attacked; they grow as suspicious of the accusation as of the offense; it becomes well-nigh hopeless to stir them either to wrath against wrong-doing or to enthusiasm for what is right; and such a mental attitude in the public gives hope to every knave, and is the despair of honest men.[42]

17. Campaign of 1904

To George Otto Trevelyan[43]

Washington, May 28, 1904

The Presidential campaign is now opening. Apparently I shall be nominated without opposition at the Republican Convention. Whom the Democrats will put up I do not know, and of course no one can forecast the results of the contest at this time. There is one point of inferiority in our system to yours which has been very little touched on, and that is the way in which the Presidential office tends to put a premium upon a man's

[42] Works XVI, pp. 415–8.
[43] British historian.

keeping out of trouble rather than upon his accomplishing results. If a man has a very decided character, has a strongly accentuated career, it is normally the case of course that he makes ardent friends and bitter enemies; and unfortunately human nature is such that more enemies will leave their party because of enmity to its head than friends will come in from the opposite party because they think well of that same head. In consequence, the dark horse, the neutral-tinted individual, is very apt to win against the man of pronounced views and active life. The electorate is very apt to vote with its back to the future! Now all this does not apply to the same extent with your Prime Minister. It is not possible for the politicians to throw over the real party leader and put up a dummy or some gray-tinted person under your system; or at least, though perhaps it is possible, the opportunity and the temptation are much less.

In my own case, for instance, I believe that most of my policies commanded the support of a great majority of my fellow-countrymen, but in each case I have made a certain number of determined foes. Thus, on Panama I had an overwhelming majority of the country with me; but whereas I am not at all sure that any Democrat will vote for me because of my attitude on Panama, there are a certain number of mugwumps who will undoubtedly vote against me because of it. So as regards Cuban reciprocity. The country backed me up in the matter, but there is not a Democrat who will vote for me because I got Cuban reciprocity, while there are now a few beet sugar men who will vote against me because of it. In the same way the whole country breathed freer, and felt as if a nightmare had been lifted, when I settled the anthracite coal strike; but the number of votes I shall gain thereby will be small indeed, while the interests to which I gave mortal offense will make their weight felt as of real moment. Thus I could go on indefinitely. However, I certainly would not be willing to hold the Presidency at the cost of failing to do the things which make the real reason why I care to hold it at all. I had much rather be a real President for three years and a half than a figurehead for seven years and a half. I think I can truthfully say that I now have to my credit a sum of substantial achievement—and the rest must take care of itself.[44]

To Lyman Abbott[45]

Oyster Bay, July 26, 1904

Normally I disbelieve in the extreme view, the fanatical view. For instance I would not be willing to die for what I regard as the untrue ab-

[44] *Letters IV*, pp. 806–7.
[45] Religious leader; editor, *The Outlook.*

stract statement that all men are in all respects equal, and are all alike entitled to the same power; but I would be quite willing to die—or better still, to fight so effectively that I should live—for the proposition that each man has certain rights which no other man should be allowed to take away from him, and that in certain great and vital matters all men should be treated as equal before the law and before the bar of public opinion. In government generally I have a feeling of distaste and impatience for those who indulge in declamatory statements about an impossible righteousness; but I believe that a high standard of righteousness is eminently possible, and I should be entirely willing to face any defeat in fighting for such a standard.[46]

To George B. Cortelyou[47]

Washington, August 11, 1904

I know the stress you are under, but as regards this Northern Securities business no stress must make us go one hand's breadth out of our path. I should hate to be beaten in this contest; but I should not merely hate, I should not be able to bear being beaten under circumstances which implied ignominy. To give any color for misrepresentation to the effect that we were now weakening in the Northern Securities matter would be ruinous. The Northern Securities suit is one of the great achievements of my administration. I look back upon it with great pride, for through it we emphasized in signal fashion, as in no other way could be emphasized, the fact that the most powerful men in this country were held to accountability before the law. Now we must not spoil the effect of this lesson. Moody is to do nothing without my full knowledge and consent.[48]

To Kermit Roosevelt

Washington, November 10, 1904

I am stunned by the overwhelming victory we have won. I had no conception that such a thing was possible. I thought it probable we should win, but was quite prepared to be defeated, and of course had not the slightest idea that there was such a tidal wave. If you will look back at my letter you will see that we carried not only all the states I put down as probably Republican, but all those that I put down as doubtful, and all but one of those that I put down as probably Democratic. The only

[46] *Letters IV*, p. 866.
[47] Secretary of Commerce and Labor and Secretary of The Treasury in Roosevelt's cabinet; chairman of Republican campaign committee, 1904.
[48] *Letters IV*, p. 886.

States that went against me were those in which no free discussion is allowed and in which fraud and violence have rendered the voting a farce. I have the greatest popular majority and the greatest electoral majority ever given to a candidate for President.

On the evening of the election I got back from Oyster Bay, where I had voted, soon after half past six. At that time I knew nothing of the returns and did not expect to find out anything definite for two or three hours; and had been endeavoring not to think of the result, but to school myself to accept it as a man ought to, whichever way it went. But as soon as I got in the White House Ted met me with the news that Buffalo and Rochester had sent in their returns already and that they showed enormous gains for me. Within the next twenty minutes enough returns were received from precincts and districts in Chicago, Connecticut, New York and Massachusetts to make it evident that there was a tremendous drift my way, and by the time we sat down to dinner at half past seven my election was assured. . . . Right after dinner members of the Cabinet and friends began to come in, and we had a celebration that would have been perfect if only you had been present. Archie, fairly plastered with badges, was acting as messenger between the telegraph operators and me, and bringing me continually telegram after telegram which I read aloud. I longed for you very much, as all of us did, for of course this was the day of greatest triumph I ever had had or ever could have, and I was very proud and happy. But I tell you, Kermit, it was a great comfort to feel, all during the last days when affairs looked doubtful that, no matter how things came out, the really important thing was the lovely life I have with your mother and with you children, and that compared to this home life everything else was of very small importance from the standpoint of happiness.[49]

18. "They will speak ill of me soon enough . . ."

To Douglas Robinson

Oyster Bay, August 31, 1905

That was an awfully nice letter of yours, old fellow, and I deeply thank you for it. But don't you be misled by the fact that just at the moment men are speaking well of me. They will speak ill soon enough. As Mr. Loeb remarked to me today, sometime soon I shall have to spank some little brigand of a South American republic, and then all the well-meaning idiots will turn and shriek that this is inconsistent with what I

[49] *Ibid.*, pp. 1024–5.

did with the peace conference, whereas it will be exactly in line with it, in reality. Of course I am very much pleased with the outcome. I tried as far as it was humanly possible to get the chances my way, and I looked the ground over very carefully before I took action. Nevertheless, I was taking big chances and I knew it, and I am very glad things came out as they did. I can honestly say, however, that my personal feelings in the matter have seemed to be of very, very small account compared to the great need of trying to do something which it seemed to me the interests of the whole world demanded to have done.[50]

19. "Why should I care . . . who gets the credit?"

To Albert Jeremiah Beveridge[51]

Oyster Bay, July 11, 1905

It was very kind of you to write and to be so thoughtful as to my reputation. But, my dear fellow, I do not care a rap as to who gets the credit for the work, provided the work is done. Hay was a really great man, and the more credit is given him the more I am delighted, while the result at the last election showed how futile it was for the Evening Post, the Sun, and the rest of my enemies to try to draw the distinction between what Hay did and what I did. Whether I originated the work, or whether he did and merely received my backing and approval, is of no consequence to the party, and what is said about it is of no earthly consequence to me. The same people who, not because they cared for Hay, but because they hated me, insisted that everything of which they approved in the management of the State Department was due to him will now make exactly the same claim in reference to Root and will hope thereby to damage or irritate me, whereas in reality they will not be making the slightest impression upon either my fortunes or my temper.

A year and a half ago these people said that with Root out of the Cabinet I would be wholly unable to run the country. Root has been out a year and a half and now when he comes back they will at once forget the intervening eighteen months and make the same assertion. They have already forgotten that Hay was on the other side of the water during these last peace negotiations; and, my dear fellow, why in the name of Heaven should I care? I wished Root as Secretary of State partly because I am extremely fond of him and prize his companionship as well as his advice, but primarily because I think that in all the country he is the best

[50] Ibid., p. 1328.
[51] U.S. Senator from Indiana; biographer of John Marshall and Abraham Lincoln.

man for the position and that no minister of foreign affairs in any other country at this moment in any way compares with him. Nobody can praise him too highly to suit me; and right away he will begin to help me in connection with the Venezuelan and Santo Domingan affairs. As for which of us gets the credit for settling them, I honestly think you will find Root quite as indifferent as I am. What we want is to get them *settled,* and *settled right.*[52]

20. *"Each man knows where the shoe pinches . . ."*

To George Otto Trevelyan

Washington, May 13, 1905

I suppose each of us is inclined to envy the advantages of a system different from that under which he himself lives. I was much struck by your congratulations upon my being free from the "wearing, distracting, and sometimes ignoble details of parliamentary warfare." They must be wearing and distracting, and often ignoble, but upon my word I can hardly believe they are worse than what comes to any American President in the matter of patronage. I have done all I could, and I think I may say more than any other President has ever done, in the direction of getting rid of the system of appointing and removing men for political considerations. But enough remains to cause me many hours of sordid and disagreeable work, which yet must be done under penalty of losing the good will of men with whom it is necessary that I should work. I can quite understand how Mr. Gladstone suffered at some great crisis like that with Russia, or in the Egyptian matter, or the Irish matter, when he was forced to submit to the insolence of men his inferiors in every respect, men not deserving serious notice by him, who yet had the power to force him into controversy. But, as I say, each man knows where his own shoe pinches.

I have had a most vivid realization of what it must have meant to Abraham Lincoln, in the midst of the heartbreaking anxieties of the civil war, to have to take up his time in trying to satisfy the candidates for postmaster at Chicago, or worse still in meeting the demands of the Germans or the Irish, one section or another of the Republicans or war Democrats, that such and such an officer should be given promotion or some special position. It is of course easy for the mugwump or googoo who has no knowledge whatever of public affairs to say that the proper thing is to refuse to deal with such men or to pay any heed to such considera-

[52] *Letters IV,* pp. 1269–1270.

tions. But in practical life one has to work with the instruments at hand, and it is impossible wholly to disregard what have by long usage come to be established customs. Lincoln had to face the fact that great bodies of his supporters would have been wholly unable to understand him if he had refused to treat them with consideration when they wished to discuss such questions of patronage.

You have your difficulties from men who are thrust into positions to which they are not entitled because of their social standing, or the social standing of those on whom they are dependent, or with whom they are connected. We have our difficulties with men of an entirely different class for whom the demands are made because of the political services which they have rendered. I suppose that those suffering from either system are tempted at times to think that they would prefer the other. But, after all, the great fact to remember is that really we are both living under free government, and while both of these governments, and the people behind the governments, differ somewhat from one another, they are closer kin than either is to any other folk. There are numerous and grave evils incident to free government, but after all is said and done I cannot imagine any real man being willing to live under any other system.[53]

21. "Man's place in history . . ."

To William Allen White[54]

Washington, November 28, 1906

I have been reading the advance sheets of your article about me, and I need hardly say that I very sincerely appreciate what you have written. Whether I deserve what you say or not, I am at any rate very glad that a man whom I respect and admire as much as I do you should think I deserve it. There is one thing which I did not like, and that is your even by implication assuming that I or my friends could think of my position as being in any shape or way akin to that of Washington or Lincoln or Franklin—the men of the great crises, the men who I think we can truthfully say are great figures in the history of the world.

Down at bottom I think you and I feel much alike as to this question of man's place in history, his place in literature. I am not in the least concerned as to whether I will have any place in history, and, indeed, I do not remember ever thinking about it. Without being able clearly to formulate the reasons for my philosophy, I am perfectly clear as to the phi-

[53] *Ibid.*, pp. 1173–4.
[54] Kansas editor, journalist and novelist.

189

losophy itself. I want to be a straight and decent man and do good service; and just as the officers and crew of a big battleship feel, each of them, if they are worth their salt, that it is quite enough reward to be one of the men actively engaged in doing the work aboard that battleship, so I feel it is in itself an ample reward to have been engaged with Root and Taft and Moody and Garfield and all the honest, brave, decent fellows who are trying in practical fashion to realize ideals of good government.[55]

To Oliver Wendell Holmes[56]

Washington, December 5, 1904

DEAR MR. JUSTICE: I am immensely pleased with President Eliot's little book,[57] which you sent me, and I agree with you absolutely as to its worth. It is very unsafe to say of anything contemporary that it will be a classic, but I am inclined to venture the statement in this case. It seems to me pre-eminently worth while to have such a biography of a typical American. How I wish President Eliot could write in the same shape biographies of a brakeman or railroad locomotive engineer, of an ordinary Western farmer, of a carpenter or blacksmith in one of our small towns, of a storekeeper in one of our big cities, of a miner—of half a dozen typical representatives of the forgotten millions who really make up American life. . . .

I was rather struck at what President Eliot said about oblivion so speedily overtaking almost everyone. But after all, what does the fact amount to that here and there a man escapes oblivion longer than his fellows? Ozymandias in the Desert—when a like interval has gone by who will know more of any man of the present day than Shelley knew of him? I suppose it is only about ten thousand years since the last glacial epoch (at least that is, I understand, the newest uncertain guess of the geologists); and this covers more than the period in which there is anything that we can even regard as civilization. Of course, when we go back even half that time we get past the period when any man's memory, no matter how great the man, is more than a flickering shadow to us; yet this distance is too small to be measured when we look at the ages even at rather short range—not astronomically but geometrically. That queer creature, Ware, my Pension Commissioner, who always uses the terminology of his Kansas environment, but who has much philosophy of his own, once wrote the following verses on this very question:

[55] *Letters V*, p. 517.
[56] Associate Justice, U.S. Supreme Court.
[57] Charles William Eliot, *John Gilley, Maine Farmer and Fisherman* (Boston, 1904).

HISTORY

Over the infinite prairie of level eternity,
  Flying as flies the deer,
Time is pursued by a pitiless, cruel oblivion,
  Following fast and near.
Ever and ever the famished coyote is following
  Patiently in the rear;
Trifling the interval, yet we are calling it "History"—
  Distance from wolf to deer.

Whether the distance from the wolf to the deer is a couple of inches or a quarter of a mile is not really of much consequence in the end. It is passed over mighty quickly in either event, and it makes small odds to any of us after we are dead whether the next generation forgets us, or whether a number of generations pass before our memory, steadily growing more and more dim, at last fades into nothing. On this point it seems to me that the only important thing is to be able to feel, when our time comes to go out into the blackness, that those survivors who care for us and to whom it will be a pleasure to think well of us when we are gone, shall have that pleasure. Save in a few wholly exceptional cases, cases of men such as are not alive at this particular time, it is only possible in any event that a comparatively few people can have this feeling for any length of time. But it is a good thing if as many as possible feel it even for a short time, and it is surely a good thing that those whom we love should feel it as long as they too live.

I should be quite unable to tell you why I think it would be pleasant to feel that one had lived manfully and honorably when the time comes after which all things are the same to every man; yet I am very sure that it is well so to feel, that it is well to have lived so that at the end it may be possible to know that on the whole one's duties have not been shirked, that there has been no flinching from foes, no lack of gentleness and loyalty to friends, and a reasonable measure of success in the effort to do the tasks allotted. This is just the kind of feeling that President Eliot's hero had the right to have; and a Justice of the Supreme Court or a President or a General or an Admiral, may be mighty thankful if at the end he has earned a similar right! [58]

[58] *Letters IV*, pp. 1059–60.

22. *"I have thoroughly enjoyed being President . . ."*

To George Otto Trevelyan

Washington, March 9, 1905

Well, I have just been inaugurated and have begun my second term. Of course I greatly enjoyed inauguration day, and indeed I have thoroughly enjoyed being President. But I believe I can also say that I am thoroughly alive to the tremendous responsibilities of my position. Life is a long campaign where every victory merely leaves the ground free for another battle, and sooner or later defeat comes to every man, unless death forestalls it. But the final defeat does not and should not cancel the triumphs, if the latter have been substantial and for a cause worth championing.

It has been peculiarly pleasant to me to find that my supporters are to be found in the overwhelming majority among those whom Abraham Lincoln called the plain people. As I suppose you know, Lincoln is my hero. He was a man of the people who always felt with and for the people, but who had not the slightest touch of the demagogue in him. It is probably difficult for his countrymen to get him exactly in the right perspective as compared with the great men of other lands. But to me he does seem to be one of the great figures who loom ever larger as the centuries go by. His unfaltering resolution, his quiet, unyielding courage, his infinite patience and gentleness, and the heights of disinterestedness which he attained whenever the crisis called for putting aside self, together with his farsighted, hardheaded common sense, point him out as just the kind of chief who can do most good in a democratic republic like ours.

Having such an admiration for the great rail-splitter, it has been a matter of keen pride to me that I have appealed peculiarly to the very men to whom he most appealed and who gave him their heartiest support. I am a college-bred man, belonging to a well-to-do family so that, as I was more than contented to live simply, and was fortunate enough to marry a wife with the same tastes, I have not had to make my own livelihood; though I have always had to add to my private income by work of some kind. But the farmers, lumbermen, mechanics, ranchmen, miners, of the North, East and West, have felt that I was just as much in sympathy with them, just as devoted to their interests, and as proud of them and as representative of them, as if I had sprung from among their own ranks; and I certainly feel that I do understand them and believe in them and feel for them and try to represent them just as much as if I had from earliest childhood made each day's toil pay for that day's existence or achievement. How long this feeling toward me will last I cannot say. It was overwhelming at the time of the election last November, and I judge by the extraordinary turnout for the inauguration it is overwhelming now. Inasmuch as the crest of the wave is invariably succeeded by the hollow, this means that there will be a reaction. But meanwhile I shall have accomplished something worth accomplishing, I hope.[59]

23. The Question of a Third Term

To George Otto Trevelyan

Washington, June 19, 1908

Well, the convention is over and Taft is nominated. . . .

It has been a curious contest, for I have had to fight tooth and nail against being nominated myself, and in the last three weeks it has needed very resolute effort on my part to prevent a break among the delegations, which would have meant a stampede for me and my nomination. I could not have prevented it at all unless I had thrown myself heart and soul into the business of nominating Taft and had shown to the country that he stood for exactly the same principles and policies that I did, and that I believed with all my heart and soul that under him we would progress steadily along the road this administration has traveled. . . .

When I made my announcement three years ago last November, just after the election, that I would under no circumstances again be a candidate, I of course acted on a carefully thought-out and considered theory. Having made it and having given my word to the people at large as to what I would do, and other men, including Taft, having entered the field on the strength of this statement of mine, I never felt the slightest hesitancy, the slightest wavering, as to the proper course to follow. But the developments of the last year or two have been so out of the common that at times I have felt a little uncomfortable as to whether my announced decision had been wise. But I think it was wise; and now I want to give you my reasons in full.

In the first place, I will freely admit what there is to say against it. I have a good deal of contempt for the type which Mirabeau condemned in Lafayette as the "Cromwell-Grandison" type, for those who, like Dante's Pope, are guilty of *"il gran refinto"*. . . . I do not like any man who flinches from work, and I like him none the better if he covers his flinching under the title of self-abnegation or renunciation or any other

[59] *Ibid.*, pp. 1132–3.

193

phrase, which may mean merely weakness, or else that he is willing to subordinate great and real public interests to a meticulous and fantastic morality in which he is concerned chiefly for the sake of his own shriveled soul. There is very much to be said in favor of the theory that the public has the right to demand as long service from any man who is doing good service as it thinks will be useful; and during the last year or two I have been rendered extremely uncomfortable both by the exultation of my foes over my announced intention to retire, and by the real uneasiness and chagrin felt by many good men because, as they believed, they were losing quite needlessly the leader in whom they trusted, and who they believed could bring to a successful conclusion certain struggles which they regarded as of vital concern to the national welfare. Moreover, it was of course impossible to foresee, and I did not foresee, when I made my public announcement of my intention, that the then leadership I possessed would continue (as far as I am able to tell) unbroken, as has actually been the case; and that the people who believed in me and trusted me and followed me would three or four years later still feel that I was the man of all others whom they wished to see President. Yet such I think has been the case; and therefore, when I felt obliged to insist on retiring and abandoning the leadership, now and then I felt ugly qualms as to whether I was not refusing to do what I ought to do, and abandoning great work on a mere fantastic point of honor.

These are strong reasons why my course should be condemned; yet I think that the countervailing reasons are still stronger. Of course when I spoke I had in view the precedent set by Washington and continued ever since, the precedent which recognizes the fact that, as there inheres in the Presidency more power than in any other office in any great republic or constitutional monarchy of modern times, it can only be saved from abuse by having the people as a whole accept as axiomatic the position that one man can hold it for no more than a limited time. I don't think that any harm comes from the concentration of powers in one man's hands, provided the holder does not keep it for more than a certain, definite time, and then returns to the people from whom he sprang. In the great days of the Roman Republic no harm whatever came from the dictatorship, because great though the power of the dictator was, after a comparatively short period he surrendered it back to those from whom he had gained it. On the other hand, the history of the first and second French Republics, not to speak of the Spanish-American Republics, not to speak of the Commonwealth, in Seventeenth-Century England, has shown that the strong man, and even the strong man who is good, may very readily subvert free institutions if he and the people at large grow to accept his continued possession of vast power as being necessary to good government. It is a very unhealthy thing that any man should be considered necessary to the people as a whole, save in the way of meeting some given crisis. Moreover, in a republic like ours the vital need is that there shall be a general recognition of the moral law, of the law which, as regards public men, means belief in efficient and disinterested service for the public rendered without thought of personal gain, and above all without the thought of self-perpetuation in office. I regard the memories of Washington and Lincoln as priceless heritages for our people, just because they are the memories of strong men, of men who cannot be accused of weakness or timidity. . . .

Now, my ambition is that, in however small a way, the work I do shall be along the Washington and Lincoln lines. While President I have *been* President, emphatically; I have used every ounce of power there was in the office and I have not cared a rap for the criticisms of those who spoke of "my usurpation of power"; for I knew that the talk was all nonsense and that there was no usurpation. I believe that the efficiency of this Government depends upon its possessing a strong central executive, and wherever I could establish a precedent for strength in the executive. . . .

I have felt not merely that my action was right in itself, but that in showing the strength of, or in giving strength to, the executive, I was establishing a precedent of value. I believe in a strong executive; I believe in power; but I believe that responsibility should go with power, and that it is not well that the strong executive should be a perpetual executive. Above all and beyond all I believe as I have said before that the salvation of this country depends upon Washington and Lincoln representing the type of leader to which we are true.

I hope that in my acts I have been a good President, a President who has deserved well of the Republic; but, most of all, I believe that whatever value my service may have comes even more from what I *am* than from what I *do*. I may be mistaken, but it is my belief that the bulk of my countrymen, the men whom Abraham Lincoln called "the plain people"—the farmers, mechanics, small tradesmen, hard-working professional men—feel that I am in a peculiar sense their President, that I represent the democracy in somewhat the fashion that Lincoln did, that is, not in any demagogic way but with the sincere effort to stand for a government by the people and for the people. Now the chief service I can render these plain people who believe in me is, not to destroy their ideal of me. They have followed me for the past six or seven years, indeed for some years previously, because they thought they recognized in me certain qualities in which they believed, because they regarded me as honest and disinterested, as having courage and common sense. Now I wouldn't for anything in the world shatter this belief of theirs in me. . . .

195

I do not want to make them think that after all I am actuated by selfish motives, by motives of self-interest, that my championship of their cause, that my opposition to the plutocracy, is simply due to the usual demagogue's desire to pander to the mob, or to the no more dangerous, but even more sinister, desire to secure self-advancement under the cloak of championship of popular rights. Of course I may be wrong in my belief, but my belief is that a great many honest people in this country who lead hard lives are helped in their efforts to keep straight and avoid envy and hatred and despair by their faith in me and in the principles I preach and in my practice of these principles. I would not for anything do the moral damage to these people that might come from shattering their faith in my personal disinterestedness. . . . However certain I might be that in seeking or accepting a third term I was actuated by a sincere desire to serve my fellow countrymen, I am very much afraid that multitudes of thoroughly honest men who have believed deeply in me . . . would . . . have a feeling of disappointment if I did try to occupy the Presidency for three consecutive terms, to hold it longer than it was deemed wise that Washington should hold it.[60]

To George Bruce Cortelyou

Washington, November 19, 1907

I have been informed that certain officeholders in your Department are proposing to go to the National Convention as delegates in favor of renominating me for the Presidency, or are proposing to procure my endorsement for such renomination by State conventions. This must not be. I wish you to inform such officers as you may find it advisable or necessary to inform in order to carry out the spirit of this instruction, that such advocacy of my renomination, or acceptance of an election as a delegate for that purpose, will be regarded as a serious violation of official propriety and will be dealt with accordingly.[61]

24. "The fringe of departing greatness . . ."

To John St. Loe Strachey[62]

Washington, November 28, 1908

Let me say how interested I was in your article on American ex-Presidents. I am not sure, however, that I altogether agree with you. When

[60] *Letters VI,* pp. 1085–9.
[61] *Letters V,* p. 852.
[62] British journalist, editor of *The Spectator.*

people have spoken to me as to what America should do with its ex-Presidents, I have always answered that there was one ex-President as to whom they need not concern themselves in the least, because I would do for myself. It would be to me personally an unpleasant thing to be pensioned and given some honorary position. I emphatically do not desire to clutch at the fringe of departing greatness. Indeed, to me there is something rather attractive, something in the way of living up to a proper democratic ideal, in having a President go out of office just as I shall go, and become abolutely and without reservation a private man, and do any honorable work which he finds to do.

My first work will be to go to Africa for the National Museum. I am fifty, I have led a very sedentary life for ten years, and I feel that this is my last chance for something in the nature of a "great adventure." If a war should occur while I am still physically fit, I should certainly try to raise a brigade, and if possible a division, of cavalry, mounted riflemen, such as those in my regiment ten years ago. But if, as I most earnestly hope, there is peace, then, after my return from Africa, and in view of the fact that I am not fit any longer for really arduous exploration, the work open to me which is best worth doing is fighting for political, social and industrial reform, just as I have been fighting for it for the twenty-eight years that I have been in politics.

Now, the money consideration, except as an entirely subordinate way, does not enter into the matter at all. For my connection with the *Outlook* I will receive less than a fourth of what I have been offered to go on other publications, and less than an eighth of what I have been requested to consider if I would go into business. I feel very strongly that one great lesson to be taught here in America is that while the first duty of every man is to earn enough for his wife and children, that when once this has been accomplished no man should treat money as the primary consideration. He is very foolish unless he makes it the first consideration, up to the point of supporting his family; but normally, thereafter it should come secondary. Now, I feel that I can still for some years command a certain amount of attention from the American public and, during those years and before my influence totally vanishes, I want to use it so far as possible to help onward certain movements for the betterment of our people. The character of the men associated with the *Outlook* makes the *Outlook* the best instrument with which I can work. My agreement is simply that whatever I have to say shall be said through their columns. It may be a good deal and it may be a very little. In any event, it won't interfere with anything else that I am doing, as is sufficiently shown by the fact that during my first year I go to Africa. All this is true; and yet I entirely agree with you that as regards the average President he should

197

not be thrown out where he may have to earn his livelihood in ways not quite advisable for an ex-President. The subject is far from being without its difficulties.[63]

25. "Full President right up to the end . . ."

To Theodore Roosevelt, Jr.

Washington, January 31, 1909

I have entered on the last month of my Presidency and I think I can hold Congress down so that no disastrous breakup can occur during that period. But they have been anxious to see if they could not do me up this winter. I have a very strong feeling that it is a President's duty to get on with Congress if he possibly can, and that it is a reflection upon him if he and Congress come to a complete break. For seven sessions I was able to prevent such a break. This session, however, they felt that it was safe utterly to disregard me because I was going out and my successor had been elected; and I made up my mind that it was just a case where the exception to the rule applied and that if I did not fight, and fight hard, I should be put in a contemptible position; while inasmuch as I was going out on the 4th of March I did not have to pay heed to our ability to co-operate in the future. The result has, I think, justified my wisdom. I have come out ahead so far, and I have been full President right up to the end—which hardly any other President ever has been.[64]

26. "I have had a great run for my money . . ."

To Kermit Roosevelt

Washington, January 14, 1909

I have had a great run for my money, and I should have liked to stay in as President if I had felt it was right for me to do so; but there are many compensations about going, and Mother and I are in the curious and very pleasant position of having enjoyed the White House more than any other President and his wife whom I recall, and yet being entirely willing to leave it, and looking forward to a life of interest and happiness after we leave.[65]

[63] *Letters VI*, pp. 1388–9.
[64] *Ibid.*, pp. 1498–9.
[65] *Ibid.*, p. 1476.

Father of a Family

The relations of Mr. Roosevelt to his family were the subject of legendry during his Presidency, but it was only after his death, when his letters to his children were published, that the public learned how close and how attractive the relationship between this busy father and his family had been.

1. "The children are darlings . . ."

To Gertrude Tyler Carow[1]

Washington, October 18, 1890

Edith . . . looks just as well and young and pretty and happy as she did four years ago when I married her—indeed, I sometimes almost think she looks if possible even sweeter and prettier, and she is as healthy as possible, and so young-looking and slender to be the mother of those two sturdy little scamps, Ted and Kermit. We have had a lovely year, though we have minded being away from Sagamore. . . .

The children are darlings. Alice has grown more and more affectionate, and is devoted to, and worshiped by, both the boys; Kermie holds out his little arms to her whenever she comes near, and she really takes care of him like a little mother. Ted eyes him with some suspicion; and when I take the wee fellow up in my arms Ted clings tightly to one of my legs, so that I can hardly walk. Kermie crawls with the utmost rapidity; and when he is getting towards some forbidden spot and we call him to stop Ted always joins in officiously and, overtaking the small yellow-haired wanderer, seizes him with his chubby hands round the neck and tries to drag him back—while the enraged Kermie endeavours in vain to retaliate. . . . As for blessed Ted he is just as much of a comfort as he ever was. I think he really loves me, and when I come back after an

[1] Mother of Edith Kermit Roosevelt.

199

absence he greets me with wild enthusiasm, due, however, I fear, in great part to knowledge that I am sure to have a large paper bundle of toys—which produces the query of "Fats in de bag," while he dances like an expectant little bear. When I come in to afternoon tea, he and Alice sidle hastily round to my chair, knowing that I will surreptitiously give them all the icing off the cake, if I can get Edith's attention attracted elsewhere; and every evening I have a wild romp with them, usually assuming the rôle of "a very big bear" while they are either little bears, or a "raccoon and a badger, papa." Ted has a most warm, tender, loving little heart; but I think he is a manly little fellow too. In fact I take the utmost possible enjoyment out of my three children; and so does Edith.[2]

2. Sagamore Hill

There could be no healthier and pleasanter place in which to bring up children than in that nook of old-time America around Sagamore Hill. Certainly I never knew small people to have a better time or a better training for their work in after-life than the three families of cousins at Sagamore Hill. It was real country, and—speaking from the somewhat detached point of view of the masculine parent—I should say there was just the proper mixture of freedom and control in the management of the children. They were never allowed to be disobedient or to shirk lessons or work; and they were encouraged to have all the fun possible. They often went barefoot, especially during the many hours passed in various enthralling pursuits along and in the waters of the bay. They swam, they tramped, they boated, they coasted and skated in winter, they were intimate friends with the cows, chickens, pigs, and other live stock. . . .

One of the stand-bys for enjoyment, especially in rainy weather, was the old barn. This had been built nearly a century previously, and was as delightful as only the pleasantest kind of old barn can be. It stood at the meeting-spot of three fences. A favorite amusement used to be an obstacle race when the barn was full of hay. The contestants were timed and were started successively from outside the door. They rushed inside, clambered over or burrowed through the hay, as suited them best, dropped out of a place where a loose board had come off, got over, through, or under the three fences, and raced back to the starting-point. When they were little, their respective fathers were expected also to take part in the obstacle race, and when with the advance of years the fathers finally refused to be contestants, there was a general feeling of pained regret among the children at such a decline in the sporting spirit.

[2] *Letters I,* pp. 233–4.

Another famous place for handicap races was Cooper's Bluff, a gigantic sand-bank rising from the edge of the bay, a mile from the house. If the tide was high there was an added thrill, for some of the contestants were sure to run into the water.[3]

3. "About small Ted's fighting . . ."

To Edward Sanford Martin[4]

Albany, November 26, 1900

Now, about small Ted's fighting. I believe you will find that he is not quarrelsome, and that above all, he is not a bully. I think it has been in amicable wrestling and boxing bouts that in your boy's words he has "licked all the boys in his form." In a measure, I am responsible for some of his fighting proclivities, but most of them came naturally. For instance, my two youngest small boys are not in the least fighters like Ted, although I think I have succeeded in instilling into them the theory that they ought not to shirk any quarrel forced upon them.

Now, do you want to know the real underlying feeling which has made me fight myself and want Ted to fight? Well, I summed it up to Ted once or twice when I told him, apropos of lessons of virtue, that he could be just as virtuous as he wished *if only he was prepared to fight*. Fundamentally this has been my own theory. I am not naturally at all a fighter. So far as any man is capable of analyzing his own impulses and desires, mine incline me to amiable domesticity and the avoidance of effort and struggle and any kind of roughness and to the practice of home virtues. Now, I believe that these are good traits, not bad ones. But I also believe that, if unsupported by something more virile, they may tend to evil rather than good. The man who merely possesses these traits, and in addition is timid and shirks effort, attracts and deserves a good deal of contempt. He attracts more, though he deserves less, contempt than the powerful, efficient man who is not at all virtuous, but is merely a strong, selfish, self-indulgent brute. . . .

I was fortunate enough in having a father whom I have always been able to regard as an ideal man. It sounds a little like cant to say what I am going to say, but he really did combine the strength and courage and will and energy of the strongest man with the tenderness, cleanness and purity of a woman. I was a sickly and timid boy. He not only took great and loving care of me—some of my earliest remembrances are of nights

[3] Autobiography, *Works XX*, pp. 331–3.
[4] Writer in *Harper's Weekly,* and humorous weekly, *Life.*

when he would walk up and down with me for an hour at a time in his arms when I was a wretched mite suffering acutely with asthma—but he also most wisely refused to coddle me, and made me feel that I must force myself to hold my own with other boys and prepare to do the rough work of the world. I cannot say that he ever put it into words, but he certainly gave me the feeling that I was always to be both decent and manly, and that if I were manly nobody would long laugh at my being decent. In all my childhood he never laid hand on me but once, but I always knew perfectly well that in case it became necessary he would not have the slightest hesitancy to do so again, and alike from my love and respect, and in a certain sense, from my fear of him, I would have hated and dreaded beyond measure to have him know that I had been guilty of a lie, or of cruelty, or of bullying, or of uncleanness, or of cowardice. Gradually I grew to have the feeling on my own account, and not merely on his. . . .

My ordinary companions in college would, I think, have had a tendency to look down upon me for doing Sunday school work if I had not also been a corking boxer, a good runner, and a genial member of the Porcellian Club. I went in for boxing and wrestling a good deal, and I really think that while this was partly because I liked them as sports, it was even more because I intended to be a middling decent fellow, and I did not intend that anyone should laugh at me with impunity because I was decent. . . .

Well, I have wanted to pass on to my boys some of what I got from my own father. I loathe cruelty and injustice. To see a boy or man torture something helpless whether in the shape of a small boy or little girl or dumb animal makes me rage. So far as I know my children have never been cruel, though I have had to check a certain amount of bullying. Ted is a little fellow, under the usual size, and wears spectacles, so that strange boys are rather inclined to jump on him first. When in addition to this I have trained him so that he objects strongly to torturing cats or hurting little girls, you can see that there are chances for life to be unpleasant for him when among other boys. Now I have striven to make him feel that if he only fights hard enough he is perfectly certain to secure the respect of all his associates for his virtues. I do not believe he is quarrelsome. I do not think your little boy has found him so. I do not think he oppresses smaller boys, but he does hold his own. . . .[5]

[5] *Letters III*, pp. 1442–4.

4. The Father Writes to the Children

Keystone Ranch, Jan. 18, 1901

DARLING LITTLE ETHEL:[6]

I have had great fun. Most of the trip neither you nor Mother nor Sister would enjoy; but you would all of you be immensely amused with the dogs. There are eleven all told, but really only eight do very much hunting. These eight are all scarred with the wounds they have received this very week in battling with the cougars and lynxes, and they are always threatening to fight one another; but they are as affectionate toward men (and especially toward me, as I pet them) as our own home dogs. At this moment a large hound and a small half-breed bull-dog, both of whom were quite badly wounded this morning by a cougar, are shoving their noses into my lap to be petted, and humming defiance to one another. They are on excellent terms with the ranch cat and kittens. The three chief fighting dogs, who do not follow the trail, are the most affectionate of all, and, moreover, they climb trees! Yesterday we got a big lynx in the top of a piñon tree—a low, spreading kind of pine—about thirty feet tall. Turk, the bloodhound, followed him up, and after much sprawling actually got to the very top, within a couple of feet of him. Then, when the lynx was shot out of the tree, Turk, after a short scramble, took a header down through the branches, landing with a bounce on his back. Tony, one of the half-breed bull-dogs, takes such headers on an average at least once for every animal we put up a tree. We have nice little horses which climb the most extraordinary places you can imagine. Get Mother to show you some of Gustave Doré's trees; the trees on these mountains look just like them.

Keystone Ranch, Jan. 29, 1901

DARLING LITTLE ETHEL:

You would be much amused with the animals round the ranch. The most thoroughly independent and self-possessed of them is a large white pig which we have christened Maude. She goes everywhere at her own will; she picks up scraps from the dogs, who bay dismally at her, but know they have no right to kill her; and then she eats the green alfalfa hay from the two milch cows who live in the big corral with the horses. One of

[6] Younger daughter of Theodore and Edith Roosevelt.

the dogs has just had a litter of puppies; you would love them, with their little wrinkled noses and squeaky voices.

Oyster Bay, May 7th, 1901

BLESSED TED:[7]

It was the greatest fun seeing you, and I really had a satisfactory time with you, and came away feeling that you were doing well. I am entirely satisfied with your standing, both in your studies and in athletics. I want you to do well in your sports, and I want even more to have you do well with your books; but I do not expect you to stand first in either, if so to stand could cause you overwork and hurt your health. I always believe in going hard at everything, whether it is Latin or mathematics, boxing or football, but at the same time I want to keep the sense of proportion. It is never worth while to absolutely exhaust one's self or to take big chances unless for an adequate object. I want you to keep in training the faculties which would make you, if the need arose, able to put your last ounce of pluck and strength into a contest. But I do not want you to squander these qualities. To have you play football as well as you do, and make a good name in boxing and wrestling, and be cox of your second crew, and stand second or third in your class in the studies, is all right. I should be rather sorry to see you drop too near the middle of your class, because, as you cannot enter college until you are nineteen, and will therefore be a year later in entering life, I want you to be prepared in the best possible way, so as to make up for the delay. But I know that all you can do you will do to keep substantially the position in the class that you have so far kept, and I have entire trust in you, for you have always deserved it.

The weather has been lovely here. The cherry trees are in full bloom, the peach trees just opening, while the apples will not be out for ten days. The May flowers and bloodroot have gone, the anemones and bellwort have come and the violets are coming. All the birds are here, pretty much, and the warblers troop through the woods. . . .

Dewey Jr. is a very cunning white guinea pig. I wish you could see Kermit taking out Dewey Sr. and Bob Evans to spend the day on the grass. Archie is the sweetest little fellow imaginable. He is always thinking of you. He has now struck up a great friendship with Nicholas, rather to Mame's [the nurse's] regret, as Mame would like to keep him purely for Quentin. The last-named small boisterous person was in fearful disgrace this morning, having flung a block at his mother's head. It was done in sheer playfulness, but of course could not be passed over lightly, and after the enormity of the crime had been brought fully home to him, he fled

[7] Theodore Roosevelt, Jr.

with howls of anguish to me and lay in an abandon of yellow-headed grief in my arms. Ethel is earning money for the purchase of the Art Magazine by industriously hoeing up the weeds in the walk. Alice is going to ride Yagenka bareback this afternoon, while I try to teach Ethel on Diamond, after Kermit has had his ride.

Yesterday at dinner we were talking of how badly poor Mrs. Blank[8] looked, and Kermit suddenly observed in an aside to Ethel, entirely unconscious that we were listening: "Oh, Effel, I'll tell you what Mrs. Blank looks like: Like Davis' hen dat died—you know, de one dat couldn't hop up on de perch." Naturally, this is purely a private anecdote.

Del Monte, Cal., May 10, 1903

Darling Ethel:

I have thought it very good of you to write me so much. Of course I am feeling rather fagged, and the next four days, which will include San Francisco, will be tiresome; but I am very well. This is a beautiful hotel in which we are spending Sunday, with gardens and a long seventeen-mile drive beside the beach and the rocks and among the pines and cypresses. I went on horseback. My horse was a little beauty, spirited, swift, surefooted, and enduring. As is usually the case here they had a great deal of silver on the bridle and headstall, and much carving on the saddle. We had some splendid gallops. By the way, tell mother that everywhere out here, from the Mississippi to the Pacific, I have seen most of the girls riding astride, and most of the grown-up women. I must say I think it very much better for the horses' backs. I think by the time that you are an old lady the side-saddle will almost have vanished—I am sure I hope so. I have forgotten whether you like the side-saddle or not.

It was very interesting going through New Mexico and seeing the strange old civilization of the desert, and next day the Grand Canyon of Arizona, wonderful and beautiful beyond description. I could have sat and looked at it for days. It is a tremendous chasm, a mile deep and several miles wide, the cliffs carved into battlements, amphitheatres, towers and pinnacles, and the coloring wonderful, red and yellow and gray and green. Then we went through the desert, passed across the Sierras and came into this semi-tropical country of southern California, with palms and orange groves and olive orchards and immense quantities of flowers.

[8] "Mrs. Blank" actually was Mrs. McKinley.

Del Monte, Cal., May 10, 1903

BLESSED KERMIT:

The last weeks' travel I have really enjoyed. Last Sunday and to-day (Sunday) and also on Wednesday at the Grand Canyon I had long rides, and the country has been strange and beautiful. I have collected a variety of treasures, which I shall have to try to divide up equally among you children. One treasure, by the way, is a very small badger, which I named Josiah, and he is now called Josh for short. He is very cunning and I hold him in my arms and pet him. I hope he will grow up friendly—that is if the poor little fellow lives to grow up at all. Dulany is taking excellent care of him, and we feed him on milk and potatoes. . . .

I was much interested in your seeing the wild deer. That was quite remarkable. To-day, by the way, as I rode along the beach I saw seals, cormorants, gulls and ducks, all astonishingly tame.

Del Monte, Cal., May 10, 1903

BLESSED ARCHIE:[9]

I think it was very cunning for you and Quentin to write me that letter together. I wish you could have been with me to-day on Algonquin, for we had a perfectly lovely ride. Dr. Rixey and I were on two very handsome horses, with Mexican saddles and bridles; the reins of very slender leather with silver rings. The road led through pine and cypress forests and along the beach. The surf was beating on the rocks in one place and right between two of the rocks where I really did not see how anything could swim a seal appeared and stood up on his tail half out of the foaming water and flapped his flippers, and was as much at home as anything could be. Beautiful gulls flew close to us all around, and cormorants swam along the breakers or walked along the beach.

I have a number of treasures to divide among you children when I get back. One of the treasures is Bill the Lizard. He is a little live lizard, called a horned frog, very cunning, who lives in a small box. The little badger, Josh, is very well and eats milk and potatoes. We took him out and gave him a run in the sand to-day. So far he seems as friendly as possible. When he feels hungry he squeals and the colored porters insist that he says "Dula-ny, Du-la-ny," because Dulany is very good to him and takes care of him.

[9] Third son of Theodore and Edith Roosevelt.

206

Del Monte, Cal., May 10, 1903

DEAREST QUENTY-QUEE:[10]

I loved your letter. I am very homesick for mother and for you children; but I have enjoyed this week's travel. I have been among the orange groves, where the trees have oranges growing thick upon them, and there are more flowers than you have ever seen. I have a gold top which I shall give you if Mother thinks you can take care of it. Perhaps I shall give you a silver bell instead. Whenever I see a little boy being brought up by his father or mother to look at the procession as we pass by, I think of you and Archie and feel very homesick. Sometimes little boys ride in the procession on their ponies, just like Archie on Algonquin.

White House, Oct. 4, 1903

DEAR TED:

In spite of the "Hurry! Hurry!" on the outside of your envelope, I did not like to act until I had consulted Mother and thought the matter over; and to be frank with you, old fellow, I am by no means sure that I am doing right now. If it were not that I feel you will be so bitterly disappointed, I would strongly advocate your acquiescing in the decision to leave you off the second squad this year. I am proud of your pluck, and I greatly admire football—though it was not a game I was ever able to play myself, my qualities resembling Kermit's rather than yours. But the very things that make it a good game make it a rough game, and there is always the chance of your being laid up. Now, I should not in the least object to your being laid up for a season if you were striving for something worth while, to get on the Groton school team, for instance, or on your class team when you entered Harvard—for of course I don't think you will have the weight to entitle you to try for the 'varsity. But I am by no means sure that it *is* worth your while to run the risk of being laid up for the sake of playing in the second squad when you are a fourth former, instead of when you are a fifth former. I do not know that the risk is balanced by the reward. However, I have told the Rector that as you feel so strongly about it, I think that the chance of your damaging yourself in body is outweighed by the possibility of bitterness of spirit if you could not play. Understand me, I should think mighty little of you if you permitted chagrin to make you bitter on some point where it was evidently right for you to suffer the chagrin. But in this case I am uncertain, and I shall give you the benefit of the doubt. If, however, the coaches at any time come to the conclusion

---

[10] Quentin Roosevelt, youngest child of Theodore and Edith Roosevelt.

that you ought not to be in the second squad, why you must come off without grumbling.

I am delighted to have you play football. I believe in rough, manly sports. But I do not believe in them if they degenerate into the sole end of any one's existence. I don't want you to sacrifice standing well in your studies to any over-athleticism; and I need not tell you that character counts for a great deal more than either intellect or body in winning success in life. Athletic proficiency is a mighty good servant, and like so many other good servants, a mighty bad master. Did you ever read Pliny's letter to Trajan, in which he speaks of its being advisable to keep the Greeks absorbed in athletics, including soldiering, and prevented their ever being dangerous to the Romans? . . . A man must develop his physical prowess up to a certain point; but after he has reached that point there are other things that count more. . . .

I am glad you should play football; I am glad that you should box; I am glad that you should ride and shoot and walk and row as well as you do. I should be very sorry if you did not do these things. But don't ever get into the frame of mind which regards these things as constituting the end to which all your energies must be devoted, or even the major portion of your energies.

White House, Oct. 19, 1903

DEAR KERMIT:

I was much pleased at your being made captain of your eleven. I would rather have you captain of the third eleven than playing on the second.

Yesterday afternoon Ethel on Wyoming, Mother on Yagenka, and I on Renown had a long ride, the only incident being meeting a large red automobile, which much shook Renown's nerves, although he behaved far better than he has hitherto been doing about automobiles. In fact, he behaved so well that I leaned over and gave him a lump of sugar when he had passed the object of terror—the old boy eagerly turning his head around to get it. It was lovely out in the country, with the trees at their very best of the fall coloring. There are no red maples here, but the Virginia creepers and some of the dogwoods give the red, and the hickories, tulip trees and beeches a brilliant yellow, sometimes almost orange.

When we got home Mother went up-stairs first and was met by Archie and Quentin, each loaded with pillows and whispering not to let me know that they were in ambush; then as I marched up to the top they assailed me with shrieks and chuckles of delight and then the pillow fight raged up and down the hall. After my bath I read them from Uncle Remus. Usually

Mother reads them, but now and then, when I think she really must have a holiday from it, I read them myself.

White House, Oct. 24, 1903

DEAR KERMIT:

Yesterday I felt rather seedy, having a touch of Cuban fever, my only unpleasant reminiscence of the Santiago campaign. Accordingly, I spent the afternoon in the house lying on the sofa, with a bright fire burning and Mother in the rocking-chair with her knitting, beside me. I felt so glad that I was not out somewhere in the wilderness, campaigning or hunting, where I would have to walk or ride all day in the rain and then lie out under a bush at night!

When Allan will come from the trainer's I do not know. Rather to my surprise, Ronald has won golden opinions and really is a very nice dog. Pinckney loves him, and he sits up in the express wagon just as if it was what he had been born to.

Quentin is learning to ride the pony. He had one tumble, which, he remarked philosophically, did not hurt him any more than when I whacked him with a sofa cushion in one of our pillow fights. I think he will very soon be able to manage the pony by himself.

Mother has just taken the three children to spend the afternoon at Dr. Rixey's farm. I am hard at work on my message to Congress, and accordingly shall not try to go out, or see any one either this afternoon or this evening. All of this work is terribly puzzling at times, but I peg away at it, and every now and then, when the dust clears away and I look around, I feel that I really have accomplished a little, at any rate.

I think you stood well in your form, taking everything into account. I feel you deserve credit for being captain of your football eleven and yet standing as high as you do in your class.

White House, Feb. 27, 1904

DEAR KERMIT:

Mother went off for three days to New York and Mame and Quentin took instant advantage of her absence to fall sick. Quentin's sickness was surely due to a riot in candy and ice-cream with chocolate sauce. He was a very sad bunny next morning and spent a couple of days in bed. Ethel, as always, was as good as gold both to him and to Archie, and largely relieved me of my duties as vice-mother. I got up each morning in time to breakfast with Ethel and Archie before they started for school, and I read

209

a certain amount to Quentin, but this was about all. I think Archie escaped with a minimum of washing for the three days. One day I asked him before Quentin how often he washed his face, whereupon Quentin interpolated, "very seldon, I fear," which naturally produced from Archie violent re-criminations of a strongly personal type. Mother came back yesterday, having thoroughly enjoyed Parsifal. All the horses continue sick.

White House, March 5, 1904

DEAR KERMIT:

I am wrestling with two Japanese wrestlers three times a week. I am not the age or the build one would think to be whirled lightly over an opponent's head and batted down on a mattress without damage. But they are so skilful that I have not been hurt at all. My throat is a little sore, because once when one of them had a strangle hold I also got hold of his windpipe and thought I could perhaps choke him off before he could choke me. However, he got ahead.

White House, April 9, 1904

DEAR TED:

I am very glad I have been doing this Japanese wrestling, but when I am through with it this time I am not at all sure I shall ever try it again while I am so busy with other work as I am now. Often by the time I get to five o'clock in the afternoon I will be feeling like a stewed owl, after an eight hours' grapple with Senators, Congressmen, etc. Then I find the wrestling a trifle too vehement for mere rest. My right ankle and my left wrist and one thumb and both great toes are swollen sufficiently to more or less impair their usefulness, and I am well mottled with bruises elsewhere. Still I have made good progress, and since you left they have taught me three new throws that are perfect corkers.

White House, June 12th, 1904

BLESSED ARCHIE-KINS:

Give my love to Mademoiselle; I hope you and Quenty are *very* good with her—and don't play in the library!

I loved your letter, and think you were very good to write.

All kinds of live things are sent me from time to time. The other day an eagle came; this morning an owl.

210

(I have drawn him holding
a rat in one claw)
   We sent both to the Zoo.
   The other day while walking with Mr. Pinchot and Mr. Garfield we
climbed into the Blagden deer park and almost walked over such a pretty
wee fawn, all spotted; it ran off like a little race horse.

   It made great jumps and held its white tail straight in the air.

White House, June 21, 1904

DEAR QUENTY-QUEE:

   The other day when out riding what should I see in the road ahead of
me but a real B'rer Terrapin and B'rer Rabbit. They were sitting solemnly
beside one another and looked just as if they had come out of a book;
but as my horse walked along

B'rer Rabbit went lippity lippity lippity off into the bushes and B'rer Terrapin drew in his head and legs till I passed.

Divide Creek, Colo., April 26, 1905

DARLING ETHEL:

   Of course you remember the story of the little prairie girl. I always
associate it with you. Well, again and again on this trip we would pass

211

through prairie villages—bleak and lonely—with all the people in from miles about to see me. Among them were often dozens of young girls, often pretty, and as far as I could see much more happy than the heroine of the story. One of them shook hands with me, and then, after much whispering, said: "We want to shake hands with the guard!" The "guard" proved to be Roly, who was very swell in his uniform, and whom they evidently thought much more attractive than the President, both in age and looks.

There are plenty of ranchmen round here; they drive over to camp to see me, usually bringing a cake, or some milk and eggs, and are very nice and friendly. About twenty of the men came out with me, "to see the President shoot a bear"; and fortunately I did so in the course of an exhausting twelve hours' ride. I am very homesick for you all.

White House, May 14, 1905

DEAR KERMIT:

Here I am back again, and mighty glad to be back. It was perfectly delightful to see Mother and the children, but it made me very homesick for you. Of course I was up to my ears in work as soon as I reached the White House, but in two or three days we shall be through it and can settle down into our old routine. . . .

Skip accompanied me to Washington. He is not as yet entirely at home in the White House and rather clings to my companionship. I think he will soon be fond of Archie, who loves him dearly. Mother is kind to Skip, but she does not think he is an aristocrat as Jack is. He is a very cunning little dog all the same.

Mother walked with me to church this morning and both the past evenings we have been able to go out into the garden and sit on the stone benches near the fountain. The country is too lovely for anything, everything being a deep, rich, fresh green.

I had a great time in Chicago with the labor union men. They made what I regarded as a rather insolent demand upon me, and I gave them some perfectly straight talk about their duty and about the preservation of law and order. The trouble seems to be increasing there, and I may have to send Federal troops into the city—though I shall not do so unless it is necessary.

White House, May 14, 1905

DEAR KERMIT:

That was a good mark in Latin, and I am pleased with your steady improvement in it.

212

Skip is housebroken, but he is like a real little Indian. He can stand any amount of hard work if there is a bear or bobcat ahead, but now that he is in the White House he thinks he would much rather do nothing but sit about all day with his friends, and threatens to turn into a lap-dog. But when we get him to Oyster Bay I think we can make him go out riding with us, and then I think he will be with Archie a great deal. He and Jack are rather jealous of one another. He is very cunning and friendly. I am immensely pleased with Mother's Virginia cottage and its name. I am going down there for Sunday with her some time soon.

P.S.—Your marks have just come! By George, you have worked hard and I am delighted. Three cheers!

White House, June 11, 1905

DEAR KERMIT:

Mother and I have just come home from a lovely day to "Pine Knot." It is really a perfectly delightful little place; the nicest little place of the kind you can imagine. Mother is a great deal pleased with it than any child with any toy I ever saw. She went down the day before, Thursday, and I followed on Friday morning. Good Mr. Joe Wilmer met me at the station and we rode on horseback to "Round Top," where we met Mother and Mr. Willie Wilmer. We all had tea there and then drove to "Plain Dealing," where we had dinner. Of course I loved both "Round Top" and "Plain Dealing," and as for the two Mr. Wilmers, they are the most generous, thoughtful, self-effacing friends that any one could wish to meet. After dinner we went over to "Pine Knot," put everything in order and went to bed. Next day we spent all by ourselves at "Pine Knot." In the morning I fried bacon and eggs, while Mother boiled the kettle for tea and laid the table. Breakfast was most successful, and then Mother washed the dishes and did most of the work, while I did odd jobs. Then we walked about the place, which is fifteen acres in all, saw the lovely spring, admired the pine trees and the oak trees, and then Mother lay in the hammock while I cut away some trees to give us a better view from the piazza. The piazza is the real feature of the house. It is broad and runs along the whole length and the roof is high near the wall, for it is a continuation of the roof of the house. It was lovely to sit there in the rocking-chairs and hear all the birds by day-time and at night the whippoorwills and owls and little forest folk.

Inside the house is just a bare wall with one big room below, which is nice now, and will be still nicer when the chimneys are up and there is a fireplace in each end. A rough flight of stairs leads above, where there are two rooms, separated by a passageway. We did everything for ourselves,

213

but all the food we had was sent over to us by the dear Wilmers, together with milk. We cooked it ourselves, so there was no one around the house to bother us at all. As we found that cleaning dishes took up an awful time we only took two meals a day, which was all we wanted. On Saturday evening I fried two chickens for dinner, while Mother boiled the tea, and we had cherries and wild strawberries, as well as biscuits and cornbread. To my pleasure Mother greatly enjoyed the fried chicken and admitted that what you children had said of the way I fried chicken was all true. In the evening we sat out a long time on the piazza, and then read indoors and then went to bed. Sunday morning we did not get up until nine. Then I fried Mother some beefsteak and some eggs in two frying-pans, and she liked them both very much. We went to church at the dear little church where the Wilmers' father and mother had been married, dined soon after two at "Plain Dealing," and then were driven over to the station to go back to Washington. I rode the big black stallion—Chief—and enjoyed it thoroughly. Altogether we had a very nice holiday.

I was lucky to be able to get it, for during the past fortnight, and indeed for a considerable time before, I have been carrying on negotiations with both Russia and Japan, together with side negotiations with Germany, France and England, to try to get the present war stopped. With infinite labor and by the exercise of a good deal of tact and judgment—if I do say it myself—I have finally gotten the Japanese and Russians to agree to meet to discuss the terms of peace. Whether they will be able to come to an agreement or not I can't say. But it is worth while to have obtained the chance of peace, and the only possible way to get this chance was to secure such an agreement of the two powers that they would meet and discuss the terms direct. Of course, Japan will want to ask more than she ought to ask, and Russia to give less than she ought to give. Perhaps both sides will prove impracticable. Perhaps one will. But there is the chance that they will prove sensible, and make a peace, which will really be for the interest of each as things are now. At any rate the experiment was worth trying. I have kept the secret very successfully, and my dealings with the Japanese in particular have been known to no one, so that the result is in the nature of a surprise.

To Archibald Bulloch Roosevelt[11]

Washington, January 10, 1904

Quentin turned up last night. He had fallen thru the ice while playing hockey and has a cough in consequence; but as he did not drown I do not really mind the cough much. This morning he discreetly vanished before

[11] Otherwise known as "Archie."

church, and when I left to go to my church the ushers were vainly seeking to round him up.

The roads are so bad that I can get only a little riding and walking now. I have an ex-prize fighter come in to give me physical exercise and to box with me in the evening. He has a wife of whom he is very proud, and I sent her some flowers by him. He was much pleased, and described in a burst of confidence how he fell in love with her, and then remarked thoughtfully: "I guess it must have been her intellect. It sure wasn't her looks, for she ain't any better looking than I am!" [12]

[12] Theodore Roosevelt's Letters to His Children." *Works XIX*, pp. 417ff.

Man of Letters

*A man of letters, says the Century Dictionary, is "one de-
voted to literature; a scholar and writer." The definition fits
Mr. Roosevelt from his youth up. He was seldom without a
book—in his hand or his pocket or within arm's reach, even
in the Brazilian wilderness. His histories attest his scholarship.
His formal writings fill twenty-four volumes; his selected letters eight more. He was a man of letters, too, inasmuch as his
reading gave him a wide background for critical judgment.*

1. The Books that I Read

I am asked to tell when and how I do my reading, and what books I
read. I am afraid my answer will not be so instructive as it ought to be,
for I have never followed any definite plan in reading; and it seems to
me that no plan can be laid down that will be generally applicable. If a
man is not fond of books, to him reading of any kind will be drudgery. I
most sincerely commiserate such a person, but I do not know how to help
him. If a man or a woman is fond of books he or she will naturally seek the
books that the mind and soul demand. Suggestions of a possibly helpful
character can be made by outsiders, but only suggestions; and they will
probably be helpful about in proportion to the outsider's knowledge of the
mind and soul of the person to be helped. . . .

The equation of personal taste is as powerful in reading as in eating;
and within certain broad limits the matter is merely one of individual
preference, having nothing to do with the quality either of the book or of
the reader's mind. I like apples, pears, oranges, pineapples and peaches.
I dislike bananas, alligator pears and prunes. The first fact is certainly
not to my credit, although it is to my advantage; and the second at least
does not show moral turpitude. At times in the tropics I have been exceedingly sorry I could not learn to like bananas, and on round-ups, in the
cow country in the old days, it was even more unfortunate not to like

217

prunes; but I simply could not make myself like either, and that was all there was to it.

In the same way I read over and over again "Guy Mannering," "The Antiquary," "Pendennis," "Vanity Fair," "Our Mutual Friend," and the "Pickwick Papers"; whereas I make heavy weather of most parts of the "Fortunes of Nigel," "Esmond," and the "Old Curiosity Shop"—to mention only books I have tried to read during the last month. I have no question that the latter three books are as good as the first six; doubtless for some people they are better; but I do not like them, any more than I like prunes or bananas.

In the same way I read and re-read "Macbeth" and "Othello"; but not "King Lear" nor "Hamlet." I know perfectly well that the latter are as wonderful as the former—I wouldn't venture to admit my shortcomings regarding them if I couldn't proudly express my appreciation of the other two! But at my age I might as well own up, at least to myself, to my limitations, and read the books I thoroughly enjoy. . . .

Within broad limits, therefore, the reader's personal and individual taste must be the guiding factor. I like hunting books and books of exploration and adventure. I do not ask anyone else to like them. I distinctly do not hold my own preferences as anything whatever but individual preferences; and this article is to be accepted as confessional rather than didactic. With this understanding I admit a liking for novels where something happens; and even among these novels I can neither explain nor justify why I like some and do not like others; why, among the novels of Sienkiewicz, I cannot stand "Quo Vadis," and never tire of "With Fire and Sword," "Pan Michael," the "Deluge" and the "Knights of the Cross."

Of course, I know that the best critics scorn the demand among novel readers for "the happy ending." Now, in really great books, in an epic like Milton's, in dramas like those of Æschylus and Sophocles, I am entirely willing to accept and even demand tragedy; and also in poetry that cannot be called great. But not in good readable novels, of sufficient length to enable me to get interested in the hero and heroine!

There are enough horror and grimness and sordid squalor in real life with which an active man has to grapple; and when I turn to the world of literature—of books considered as books, and not as instruments of my profession—I do not care to study suffering unless for some sufficient purpose. It is only a very exceptional novel which I will read if He does not marry Her; and even in exceptional novels I much prefer this consummation. I am not defending my attitude. I am merely stating it.

Therefore it would be quite useless for me to try to explain why I read certain books. As to how and when, my answers must be only less vague.

I almost always read a good deal in the evening; and if the rest of the evening is occupied I can at least get half an hour before going to bed. But all kinds of odd moments turn up during even a busy day, in which it is possible to enjoy a book; and then there are rainy afternoons in the country in autumn, and stormy days in winter, when one's work outdoors is finished and after wet clothes have been changed for dry, the rocking chair in front of the open wood fire simply demands an accompanying book.

Railway and steamboat journeys were, of course, predestined through the ages as aids to the enjoyment of reading. I have always taken books with me when on hunting and exploring trips. In such cases the literature should be reasonably heavy, in order that it may last. You can under these conditions read Herbert Spencer, for example, or the writings of Turgot, or a German study of the Mongols, or even a German edition of Aristophanes, with erudite explanations of the jokes, as you never would if surrounded by less formidable authors in your own library; and when you do reach the journey's end you grasp with eager appetite at old magazines, or at the lightest of literature.

Then, if one is worried by all kinds of men and events—during critical periods in administrative office, or at national conventions, or during congressional investigations or in hard-fought political campaigns—it is the greatest relief and unalloyed delight to take up some really good, some really enthralling book—Tacitus, Thucydides, Herodotus, Polybius, or Goethe, Keats, Gray or Lowell—and lose all memory of everything grimy, and of the baseness that must be parried or conquered.

Like every one else I am apt to read in streaks. If I get interested in any subject I read different books connected with it, and probably also read books on subjects suggested by it. Having read Carlyle's "Frederick the Great"—with its splendid description of the battles, and of the unyielding courage and thrifty resourcefulness of the iron-tempered king; and with its screaming deification of able brutality in the name of morality, and its practice of the suppression and falsification of the truth under the pretense of preaching veracity—I turned to Macaulay's essay on this subject, and found that the historian whom it has been the fashion of the intellectuals to patronize or deride showed a much sounder philosophy and an infinitely greater appreciation of and devotion to truth than was shown by the loquacious apostle of the doctrine of reticence.

Then I took up Waddington's "Guerre de Sept Ans," then I read all I could about Gustavus Adolphus; and, gradually dropping everything but the military side, I got hold of quaint little old histories of Eugene of Savoy and Turenne. In similar fashion my study of and delight in Mahan sent

219

me farther afield, to read queer old volumes about de Ruyter and the daring warrior-merchants of the Hansa, and to study, as well as I could, the feats of Suffren and Tegethoff. I did not need to study Farragut. Mahaffy's books started me to re-read—in translation, alas!—the post-Athenian Greek authors. After Ferrero I did the same thing as regards the Latin authors, and then industriously read all kinds of modern writers on the same period, finishing with Oman's capital essay on "Seven Roman Statesmen." Gilbert Murray brought me back from Greek history to Greek literature, and thence by a natural suggestion to parts of the Old Testament, to the Nibelungenlied, to the Roland lay and the *chansons de gestes,* to Beowulf and finally to the great Japanese hero-tale, the story of the Forty-Nine Ronins.

Now, I read Burroughs too often to have him suggest anything save himself; but I am exceedingly glad that at last Charles Sheldon has arisen to show what a hunter-naturalist, who adds the ability of the writer to the ability of the trained observer and outdoor adventurer, can do for our last great wilderness, Alaska. From Sheldon I turned to Stewart Edward White, and then began to wander afar, with Herbert Ward's "Voice From the Congo," and Mary Kingsley's writings, and Hudson's "El Ombu," and Cunningham Grahame's sketches of South America. A rereading of The Federalist led me to Burke, to Trevelyan's history of Fox and of our own Revolution, to Lecky; and finally by way of Malthus and Adam Smith and Lord Acton and Bagehot to my own contemporaries, to Ross and George Alger.

Even in pure literature, having nothing to do with history, philosophy, sociology or economy, one book will often suggest another, so that one finds one has unconsciously followed a regular course of reading. Once I traveled steadily from Montaigne through Addison, Swift, Steele, Lamb, Irving and Lowell to Crothers and Kenneth Grahame—and if it be objected that some of these *could* not have suggested the others, I can only answer that they *did* suggest them.

I suppose that every one passes through periods during which he reads no poetry; and some people, of whom I am one, also pass through periods during which they voraciously devour poets of widely different kinds. Now it will be Horace and Pope; now Schiller, Scott, Longfellow, Körner; now Bret Harte or Kipling; now Shelley or Herrick or Tennyson; now Poe and Coleridge; and again Emerson or Browning or Whitman.

Sometimes one wishes to read for the sake of contrast. To me Owen Wister is the writer I wish when I am hungry with the memories of lonely mountains, of vast sunny plains with seas of wind-rippled grass, of springing wild creatures, and lithe sun-tanned men who ride with utter ease on ungroomed, half-broken horses. But when I lived much in cow camps

I often carried a volume of Swinburne, as a kind of antiseptic to alkali dust, tepid muddy water, frying-pan bread, sow-belly bacon, and the too-infrequent washing of sweat-drenched clothing.[1]

2. The Books Are Everywhere

At Sagamore Hill we love a great many things—birds and trees and books, and all things beautiful, and horses and rifles and children and hard work and the joy of life. . . . The books are everywhere. There are as many in the North Room and in the parlor—is drawing-room a more appropriate name than parlor?—as in the library; the gun-room at the top of the house, which incidentally has the loveliest view of all, contains more books than any of the other rooms; and they are particularly delightful books to browse among, just because they have not much relevance to one another, this being one of the reasons why they are relegated to their present abode. But the books have overflowed into all the other rooms too.

I could not name any principle upon which the books have been gathered. Books are almost as individual as friends. There is no earthly use in laying down general laws about them. Some meet the needs of one person, and some of another. . . .

A book must be interesting to the particular reader at that particular time. But there are tens of thousands of interesting books, and some of them are sealed to some men and some are sealed to others; and some stir the soul at some given point of a man's life and yet convey no message at other times. The reader, the book-lover, must meet his own needs without paying too much attention to what his neighbors say those needs should be. He must not hypocritically pretend to like what he does not like. . . .

I still read a number of Scott's novels over and over again, whereas if I finish anything by Miss Austen I have a feeling that duty performed is a rainbow to the soul. But other book-lovers who are very close kin to me, and whose taste I know to be better than mine, read Miss Austen all the time—and, moreover, they are very kind, and never pity me in too offensive a manner for not reading her myself.[2]

[1] *Ladies' Home Journal*, April, 1915.
[2] Autobiography, *Works XX*, pp. 319–26.

3. "I find reading a great comfort . . ."

To George Otto Trevelyan

Washington, May 28, 1904

I find reading a great comfort. People often say to me that they do not see how I find time for it, to which I answer them (much more truthfully than they believe) that to me it is a dissipation, which I have sometimes to try to avoid, instead of an irksome duty. Of course I have been so busy for the last ten years, so absorbed in political work, that I have simply given up reading any book that I do not find interesting. But there are a great many books which ordinarily pass for "dry" which to me do possess much interest—notably history and anthropology; and these give me ease and relaxation that I can get in no other way, not even on horseback! [3]

To Jean Jules Jusserand [4]

Washington, February 8, 1904

Herewith I send you back the Chanson de Roland. I have enjoyed it particularly because it is the first copy I ever read which had the old French and the modern French interpaged; so that I was able to read the old French, which I could not otherwise have done. There are a dozen points that I want to talk over with you, and as soon as the social season is over I shall get Madame Jusserand and you to come around to lunch.

Do you regard the Venetian manuscript as being as authentic as the older English manuscript? I hope so, because I particularly like a certain generous side to that description of the Moorish king, Margaris, who "would have been so great a baron if he had only been a Christian," and who seems to me to have more individuality than any of the other characters, after the three great heroes of the epic and Charlemagne.

It seems to me that it is somewhat doubtful to put the poem after the Norman conquest, and by an Anglo-Norman, on so slender a ground as the mention of the conquest of England; for Poland and Byzantium are also mentioned as having been conquered.[5]

[3] *Letters IV*, p. 806.
[4] French ambassador to the United States.
[5] *Letters IV*, p. 718.

To Benjamin Ide Wheeler[6]

Washington, May 11, 1904

MY DEAR PRESIDENT WHEELER: Speaking from the standpoint of utterly superficial knowledge, I had come to just the conclusion that you had about the Bérard,[7] excepting that I think it perfectly possible that the Greek poet or poets had used Phoenician recitals of trading voyages, or explorations in search of trade, as giving material for the framework of certain incidents.

Your speaking of relaxing yourself by reading philosophical works suggests that I have been reading an interesting Italian book on the Indo-Europeans recently by de Michelis. As I have never studied Italian I have read it very slowly, and in some cases imperfectly. But I have been much impressed with it, owing to the clear grasp by the author of the [conditions] . . . and relationships between languages and races—his understanding, for instance, that Aryan is a linguistic and not a biological term.[8]

4. Dante and the Bowery

It is the conventional thing to praise Dante because he of set purpose "used the language of the market-place," so as to be understanded of the common people; but we do not in practice either admire or understand a man who writes in the language of our own market-place. It must be the Florentine market-place of the thirteenth century—not Fulton Market of to-day. What infinite use Dante would have made of the Bowery! Of course, he could have done it only because not merely he himself, the great poet, but his audience also, would have accepted it as natural. The nineteenth century was more apt than the thirteenth to boast of itself as being the greatest of the centuries; but, save as regards purely material objects, ranging from locomotives to bank buildings, it did not wholly believe in its boasting. A nineteenth-century poet, when trying to illustrate some point he was making, obviously felt uncomfortable in mentioning nineteenth-century heroes if he also referred to those of classic times, lest he should be suspected of instituting comparisons between them. A thirteenth-century poet was not in the least troubled by any such misgivings, and quite simply illustrated his point by illusions to any character in history or romance, ancient or contemporary, that happened to occur to him.

[6] President, University of California.
[7] Vicyor Bérard, *Les Phéniciens et l'Odyssée* (Paris, 1902–1903).
[8] *Letters IV*, p. 795.

Of all the poets of the nineteenth century, Walt Whitman was the only one who dared use the Bowery—that is, use anything that was striking and vividly typical of the humanity around him—as Dante used the ordinary humanity of his day; and even Whitman was not quite natural in doing so, for he always felt that he was defying the conventions and prejudices of his neighbors, and his self-consciousness made him a little defiant. Dante was not defiant of conventions: the conventions of his day did not forbid him to use human nature just as he saw it, no less than human nature as he read about it. The Bowery is one of the great highways of humanity, a highway of seething life, of varied interest, of fun, of work, of sordid and terrible tragedy; and it is haunted by demons as evil as any that stalk through the pages of the "Inferno." But no man of Dante's art and with Dante's soul would write of it nowadays; and he would hardly be understood if he did. Whitman wrote of homely things and every-day men, and of their greatness, but his art was not equal to his power and his purpose; and, even as it was, he, the poet, by set intention, of the democracy, is not known to the people as widely as he should be known; and it is only the few . . . who prize him as he ought to be prized.

Nowadays, at the outset of the twentieth century, cultivated people would ridicule the poet who illustrated fundamental truths, as Dante did six hundred years ago, by examples drawn alike from human nature as he saw it around him and from human nature as he read of it. I suppose that this must be partly because we are so self-conscious as always to read a comparison into any illustration, forgetting the fact that no comparison is implied between two men, in the sense of estimating their relative greatness or importance, when the career of each of them is chosen merely to illustrate some given quality that both possess. It is also probably due to the fact that an age in which the critical faculty is greatly developed often tends to develop a certain querulous inability to understand the fundamental truths which less critical ages accept as a matter of course. To such critics it seems improper, and indeed ludicrous, to illustrate human nature by examples chosen alike from the Brooklyn Navy Yard or Castle Garden and the Piræus, alike from Tammany and from the Roman mob organized by the foes or friends of Cæsar. To Dante such feeling itself would have been inexplicable.

Dante dealt with those tremendous qualities of the human soul which dwarf all differences in outward and visible form and station, and therefore he illustrated what he meant by any example that seemed to him apt. Only the great names of antiquity had been handed down, and so, when he spoke of pride or violence or flattery, and wished to illustrate his thesis by an appeal to the past, he could speak only of great and prominent characters; but in the present of his day most of the men he knew, or knew of, were naturally people of no permanent importance—just as is the case in the present of our own day. Yet the passions of these men were the same as those of the heroes of old, godlike or demoniac; and so he unhesitatingly used his contemporaries, or his immediate predecessors, to illustrate his points, without regard to their prominence or lack of prominence. He was not concerned with the differences in their fortunes and careers, with their heroic proportions or lack of such proportions; he was a mystic whose imagination soared so high and whose thoughts plumbed so deeply the far depths of our being that he was also quite simply a realist; for the eternal mysteries were ever before his mind, and, compared to them, the differences between the careers of the mighty masters of mankind and the careers of even very humble people seemed trivial. If we translate his comparisons into the terms of our day, we are apt to feel amused over this trait of his, until we go a little deeper and understand that we are ourselves to blame, because we have lost the faculty simply and naturally to recognize that the essential traits of humanity are shown alike by big men and by little men, in the lives that are now being lived and in those that are long ended.

Probably no two characters in Dante impress the ordinary reader more than Farinata and Capaneus: the man who raises himself waist-high from out his burning sepulchre, unshaken by torment, and the man who, with scornful disdain, refuses to brush from his body the falling flames; the great souls—magnanimous, Dante calls them—whom no torture, no disaster, no failure of the most absolute kind could force to yield or to bow before the dread powers that had mastered them. Dante has created these men, has made them permanent additions to the great figures of the world; they are imaginary only in the sense that Achilles and Ulysses are imaginary—that is, they are now as real as the figures of any men that ever lived. One of them was a mythical hero in a mythical feat, the other a second-rate faction leader in a faction-ridden Italian city of the thirteenth century, whose deeds have not the slightest importance aside from what Dante's mention gives. Yet the two men are mentioned as naturally as Alexander and Cæsar are mentioned. Evidently they are dwelt upon at length because Dante felt it his duty to express a peculiar horror for that fierce pride which could defy its overlord, while at the same time, and perhaps unwillingly, he could not conceal a certain shuddering admiration for the lofty courage on which this evil pride was based.

The point I wish to make is the simplicity with which Dante illustrated one of the principles on which he lays most stress, by the example of a man who was of consequence only in the history of the parochial politics of Florence. Farinata will now live forever as a symbol of the soul; yet as an historical figure he is dwarfed beside any one of hundreds of the

225

leaders in our own Revolution and Civil War. Tom Benton, of Missouri, and Jefferson Davis, of Mississippi, were opposed to one another with a bitterness which surpassed that which rived asunder Guelph from Ghibellin, or black Guelph from white Guelph. They played mighty parts in a tragedy more tremendous than any which any mediæval city ever witnessed or could have witnessed. Each possessed an iron will and undaunted courage, physical and moral; each led a life of varied interest and danger, and exercised a power not possible in the career of the Florentine. One, the champion of the Union, fought for his principles as unyieldingly as the other fought for what he deemed right in trying to break up the Union. Each was a colossal figure. Each, when the forces against which he fought overcame him—for in his latter years Benton saw the cause of disunion triumph in Missouri, just as Jefferson Davis lived to see the cause of union triumph in the Nation—fronted an adverse fate with the frowning defiance, the high heart, and the stubborn will which Dante has commemorated for all time in his hero who "held hell in great scorn." Yet a modern poet who endeavored to illustrate such a point by reference to Benton and Davis would be uncomfortably conscious that his audience would laugh at him. He would feel ill at ease, and therefore would convey the impression of being ill at ease, exactly as he would feel that he was posing, was forced and unnatural, if he referred to the deeds of the evil heroes of the Paris Commune as he would without hesitation refer to the many similar but smaller leaders of riots in the Roman forum.

Dante speaks of a couple of French troubadours, or of a local Sicilian poet, just as he speaks of Euripides; and quite properly, for they illustrate as well what he as to teach; but we of to-day could not possibly speak of a couple of recent French poets or German novelists in the same connection without having an uncomfortable feeling that we ought to defend ourselves from possible misapprehension; and therefore we could not speak of them naturally. When Dante wishes to assail those guilty of crimes of violence, he in one stanza speaks of the torments inflicted by divine justice on Attila (coupling him with Pyrrhus and Sextus Pompey —a sufficiently odd conjunction in itself, by the way), and in the next stanza mentions the names of a couple of local highwaymen who had made travel unsafe in particular neighborhoods. The two highwaymen in question were by no means as important as Jesse James and Billy the Kid; doubtless they were far less formidable fighting men, and their adventures were less striking and varied. Yet think of the way we should feel if a great poet should now arise who would incidentally illustrate the ferocity of the human heart by allusions both to the terrible Hunnish

226

"scourge of God" and to the outlaws who in our own times defied justice in Missouri and New Mexico!

When Dante wishes to illustrate the fierce passions of the human heart, he may speak of Lycurgus, or of Saul; or he may speak of two local contemporary captains, victor or vanquished in obscure struggles between Guelph and Ghibellin; men like Jacopo del Cassero or Buonconte, whom he mentions as naturally as he does Cyrus or Rehoboam. He is entirely right! What one among our own writers, however, would be able simply and naturally to mention Ulrich Dahlgren, or Custer, or Morgan, or Raphael Semmes, or Marion, or Sumter, as illustrating the qualities shown by Hannibal, or Rameses, or William the Conqueror, or by Moses or Hercules? Yet the Guelph and Ghibellin captains of whom Dante speaks were in no way as important as these American soldiers of the second or third rank. Dante saw nothing incongruous in treating at length of the qualities of all of them; he was not thinking of comparing the genius of the unimportant local leader with the genius of the great sovereign conquerors of the past—he was thinking only of the qualities of courage and daring and of the awful horror of death; and when we deal with what is elemental in the human soul it matters but little whose soul we take. . . .

When Dante deals with the crimes which he most abhorred, simony and barratry, he flails offenders of his age who were of the same type as those who in our days flourish by political or commercial corruption; and he names his offenders, both those just dead and those still living, and puts them, popes and politicians alike, in hell. There have been trust magnates and politicians and editors and magazine-writers in our own country whose lives and deeds were no more edifying than those of the men who lie in the third and the fifth chasm of the eighth circle of the Inferno; yet for a poet to name those men would be condemned as an instance of shocking taste.

One age expresses itself naturally in a form that would be unnatural, and therefore undesirable, in another age. We do not express ourselves nowadays in epics at all; and we keep the emotions aroused in us by what is good or evil in the men of the present in a totally different compartment from that which holds our emotions concerning what was good or evil in the men of the past. An imitation of the letters of the times past, when the spirit has wholly altered, would be worse than useless; and the very qualities that help to make Dante's poem immortal would, if copied nowadays, make the copyist ridiculous. Nevertheless, it would be a good thing if we could, in some measure, achieve the mighty Florentine's high simplicity of soul, at least to the extent of recognizing in those around us the eternal qualities which we admire or condemn in the men who wrought good or evil at any stage in the world's previous history. Dante's masterpiece is one of the supreme works of art that the ages have witnessed; but he would have been the last to wish that it should be treated only as a work of art, or worshipped only for art's sake, without reference to the dread lessons it teaches mankind.[9]

5. "That book . . . 'The Octopus'"

To Owen Wister[10]

Oyster Bay, July 20, 1901

Your coming here started me to re-reading your pieces. I want to re-iterate my judgment that the "Pilgrim on the Gila," "Specimen Jones" and "The Second Missouri Compromise" are among the very best. I think they have a really very high value as historical documents which also possess an immense human interest. When you speak of the teachings of the Mormon bishop as having no resemblance to the Gospels but being right in the line of Deuteronomy, you set forth a great truth as to the whole Mormon Church. I shall always believe that Brigham Young was quite as big a man as Mahomet. But the age and the place were very unfavorable instead of highly favorable. . . .

Now, about that book by Frank Norris,[11] The Octopus. I read it with interest. He has a good idea and he has some power, but he left me with the impression that his overstatement was so utterly preposterous as to deprive his work of all value. A good part of it reads like the ravings which Altgeld and Bryan regard as denunciation of wrong. I do not know California at all, but I have seen a good deal of all the western States between the Mississippi and the western side of the Rocky Mountains. I know positively that as regards all those States—the Dakotas, Montana, Wyoming, Idaho, Colorado and New Mexico, the facts alleged in The Octopus are a wild travesty of the truth. It is just exactly as if in writing about the tyranny and corruption of Tammany Hall I should solemnly revive the stories of mediæval times and picture Mr. Croker[12] as bathing in the blood of hundreds of babies taken from the tenement houses, or of having Jacob Schiff[13] tortured in the Tombs until he handed over a couple

[9] Works XII, pp. 98–103.
[10] Harvard classmate from Philadelphia and author of The Virginian and many other books.
[11] Benjamin Franklin Norris, one of the first American novelists to exploit the possibilities of naturalism.
[12] Richard Croker, boss of Tammany Hall.
[13] Jacob H. Schiff, head of the banking firm of Kuhn, Loeb & Co., New York.

of million dollars. The overstatement would be so preposterous that I would have rendered myself powerless to call attention to the real and gross iniquity.

Of course the conditions in California may have been wholly different from those in every other western State, but, if so, Norris should have been most careful to show that what he wrote was absolutely limited by State lines and had no application to life in the west as a whole. What I am inclined to think is that conditions were worse in California than elsewhere, and that a writer of great power and vigor who was also gifted with self-restraint and with truthfulness could make out of them a great tragedy, which would not, like Norris's book, be contemptuously tossed aside by any serious man who knew western conditions, as so very hysterical and exaggerated as to be without any real value.

More and more I have grown to have a horror of the reformer who is half charlatan and half fanatic, and ruins his own cause by overstatement. If Norris's book is taken to apply to all the west, as it certainly would be taken by any ordinary man who reads it, then it stands on an exact level with some of the publications of the W.C.T.U. in which the Spanish War, our troubles in the Philippines, and civic dishonesty and social disorder, are all held to spring from the fact that sherry is drunk at the White House.[14]

6. "I have managed to combine . . ."

To Corinne Roosevelt Robinson

Medora, Dakota, May 12, 1886

If I was not afraid of being put down as cold blooded I should say that, though I honestly miss greatly, and all the time think longingly of all you dear ones, yet I really enjoy this life. I have managed to combine an out-doors life, possessing much variety and excitement and now and then a little adventure, with a literary life also. Three out of four days I spend the morning and evening in the ranch house, where I have a sitting-room all to myself, reading and working at various pieces I have now on hand. They may come to nothing whatever; but on the other hand they may succeed; at any rate, I am doing some honest work, whatever the result is. I am really pretty philosophical about success or failure now. It often amuses me when I accidentally hear that I am supposed to be harboring secret and biting regret for my political career; when as a matter of fact I have hardly ever when alone given it two thoughts since it closed, and

[14] *Letters III,* pp. 126–8.

have been quite as much wrapped up in hunting, ranching and book-making as I ever was in politics.[15]

To Anna Roosevelt

Medora, Dakota, June 19, 1886

"La Guerre et La Paix," like all Tolstoi's work, is very strong and very interesting. The descriptions of the battles are excellent, but though with one or two good ideas underneath them, the criticisms of the commanders, especially of Napoleon, and of wars in general, are absurd. Moreover, when he criticises battles (and the iniquity of war) in his capacity of author, he deprives himself of all excuse for the failure to criticise the various other immoralities he portrays. In "Anna Karénina" he let each character, good or bad, speak for itself; and while he might better have shown some reprobation of evil, at least it could be alleged in answer that he simply narrated, putting the facts before us that we ourselves might judge them. But when he again and again spends pages in descanting on the wickedness and folly of war, and passes over other vices without a word of reproach he certainly in so far acts as the apologist for the latter, and the general tone of the book does not seem to me to be in the least conducive to morality. Natacha is a bundle of contradictions, and her fickleness is portrayed as truly marvelous; how Pierre could ever have ventured to leave her alone for six weeks after he was married I can not imagine. Marie as portrayed by him is a girl that we can hardly conceive of as fascinating Rostow. Sonia is another variety of the patient Griselda type. The two men André and Pierre are wonderfully well drawn; and all through the book there are touches and descriptions that are simply masterpieces.[16]

7. "I have been a part of all that I describe . . ."

To Richard Watson Gilder[17]

Oyster Bay, July 19, 1888

MY DEAR GILDER: I am not a modest man, but I really don't know what to write you. The sketches will be on similar subjects to those in my book which the *Saturday Review*, & *Athenaeum* & *Spectator* were most flattering over. I can send you the reviews if you wish, only I would

[15] *Letters I*, p. 99.
[16] *Ibid.*, pp. 103–4.
[17] Poet, publisher, editor of *Century Magazine*.

hate to have them lost. The sketches or series will (feebly) portray a most fascinating and most evanescent phase of American life; the wild industries, and scarcely wilder sports of the great lonely plains of the far west. By the way, the title is to be "Ranch Life in the Far West," is it not?

I have been a part of all that I describe; I have seen the things and done them; I have herded my own cattle, I have killed my own food; I have shot bears, captured horse thieves, and "stood off" Indians. The descriptions are literally exact; few eastern men have seen the wild life for themselves.

Is that egotistic enough! [18]

8. Obstacles to Literary Work

To William P. Trent [19]

Washington, February 23, 1898

You touch on one of what I believe to be the most serious obstacles in the way of doing good literary work in the present generation, when you speak of the press and bustle of city life, and especially of the tendency to write "timely" articles, and the like. It is not necessary to be a mere recluse in order to do good work as a poet, a novelist, or even as a historian or a scholar; but it is absolutely necessary to be able to have the bulk of one's time to one's self, so that it can be spent on the particular study needed. Nowadays it is rather difficult to get such leisure, and indeed it can be gotten only by a man of some means and of great determination of character, if he has any widespread popularity. Prof. Lounsbury can work as a scholar should, very largely because his countrymen, as a whole, do not in the least appreciate him and his work; but if a man becomes at all popular the conditions of modern life render it the easiest thing in the world for thoughtless people to intrude upon his time, and for the man himself to fall into temptations which will interfere with his work. Even more important and more harmful is the fact that the enormous increase in the half-educated reading public, and in the half-educated caterers to this reading public, tends to divert every man capable of doing good work from that good work; because as my own experience tends to show, one's literary work is very apt to be remunerated in inverse proportion to its value. The minute that a man like Moses Coit Tyler writes a serious work on our early literature, a work which attracts attention and gives him a name, he receives all kinds of requests to do

[18] *Letters I,* pp. 143–4.
[19] Editor, critic, professor of English.

second-rate work, and unless he is very well-to-do, and very much accustomed to saying No, and to treating temporary popularity with indifference, it is exceedingly difficult for him not to yield.

I don't suppose I could ever have made "The Winning of the West" a big historical book, and a good deal of my active life has helped me in making it even what it is; but I know that if I had had more leisure I could have done much better with it; and now I have to be adamantine in refusing innumerable requests to write a manual on western history for one publisher, a manual on naval wars for another, a little book on the cowboy for a third, some articles on our navy for a newspaper syndicate, some sketches of New York police life for the magazines, etc., etc., etc. There is a plausible reason for writing each one, but if I should go into any of them while I am at work as I am in the Navy Department, it would mean the absolute surrender of the purpose of going on with "The Winning of the West," and that I am not willing to do if it can be avoided.

There! You see what you have brought on yourself by writing me as you did.[20]

9. "Good for the split infinitive!"

To Thomas R. Lounsbury[21]

Washington, March 29, 1904

MY DEAR MR. LOUNSBURY: Good for the split infinitive! Here have I been laboriously trying to avoid using it in a vain desire to look cultured; and now I shall give unbridled rein to my passions in the matter.[22]

10. The Children of the Night

The "twilight of the poets" has been especially gray in America; for poetry is of course one of those arts in which the smallest amount of work of the very highest class is worth an infinity of good work that is not of the highest class. The touch of the purple makes a poem out of verse, and if it is not there, there is no substitute. It is hard to account for the failure to produce in America of recent years a poet who in the world of letters will rank as high as certain American sculptors and painters rank in the world of art.

But individual poems appear from time to time, by Mr. Madison

[20] *Letters I*, pp. 782–3.
[21] Professor of English, Yale University.
[22] *Letters IV*, p. 765.

Cawein, by Mr. Clinton Scollard, by Doctor Maurice Egan, and others; and more rarely a little volume of poetry appears, like Bliss Carman's "Ballads of Lost Heaven." Such a book is Edwin Arlington Robinson's "The Children of the Night."

It is rather curious that Mr. Robinson's volume should not have attracted more attention. There is an undoubted touch of genius in the poems collected in this volume, and a curious simplicity and good faith, all of which qualities differentiate them sharply from ordinary collections of the kind. There is in them just a little of the light that never was on land or sea, and in such light the objects described often have nebulous outlines; but it is not always necessary in order to enjoy a poem that one should be able to translate it into terms of mathematical accuracy. Indeed, those who admire the coloring of Turner, those who like to read how—and to wonder why—Childe Roland to the Dark Tower came, do not wish always to have the ideas presented to them with cold, hard, definite outlines; and to a man with the poetic temperament it is inevitable that life should often appear clothed with a certain sad mysticism. In the present volume I am not sure that I understand "Luke Havergal"; but I am entirely sure that I like it.

Whoever has lived in country America knows the gray, empty houses from which life has gone. It is of one of these that "The House on the Hill" was written.

> "They are all gone away,
>   The House is shut and still,
> There is nothing more to say.
>
> Through broken walls and gray
>   The winds blow bleak and shrill:
> They are all gone away.
>
> Nor is there one to-day
>   To speak them good or ill:
> There is nothing more to say.
>
> Why is it then we stray
>   Around that sunken sill?
> They are all gone away,
>
> And our poor fancy-play
>   For them is wasted skill:
> There is nothing more to say.
>
> There is ruin and decay
>   In the House on the Hill:
> They are all gone away,
> There is nothing more to say."

The next poem, "Richard Cory," illustrates a very ancient but very profound philosophy of life with a curiously local touch which points its keen insight. Those who feel poetry in their marrow and fibre are the spiritual heirs of the ages; and so it is natural that this man from Maine, many of whose poems could have been written only by one to whom the most real of lives is the life of the American small town, should write his "Ballade of Broken Flutes"—where "A lonely surge of ancient spray told of an unforgetful sea"—should write the poem beginning:

> "Since Persia fell at Marathon,
>   The yellow years have gathered fast:
> Long centuries have come and gone";

and the very original sonnet on Amaryllis, the last three lines of which are:

> "But though the trumpets of the world were glad,
>   It made me lonely and it made me sad
> To think that Amaryllis had grown old."

Some of his images stay fixed in one's mind, as in "The Pity of the Leaves," the lines running:

> "The brown, thin leaves that on the stones outside
>   Skipped with a freezing whisper."

Sometimes he writes, as in "The Tavern," of what most of us feel we have seen; and then again of what we have seen only with the soul's eyes. . . .

Mr. Robinson has written in this little volume not verse but poetry. Whether he has the power of sustained flight remains to be seen.[23]

To Alexander Smith Cochran

Oyster Bay, February 4, 1915

. . . Have you any acquaintance with the poems of Bliss Carman? Some of his Ballads have really been capital; and I wish to Heaven there were some way that we could be saved the discredit of having a man like him die of want, because the advertisers of automobile supplies do not think his poetry is "breezy" and "snappy" and "up-to-date." From the letter you will see that what is wanted is some employment at a salary of five hundred dollars a year for Carman or five thousand dollars to get him the annuity.

When I was President, I cheerfully outraged the feelings of the ultra-

[23] *Works XII*, pp. 296–8.

Civil-Service reformers by fishing a similar poet—I think an even better man—Arlington Robinson, out of a Boston Millinery store, where he was writing metrical advertisements for spring hats, and put him in the Customs House. This got him a start; and he has done well ever since. . . . I write you chiefly as founder of the Elizabethan Club. Would there be anything he could do at a salary of five hundred dollars a year annually that could be given him or any steps that could be taken toward getting that annuity for him? [24]

11. "Painstaking little pedants . . ."

To George Otto Trevelyan

Washington, January 25, 1904

On the whole we have cause to be grateful to Professor Bury for his address inasmuch as it called out your really noble article on history. . . .

Aside from your actually showing what history should be, I am exceedingly glad that you spoke so plainly of Mr. Bury's proposition to make it what it should not be. I am sorry to say that I think the Burys are doing much damage to the cause of historic writing. . . . Fortunately I had enough good sense, or obstinacy, or something, to retain a subconscious belief that, inasmuch as books were meant to be read, good books ought to be interesting, and the best books capable in addition of giving one a lift upward in some direction. After a while it dawned on me that all of the conscientious, industrious, painstaking little pedants, who would have been useful people in a rather small way if they had understood their own limitations, had become, because of their conceit, distinctly noxious. They solemnly believed that if there were only enough of them, and that if they only collected enough facts of all kinds and sorts, there would cease to be any need hereafter for great writers, great thinkers. They looked for instance at Justin Winsor's conglomerate narrative history of America —a book which is either literature or science in the sense in which a second-rate cyclopedia is literature and science—as showing an "advance" upon Francis Parkman— Heaven save the mark! Each of them was a good-enough day laborer, trundling his barrowful of bricks and worthy of his hire; as long as they saw themselves as they were they were worthy of all respect; but when they imagined that by their activity they rendered the work of an architect unnecessary they became both absurd and mischievous.

Unfortunately, with us, it is these small men who do most of the his-

[24] *Letters VIII*, p. 887.

toric teaching in the colleges. They have done much real harm in preventing the development of students who might have a large grasp of what history should really be. They represent what is in itself the excellent revolt against superficiality and lack of research, but they have grown into the opposite and equally noxious belief that research is all in all, that accumulation of facts is everything, and that the ideal history of the future will consist not even of the work of one huge pedant but of a multitude of articles by a multitude of small pedants. They are honestly unconscious that all they are doing is to gather bricks and stones, and that whether their work will or will not amount to anything really worthy depends entirely upon whether or not some great master builder hereafter arrives who will be able to go over their material, to reject the immense majority of it, and out of what is left to fashion some edifice of majesty and beauty instinct with the truth that both charms and teaches. A thousand Burys, and two thousand of the corresponding Germans whom he reverentially admires, would not in the aggregate begin to add to the wisdom of mankind what another Macaulay, should one arise, would add. The great historian must of course have the scientific spirit which gives the power of research, which enables one to marshal and weigh the facts, but unless his finished work is literature of a very high type small will be his claim to greatness.[25]

12. History as Literature

There has been much discussion as to whether history should not henceforth be treated as a branch of science rather than of literature. As with most such discussions, much of the matter in dispute has referred merely to terminology. Moreover, as regards part of the discussion, the minds of the contestants have not met, the propositions advanced by the two sides being neither mutually incompatible nor mutually relevant. There is, however, a real basis for conflict in so far as science claims exclusive possession of the field.

There was a time—we see it in the marvellous dawn of Hellenic life—when history was distinguished neither from poetry, from mythology, nor from the first dim beginnings of science. There was a more recent time, at the opening of Rome's brief period of literary splendor, when poetry was accepted by a great scientific philosopher as the appropriate vehicle for teaching the lessons of science and philosophy. There was a more recent time still—the time of Holland's leadership in arms and arts—when one of the two or three greatest world painters put his genius at the service of anatomists.

[25] *Letters III*, pp. 706–8.

In each case the steady growth of specialization has rendered such combination now impossible. Virgil left history to Livy; and when Tacitus had become possible Lucan was a rather absurd anachronism. The elder Darwin, when he endeavored to combine the functions of scientist and poet, may have thought of Lucretius as a model; but the great Darwin was incapable of such a mistake. The surgeons of to-day would prefer the services of a good photographer to those of Rembrandt—even were those of Rembrandt available.

As regards philosophy, as distinguished from material science and from history, the specialization has been incomplete. Poetry is still used as a vehicle for the teaching of philosophy. Goethe was as profound a thinker as Kant. He has influenced the thought of mankind far more deeply than Kant because he was also a great poet. . . .

Philosophy is a science just as history is a science. There is need in one case as in the other for vivid and powerful presentation of scientific matter in literary form.

This does not mean that there is the like need in the two cases. History can never be truthfully presented if the presentation is purely emotional. It can never be truthfully or usefully presented unless profound research, patient, laborious, painstaking, has preceded the presentation. No amount of self-communion and of pondering on the soul of mankind, no gorgeousness of literary imagery, can take the place of cool, serious, widely extended study. The vision of the great historian must be both wide and lofty. But it must be sane, clear, and based on full knowledge of the facts and of their interrelations. Otherwise we get merely a splendid bit of serious romance-writing, like Carlyle's "French Revolution." Many hard-working students, alive to the deficiencies of this kind of romance-writing, have grown to distrust not only all historical writing that is romantic, but all historical writing that is vivid. They feel that complete truthfulness must never be sacrificed to color. In this they are right. They also feel that complete truthfulness is incompatible with color. In this they are wrong. The immense importance of full knowledge of a mass of dry facts and gray details has so impressed them as to make them feel that the dryness and the grayness are in themselves meritorious.

These students have rendered invaluable service to history. They are right in many of their contentions. They see how literature and science have specialized. They realize that scientific methods are as necessary to the proper study of history as to the proper study of astronomy or zoology. They know that in many, perhaps in most, of its forms, literary ability is divorced from the restrained devotion to the actual fact which is as essential to the historian as to the scientist. They know that nowadays

237

science ostentatiously disclaims any connection with literature. They feel that if this is essential for science, it is no less essential for history.

There is much truth in all these contentions. Nevertheless, taking them all together, they do not indicate what these hard-working students believed that they indicate. Because history, science, and literature have all become specialized, the theory now is that science is definitely severed from literature and that history must follow suit. Not only do I refuse to accept this as true for history, but I do not even accept it as true for science.

Literature may be defined as that which has permanent interest because both of its substance and its form, aside from the mere technical value that inheres in a special treatise for specialists. For a great work of literature there is the same demand now that there always has been; and in any great work of literature the first element is great imaginative power. The imaginative power demanded for a great historian is different from that demanded for a great poet; but it is no less marked. Such imaginative power is in no sense incompatible with minute accuracy. On the contrary, very accurate, very real and vivid, presentation of the past can come only from one in whom the imaginative gift is strong. The industrious collector of dead facts bears to such a man precisely the relation that a photographer bears to Rembrandt. There are innumerable books, that is, innumerable volumes of printed matter between covers, which are excellent for their own purposes, but in which imagination would be as wholly out of place as in the blueprints of a sewer system or in the photographs taken to illustrate a work on comparative osteology. But the vitally necessary sewer system does not take the place of the cathedral of Rheims or of the Parthenon; no quantity of photographs will ever be equivalent to one Rembrandt; and the greatest mass of data, although indispensable to the work of a great historian, is in no shape or way a substitute for that work.

History, taught for a directly and immediately useful purpose to pupils and the teachers of pupils, is one of the necessary features of a sound education in democratic citizenship. A book containing such sound teaching, even if without any literary quality, may be as useful to the student and as creditable to the writer as a similar book on medicine. I am not slighting such a book when I say that, once it has achieved its worthy purpose, it can be permitted to lapse from human memory as a good book on medicine, which has outlived its usefulness, lapses from memory. But the historical work which does possess literary quality may be a permanent contribution to the sum of man's wisdom, enjoyment and inspiration. The writer of such a book must add wisdom to knowledge, and the gift of expression to the gift of imagination. . . . of history, a man who has at his finger-tips all the accumulated facts from the treasure-houses of the dead past. But he must also possess the power to marshal what is dead so that before our eyes it lives again.

Do not misunderstand me. In the field of historical research an immense amount can be done by men who have no literary power whatever. Moreover, the most painstaking and laborious research, covering long periods of years, is necessary in order to accumulate the material for any history worth writing at all. There are important bypaths of history, moreover, which hardly admit of treatment that would make them of interest to any but specialists. All this I fully admit. In particular I pay high honor to the patient and truthful investigator. He does an indispensable work. My claim is merely that such work should not exclude the work of the great master who can use the materials gathered, who has the gift of vision, the quality of the seer, the power himself to see what has happened and to make what he has seen clear to the vision of others. . . .

The great historian of the future will have easy access to innumerable facts patiently gathered by tens of thousands of investigators, whereas the great historian of the past had very few facts, and often had to gather most of these himself. The great historian of the future cannot be excused if he fails to draw on the vast storehouses of knowledge that have been accumulated, if he fails to profit by the wisdom and work of other men, which are now the common property of all intelligent men. He must use the instruments which the historians of the past did not have ready to hand. Yet even with these instruments he cannot do as good work as the best of the elder historians unless he has vision and imagination, the power to grasp what is essential and to reject the infinitely more numerous non-essentials, the power to embody ghosts, to put flesh and blood on dry bones, to make dead men living before our eyes. In short, he must have the power to take the science of history and turn it into literature. . . .

The work of the archæologist, the work of the anthropologist, the work of the palæo-ethnologist—out of all these a great literary historian may gather material indispensable for his use. He, and we, ought fully to acknowledge our debt to the collectors of these indispensable facts. The investigator in any line may do work which puts us all under lasting obligation to him, even though he be totally deficient in the art of literary expression, that is, totally deficient in the ability to convey vivid and life-like pictures to others of the past whose secrets he has laid bare. I would give no scanty or grudging acknowledgment to the deeds of such a man. He does a lasting service; whereas the man who tries to make literary expression cover his ignorance or misreading of facts renders less than no service. But the service done is immeasurably increased in value when

239

the man arises who from his study of a myriad dead fragments is able to paint some living picture of the past.

This is why the record as great writers preserve it has a value immeasurably beyond what is merely lifeless. Such a record pulses with immortal life. It may recount the deed or the thought of a hero at some supreme moment. It may be merely the portrayal of homely every-day life. This matters not, so long as in either event the genius of the historian enables him to paint in colors that do not fade. The cry of the Ten Thousand when they first saw the sea still stirs the hearts of men. The ruthless death-scene between Juhu and Jezebel; wicked Ahab, smitten by the chance arrow, and propped in his chariot until he died at sundown; Josiah, losing his life because he would not heed the prophet's solemn warning, and mourned by all the singing men and all the singing women—the fates of these kings and of this king's daughter, are part of the common stock of knowledge of mankind. They were petty rulers of petty principalities; yet, compared with them, mighty conquerors, who added empire to empire, Shalmaneser and Sargon, Amenhotep and Rameses, are but shadows; for the deeds and the deaths of the kings of Judah and Israel are written in words that, once read, cannot be forgotten. The Peloponnesian War bulks of unreal size to-day because it once seemed thus to bulk to a master mind. Only a great historian can fittingly deal with a very great subject; yet because the qualities of chief interest in human history can be shown on a small field no less than on a large one, some of the greatest historians have treated subjects that only their own genius rendered great.

So true is this that if great events lack a great historian, and a great poet writes about them, it is the poet who fixes them in the mind of mankind, so that in after-time importance the real has become the shadow and the shadow the reality. Shakespeare has definitely fixed the character of the Richard III of whom ordinary men think and speak. Keats forgot even the right name of the man who first saw the Pacific Ocean; yet it is his lines which leap to our minds when we think of the "wild surmise" felt by the indomitable explorer-conqueror from Spain when the vast new sea burst on his vision.

When, however, the historian has spoken, his work will never be undone. No poet can ever supersede what Napier wrote of the storming of Badajoz, of the British infantry at Albuera, and of the light artillery at Fuentes d'Oñoro. After Parkman had written of Montcalm and Wolfe there was left for other writers only what FitzGerald left for other translators of Omar Khayyàm. Much new light has been thrown on the history of the Byzantine Empire by the many men who have studied it of recent years; we read each new writer with pleasure and profit; and after reading each we take down a volume of Gibbon, with renewed thankfulness that a great writer was moved to do a great task.

The greatest of future archæologists will be the great historian who instead of being a mere antiquarian delver in dust-heaps has the genius to reconstruct for us the immense panorama of the past. He must possess knowledge. He must possess that without which knowledge is of so little use, wisdom. What he brings from the charnel-house he must use with such potent wizardry that we shall see the life that was and not the death that is. For remember that the past was life just as much as the present is life. Whether it be Egypt, or Mesopotamia, or Scandinavia with which he deals, the great historian, if the facts permit him, will put before us the men and women as they actually lived so that we shall recognize them for what they were, living beings. Men like Maspero, Breasted, and Weigall have already begun this work for the countries of the Nile and the Euphrates. For Scandinavia the groundwork was laid long ago in the "Heimskringla" and in such sagas as those of Burnt Njal and Gisli Soursop. Minute descriptions of mummies and of the furniture of tombs help us as little to understand the Egypt of the mighty days, as to sit inside the tomb of Mount Vernon would help us to see Washington the soldier leading to battle his scarred and tattered veterans, or Washington the statesman, by his serene strength of character, rendering it possible for his countrymen to establish themselves as one great nation.

The great historian must be able to paint for us the life of the plain people, the ordinary men and women, of the time of which he writes. He can do this only if he possesses the highest kind of imagination. Collections of figures no more give us a picture of the past than the reading of a tariff report on hides or woolens gives us an idea of the actual lives of the men and women who live on ranches or work in factories. The great historian will in as full measure as possible present to us the everyday life of the men and women of the age which he describes. Nothing that tells of this life will come amiss to him. The instruments of their labor and the weapons of their warfare, the wills that they wrote, the bargains that they made, and the songs that they sang when they feasted and made love: he must use them all. He must tell us of the toil of the ordinary times, and of the play by which that ordinary toil was broken. He must never forget that no event stands out entirely isolated. He must trace from its obscure and humble beginnings each of the movements that in its hour of triumph has shaken the world.

Yet he must not forget that the times that are extraordinary need especial portrayal. In the revolt against the old tendency of historians to deal exclusively with the spectacular and the exceptional, to treat only of war and oratory and government, many modern writers have gone to

241

the opposite extreme. They fail to realize that in the lives of nations as in the lives of men there are hours so fraught with weighty achievement, with triumph or defeat, with joy or sorrow, that each such hour may determine all the years that are to come thereafter, or may outweigh all the years that have gone before. In the writings of our historians, as in the lives of our ordinary citizens, we can neither afford to forget that it is the ordinary every-day life which counts most; nor yet that seasons come when ordinary qualities count for but little in the face of great contending forces of good and of evil, the outcome of whose strife determines whether the nation shall walk in the glory of the morning or in the gloom of spiritual death.

The historian must deal with the days of common things, and deal with them so that they shall interest us in reading of them as our own common things interest us as we live among them. He must trace the changes that come almost unseen, the slow and gradual growth that transforms for good or for evil the children and grandchildren so that they stand high above or far below the level on which their forefathers stood. He must also trace the great cataclysms that interrupt and divert this gradual development. He can no more afford to be blind to one class of phenomena than to the other. He must ever remember that while the worst offense of which he can be guilty is to write vividly and inaccurately, yet that unless he writes vividly he cannot write truthfully; for no amount of dull, painstaking detail will sum up as the whole truth unless the genius is there to paint the truth. . . .

The true historian will bring the past before our eyes as if it were the present. He will make us see as living men the hard-faced archers of Agincourt, and the war-worn spearmen who followed Alexander down beyond the rim of the known world. We shall hear grate on the coast of Britain the keels of the Low-Dutch sea-thieves whose children's children were to inherit unknown continents. We shall thrill to the triumphs of Hannibal. Gorgeous in our sight will rise the splendor of dead cities, and the might of the elder empires of which the very ruins crumbled to dust ages ago. Along ancient trade-routes, across the world's waste spaces, the caravans shall move; and the admirals of uncharted seas shall furrow the oceans with their lonely prows. Beyond the dim centuries we shall see the banners float above armed hosts. We shall see conquerors riding forward to victories that have changed the course of time. We shall listen to the prophecies of forgotten seers. Ours shall be the dreams of dreamers who dreamed greatly, and who saw in their vision peaks so lofty that never yet have they been reached by the sons and daughters of men. Dead poets shall sing to us the deeds of men of might and the love and the beauty of women. We shall see the dancing girls of Memphis. The scent of the flowers in the

Hanging Gardens of Babylon will be heavy to our senses. We shall sit at feast with the kings of Nineveh when they drink from ivory and gold. With Queen Meave in her sun-parlor we shall watch the nearing chariots of the champions. For us the war-horns of King Olaf shall wail across the flood, and the harps sound high at festivals in forgotten halls. The frowning strongholds of the barons of old shall rise before us, and the white palace-castles from whose windows Syrian princes once looked across the blue Ægean. We shall know the valor of the two-sworded Samurai. Ours shall be the hoary wisdom and the strange, crooked folly of the immemorial civilizations which tottered to a living death in India and in China. We shall see the terrible horsemen of Timour the Lame ride over the roof of the world; we shall hear the drums beat as the armies of Gustavus and Frederick and Napoleon drive forward to victory. Ours shall be the woe of burgher and peasant, and ours the stern joy when freemen triumph and justice comes to her own. The agony of the galley-slaves shall be ours, and the rejoicing when the wicked are brought low and the men of evil days have their reward. We shall see the glory of triumphant violence, and the revel of those who do wrong in high places; and the broken-hearted despair that lies beneath the glory and the revel. We shall also see the supreme righteousness of the wars for freedom and justice, and know that the men who fell in these wars made all mankind their debtors.

Some day the historians will tell us of these things.[26]

[26] "History as Literature" (1913). *Works XII,* pp. 3–23.

Adventurer in the Wide Waste Spaces

The lure that the "wild waste spaces" exercised on Theodore Roosevelt in his youth lost none of its pulling power as the years passed, though the slender frame grew portly. As President, Mr. Roosevelt went on extensive hunting trips in Louisiana, Colorado and elsewhere in the United States. Six weeks after he left the Presidency in 1909, he embarked with his son, Kermit, for Africa, for a year's hunt of big game. He undertook the exploration of the River of Doubt in Brazil at the age of fifty-five. "It was my last chance," he explained, "to be a boy."

1. The Joy of Living

The man should have youth and strength who seeks adventure in the wide, waste spaces of the earth, in the marshes, and among the vast mountain masses, in the northern forests, amid the steaming jungles of the tropics, or on the deserts of sand or of snow. He must long greatly for the lonely winds that blow across the wilderness, and for sunrise and sunset over the rim of the empty world. His heart must thrill for the saddle and not for the hearthstone. He must be helmsman and chief, the cragsman, the rifleman, the boat steerer. He must be the wielder of axe and of paddle, the rider of fiery horses, the master of the craft that leaps through white water. His eye must be true and quick, his hand steady and strong. His heart must never fail nor his head grow bewildered, whether he face brute and human foes, or the frowning strength of hostile nature, or the awful fear that grips those who are lost in trackless lands. Wearing toil and hardship shall be his; thirst and famine he shall face, and burning fever. Death shall come to greet him with poison-fang or poison-arrow, in shape of charging beast or of scaly things that lurk in lake and river; it shall lie in wait for him among untrodden forests, in the swirl of wild waters, and in the blast of snow blizzard or thunder-shattered hurricane.

Not many men can with wisdom make such a life their permanent and serious occupation. Those whose tasks lie along other lines can lead it for but a few years. For them it must normally come in the hardy vigor of their youth, before the beat of the blood has grown sluggish in their veins.

Nevertheless, older men also can find joy in such a life, although in their case it must be led only on the outskirts of adventure, and although the part they play therein must be that of the onlooker rather than that of the doer. The feats of prowess are for others. It is for other men to face the peril of unknown lands, to master unbroken horses, and to hold their own among their fellows with bodies of supple strength. But much, very much, remains for the man who has "warmed both hands before the fire of life," and who, although he loves the great cities, loves even more the fenceless grass-land, and the forest-clad hills.

The grandest scenery of the world is his to look at if he chooses; and he can witness the strange ways of tribes who have survived into an alien age from an immemorial past, tribes whose priests dance in honor of the serpent and worship the spirits of the wolf and the bear. Far and wide, all the continents are open to him as they never were to any of his forefathers; the Nile and the Paraguay are easy of access, and the border-land between savagery and civilization; and the veil of the past has been lifted so that he can dimly see how, in time immeasurably remote, his ancestors—no less remote—led furtive lives among uncouth and terrible beasts, whose kind has perished utterly from the face of the earth. He will take books with him as he journeys; for the keenest enjoyment of the wilderness is reserved for him who enjoys also the garnered wisdom of the present and the past. He will take pleasure in the companionship of the men of the open; in South America, the daring and reckless horsemen who guard the herds of the grazing country, and the dark-skinned paddlers who guide their clumsy dugouts down the dangerous equatorial rivers; the white and red and half-breed hunters of the Rockies, and of the Canadian woodland; and in Africa the faithful black gun-bearers who have stood steadily at his elbow when the lion came on with coughing grunts, or when the huge mass of the charging elephant burst asunder the vine-tangled branches.

The beauty and charm of the wilderness are his for the asking, for the edges of the wilderness lie close beside the beaten roads of present travel. He can see the red splendor of desert sunsets, and the unearthly glory of the afterglow on the battlements of desolate mountains. In sapphire gulfs of ocean he can visit islets, above which the wings of myriads of sea-fowl make a kind of shifting cuneiform script in the air. He can ride along the brink of the stupendous cliff-walled canyon, where eagles soar below him, and cougars make their lairs on the ledges and harry the big-horned sheep. He can journey through the northern forests, the home of the giant

246

moose, the forests of fragrant and murmuring life in summer, the iron-bound and melancholy forests of winter.

The joy of living is his who has the heart to demand it.[1]

2. The Hunter Hunted

It was shortly after three when we again pushed off in the canoe, and headed for the western end of the lake, for the landing from which the portage led to our cabin. It had been a red-letter day, of the ordinary hunting red-letter type. I had no conception that the real adventure still lay in front of us.

When half a mile from the landing we saw another big bull moose on the edge of the shore ahead of us. It looked and was—if anything—even bigger-bodied than the one I had shot in the morning, with antlers almost as large and rather more palmated. We paddled up to within a hundred yards of it, laughing and talking, and remarking how eager we would have been if we had not already got our moose. At first it did not seem to notice us. Then it looked at us, but paid us no further heed. We were rather surprised at this but paddled on past it, and it then walked along the shore after us. We still supposed that it did not realize what we were. But another hundred yards put us to windward of it. Instead of turning into the forest when it got our wind, it merely bristled up the hair on its withers, shook its head, and continued to walk after the canoe, along the shore. I had heard of bull moose, during the rut, attacking men unprovoked, if the men were close up, but never of anything as wanton and deliberate as this action, and I could hardly believe the moose meant mischief, but Arthur said it did; and obviously we could not land with the big, evil-looking beast coming for us—and, of course, I was most anxious not to have to shoot it. So we turned the canoe round and paddled on our back track. But the moose promptly turned and followed us along the shore. We yelled at him, and Odilon struck the canoe with his paddle, but with no effect. After going a few hundred yards we again turned and resumed our former course; and as promptly the moose turned and followed us, shaking his head and threatening us. He seemed to be getting more angry, and evidently meant mischief. We now continued our course until we were opposite the portage landing, and about a hundred yards away from it; the water was shallow and we did not wish to venture closer, lest the moose might catch us if he charged. When he came to the portage trail he turned up it, sniffing at our footsteps of the morning, and walked along it into the woods; and we hoped that now he would become uneasy and go off. After waiting a few minutes we paddled slowly toward the landing, but before

[1] "A Booklover's Holidays in the Open" (1916). *Works III*, pp. 181-3.

reaching it we caught his loom in the shadow, as he stood facing us some distance down the trail. As soon as we stopped he rushed down the trail toward us, coming in to the lake; and we backed hastily into deep water. He vented his rage on a small tree, which he wrecked with his antlers. We continued to paddle round the head of the bay, and he followed us; we still hoped we might get him away from the portage, and that he would go into the woods. But when we turned he followed us back, and thus went to and fro with us. Where the water was deep near shore we pushed the canoe close in to him, and he promptly rushed down to the water's edge, shaking his head, and striking the earth with his fore hoofs. We shouted at him, but with no effect. As he paraded along the shore he opened his mouth, lolling out his tongue; and now and then when he faced us he ran out his tongue and licked the end of his muzzle with it. Once, with head down, he bounded or galloped round in a half-circle; and from time to time he grunted or uttered a low, menacing roar. Altogether the huge black beast looked like a formidable customer, and was evidently in a most evil rage and bent on man-killing.

For over an hour he thus kept us from the shore, running to meet us wherever we tried to go. The afternoon was waning, a cold wind began to blow, shifting as it blew. He was not a pleasant-looking beast to meet in the woods in the dusk. We were at our wits' end what to do. At last he turned, shook his head, and with a flourish of his heels galloped—not trotted—for fifty yards up beside the little river which paralleled the portage trail. I called Arthur's attention to this, as he had been telling me that a big bull never galloped. Then the moose disappeared at a trot around the bend. We waited a few minutes, cautiously landed, and started along the trail, watching to see if the bull was lying in wait for us; Arthur telling me that if he now attacked us I must shoot him at once or he would kill somebody.

A couple of hundred yards on, the trail led within a few yards of the little river. As we reached this point a smashing in the brush beyond the opposite bank caused us to wheel; and the great bull came headlong for us, while Arthur called to me to shoot. With a last hope of frightening him I fired over his head, without the slightest effect. At a slashing trot he crossed the river, shaking his head, his ears back, the hair on his withers bristling. "Tirez, m'sieu, tirez; vite, vite!" called Arthur, and when the bull was not thirty feet off I put a bullet into his chest, in the sticking-point. It was a mortal wound, and stopped him short; I fired into his chest again, and this wound, too, would by itself have been fatal. He turned and recrossed the stream, falling to a third shot, but as we approached he struggled to his feet, grunting savagely, and I killed him as he came toward us.

248

I was sorry to have to kill him, but there was no alternative. As it was, I only stopped him in the nick of time, and had I not shot straight, at least one of us would have paid forfeit with his life in another second. Even in Africa I have never known anything but a rogue elephant or buffalo, or an occasional rhinoceros, to attack so viciously or with such premeditation when itself neither wounded nor threatened.[2]

3. Prologue to Africa

To Cecil A. Spring-Rice

Oyster Bay, September 17, 1908

Oh, you beloved Mrs. Gummidge! If you feel as melancholy over my trip in Africa as you do over the future of the race generally, at least you must not share the feeling too fully with Mrs. Roosevelt. I laughed until I almost cried over your sending her the pamphlet upon the "sleeping sickness," and explaining in your letter that it was perfectly possible that I would not die of that, because (in the event of my not previously being eaten by a lion or crocodile, or killed by an infuriated elephant or buffalo) malarial fever or a tribe of enraged savages might take me off before the sleeping sickness got at me! I am bound to say, however, that the letter gave Mrs. Roosevelt a keen tho melancholy enjoyment, and she will now have the feeling that she is justified in a Roman-matron-like attitude of heroically bidding me to my death when I sail in a well-equipped steamer for an entirely comfortable and mild little hunting trip.

Seriously, both of us were really touched and pleased with your letters and with your thought of me. I feel excessively melancholy at being separated for so long from Mrs. Roosevelt, and I shall be so homesick, especially when, as I suppose will be the case, I have a slight attack of fever or something of the kind, that I shall not know quite what to do with myself. But I am convinced that it is the wise thing for me to go; and also I freely admit that I am looking forward to the trip! I should like to have stayed on in the Presidency, and I make no pretense that I am glad to be relieved of my official duties. The only reason I did not stay on was because I felt that I ought not to; and I am exceedingly glad that I am to have the interest of this African trip before me. I think I wrote you that I am going for the National Museum. I shall take a couple of naturalists who are field taxidermists with me, and any specimens I shoot will be sent to the Museum. The Sirdar has been most kind, and he is going to give me a little boat which will enable me to get up the smaller tributaries of the Nile.

[2] *Ibid.*, pp. 396–9.

Outside of this I do not believe I shall need any Government assistance; but a number of Englishmen, Selous, Buxton, Pease and others, have been too kind for anything in advising me and helping me secure my equipment.[3]

4. "I speak of Africa"

"I speak of Africa and golden joys"; the joy of wandering through lonely lands; the joy of hunting the mighty and terrible lords of the wilderness, the cunning, the wary, and the grim.

In these greatest of the world's great hunting-grounds there are mountain peaks whose snows are dazzling under the equatorial sun; swamps where the slime oozes and bubbles and festers in the steaming heat; lakes like seas; skies that burn above deserts where the iron desolation is shrouded from view by the wavering mockery of the mirage; vast grassy plains where palms and thorn-trees fringe the dwindling streams; mighty rivers rushing out of the heart of the continent through the sadness of endless marshes; forests of gorgeous beauty, where death broods in the dark and silent depths.

There are regions as healthy as the northland; and other regions, radiant with bright-hued flowers, birds, and butterflies, odorous with sweet and heavy scents, but treacherous in their beauty, and sinister to human life. On the land and in the water there are dread brutes that feed on the flesh of man; among the lower things that crawl and fly and sting and bite, he finds swarming foes far more evil and deadly than any beast or reptile; foes that kill his crops and his cattle, foes before which he himself perishes in his hundreds of thousands. . . .

The land teems with beasts of the chase, infinite in number and in-incredible in variety. It holds the fiercest beasts of ravin, and the fleetest and most timid of those beings that live in undying fear of talon and fang. It holds the largest and the smallest of hoofed animals. It holds the mightiest creatures that tread the earth or swim in its rivers; it also holds distant kinsfolk of these same creatures, no bigger than woodchucks, which dwell in crannies of the rocks and in the tree-tops. There are antelope smaller than hares, and antelope larger than oxen. There are creatures which are the embodiments of grace; and others whose huge ungainliness is like that of a shape in a nightmare. . . .

These things can be told. But there are no words that can tell the hidden spirit of the wilderness, that can reveal its mystery, its melancholy, and its charm. There is delight in the hardy life of the open, in long rides rifle in hand, in the thrill of the fight with dangerous game. Apart from this, yet

[3] *Letters VI,* pp. 1241–2.

250

mingled with it, is the strong attraction of the silent places, of the large tropic moons, and the splendor of the new stars; where the wanderer sees the awful glory of sunrise and sunset in the wide waste spaces of the earth, unworn of man, and changed only by the slow change of the ages through time everlasting.[4]

5. Primeval Man

It was my good fortune throughout one year of my life to roam, rifle in hand, over the empty, sunlit African wastes, and at night to camp by palm and thorn tree on the banks of the African rivers. Day after day I watched the thronging herds of wild creatures and the sly, furtive human life of the wilderness. Often and often, as I so watched, my thoughts went back through measureless time to the ages when the western lands where my people now dwell, and the northern lands of the eastern world where their remote forefathers once dwelt, were filled with just such a wild life. In those days these far-back ancestors of ours led the same lives of suspicion and vigilant cunning among the beasts of the forest and plain that are now led by the wildest African savages. In that immemorial past the beasts conditioned the lives of men as they conditioned the lives of one another; for the chief factors in man's existence were then the living things upon which he preyed and the fearsome creatures which sometimes made prey of him. Ages were to pass before his mastery grew to such a point that the fanged things he once had feared, and the hoofed things success in the chase of which had once meant to him life or death, became negligible factors in his existence.

Some of the naked or half skin-clad savages whom I met and with whom I hunted were still leading precisely the life of these ages-dead forebears of ours. More than once I spent days in heavy forests at the foot of equatorial mountains in company with small parties of 'Ndorobo hunters. They were men of the deep woods, as stealthy and wary as any of the woodland creatures. In each case they knew and trusted my companion—who was in one instance a settler, a famous lion-hunter, and in the other a noted professional elephant-hunter. Yet even so their trust did not extend to letting a stranger like himself see their women and children, who had retreated into some forest fastness from which we were kept aloof. The men wore each a small fur cape over the shoulders. Otherwise they were absolutely naked. Each carried a pouch and a spear. The spear head was of iron, obtained from some of the settled tribes. Except this iron spear head, not one of their few belongings differed from what it doubtless was long prior to the age of metals. They carried bows, strung with zebra gut, and arrows of

[4] "Africa Game Trails" (1910). *Works IV,* pp. XXII–XXV.

which the wooden tips were poisoned. They did not cultivate the earth; they owned a few dogs; and they lived on honey and game. They killed monkeys and hyraxes, occasionally forest hog and bongo—a beautifully striped forest antelope as big as a Jersey cow—and now and then elephant, rhino, and buffalo, and, on the open plains at the edge of the forest, zebra. . . . Very rarely the hunters killed a leopard, and sometimes a leopard pounced on one of them. The lion they feared greatly, but it did not enter the woods, and they were in danger from it only if they ventured on the plain. . . . They were able to exist at all only because they had developed their senses and powers to a degree that placed them level with the creatures they dreaded or preyed upon. They climbed the huge trees almost as well as the big black-and-white monkey. I had with me gun-bearers from the hunting tribes of the plains, men accustomed to the chase, but brought up in villages where there was tillage and where goats and cattle were raised. These gun-bearers of mine were good trackers and at home in the ordinary wilderness. But compared to these true wild men of the forest they might almost as well have been town-bred. The 'Ndorobo trackers would take me straight to some particular tree or spot of ground, through miles of dense, steaming woodland every rod of which looked like every other, returning with unerring precision to a goal which my gun-bearers would have been as helpless to find again as I was myself; and they interpreted trails and signs and footprint-scrapes which we either hardly saw or else misread.

Doubtless the ancestors, or some of the ancestors, of these men had lived in the land just as they themselves now did, for untold generations before the soil-tillers and cattle-owners came into it. They had shrunk from the advent of the latter, and as a rule were found only in isolated tracts which were useless for tillage or pasturage, the dense forest forming their habitual dwelling-place and retreat of safety. From the best hunting-grounds, those where the great game teemed, they had been driven; yet these hunting-grounds were often untenanted by human beings for much of the year, being visited only at certain seasons by the cattle-growing nomads.

Often these hunting-grounds offered sights of wonder and enchantment. Day after day I rode across them without seeing, from dawn to sundown, a human being save the faithful black followers, hawk-eyed and steel-thewed, who trudged behind me. Sometimes the plains were seas of wind-rippled grass. Sometimes they were dotted with clumps of low thorn-trees or broken by barren, boldly outlined hills. Our camp might be pitched by a muddy pool, with only stunted thorns near by; or on the edge of a shrunken river, under the dense shade of some great, brilliantly green fig-tree; or in a grove of huge, flat-topped acacias with yellow trunks and foliage like the most delicate lace; or where the long fronds of palms moved with a ceaseless, dry rustle in the evening breeze. At the drinking-holes, in pond or river, as the afternoon waned, or occasionally after nightfall when the moon was bright, I sometimes lay to see the game filing down to drink. . . .

Africa is a country of trails. Across the high velt, in every direction run the tangled trails of the multitudes of game that have lived thereon from time immemorial. The great beasts of the marsh and the forest made therein broad and muddy trails which often offer the only pathway by which a man can enter the sombre depths. In wet ground and dry alike are also found the trails of savage man. They lead from village to village, and in places they stretch for hundreds of miles, where trading parties have worn them in the search for ivory, or in the old days when raiding or pur-chasing slaves. The trails made by the men are made much as the beasts make theirs. They are generally longer and better defined, although I have seen hippo tracks more deeply marked than any made by savage man. But they are made simply by men following in one another's footsteps, and they are never quite straight. They bend now a little to one side, now a little to the other, and sudden loops mark the spot where some vanished obstacle once stood; around it the first trail-makers went, and their succes-sors have ever trodden in their footsteps even though the need for so doing has long passed away. . . .[5]

Death by violence, death by cold, death by starvation—these are the normal endings of the stately and beautiful creatures of the wilderness. The sentimentalists who prattle about the peaceful life of nature do not realize its utter mercilessness; although all they would have to do would be to look at the birds in the winter woods, or even at the insects on a cold morning or cold evening. Life is hard and cruel for all the lower crea-tures, and for man also in what the sentimentalists call a "state of nature." The savage of today shows us what the fancied age of gold of our ances-tors was really like; it was an age when hunger, cold, violence, and iron cruelty were the ordinary accompaniments of life. . . .[6]

In this desolate and lonely land the majesty of the storms impressed on the beholder a sense of awe and solemn exaltation. Tossing their crests, and riven by lightning, they gathered in their wrath from every quarter of the heavens, and darkness was before and under them; then, in the lull of a moment, they might break apart, while the sun turned the rain to silver and the rainbows were set in the sky; but always they gathered again, menacing and mighty—for the promise of the bow was never kept, and ever the clouds returned after the rain. Once as I rode facing Kenia the

[5] *Works III*, pp. 303–6.
[6] *Works IV*, p. 169.

253

clouds tore asunder, to right and left, and the mountain towered between, while across its base was flung a radiant arch. But almost at once the many-colored glory was dimmed; for in splendor and terror the storm strode in front, and shrouded all things from sight in thunder-shattered sheets of rain.[7]

6. Lion

In a few minutes Tarlton pointed out the lion, a splendid old fellow, a heavy male wih a yellow-and-black mane; and after him we went. There was no need to go fast; he was too burly and too savage to run hard, and we were anxious that our hands should be reasonably steady when we shot; all told, the horses, galloping and cantering, did not take us two miles.

The lion stopped and lay down behind a bush; jumping off I took a shot at him at two hundred yards, but only wounded him slightly in one paw; and after a moment's sullen hesitation off he went, lashing his tail. We mounted our horses and went after him; Tarlton lost sight of him, but I marked him lying down behind a low grassy ant-hill. Again we dismounted at a distance of two hundred yards; Tarlton telling me that now he was sure to charge. . . .

Again I knelt and fired; but the mass of hair on the lion made me think he was nearer than he was, and I undershot, inflicted a flesh wound that was neither crippling nor fatal. He was already grunting savagely and toss-ing his tail erect, with his head held low; and at the shot the great sinewy beast came toward us with the speed of a greyhound. Tarlton then, very properly, fired, for lion-hunting is no child's play, and it is not good to run risks. Ordinarily it is a very mean thing to experience joy at a friend's miss; but this was not an ordinary case, and I felt keen delight when the bullet from the badly sighted rifle missed, striking the ground many yards short. I was sighting carefully, from my knee, and I knew I had the lion all right; for though he galloped at a great pace, he came on steadily—ears laid back, and uttering terrific coughing grunts—and there was now no question of making allowance for distance, nor, as he was out in the open, for the fact that he had not before been distinctly visible. The bead of my fore-sight was exactly on the centre of his chest as I pressed the trigger, and the bullet went as true as if the place had been plotted with dividers. The blow brought him up all standing, and he fell forward on his head. The soft-nosed Winchester bullet had gone straight through the chest cavity, smashing the lungs and the big blood-vessels of the heart. Painfully he recovered his feet, and tried to come on, his ferocious courage holding out to the last; but he staggered, and turned from side to side,

[7] *Ibid.*, p. 231.

unable to stand firmly, still less to advance at a faster pace than a walk. He had not ten seconds to live; but it is a sound principle to take no chances with lions. Tarlton hit him with his second bullet, probably in the shoulder; and with my next shot I broke his neck. I had stopped him when he was still a hundred yards away; and certainly no finer sight could be imagined than that of this great maned lion as he charged. . . .

The lion was a big old male, still in his prime. Between uprights his length was nine feet four inches, and his weight 410 pounds, for he was not fat. We skinned him and started for camp, which we reached after dark. There was a thunderstorm in the southwest, and in the red sunset that burned behind us the rain-clouds turned to many gorgeous hues. Then daylight failed, the clouds cleared, and, as we made our way across the formless plain, the half-moon hung high overhead, strange stars shone in the brilliant heavens, and the Southern Cross lay radiant above the skyline.[8]

7. Elephants

We could hear the elephants, and under Cuninghame's lead we walked more cautiously than ever. The wind was right, and the trail of one elephant led close alongside that of the rest of the herd, and parallel thereto. It was about noon. The elephants moved slowly, and we listened to the boughs crack, and now and then to the curious internal rumblings of the great beasts. Carefully, every sense on the alert, we kept pace with them. My double-barrel was in my hands, and, whenever possible, as I followed the trail, I stepped in the huge footprints of the elephant, for where such a weight had pressed there were no sticks left to crack under my feet.

It made our veins thrill thus for half an hour to creep stealthily along, but a few rods from the herd, never able to see it, because of the extreme denseness of the cover, but always hearing first one and then another of its members, and always trying to guess what each one might do, and keeping ceaselessly ready for whatever might befall. A flock of hornbills flew up with noisy clamor, but the elephants did not heed them.

At last we came in sight of the mighty game. The trail took a twist to one side, and there, thirty yards in front of us, we made out part of the gray and massive head of an elephant resting his tusks on the branches of a young tree. A couple of minutes passed before, by cautious scrutiny, we were able to tell whether the animal was a cow or a bull, and whether, if a bull, it carried heavy enough tusks. Then we saw that it was a big bull with good ivory. It turned its head in my direction and I saw its eye; and I fired a little to one side of the eye, at a spot which I thought would lead

[8] *Ibid.*, pp. 162–3.

to the brain. I struck exactly where I aimed, but the head of an elephant is enormous and the brain small, and the bullet missed it. However, the shock momentarily stunned the beast. He stumbled forward, half falling, and as he recovered I fired with the second barrel, again aiming for the brain. This time the bullet sped true, and as I lowered the rifle from my shoulder, I saw the great lord of the forest come crashing to the ground.

But at that very instant, before there was a moment's time in which to reload, the thick bushes parted immediately on my left front, and through them surged the vast bulk of a charging bull elephant, the matted mass of tough creepers snapping like packthread before his rush. He was so close that he could have touched me with his trunk. I leaped to one side and dodged behind a tree trunk, opening the rifle, throwing out the empty shells, and slipping in two cartridges. Meanwhile Cuninghame fired right and left, at the same time throwing himself into the bushes on the other side. Both his bullets went home, and the bull stopped short in his charge, wheeled, and immediately disappeared in the thick cover. We ran forward, but the forest had closed over his wake. We heard him trumpet shrilly, and then all sounds ceased.

So back we turned to where the dead tusker lay. . . . There was the usual scene of joyful excitement among the gun-bearers—who had behaved excellently—and among the wild bush people who had done the tracking for us. . . . Chattering like monkeys, and as happy as possible, all, porters, gun-bearers, and 'Ndorobo alike, began the work of skinning and cutting up the quarry, under the leadership and supervision of Heller and Cuninghame, and soon they were all splashed with blood from head to foot. One of the trackers took off his blanket and squatted stark naked inside the carcass the better to use his knife. Each laborer rewarded himself by cutting off strips of meat for his private store, and hung them in red festoons from the branches round about. There was no let-up in the work until it was stopped by darkness.

Our tents were pitched in a small open glade a hundred yards from the dead elephant. The night was clear, the stars shone brightly, and in the west the young moon hung just above the line of tall tree-tops. Fires were speedily kindled and the men sat around them, feasting and singing in a strange minor tone until late in the night. The flickering light left them at one moment in black obscurity, and the next brought into bold relief their sinewy crouching figures, their dark faces, gleaming eyes and flashing teeth. . . .[9]

It was mid-afternoon when Kermit and I reached our new camping-place. Soon afterward word was brought us that some elephants were near by; we were told that the beasts were in the habit of devastating the sham-

[9] *Ibid.*, pp. 210–12.

bas, and were bold and truculent, having killed a man who had tried to interfere with them. Kermit and I at once started after them, just as the last of the safari came in. . . .

In half an hour we came on fresh sign, and began to work cautiously along it. Our guide, a wild-looking savage with a blunt spear, went first, followed by my gun-bearer, Kongoni, who is excellent on spoor; then I came, followed by Kermit, and by the other gun-bearers. The country was covered with tall grass, and studded with numerous patches of jungle and small forest. In a few minutes we heard the elephants, four or five of them, feeding in thick jungle where the vines that hung in tangled masses from the trees and that draped the bushes made dark caves of greenery. It was difficult to find any space clear enough to see thirty yards ahead. Fortunately there was no wind whatever. We picked out the spoor of a big bull and for an hour and a half we followed it, Kongoni usually in the lead. Two or three times, as we threaded our way among the bushes, as noiselessly as possible, we caught glimpses of gray, shadowy bulks, but only for a second at a time, and never with sufficient distinctness to shoot. The elephants were feeding, tearing down the branches of a rather large-leaved tree with bark like that of a scrub-oak and big pods containing beans; evidently these beans were a favorite food. They fed in circles and zigzags, but toward camp, until they were not much more than half a mile from it, and the noise made by the porters in talking and gathering wood was plainly audible; but the elephants paid no heed to it, being evidently too much accustomed to the natives to have much fear of man. We continually heard them breaking branches, and making rumbling or squeaking sounds. They then fed slowly along in the opposite direction, and got into rather more open country; and we followed faster in the big footprints of the bull we had selected.

Suddenly in an open glade Kongoni crouched and beckoned to me, and through a bush I caught the loom of the tusker. But at that instant he either heard us, saw us, or caught a whiff of our wind, and without a moment's hesitation he himself assumed the offensive. With his huge ears cocked at right angles to his head, and his trunk hanging down, he charged full tilt at us, coming steadily, silently, and at a great pace, his feet swishing through the long grass; and a formidable monster he looked.

At forty yards I fired the right barrel of the Holland into his head, and though I missed the brain the shock dazed him and brought him to an instant halt. Immediately Kermit put a bullet from the Winchester into his head; as he wheeled I gave him the second barrel between the neck and shoulder, through his ear; and Kermit gave him three more shots before he slewed round and disappeared.

There were not many minutes of daylight left, and we followed hard on his trail, Kongoni leading. At first there was only an occasional gout of dark blood; but soon we found splashes of red froth from the lungs; then we came to where he had fallen, and then we heard him crashing among the branches in thick jungle to the right. In we went after him, through the gathering gloom, Kongoni leading and I close behind, with the rifle ready for instant action; for though his strength was evidently fast failing, he was also evidently in a savage temper, anxious to wreak his vengeance before he died. On we went, following the bloody trail through the dim, cavernous windings in the dark, vine-covered jungle; we heard him smash the branches but a few yards ahead, and fall and rise; and stealing forward Kermit and I slipped up to within a dozen feet of him as he stood on the other side of some small twisted trees, hung with a mat of creepers. I put a bullet into his heart, Kermit fired, each of us fired again on the instant; the mighty bull threw up his trunk, crashed over backward, and lay dead on his side among the bushes . . . a giant in death.[10]

8. *Across the Navajo Desert*

The sun rose in burning glory, and through the breathless heat we drove the pack-train before us toward the crossing of the Colorado. Hour after hour we plodded ahead. The cliff line bent back at an angle, and we followed into the valley of the Colorado. The trail edged in toward the high cliffs as they gradually drew toward the river. At last it followed along the base of the frowning rock masses. Far off on our right lay the Colorado; on its opposite side the broad river-valley was hemmed in by another line of cliffs, at whose foot we were to travel for two days after crossing the river.

The landscape had become one of incredible wildness, of tremendous and desolate majesty. No one could paint or describe it save one of the great masters of imaginative art or literature—a Turner or Browning or Poe. The sullen rock walls towered hundreds of feet aloft, with something about their grim savagery that suggested both the terrible and the grotesque. All life was absent, both from them and from the fantastic barrenness of the boulder-strewn land at their bases. The ground was burned out or washed bare. In one place a little stream trickled forth at the bottom of a ravine, but even here no grass grew—only little clusters of a coarse weed with flaring white flowers that looked as if it throve on poisoned soil. In the still heat "we saw the silences move by and beckon." The cliffs were channelled into myriad forms—battlements, spires, pillars, buttressed towers, flying arches; they looked like the ruined castles and temples of the monstrous devil-deities of some vanished race. All were

[10] *Ibid.,* pp. 321–2.

ruins—ruins vaster than those of any structures ever reared by the hands of men—as if some magic city, built by warlocks and sorcerers, had been wrecked by the wrath of the elder gods. Evil dwelt in the silent places; from battlement to lonely battlement fiends' voices might have raved; in the utter desolation of each empty valley the squat blind tower might have stood, and giants lolled at length to see the death of a soul at bay.

As the afternoon wore on, storm boded in the south. The day grew sombre; to the desolation of the blinding light succeeded the desolation of utter gloom. The echoes of the thunder rolled among the crags, and lightning jagged the darkness. The heavens burst, and the downpour drove in our faces; then through cloud rifts the sun's beams shone again and we looked on "the shining face of rain whose hair a great wind scattereth."

At Lee's Ferry . . . the cliffs, a medley of bold colors and striking forms, come close to the river's brink on either side; but at this one point there is a break in the canyon walls and a ferry can be run. . . .

For two days we drove southward through the desert country, along the foot of a range of red cliffs. In places the sand was heavy; in others the ground was hard, and the teams made good progress. There were little water-holes, usually more or less alkaline, ten or fifteen miles apart. At these the Navajos were watering their big flocks of sheep and goats, their horses and donkeys, and their few cattle. . . .

During the second day of our southward journey the Painted Desert, in gaudy desolation, lay far to our right; and we crossed tongues and patches of the queer formation, with its hard, bright colors. Red and purple, green and bluish, orange and gray and umber brown, the streaked and splashed clays and marls had been carved by wind and weather into a thousand outlandish forms. Funnel-shaped sand-storms moved across the waste. We climbed gradually upward to the top of the mesa. The yellow sand grew heavier and deeper. There were occasional short streams from springs; but they ran in deep gullies, with nothing to tell of their presence; never a tree near by and hardly a bush or a tuft of grass, unless planted and tended by man. We passed the stone walls of an abandoned trading-post. The desert had claimed its own. The ruins lay close to a low range of cliffs; the white sand, dazzling under the sun, had drifted everywhere; there was not a plant, not a green thing in sight—nothing but the parched and burning lifelessness of rock and sand. . . .

All next day we travelled through a parched, monotonous landscape, now and then meeting Navajos with their flocks and herds, and passing by an occasional Navajo "hogan," or hovel-like house, with its rough corral near by. . . .

That night . . . we camped in Bubbling Spring Valley. It would be hard to imagine a wilder or more beautiful spot; if in the Old World, the valley would surely be celebrated in song and story; here it is one among many others, all equally unknown. We camped by the bubbling spring of pure cold water from which it derives its name. The long, winding valley was carpeted with emerald green, varied by wide bands and ribbons of lilac, where the tall ranks of bee-blossoms haunted by humming-birds, grew thickly, often for a quarter of a mile at a stretch. The valley was walled in by towering cliffs, a few of them sloping, most of them sheer-sided or with the tops overhanging; and there were isolated rock domes and pinnacles. As everywhere round about, the rocks were of many colors, and the colors varied from hour to hour, so that the hues of sunrise differed from those of noonday, and yet again from the long lights of sunset. The cliffs seemed orange and purple; and again they seemed vermilion and umber; or in the white glare they were white and yellow and light red. . . .

On we went, under the pitiless sun, through a contorted wilderness of scalped peaks and ranges, barren passes, and twisted valleys of sun-baked clay. We worked up and down steep hill slopes, and along tilted masses of sheet rock ending in cliffs. . . .

The last four miles were the worst of all for the horses. They led along the bottom of the Bridge canyon. It was covered with a torrent-strewn mass of smooth rocks, from pebbles to boulders of a ton's weight. It was a marvel that the horses got down without breaking their legs; and the poor beasts were nearly worn out.

Huge and bare the immense cliffs towered, on either hand, and in front and behind as the canyon turned right and left. They lifted straight above us for many hundreds of feet. The sunlight lingered on their tops; far below, we made our way like pigmies through the gloom of the great gorge. As we neared the Bridge the horse trail led up to one side, and along it the Indians drove the horses; we walked at the bottom of the canyon so as to see the Bridge first from below and realize its true size; for from above it is dwarfed by the immense mountain masses surrounding it.

At last we turned a corner, and the tremendous arch of the Bridge rose in front of us. It is surely one of the wonders of the world. It is a triumphal arch rather than a bridge, and spans the torrent bed in a majesty never shared by any arch ever reared by the mightiest conquerors among the nations of mankind. At this point there were deep pools in the rock bed of the canyon, with overhanging shelves under which grew beautiful ferns and hanging plants. Hot and tired, we greeted the chance for a bath, and as I floated on my back in the water the Bridge towered above me. Then we made camp. We built a blazing fire under one of the giant buttresses of the arch, and the leaping flame brought it momentarily into sudden re-lief. We white men talked and laughed by the fire, and the two silent Indians sat by and listened to us. The night was cloudless. The round moon rose under the arch and flooded the cliffs behind us with her radiance. After she passed behind the mountains the heavens were still brilliant with starlight, and whenever I waked I turned and gazed at the loom of the mighty arch against the clear night sky.[11]

9. The Hopi Snake-Dance

The snake-dance and antelope-dance, which we had come to see . . . are prayers or invocations for rain, the crowning blessing in this dry land. The rain is adored and invoked both as male and female; the gentle steady downpour is the female, the storm with lightning the male. The lightning-stick is "strong medicine," and is used in all these religious ceremonies. The snakes, the brothers of men, as are all living things in the Hopi creed, are besought to tell the beings of the underworld man's need of water.

As a former great chief at Washington I was admitted to the sacred room, or one-roomed house, the kiva, in which the chosen snake priests had for a fortnight been getting ready for the sacred dance. Very few white men have been thus admitted, and never unless it is known that they will treat with courtesy and respect what the Indians revere. Entrance to the house, which was sunk in the rock, was through a hole in the roof, down a ladder across whose top hung a cord from which fluttered three eagle plumes and dangled three small animal skins. Below was a room perhaps fifteen feet by twenty-five. One end of it, occupying perhaps a third of its length, was raised a foot above the rest, and the ladder led down to this raised part. Against the rear wall of this raised part or dais lay thirty odd rattlesnakes, most of them in a twined heap in one corner, but a dozen by themselves scattered along the wall. There was also a pot containing several striped ribbon-snakes, too lively to be left at large. Eight or ten priests, some old, some young, sat on the floor in the lower and larger two-thirds of the room, and greeted me with grave courtesy; they spread a blanket on the edge of the dais, and I sat down, with my back to the snakes and about eight feet from them; a little behind and to one side of me sat a priest with a kind of fan or brush made of two or three wing-plumes of an eagle, who kept quiet guard over his serpent wards. At the farther end of the room was the altar; the rude picture of a coyote was painted on the floor, and on the four sides of this coyote picture were paintings of snakes; on three sides it was hemmed in by lightning-sticks, or thunder-sticks, standing upright in little clay cups and on the fourth side by eagle plumes held similarly erect. . . .

The snakes behind me never rattled or showed any signs of anger; the

[11] *Works III*, pp. 205–16.

translator volunteered the remark that they were peaceable because they had been given medicine—whatever that might mean, supposing the statement to be true according to the sense in which the words are accepted by plainsmen. But several of them were active in the sluggish rattlesnake fashion. One glided sinuously toward me; when he was a yard away, I pointed him out to the watcher with the eagle feathers; the watcher quietly extended the feathers and stroked and pushed the snake's head back, until it finally turned and crawled back to the wall. Half a dozen times different snakes thus crawled out toward me and were turned back, without their ever displaying a symptom of irritation. One snake got past the watcher and moved slowly past me about six inches away, whereupon the priest on my left leaned across me and checked its advance by throwing pinches of dust in its face until the watcher turned round with his feather sceptre. Every move was made without hurry and with quiet unconcern; neither snake nor man, at any time, showed a trace of worry or anger; all, human beings and reptiles, were in an atmosphere of quiet peacefulness. . . .

That night fires flared from the villages on the top of the mesa. Before there was a hint of dawn we heard the voice of the crier summoning the runners to get ready for the snake-dance; and we rose and made our way to the mesa top. . . .

There were twenty Indians in the kiva, all stripped to their breechclouts; only about ten actually took part in handling the snakes, or in any of the ceremonies except the rhythmic chant, in which all joined. Eighty or a hundred snakes, half of them rattlers, the others bull-snakes or ribbonsnakes, lay singly or in tangled groups against the wall at the raised end of the room. They were quiet and in no way nervous or excited. Two men stood at this end of the room. Two more stood at the other end, where the altar was; there was some sand about the altar, and the eagle feathers . . . had been removed, but the upright thunder-sticks remained. The other Indians were squatted in the middle of the room, and half a dozen of them were in the immediate neighborhood of a very big, ornamental wooden bowl of water, placed on certain white-painted symbols on the floor. Two of these Indians held sacred rattles, and there was a small bowl of sacred meal beside them. There was some seemingly ceremonial pipe-smoking.

After some minutes of silence, one of the squatting priests, who seemed to be the leader, and who had already puffed smoke toward the bowl, began a low prayer, at the same time holding and manipulating in his fingers a pinch of the sacred meal. The others once and again during this prayer uttered in unison a single world or exclamation—a kind of selah or amen. At the end he threw the meal into the bowl of water; he had already put some in at the outset of the prayer. Then he began a rhythmic chant, in which all the others joined, the rattles being shaken and the hands moved in harmony with the rhythm. The chant consisted seemingly of a few words repeated over and over again. It was a strange scene, in the half-light of the ancient temple-room. The copper-red bodies of the priests swayed, and their strongly marked faces, hitherto changeless, gained a certain quiet intensity of emotion. The chanting grew in fervor; yet it remained curiously calm throughout (except for a moment at a time, about which I shall speak later). Then the two men who stood near the snakes stooped over, and each picked up a handful of them, these first handfuls being all rattlesnakes. It was done in tranquil, matter-of-fact fashion, and the snakes behaved with equally tranquil unconcern. All was quiet save for the chanting. The snakes were handed to two of the men squatting round the bowl, who received them as if they had been harmless, holding them by the middle of the body, or at least well away from the head. This was repeated until half a dozen of the squatting priests held each three or four poisonous serpents in his hands. The chanting continued, in strongly accented but monotonous rhythm, while the rattles were shaken, and the snakes moved up and down or shaken, in unison with it. Then suddenly the chant quickened and rose to a scream, and the snakes were all plunged into the great bowl of water, a writhing tangle of snakes and hands. Immediately afterward they were withdrawn, as suddenly as they had been plunged in, and were hurled half across the room, to the floor, on and around the altar. They were hurled from a distance of a dozen feet, with sufficient violence to overturn the erect thunder-sticks. That the snakes should have been quiet and inoffensive under the influence of the slow movements and atmosphere of calm that had hitherto obtained was understandable; but the unexpected violence of the bathing and then of the way in which they were hurled to the floor, together with the sudden screaming intensity of the chant, ought to have upset the nerves of every snake there. However, it did not. The snakes woke to an interest in life, it is true, writhed themselves free of one another and of the upset lightning-sticks, and began to glide rapidly in every direction. But only one showed symptoms of anger, and these were not marked. The two standing Indians at this end of the room herded the snakes with their eagle feathers, gently brushing and stroking them back as they squirmed toward us, or toward the singing, sitting priests.

The process was repeated until all the snakes, venomous and nonvenomous alike, had been suddenly bathed and then hurled on the floor, filling the other end of the room with a wriggling, somewhat excited serpent population, which was actively, but not in any way nervously, shepherded by the two Indians stationed for that purpose. These men were, like the others, clad only in a breech-clout, but they moved about among the snakes, barelegged and barefooted, with no touch of concern. One or two of the rattlers became vicious under the strain, and coiled and struck. I thought I saw one of the two shepherding watchers struck in the hand by a recalcitrant side-winder which refused to be soothed by the feathers and which he finally picked up; but, if so, the man gave no sign and his placidity remained unruffled. Most of the snakes showed no anger at all; it seemed to me extraordinary that they were not all of them maddened.

When the snakes had all been washed, the leading priest again prayed. Afterward he once more scattered meal in the bowl, in lines east, west, north, and south, and twice diagonally. The chant was renewed; it grew slower; the rattles were rattled more slowly; then the singing stopped and all was over. . . .

The snake-dance itself took place in the afternoon at five o'clock. There were many hundreds of onlookers, almost as many whites as Indians, and most of the Indian spectators were in white man's dress, in strong contrast to the dancers. The antelope priests entered first and ranged themselves by a tree-like bundle of cottonwood branches against the wall of buildings to one side of the open place where the dance takes place; the other side is on the cliff edge. The snakes, in a bag, were stowed by the bundle of cottonwood branches. Young girls stood near the big pillar of stone with sacred meal to scatter at the foot of the pillar after the snakes had been thrown down there and taken away. Then the snake priests entered in their fringed leather kilts and eagle-plume head-dresses; fox-skins hung at the backs of their girdles, their bodies were splashed and streaked with white, and on each of them the upper part of the face was painted black and the lower part white. Chanting, and stepping in rhythm to the chant, and on one particular stone slab stamping hard as a signal to the underworld, they circled the empty space and for some minutes danced opposite the line of antelope priests. Then, in couples, one of each couple seizing and carrying in his mouth a snake, they began to circle the space again. The leading couple consisted of one man who had his arm across the shoulder of another, while this second man held in his teeth, by the upper middle of its body, a rattlesnake four feet long, the flat, ace-of-clubs-shaped head and curving neck of the snake being almost against the man's face. Rattlesnakes, bull-snakes, ribbon-snakes, all were carried in the same way. One man carried at the same time two small sidewinder rattlesnakes in his mouth. After a while each snake was thrown on the rock and soon again picked up and held in the hand, while a new snake was held in the mouth. Finally each man carried a bundle of snakes in his hand, all so held as to leave the head free, so that the snake could strike if it wished. Most of the snakes showed no anger or resentment. But occasionally one, usually a small sidewinder, half coiled or rattled when

264

thrown down; and in picking these up much caution was shown, the Indian stroking the snake with his eagle feathers and trying to soothe it and get it to straighten out; and if it refused to be soothed, he did his best to grasp it just back of the head; and when he had it in his hand, he continued to stroke the body with the feathers, obviously to quiet it. But whether it were angry or not, he always in the end grasped and lifted it—besides keeping it from crawling among the spectators. Several times I saw the snakes strike at the men who were carrying them, and twice I was sure they struck home—once a man's wrist, once his finger. Neither man paid any attention or seemed to suffer in any way. I saw no man struck in the face; but several of my friends had at previous dances seen men so struck. In one case the man soon showed that he was in much pain, although he continued to dance, and he was badly sick for days; in the other cases no bad result whatever followed.

At last all the snakes were in the hands of the dancers. Then all were thrown at the foot of the natural stone pillar, and immediately, with a yell, the dancers leaped in, seized, each of them, several snakes, and rushed away, east, west, north, and south, dashing over the edge of the cliff and jumping like goats down the precipitous trails. At the foot of the cliff, or on the plain, they dropped the snakes, and then returned to purify themselves by drinking and washing from pails of dark sacred water—medicine water—brought by the women.[12]

10. The River of Doubt

On February 27, 1914, shortly after midday, we started down the River of Doubt into the unknown. We were quite uncertain whether after a week we should find ourselves in the Gy-Paraná, or after six weeks in the Madeira, or after three months we knew not where. That was why the river was rightly christened the Dúvida.

We had been camped close to the river, where the trail that follows the telegraph-line crosses it by a rough bridge. . . . It was the height of the rainy season, and the swollen torrent was swift and brown. Our camp was at about twelve degrees one minute latitude south and sixty degrees fifteen minutes longitude west of Greenwich. Our general course was to be northward toward the equator, by waterway through the vast forest.

We had seven canoes, all of them dugouts. One was small, one was cranky, and two were old, water-logged, and leaky. The other three were good. The two old canoes were lashed together, and the cranky one was lashed to one of the others. Kermit with two paddlers went in the smallest of the good canoes; Colonel Rondon and Lyra with three other paddlers

[12] *Ibid.*, pp. 233–43.

in the next largest; and the doctor, Cherrie, and I in the largest with three paddlers. The remaining eight camaradas—there were sixteen in all—were equally divided between our two pairs of lashed canoes. Although our personal baggage was cut down to the limit necessary for health and efficiency, yet on such a trip as ours, where scientific work has to be done and where food for twenty-two men for an unknown period of time has to be carried, it is impossible not to take a good deal of stuff; and the seven dugouts were too heavily laden.

The paddlers were a strapping set. They were expert rivermen of the forest, skilled veterans in wilderness work. They were lithe as panthers and brawny as bears. They swam like water-dogs. They were equally at home with pole and paddle, with axe and machete; and one was a good cook and others were good men around camp. They looked like pirates in the pictures of Howard Pyle or Maxfield Parrish; one or two of them were pirates, and one worse than a pirate; but most of them were hard-working, willing, and cheerful. They were white—or, rather, the olive of southern Europe—black, copper-colored, and of all intermediate shades. In my canoe Luiz the steersman, the head man, was a Matto Grosso negro; Julio the bowsman was from Bahia and of pure Portuguese blood; and the third man, Antonio, was a Parecís Indian.

The actual surveying of the river was done by Colonel Rondon and Lyra, with Kermit as their assistant. . . . The first half-day's work was slow. The general course of the stream was a trifle east of north, but at short intervals it bent and curved literally toward every point of the compass. . . .

My canoe ran ahead of the surveying canoes. The height of the water made the going easy, for most of the snags and fallen trees were well beneath the surface. Now and then, however, the swift water hurried us toward ripples that marked ugly spikes of sunken timber, or toward uprooted trees that stretched almost across the stream. Then the muscles stood out on the backs and arms of the paddlers as stroke on stroke they urged us away from and past the obstacle. If the leaning or fallen trees were the thorny, slender-stemmed boritana palms, which love the wet, they were often, although plunged beneath the river, in full and vigorous growth, their stems curving upward, and their frond-crowned tops shaken by the rushing water. It was interesting work, for no civilized man, no white man, had ever gone down or up this river or seen the country through which we were passing. The lofty and matted forest rose like a green wall on either hand. The trees were stately and beautiful. The looped and twisted vines hung from them like great ropes. Masses of epiphytes grew both on the dead trees and the living; some had huge leaves like elephants' ears. Now and then fragrant scents were blown to us from flowers on the banks.

266

There were not many birds, and for the most part the forest was silent; rarely, we heard strange calls from the depths of the woods, or saw a cormorant or ibis. . . .

We spent March 3 and 4 and the morning of the 5th in portaging around rapids. . . . It rained heavily. The little bees were in such swarms as to be a nuisance. . . . We were bitten by huge horse-flies, the size of bumblebees. More serious annoyance was caused by the pium and boroshuda flies during the hours of daylight, and by the polvora, the sand-flies, after dark. There were a few mosquitoes. The boroshudas were the worst pests; they brought the blood at once, and left marks that lasted for weeks. I did my writing in head net and gauntlets. . . .

Packing the loads across was simple. Dragging the heavy dugouts was labor. The bigger of the two water-logged ones was the heavier. . . . All the men were employed at it except the cook, and one man who was down with fever. A road was chopped through the forest and a couple of hundred stout six-foot poles, or small logs, were cut as rollers and placed about two yards apart. With block and tackle the seven dugouts were hoisted out of the river up the steep banks, and up the rise of ground until the level was reached. Then the men harnessed themselves two by two on the drag-rope, while one of their number pried behind with a lever, and the canoe, bumping and sliding, was twitched through the woods. . . .

We started downstream again early in the afternoon of March 5. Our hands and faces were swollen from the bites and stings of the insect pests at the sand-flat camp, and it was a pleasure once more to be in the middle of the river, where they did not come, in any numbers, while we were in motion. The current was swift, but the river was so deep that there were no serious obstructions. . . . The course wound hither and thither, sometimes in sigmoid curves. . . .

On the second day the canoes and loads were brought down to the foot of the first rapids . . . to the little beach by the three palms where our tents were pitched. . . . I went into the woods, but in the tangle of vegetation it would have been a mere hazard had I seen any big animal. Generally the woods were silent and empty. Now and then little troops of birds of many kinds passed—woodhewers, ant-thrushes, tanagers, flycatchers; as in the spring and fall similar troops of warblers, chickadees, and nuthatches pass through our northern woods. On the rocks and on the great trees by the river grew beautiful white and lilac orchids—the sobralia, of sweet and delicate fragrance. For the moment my own books seemed a trifle heavy, and perhaps I would have found the day tedious if Kermit had not lent me the Oxford Book of French Verse. Eustache Deschamp, Joachim du Bellay, Ronsard, the delightful La Fontaine, the delightful but appalling Villon, Victor Hugo's "Guitare," Madame Desbordes-Val-

267

more's lines on the little girl and her pillow, as dear little verses about a child as ever were written—these and many others comforted me much, as I read them in head net and gauntlets, sitting on a log by an unknown river in the Amazonian forest. . . .

We again embarked and made a kilometre and a half, spending most of the time in getting past two more rapids. . . . At each set of rapids the canoes were unloaded and the loads borne past on the shoulders of the camaradas; three of the canoes were paddled down by a couple of naked paddlers apiece; and the two sets of double canoes were let down by ropes, one of one couple being swamped but rescued and brought safely to shore on each occasion. . . . Lyra and Kermit did the actual work with the camaradas. Kermit, dressed substantially like the camaradas themselves, worked in the water, and, as the overhanging branches were thronged with crowds of biting and stinging ants, he was marked and blistered over his whole body. Indeed, we all suffered more or less from these ants; while the swarms of biting flies grew constantly more numerous. The termites ate holes in my helmet and also in the cover of my cot. . . .

Next morning we found that during the night we had met with a serious misfortune. We had halted at the foot of the rapids. The canoes were moored to trees on the bank, at the tail of the broken water. The two old canoes, although one of them was our biggest cargo-carrier, were waterlogged and heavy, and one of them was leaking. In the night the river rose. The leaky canoe, which at best was too low in the water, must have gradually filled from the wash of the waves. It sank, dragging down the other; they began to roll, bursting their moorings; and in the morning they had disappeared. . . .

It was not pleasant to have to stop for some days; thanks to the rapids, we had made slow progress, and with our necessarily limited supply of food, and no knowledge whatever of what was ahead of us, it was important to make good time. But there was no alternative. We had to build either one big canoe or two small ones. It was raining heavily as the men started to explore in different directions for good canoe trees. Three— which ultimately proved not very good for the purpose—were found close to camp; splendid-looking trees, one of them five feet in diameter three feet from the ground. The axemen immediately attacked this one under the superintendence of Colonel Rondon, . . . hollowing out the hard wood of the big tree, with axe and adze, while watch and ward were kept over them to see that the idlers did not shirk at the expense of the industrious. . . . I spent the day hunting in the woods, for the most part by the river, but saw nothing. In the season of the rains game is away from the river and fish are scarce and turtles absent. Yet it was pleasant to be in the great silent forest. Here and there grew immense trees, and on some of them mighty buttresses sprang from the base. The lianas and vines were of every size and shape. . . . In the shadow there was little noise. The wind rarely moved the hot, humid air. There were few flowers or birds. Insects were altogether too abundant, and even when travelling slowly it was impossible always to avoid them—not to speak of our constant companions the bees, mosquitoes, and especially the boroshudas or bloodsucking flies. . . .

All of us suffered more or less, our faces and hands swelling slightly from the boroshuda bites; and in spite of our clothes we were bitten all over our bodies, chiefly by ants and the small forest ticks. Because of the rain and the heat our clothes were usually wet when we took them off at night, and just as wet when we put them on again in the morning. . . .

The men worked at the canoe . . . until ten in the evening, as the weather was clear. After nightfall some of the men held candles and the others plied axe or adze, standing within or beside the great, half-hollowed logs, while the flicker of the lights showed the tropic forest rising in the darkness round about. The night air was hot and still and heavy with moisture. The men were stripped to the waist. Olive and copper and ebony, their skins glistened as if oiled, and rippled with the ceaseless play of the thews beneath.

On the morning of the 14th the work was resumed in a torrential tropic downpour. The canoe was finished, dragged down to the water, and launched soon after midday, and another hour or so saw us under way. The descent was marked, and the swollen river raced along. Several times we passed great whirlpools, sometimes shifting, sometimes steady. Half a dozen times we ran over rapids, and, although they were not high enough to have been obstacles to loaded Canadian canoes, two of them were serious to us. Our heavily laden, clumsy dugouts were sunk to within three or four inches of the surface of the river, and, although they were buoyed on each side with bundles of burity-palm branch stems, they shipped a great deal of water in the rapids. The two biggest rapids we only just made, and after each we had hastily to push ashore in order to bail. In one set of big ripples or waves my canoe was nearly swamped. In a wilderness, where what is ahead is absolutely unknown, alike in terms of time, space, and method—for we had no idea where we would come out, how we would get out, or when we would get out—it is of vital consequence not to lose one's outfit, especially the provisions; and yet it is of only less consequence to go as rapidly as possible lest all the provisions be exhausted and the final stages of the expedition be accomplished by men weakened from semistarvation, and therefore ripe for disaster. . . . On this occasion, of the two hazards, we felt it necessary to risk running the rapids; for our progress had been so very slow that unless we made up the time, it was probable that we would be short of food before we got where we could expect to procure any more except what little the country in the time of the rains and floods might yield. . . . We ran until after five, so that the work of pitching camp was finished in the dark. We had made nearly sixteen kilometres in a direction slightly east of north. This evening the air was fresh and cool.

The following morning, the 15th of March, we started in good season. For six kilometres we drifted and paddled down the swift river without incident. At times we saw lofty Brazil-nut trees rising above the rest of the forest on the banks; and back from the river these trees grow to enormous proportions, towering like giants. There were great rubber-trees also, their leaves always in sets of threes. Then the ground on either hand rose into boulder-strewn, forest-clad hills and the roar of broken water announced that once more our course was checked by dangerous rapids. Round a bend we came on them; a wide descent of white water, with an island in the middle, at the upper edge. . . .

Kermit, as usual, was leading in his canoe . . . the smallest and least seaworthy of all. He had in it little except a week's supply of our boxed provisions and a few tools; fortunately none of the food for the camaradas. His dog Trigueiro was with him. Besides himself, the crew consisted of two men: João, the helmsman, or pilot, as he is called in Brazil, and Simplicio, the bowsman. Both were negroes and exceptionally good men in every way. . . . Kermit took his canoe across to the island to see whether the descent could be better accomplished on the other side. Having made his investigation, he ordered the men to return to the bank he had left, and the dugout was headed upstream accordingly. Before they had gone a dozen yards, the paddlers digging their paddles with all their strength into the swift current, one of the shifting whirlpools of which I have spoken came downstream, whirled them around, and swept them so close to the rapids that no human power could avoid going over them. As they were drifting into them broadside on, Kermit yelled to the steersman to turn her head, so as to take them in the only way that offered any chance whatever of safety. The water came aboard, wave after wave, as they raced down. They reached the bottom with the canoe upright, but so full as barely to float, and the paddlers urged her toward the shore. They had nearly reached the bank when another whirlpool or whirling eddy tore them away and hurried them back to midstream, where the dugout filled and turned over. João, seizing the rope, started to swim ashore; the rope was pulled from his hand, but he reached the bank. Poor Simplicio must have been pulled under at once and his life beaten out on the boulders beneath the racing torrent. He never rose again, nor did we ever

270

recover his body. Kermit clutched his rifle, his favorite 405 Winchester with which he had done most of his hunting both in Africa and America, and climbed on the bottom of the upset boat. In a minute he was swept into the second series of rapids, and whirled away from the rolling boat, losing his rifle. The water beat his helmet down over his head and face and drove him beneath the surface; and when he rose at last he was almost drowned, his breath and strength almost spent. He was in swift but quiet water, and swam toward an overhanging branch. His jacket hindered him, but he knew he was too nearly gone to be able to get it off, and, thinking with the curious calm one feels when death is but a moment away, he realized that the utmost his failing strength could do was to reach the branch. He reached, and clutched it, and then almost lacked strength to haul himself out on the land. Good Trigueiro had faithfully swum alongside him through the rapids, and now himself scrambled ashore.

It was a very narrow escape. Kermit was a great comfort and help to me on the trip; but the fear of some fatal accident befalling him was always a nightmare to me. He was to be married as soon as the trip was over. . . .

We camped at the foot of the rapids. . . . There were many small birds here, but it was extremely difficult to see or shoot them in the lofty treetops, and to find them in the tangle beneath if they were shot. However, Cherrie got four species new to the collection . . . a tiny hummer, one of the species known as wood-stars, with dainty but not brilliant plumage . . . a very handsome trogon and an exquisite little tanager, as brilliant as a cluster of jewels; its throat was lilac, its breast turquoise, its crown and forehead topaz, while above it was glossy purple-black, the lower part of the back ruby red. . . . The fourth bird was a queer hawk of the genus *ibycter*, black, with a white belly, naked red cheeks and throat, and red legs and feet. Its crop was filled with the seeds of fruits and a few insect remains; an extraordinary diet for a hawk.

The morning of the 16th was dark and gloomy. Less than half an hour took our dugouts to the head of the rapids below. . . . While the loads were being brought down the left bank, Luiz and Antonio Correa, our two best water-men, started to take a canoe down the right side, and Colonel Rondon walked ahead to see anything he could about the river. He was accompanied by one of our three dogs, Lobo.

After walking about a kilometre he heard ahead a kind of howling noise, which he thought was made by spider-monkeys. He walked in the direction of the sound and Lobo ran ahead. In a minute he heard Lobo yell with pain, and then, still yelping, come toward him, while the creature that was howling also approached, evidently in pursuit. In a moment a second yell from Lobo, followed by silence, announced that he was dead; and the

271

sound of the howling, when near, convinced Rondon that the dog had been killed by an Indian, doubtless with two arrows. Probably the Indian was howling to lure the spider-monkeys toward him.

Rondon fired his rifle in the air, to warn off the Indian or Indians, who in all probability had never seen a civilized man, and certainly could not imagine that one was in the neighborhood. He then returned to the foot of the rapids, where the portage was still going on, and in company with Lyra, Kermit, and Antonio Parecís, the Indian, walked back to where Lobo's body lay. Sure enough, he found him, slain by two arrows. One arrow-head was in him, and near by was a strange stick used in the very primitive method of fishing of all these Indians. Antonio recognized its purpose. The Indians, who were apparently two or three in number, had fled. Some beads and trinkets were left on the spot to show that we were not angry and were friendly.

Meanwhile Cherrie stayed at the head and I at the foot of the portage as guards. Luiz and Antonio Correa brought down one canoe safely. The next was the new canoe, which was very large and heavy. . . . In the rapids the rope broke, and the canoe was lost, Luiz being nearly drowned.

It was a very bad thing to lose the canoe, but it was even worse to lose the rope and pulleys. This meant that it would be physically impossible to hoist big canoes up even small hills or rocky hillocks, such as had been so frequent beside the many rapids we had encountered. It was not wise to spend the four days necessary to build new canoes where we were, in danger of attack from the Indians. Moreover, new rapids might be very near, in which case the new canoes would hamper us. Yet the four remaining canoes would not carry all the loads and all the men, no matter how we cut the loads down; and we intended to cut everything down at once. We had been gone eighteen days. We had used over a third of our food. . . .

The following morning Colonel Rondon, Lyra, Kermit, Cherrie, and nine of the camaradas started in single file down the bank, while the doctor and I went in the two double canoes, with six camaradas, three of them the invalids with swollen feet. We halted continually, as we went about three times as fast as the walkers; and we traced the course of the river. After forty minutes' actual going in the boats we came to some rapids; the unloaded canoes ran them without difficulty, while the loads were portaged. In an hour and a half we were again under way, but in ten minutes came to other rapids, where the river ran among islands, and there were several big curls. The clumsy, heavily laden dugouts, lashed in couples, were unwieldy and hard to handle. The rapids came just round a sharp bend, and we got caught in the upper part of the swift water and had to run the first set of rapids in consequence. We in the leading pair of dugouts were within an ace of coming to grief on some big boulders against which we were swept by a cross current at the turn. All of us paddling hard—scraping and bumping—we got through by the skin of our teeth, and managed to make the bank and moor our dugouts. It was a narrow escape from grave disaster. The second pair of lashed dugouts profited by our experience, and made the run—with risk, but with less risk—and moored beside us. Then all the loads were taken out, and the empty canoes were run down through the least dangerous channels among the islands. . . .

At the foot of the rapids we camped, as there were several good canoe trees near, and we had decided to build two rather small canoes. . . .

It was three weeks since we had started down the River of Doubt. We had come along its winding course about one hundred and forty kilometres, with a descent of somewhere in the neighborhood of one hundred and twenty-four metres. It had been slow progress. We could not tell what physical obstacles were ahead of us, nor whether the Indians would be actively hostile. . . .

Next day we made thirteen kilometres. We ran, all told, a little over an hour and three-quarters. Seven hours were spent in getting past a series of rapids at which the portage, over rocky and difficult ground, was a kilometre long. The canoes were run down empty—a hazardous run, in which one of them upset.

A kilometre and a half after leaving this camp we came on a stretch of big rapids. The river here twists in loops, and we had heard the roaring of these rapids the previous afternoon. Then we passed out of earshot of them; but Antonio Correa, our best waterman, insisted all along that the roaring meant rapids worse than any we had encountered for some days. "I was brought up in the water, and I know it like a fish, and all its sounds," said he. He was right. We had to carry the loads nearly a kilometre that afternoon, and the canoes were pulled out on the bank so that they might be in readiness to be dragged overland next day. . . .

Next morning we went about three kilometres before coming to some steep hills, beautiful to look upon, clad as they were in dense, tall, tropical forest, but ominous of new rapids. Sure enough, at their foot we had to haul up and prepare for a long portage. The canoes we ran down empty. Even so, we were within an ace of losing two, the lashed couple in which I ordinarily journeyed. In a sharp bend of the rapids, between two big curls, they were swept among the boulders and under the matted branches which stretched out from the bank. They filled, and the racing current pinned them where they were, one partly on the other. All of us had to help get them clear. Their fastenings were chopped asunder with axes. Kermit and half a dozen of the men, stripped to the skin, made their

273

way to a small rock island in the little falls just above the canoes, and let down a rope which we tied to the outermost canoe. The rest of us, up to our armpits and barely able to keep our footing as we slipped and stumbled among the boulders in the swift current, lifted and shoved while Kermit and his men pulled the rope and fastened the slack to a half-submerged tree. Each canoe in succession was hauled up the little rock island, baled, and then taken down in safety by two paddlers. It was nearly four o'clock before we were again ready to start, having been de-layed by a rain-storm so heavy that we could not see across the river. Ten minutes' run took us to the head of another series of rapids; the exploring party returned with the news that we had an all-day's job ahead of us; and we made camp in the rain, which did not matter much, as we were already drenched through. . . .

The last three days of March we spent in getting to the foot of the rapids in this gorge. . . . The work was not only difficult and laborious in the extreme, but hazardous; for the walls of the gorge were so sheer that at the worst places they had to cling to narrow shelves on the face of the rock, while letting the canoes down with ropes. Meanwhile Rondon surveyed and cut a trail for the burden-bearers, and superintended the por-tage of the loads. The rocky sides of the gorge were too steep for laden men to attempt to traverse them. Accordingly the trail had to go over the top of the mountain, both the ascent and the descent of the rock-strewn, forest-clad slopes being very steep. It was hard work to carry loads over such a trail. . . . Most of the camaradas were downhearted, naturally enough, and occasionally asked one of us if we really believed that we should ever get out alive and we had to cheer them up as best we could. . . . Genuine wilderness exploration is as dangerous as warfare. The conquest of wild nature demands the utmost vigor, hardihood, and daring, and takes from the conquerors a heavy toll of life and health. . . .

The men were growing constantly weaker under the endless strain of exhausting labor. Kermit was having an attack of fever, and Lyra and Cherrie had touches of dysentery, but all three continued to work. While in the water trying to help with an upset canoe I had by my own clum-siness bruised my leg against a boulder; and the resulting inflammation was somewhat bothersome. I now had a sharp attack of fever, but thanks to the excellent care of the doctor, was over it in about forty-eight hours; but Kermit's fever grew worse and he too was unable to work for a day or two. We could walk over the portages, however. . . . There were al-ready two of the camaradas who were too weak to help the others, their condition being such as to cause us serious concern. . . .

It was a rather sorry crew that embarked the following morning, April 15. But it turned out a red-letter day. The day before, we had come across cuttings, a year old, which were probably but not certainly made by pioneer rubber men. But on this day—during which we made twenty-five kilometres—after running two hours and a half we found on the left bank a board on a post with the initials J.A., to show the farthest-up point which a rubber man had reached and claimed as his own. An hour farther down we came on a newly built house in a little planted clearing; and we cheered heartily. No one was at home, but the house of palm thatch was clean and cool. A couple of dogs were on watch, and the belongings showed that a man, and a woman, and a child lived there and had only just left. Another hour brought us to a similar house where dwelt an old black man who showed the innate courtesy of the Brazilian peasant. . . .

We had passed the period when there was a chance of peril, of disaster, to the whole expedition. . . . We now no longer had to face continual anxiety, the need of constant economy with food, the duty of labor with no end in sight, and bitter uncertainty as to the future.

It was time to get out. The wearing work, under very unhealthy conditions, was beginning to tell on every one. Half of the camaradas had been down with fever and were much weakened; only a few of them retained their original physical and moral strength. Cherrie and Kermit had recovered; but both Kermit and Lyra still had bad sores on their legs from the bruises received in the water work.

I was in worse shape. The after-effects of the fever still hung on; and the leg which had been hurt while working in the rapids with the sunken canoe had taken a turn for the bad and developed an abscess. The good doctor, to whose unwearied care and kindness I owe much, had cut it open and inserted a drainage-tube. . . . I could hardly hobble and was pretty well laid up. But "there aren't no 'stop, conductor,' while a battery's changing ground." No man has any business to go on such a trip as ours unless he will refuse to jeopardize the welfare of his associates by any delay caused by a weakness or ailment of his. It is his duty to go forward, if necessary on all fours, until he drops. Fortunately, I was put to no such test. I remained in good shape until we had passed the last of the rapids of the chasms. When my serious trouble came we had only canoe-riding ahead of us. It is not ideal for a sick man to spend the hottest hours of the day stretched on the boxes in the bottom of a small open dugout, under the well-nigh intolerable heat of the torrid sun of the mid-tropics, varied by blinding, drenching downpours of rain; but I could not be sufficiently grateful for the chance. Kermit and Cherrie took care of me as if they had been trained nurses; and Colonel Rondon and Lyra were no less thoughtful.

The north was calling strongly to the three men of the north—Rocky

275

Dell Farm to Cherrie, Sagamore Hill to me; and to Kermit the call was stronger still. After nightfall we could now see the Dipper well above the horizon—upside down, with the two pointers pointing to a north star below the world's rim; but the Dipper, with all its stars. In our home country spring had now come, the wonderful northern spring of long glorious days, of brooding twilights, of cool delightful nights. Robin and bluebird, meadow-lark and song-sparrow, were singing in the mornings at home; the maple buds were red; wind-flowers and bloodroot were blooming while the last patches of snow still lingered; the rapture of the hermit-thrush in Vermont, the serene golden melody of the wood-thrush on Long Island, would be heard before we were there to listen. Each man to his home, and to his true love! Each was longing for the homely things that were so dear to him, for the home people who were dearer still, and for the one who was dearest of all.[13]

11. "We have put upon the map a river as long as the Rhine . . ."

To Ruth Moore Lee and Arthur Hamilton Lee

Oyster Bay, May 20, 1914

Probably you have received a pencil note from me, written when I was pretty well laid up in Brazil; but I shall repeat what I then said, and a little enlarge on it. We really performed quite a feat. We have put upon the map a river as long as the Rhine or the Elbe. The worth of the accomplishment is shown by the attitude of Sir Clements Markham[14] and the other men who doubt my having done what I say I have done. If it were a case of climbing a mountain or going to one or the other pole, I might have to rely merely upon the statements of myself and my companions. But fortunately this is the case of a river nearly a thousand miles long. The river will stay there. Anybody can go and verify for himself what we have done. Kermit and myself were accompanied by three officers of the Brazilian Army, two of them engineers and one a doctor, and by a naturalist representing the American Museum of Natural History. On the twelfth parallel of latitude south we said good-by to the men who had hitherto been our companions and sixty days later met the lieutenant

[13] "Through the Brazilian Wilderness" (1914). *Works V*, pp. 199–262.
[14] Sir Clements Robert Markham, geographical director of the India office, 1867–1877, president of the Hakluyt Society, 1889–1909, and president of the Royal Geographical Society, 1893–1905, was the foremost doubter of Roosevelt's achievement.

who, on the chance of our coming down the river we actually did come down, had gone up to await us. During those sixty days it was a physical impossibility for us to get down in any way excepting by the river. We have the diaries, the photos, and the astronomical observations.[15]

[15] *Letters VII*, p. 761.

Friend of Cowboys and Kings

These letters, written in response to the pleas of friends who heard Mr. Roosevelt's accounts of certain episodes of travel in America and Europe, happily record some of his typical, rich, colorful and uninhibited table-talk.

1. "Old friends and queer characters . . ."

To John Hay

Oyster Bay, Aug. 9, 1903

As soon as I got west of the Missouri I came into my own former stamping ground. At every station there was somebody who remembered my riding in there when the Little Missouri roundup went down to the Indian reservation and then worked north across the Cannon Ball and up Knife and Green Rivers; or who had been an interested and possibly malevolent spectator when I had ridden east with other representatives of the cow men to hold a solemn council with the leading grangers on the vexed subject of mavericks; or who had been hired as a train hand when I had been taking a load of cattle to Chicago, and who remembered well how he and I at the stoppages had run frantically down the line of the cars and with our poles jabbed the unfortunate cattle who had lain down until they again stood up and thereby gave themselves a chance for their lives; and who remembered how when the train started we had to clamber hurriedly aboard and make our way back to the caboose along the tops of the cattle cars. At Mandan two of my old cow hands, Sylvane and Joe Ferris, joined me. At Dickinson all of the older people had known me and the whole town turned out with wild and not entirely sober enthusiasm. It was difficult to make them much of a speech as there were dozens of men each earnestly desirous of recalling to my mind some special incident. One man, how he helped me bring in my

279

cattle to ship, and how a blue roan steer broke away leading a bunch which it took him and me three hours to round up and bring back; another, how seventeen years before I had come in a freight train from Medora to deliver the Fourth of July oration; another, a gray-eyed individual named Paddock, who during my early years at Medora had shot and killed an equally objectionable individual named Livingstone, reminded me how just twenty years before, when I was on my first buffalo hunt, he loaned me the hammer off his Sharp's rifle to replace the broken hammer of mine; another, recalled the time when he and I worked on the roundup as partners, going with the Little Missouri outfit from the head of the Box Alder to the mouth of the Big Beaver, and then striking over to represent the Little Missouri brands on the Yellowstone roundup; yet another recalled the time when I as deputy sheriff of Billings County had brought in three cattle thieves named Red Finnigan, Dutch Chris, and the Half Breed to his keeping, he being then sheriff in Dickinson, etc., etc., etc.

At Medora, which we reached after dark, the entire population of the Bad Lands down to the smallest baby had gathered to meet me. This was formerly my home station. The older men and women I knew well; the younger ones had been wild towheaded children when I lived and worked along the Little Missouri. I had spent nights in their ranches. I still remembered meals which the women had given me when I had come from some hard expedition, half famished and sharpset as a wolf. I had killed buffalo and elk, deer and antelope with some of the men. With others I had worked on the trail, on the calf roundup, on the beef roundup. We had been together on occasions which we still remembered when some bold rider met his death in trying to stop a stampede, in riding a mean horse, or in the quicksands of some swollen river which he sought to swim. They all felt I was their man, their old friend; and even if they had been hostile to me in the old days when we were divided by the sinister bickering and jealousies and hatreds of all frontier communities, they now firmly believed they had always been my staunch friends and admirers. They had all gathered in the town hall, which was draped for a dance—young children, babies, everybody being present. I shook hands with them all and almost each one had some memory of special association with me which he or she wished to discuss. . . .

From Washington I turned eastward and when I struck northern Montana again . . . I met all kinds of queer characters with whom I had hunted and worked and slept and sometimes fought. From Helena I went southward to Butte, reaching that city in the afternoon of May 27th. By this time Seth Bullock had joined us, together with an old hunting friend, John Willis,—a Donatello of the Rocky Mountains—wholly lacking, however, the morbid self-consciousness which made Hawthorne's faun go out of his head because he had killed a man. Willis and I had been in Butte some seventeen years before at the end of a hunting trip in which we got dead broke, so that when we struck Butte we slept in an outhouse and breakfasted heartily in a two-bit Chinese restaurant. Since then I had gone through Butte in the campaign of 1900, the major part of the inhabitants receiving me with frank hostility and enthusiastic cheers for Bryan. However, Butte is mercurial and its feelings had changed. The wicked, wealthy, hospitable, full-blooded little city welcomed me with wild enthusiasm of the most disorderly kind.

The mayor, Pat Mullins, was a huge, good-humored creature, wearing for the first time in his life a top hat and a frock coat, the better to do honor to the President. National party lines count very little in Butte, where the fight was Heinze and anti-Heinze, ex-Senator Carter and Senator Clark being in the opposition. Neither side was willing to let the other have anything to do with the celebration, and they drove me wild with their appeals until I settled that the afternoon parade and speech was to be managed by the Heinze peole and the evening speech by the anti-Heinze people; and that the dinner should contain fifty of each faction and be presided over in his official capacity by the mayor. The ordinary procession in barouches was rather more exhilarating than usual and reduced the faithful secret-service men very nearly to the condition of Bedlamites. The crowd was filled with whooping enthusiasm and every kind of whisky, and in their desire to be sociable broke the lines and jammed right up to the carriage. There were a lot of the so-called "rednecks" or dynamiters, the men who had taken part in the murderous Coeur d'Alene strike, who had been indulging in threats as to what they would do to me, and of course the city is a hotbed of violent anarchy. Seth Bullock accordingly had gone down three days in advance and had organized for my personal protection a bodyguard composed of old friends of his on whom he could rely, for the most part tough citizens and all of them very quick with a gun. By occupation they were, as he casually mentioned, for the major part gamblers and "sure thing" men. But they had no sympathy whatever with anarchy in any form. They thoroughly believed in men of wealth, for they wished to prey on them. These men kept a close watch over all who approached me, and I was far less nervous about being shot myself than about their shooting some exuberant enthusiast with peaceful intentions. Seth Bullock rode close beside the rear wheel of the carriage, a splendid-looking fellow with his size and supple strength, his strongly marked aquiline face with its big mustache, and the broad brim of his soft hat drawn down over his hawk eyes. . . .

My address was felt to be honor enough for one hotel, and the dinner was given in the other. When the dinner was announced the mayor led me in—or to speak more accurately, tucked me under one arm and lifted me partially off the ground, so that I felt as if I looked like one of those limp dolls with dangling legs carried around by small children, like Mary Jane in "The Goliwogs," for instance. As soon as we got in the banquet hall and sat at the head of the table the mayor hammered lustily with the handle of his knife and announced, "Waiter, bring on the feed!" Then in a spirit of pure kindliness he added, "Waiter, pull up the curtains and let the people see the President eat!"—but to this I objected. The dinner was soon in full swing and it was interesting in many regards. Besides my own party, including Seth Bullock and Willis, there were fifty men from each of the Butte factions. In Butte every prominent man is a millionaire, a professional gambler, or a labor leader; and generally he has been all three. Of the hundred men who were my hosts I suppose at least half had killed their man in private war, or had striven to compass the assassination of an enemy. They had fought one another with reckless ferocity. They had been allies and enemies in every kind of business scheme, and companions in brutal revelry. As they drank great goblets of wine the sweat glistened on their hard, strong, crafty faces. They looked as if they had come out of the pictures in Aubrey Beardsley's *Yellow Book*. The millionaires had been laboring men once; the labor leaders intended to be millionaires in their turn or else to pull down all who were. They had made money in mines; they had spent it on the races, in other mines, or in gambling and every form of vicious luxury. But they were strong men for all that. They had worked and striven and pushed and trampled, and had always been ready, and were ready now, to fight to the death in many different kinds of conflict. They had built up their part of the West. They were men with whom one had to reckon if thrown in contact with them. There was Senator Clark with his Iscariot face; goat-bearded Carter with his cold gray eyes; Heinze, heavy-jowled, his cheeks flushed, his eyes glittering—he regarded the dinner as a triumph for him because the mayor was his man, and in pure joy he had lost twenty thousand dollars in reckless betting on horse races that afternoon. In Butte proper at the moment he was the wealthiest and most powerful man. There were plenty of those at the table who would stop at no measure to injure him in fortune, in limb or in life; and as he looked at them he would lean over and tell me the evil things he intended in turn to do to them. But though most of them hated each other, they were accustomed to taking their pleasure when they could get it, and they took it fast and hard with the meats and wines.[1]

[1] *Letters III*, pp. 551–60.

2. The ex-President Calls on Kings

To George Otto Trevelyan

Oyster Bay, Oct. 1, 1911

I doubted whether the sovereigns cared to see me. I am now inclined to think that they did, as a relief to the tedium, the dull, narrow routine of their lives. I shall always bear testimony to the courtesy and good manners, and the obvious sense of responsibility and duty, of the various sovereigns I met. But, of course, as was to be expected, they were like other human beings in that the average among them was not very high as regards intellect and force. . . .

The kings whom I saw were not as a whole very ambitious or very forceful, though fine, honest, good fellows; and the monotony of their lives evidently made them welcome any diversion in the shape of a stranger, who gave them an entirely new point of view, and with whom, because of the nature of the case, they knew they could be intimate without any danger of the intimacy being misconstrued, or leading to unpleasant situations in the future. They had made the advances, not I; they knew that I was not coming back to Europe, that I would never see them again, or try in any way to keep up relations with them; and so they felt free to treat us with an intimacy, and on a footing of equality, which would have been impossible with a European, the subject of some one of them (I think this was why they asked us to stay in the palaces). In a way, although the comparison sounds odd, these sovereigns, in their relations among themselves and with others, reminded me of the officers and their wives in one of our western army posts in the old days, when they were all shut up together and away from the rest of the world, were sundered by an impassable gulf from the enlisted men and the few scouts, hunters and settlers around about, and were knit together into one social whole, and nevertheless were riven asunder by bitter jealousies, rivalries and dislikes. Well, the feelings between a given queen and a given dowager-empress, or a small king and the emperor who on some occasion had relished bullying him, were precisely the same as those between the captain's lady and the colonel's spinster daughter, or the sporting lieutenant and the martinet major, in a lonely army post. . . .

All these small kings had vague ambitions, which they knew would never be gratified, for military distinction, and hunting dangerous game, and they always had questions to put about the Spanish War and the Afri-

283

can trip. They also all stood distinctly in awe of the German Kaiser, who evidently liked to drill them; and both the big and the small ones felt much jealousy of one another, and at the same time felt joined together and sundered from all other people by their social position. . . .

The popular reception in Vienna was even greater than the popular reception in Rome. . . . The streets and squares around the hotel were blocked with crowds, and when I drove to Schönbrunn to dine with the Emperor, the whole route was lined on both sides with onlookers. . . .

The Emperor was an interesting man. With him again I had to speak French. He did not strike me as a very able man, but he was a gentleman, he had good instincts, and in his sixty years' reign he had witnessed the most extraordinary changes and vicissitudes. He talked very freely and pleasantly, sometimes about politics, sometimes about hunting; and after my first interview, when he got up to tell me "good-by," he said that he had been particularly interested in seeing me because he was the last representative of the old system, whereas I embodied the new movement, the movement of the present and the future, and that he had wished to see me so as to know for himself how the prominent exponent of that movement felt and thought. He knew that I disliked the old king of the Belgians who was just dead, and suddenly asked me if I would have visited Belgium if he had been alive; and when I said no, he responded that he quite understood why, and added "c'était un homme absolument méchant," explaining that there were very few men who were absolutely and without qualification "méchant," but that Leopold was one.

The dinner at Schönbrunn was interesting, of course, and not as dull, as those functions are apt to be. The Emperor and all the Austrian guests had one horrid habit. The finger bowls were brought on, each with a small tumbler of water in the middle; and the Emperor and all the others proceeded to rinse their mouths, and then empty them into the finger bowls. I felt a little as if the days of Kaunitz had been revived—I believe that eminent servant of Maria Theresa used to take a complete toilet set with him to dinner, including a toothbrush, which he used at the close of the feast. However, all of the guests were delightful; and both the men and the women who came in after dinner were on the whole charming. I was told that Viennese society was frivolous, but it happened, I suppose naturally, that those men whom I saw were most of them interested in real problems of statecraft and warcraft. . . .

At Christiania we were taken at once to the palace, where we stayed; and I could hardly speak too strongly of King Haakon, Queen Maud and little Olaf. They were dears; we were genuinely sorry, when we left them, to think that we would never see them again; if ever Norway decides to turn Republic we should love to have them come to live near Sagamore Hill. Of course Norway is as funny a kingdom as was ever imagined outside of *opéra bouffe*—although it isn't *opéra bouffe* at all, for the Norwegians are a fine, serious, powerful lot of men and women. But they have the most genuinely democratic society to be found in Europe, not excepting Switzerland. . . . They have no nobles, hardly even gentry; they are peasants and small townspeople—farmers, sailors, fisherfolk, mechanics, small traders. On this community a royal family is suddenly plumped down. It is much as if Vermont should offhand try the experiment of having a king. Yet it certainly seemed as if the experiment were entirely successful. . . .

For such a kingdom . . . the entire royal family, king, queen, and prince, were just exactly what was needed. They were as simple and unpretentious as they were good and charming. Olaf was a dear little boy, and the people at large were immensely pleased with him. The King was a trump, privately and publicly; he took a keen and intelligent interest in every question affecting his people, treated them and was treated by them, with a curiously simple democracy of attitude which was free from make-believe on either side . . . and while he unhesitatingly and openly discussed questions with his ministers, never in the slightest way sought to interfere with or hamper their free action. The Queen was a dear; shy, good, kind, very much in love with her husband, devoted to her boy, anxious to do anything the people expected from her. She deeply loved both her father and mother; the news of the death of the latter came only as we were leaving, and was heartbreaking to her. She had told us much about their family relations. She was like a good simple child; she said that no wonder she was devoted to her father, for he was always kind, and had always said that he would never, for considerations of state or any other cause, try to make his daughters marry if they were not in love with the man; and that he had been so pleased when she fell in love with Haakon, then one of the Danish princes, for her marriage was a love match. . . .

In such a monarchy formal state and ceremonial at the court would have been absurd. Staying at the palace was like staying at any gentleman's house with exceptionally charming and friendly hosts. On the first afternoon, shortly after arriving, I was in the sitting room, when in came the King and Queen with Olaf. Mrs. Roosevelt was in her room, dressing. I gave Olaf various bits of bloodcurdling information about lions and elephants; and after a while his mother and father rose, and said "Come, Olaf, we must go." Olaf's face fell. "But am I not to see the wife?" he said. We assured him he should see the wife at tea. He was not a bit spoiled; his delight was a romp with his father, and he speedily pressed

Kermit and Ethel, whom he adored, into the games. In the end I too succumbed and romped with him as I used to romp with my own children when they were small. Outside of his own father and mother we were apparently the only persons who had ever really played with him in a fashion which he considered adequate; and he loudly bewailed our departure. When we reached London, where he had been brought by his father and mother to attend his grandfather's funeral, Princess Beatrice brightened up for a moment as she told me that Olaf had announced to her "I would like to marry Ethel; but I know I never shall!" Later, after the funeral, when I called to pay my respects to Queen Alexandra at Buckingham Palace, after being received by her I was taken to see her sister the Dowager-Empress of Russia. She was a very intelligent woman, and kept me nearly an hour discussing all kinds of subjects. Towards the end I began to hear little squeals in the hall, and when I left the Empress, there was Olaf patiently waiting outside the door. He had heard I was in the Palace, and had refused to go down to his dinner until he could see me—with the obvious belief that I would have a game of romps with him. I tossed him in the air, and rolled him on the floor while he shouted with delight; then happening to glance up, I saw that the noise had attracted the Empress, who had opened the door to look on; I paused for a moment, whereupon Olaf exclaimed with a woebegone face "but aren't you going on with the play?". . .

At Berlin and in Germany I was well received, that is, the Emperor and all the people high up were more than cordial. So were the professors and the people of the university and the scientific men generally; and the crowds were civil. But it was curious and interesting to notice the contrast between my reception in Germany and my reception in the other countries of Europe which I had already visited or visited afterwards. Everywhere else I was received . . . with practically as much enthusiasm as in my own country when I was President. In Germany I was treated with proper civility, all the civility which I had a right to demand and expect; and no more. In Paris the streets were decorated with French and American flags in my honor, and when I went to the theatre at the Français everyone rose and applauded so that I had to get up in the box and bow repeatedly, first to the actors, who had stopped the piece, and then to the audience. In Berlin the authorities showed me every courtesy, and the people all proper civility. But excepting the university folk, they really did not want to see me. . . .

Of course my chief interest at Berlin was in the Emperor himself. He is an able and powerful man. The first day we went out to take lunch with him. Afterwards he drove us to Potsdam, and showed us over Sans Souci. He also held army maneuvers at which I was present. On this occasion I rode with him for about five hours, and he talked steadily; and on another afternoon we spent three hours together. He was much interested to find how he was looked at by outsiders, and finally put a practically direct question to me as to how he was regarded in America; and I answered, "Well! your Majesty, I don't know whether you will understand our political terminology; but in America we think that if you lived on our side of the water you would carry your ward and turn up at the convention with your delegation behind you—and I cannot say as much for most of your fellow sovereigns!" Of course this needed a little explanation, but he was immensely pleased and amused with it when he understood it. He has a real sense of humor, as is shown by the comments he wrote on the backs of the photographs he sent me, which had been taken of us while we were at the maneuvers by his court photographer. Moreover, he is entirely modest about the many things which he thoroughly knows, such as the industrial and military conditions and needs of Germany. But he lacks all sense of humor when he comes to discuss the things that he does not know, and which he prides himself upon knowing, such as matters artistic and scientific. . . .

I said to the Emperor that it seemed to me that a war between England and Germany would be an unspeakable calamity. He answered eagerly that he quite agreed with me, that such a war he regarded as unthinkable; and he continued "I was brought up in England, very largely; I feel myself partly an Englishman. Next to Germany I care more for England than for any other country." Then with intense emphasis, "I ADORE ENGLAND!" I said that this was a stronger statement than I myself would be willing quite to make, but that I was very glad he felt so, because I believed that the English, Germans and Americans ought to be fundamentally in accord; and that nothing would so make for the peace and progress of the world. He answered that he entirely agreed with me; and then continued to speak of England with a curious mixture of admiration and resentment. . . .

I was especially interested in the Emperor, at seeing developed in him, to a much greater degree, what I had already seen traces of in some of the kings, that is, a kind of curious dual consciousness of events, a dual way of looking at them in relation to himself and his fellow sovereigns. Down at the bottom of his heart, he knew perfectly well that he himself was not an absolute sovereign. He had never had a chance to try. Taking into account the curious combination of power, energy, egotism, and restless desire to do, and to seem to do, things, which his character shows it is rather interesting to speculate on what he would have done as a really absolute sovereign, a Roman Emperor.[2]

[2] *Letters VII*, pp. 366–97.

3. *"King Edward's Wake"*

To David Gray[3]

Oyster Bay, Oct. 5, 1911

There was much that was both amusing and interesting in connection with my being special ambassador to the funeral of poor King Edward. All the special ambassadors were, of course, treated with much ceremony and pomp, and I was given a special carriage of State and a guard of six magnificent grenadiers in bearskins, who lined up and saluted me whenever I left or entered the Embassy, while the bugler sounded off—or whatever the technical expression is. . . . All of the special ambassadors were either sovereigns or princes of the blood royal, excepting Pichon, the French Minister of Foreign Affairs, and myself.

The night before the funeral there was a veritable wake—I hardly know what else to call it. King George gave a dinner to the special ambassadors in Buckingham Palace, the palace in which the dead king his father was lying in state. There was some seventy of us all told. Each man as he arrived said some word of perfunctory condolence to the king our host, and then on with the revel! It was not possible to keep up an artificial pretense of grief any longer, and nobody tried; and it was precisely like any other entertainment. The king sat in the middle of one side of the table, and the Emperor opposite him, and the rest of us were arranged elsewhere without as far as I could judge much attention being paid to rank. I sat with Prince Henry of Prussia on my right hand, and on my left a tall, shambling young man in a light blue uniform, whose card proclaimed him to be the Prince of Cumberland, or Prince Somebody of Cumberland, I forget which. For lack of other subjects of conversation, I said to him that although his title was English, yet that he himself seemed to be German; and with a melancholy glance at the very vivacious Emperor, who was diagonally opposite us, he answered that he ought to be Prince of Brunswick and King of Hanover, and would be "if it were not for him," nodding his head to indicate the Emperor. I felt like suggesting to him to relieve his feelings by throwing a carafe at the usurper.

As soon as I entered the room the Bulgarian Czar came up to speak to me, and to thank me for various things I had done for the Bulgarians, a people who have always interested me and in whom I have always believed. He is a very competent fellow, but with some unattractive traits,

[3] Journalist and lawyer; author of novels, essays and plays.

288

and at the moment all the other sovereigns were angry with him because he had suddenly christened himself czar instead of king, which they regarded as bumptious. . . .

While I was talking to the Czar, the Emperor suddenly walked up to us, thrust himself in ahead of the Czar, turned his back square to him and said to me: "Roosevelt, my friend, I want to introduce you to the King of Spain"; (then with a sudden ferocious glance over his shoulder at the Czar) "*he* is worth talking to!"

The King of Spain, by the way, *was* worth while talking to. I was much impressed by him. He at first thanked me for having behaved with such courtesy and consideration to Spain while I was President, and I told him of course that I had simply done my duty, for which I deserved no thanks, and that anyhow it was a real pleasure for me to do anything I could for Spain. He then said, looking me straight in the face, "I am glad to meet you, Mr. Roosevelt, I have admired your public career, and I have also admired your military career, though I am sorry that your honors should have been won at the expense of my countrymen." I bowed and said: "Your Majesty, I have always borne testimony, and I always shall bear testimony, to the gallantry and courage your countrymen showed in battle; although frankly I cannot speak as highly of their leadership." To which he responded: "I should think not! I should think not! but I am glad to have you speak thus of the courage of the soldiers," to which I answered that I could not speak too highly of the courage that the Spanish soldiers had shown under very depressing circumstances. . . .

Among those present at the dinner were various representatives of the royal family of France. . . . I think the consideration they were shown at the funeral was one of the reasons why Pichon was irritated. He is a queer looking creature at best, but on this particular evening anger made him look like a gargoyle. His clothes were stiff with gold lace and he wore sashes and orders, for I was the only man present in ordinary evening dress. He had all along held me as his natural companion and ally, because we represented the two republics, and were the only people present who were not royalties.

Before dinner he got me aside and asked me in French, as he did not speak English, what colored coat my coachman had worn that evening. I told him I did not know; whereupon he answered that his coachman had a black coat. I nodded and said Yes, I thought mine had a black coat also. He responded with much violence that this was an outrage, a slight upon the two great republics, as all the Royalties' coachmen wore red coats, and that he would at once make a protest on behalf of us both. I told him to hold on, that he must not make any protest on my behalf, that I did not care what kind of coat my coachman wore, and would be

289

perfectly willing to see him wear a green coat with yellow splashes—"un paletot vert avec des taches jaunes," being my effort at idiomatic rendering of the idea, for I speak French, I am sorry to say, as if it were a non-Aryan tongue, without tense or gender, although with agglutinative vividness and fluency. My incautious incursion into levity in a foreign tongue met appropriate punishment, for I spent the next fifteen minutes in eradicating from Pichon's mind the belief that I was demanding these colors as my livery. However I think it had the effect of diverting him from his own woe, and nothing more happened that evening.

But next morning when at eight o'clock, in evening dress, I turned up at the palace to go to Windsor, I found Pichon waiting for me more angry than ever. He was to go in the same carriage with me, and walking hastily up, and his voice shaking, he pointed out the very gorgeous-looking carriage in which we were to go and said that it was an outrage, that all the royalties had glass coaches and we did not. As I had never heard of a glass coach excepting in connection with Cinderella, I was less impressed by the omission than he was; and he continued that "ces Chinois" were put ahead of us. To this I answered that any people dressed as gorgeously as "ces Chinois" ought to go ahead of us; but he responded that it was not a laughing matter. Then he added that "ce Perse" had been put in with us, pointing out a Persian prince of the blood royal, a deprecatory, inoffensive-looking Levantine of Parisian education, who was obviously ill at ease, but whom Pichon insisted upon regarding as somebody who wanted to be offensive.

At this moment our coach drove up, and Pichon bounced into it. I supposed he had gotten in to take the right-hand rear seat; as to which I was totally indifferent, for my experience at the White House had given me a horror of squabbles over precedence, and the one thing upon which I had insisted with our Ambassadors was that I should sit or walk or stand whenever any of my hosts wished me to. But Pichon was scrupulous in giving me precedence, although I have no idea whether I was entitled to it or not. He sat on the left rear seat himself, stretched his arm across the right seat and motioned me to get in so that "ce Perse" should not himself take the place of honor! Accordingly I got in, and the unfortunate Persian followed, looking about as unaggressive as a rabbit in a cage with two boa constrictors.

As soon as we had started, Pichon's feelings overcame him again, and he pointed out the fact that we were following "toutes ces petites royautés," even "le roi du Portugal."

I then spoke to him seriously, and said that in my judgment France and the United States were so important that it was of no earthly consequence whether their representatives went before or behind the representatives of utterly insignificant little states like Portugal, and that I thought it a great mistake to make a fuss about it, because it showed a lack of self-confidence. He shook his head, and said that in Europe they regarded these things as of real importance, and that if I would not join him in a protest he would make one on his own account. I answered that I very earnestly hoped he would not make a row at a funeral (my French failed me at this point, and I tried alternately "funéraille" and "pompe funèbre") that it would be sure to have a bad effect, and that if he was discontented the proper thing to do was to wait until the coronation and then have France stipulate in advance how her special ambassador should rank. He asked if I would join in such a proposal; and I answered that in the first place I should not be special ambassador, and in the next place that if I were I most emphatically would not care a rap where I was placed any more than I did at the moment, for I was merely trying on behalf of the American people to show in courteous fashion their sympathy for the British people, that I wanted to do whatever the British people wished done, and did not in the least care where I was placed. I also told him to wait and see how we were treated at Windsor Castle, for I believed he would find that every effort would be made to be more than attentive to us. Sure enough, after the funeral, when we had lunch at Windsor Castle, I was at the King's table and he was at the queen's. I think my advice had a sedative effect; it certainly prevented any public explosion. . . .[4]

[4] *Letters VII*, pp. 409–13.

Preacher

~~~~~~

Mr. Roosevelt once described the White House as a "bully pulpit." He was inclined to make any platform a pulpit. If he had not been the ablest politician of his generation, and its most effective statesman, he might have been its most compelling preacher. But his sermons would not have carried so far as those that had the White House for a sounding-board, and could be, and generally were, backed by action.

~~~~~~

1. The Adventure of Living

Life is a great adventure, and I want to say to you, accept it in such a spirit. I want to see you face it ready to do the best that lies in you to win out; and resolute, if you do not win out, to go down without complaining, doing the best that is in you, and abiding by the result. What is true of the boy is also true of the girl; what is true of the young man is true of the young woman, the fundamental facts are the same.

Nothing worth having normally comes unless there is willingness to pay for it; and perhaps the highest good that comes from training of the kind which you get here is not merely training of the body, not merely the training of the mind, but the training of what counts for more than body, more than mind—the training of character, especially in the two ways of giving you the proper perspective (so that you may see what are the important and what the unimportant things) and of giving you the type of soul which will make you willing to strive, and to pay the necessary penalty, for achieving the things that are really worth while.

I do not at the moment remember any man or any woman whose life has been entirely easy, and who has at the same time led a life that under conceivable conditions I would have been willing to lead. That is true of the men; I think it is probably even more true of the women. The man or woman who has come to threescore years and ten without knowing sorrow, with no effort or risk, has, save in wholly exceptional cases, not known the highest joys. As I have said, life is a great adventure, and you cannot win the great prizes unless you are willing to run certain risks, unless you are willing to pay certain penalties. It is the same in large things as in small. If an individual starts to play football, and expects not to get bumped, he will be sadly disappointed. An individual who tries to rise to any position of prominence along any line in his college work and to surpass competitors, and expects to do so without struggle, is again in error. In the college world there is not any real prize in any field, the winning of which does not necessarily imply effort and self-denial, does not imply a certain amount of risk. As on the football-field, if you desire absolute safety, I do not think you had better play the game. And while it is the business of your elders and betters to shape conditions which shall minimize the risk, there will always be a certain amount of risk. On a larger scale it is just so in every-day life. When you graduate, when you go into your life-work, you can purchase immunity from risk, the certainty of ease, the certainty of possessing a soul that will be unruffled by any pain, only on condition of living a life not worth living, only on condition of leading the life of a vegetable.

In looking back at my companions when they were your age, and when I was your age, it is half pathetic, and all too melancholy to realize how poor the lives have been of those young men and young women of that day who declined to get their enjoyment from worthy effort, and who have devoted themselves of set purpose to lives that should consist, at best, of active pleasure, and, at worst, of the avoidance of risk and responsibility. I would not wish for any young man or young woman, or for any boy or girl of my own or of any one else for whom I care, a life of mere ease, a life which should consist merely of the absence of toil, of effort, of risk, or even of sorrow. You cannot get the highest pleasure in life without toil and effort and risk, and yours is a poor soul if you fail to pay the price for them. No nation ever yet became great unless it possessed within itself the power of effort and self-sacrifice in a great crisis. The effort and self-sacrifice are demanded, and no individual ever became great, and no individual ever led a really worthy life, unless he or she possessed within himself or herself the power, if need be, for effort long sustained, at the cost of discomfort, of pain, and hardship; and the power to face risk, to face danger and difficulty and even disaster, rather than not achieve a worthy end.

It is impossible to prophesy for any one an absolutely safe life. That cannot be done. No parents, no fathers and mothers can hope to bring up their children with the certainty that they will not meet with trials in after-life. On the contrary, if their children are to lead full lives, if they are to know what is highest and best in life, it can be set down as axiomatic that they will have to face trials, and will have to face suffering. No great joy can be achieved save with the possibility that a great sorrow may come as an alternative. No great success can ever be won save by accepting the fact that, normally, sacrifice of some kind must come in winning the success. No man or woman has ever known the extreme happiness of having and bringing up children without having to face the possibility of danger and of risk in connection with those children. And what is true of the family is true in every other expression of life. I was going to say in any other kind of life, but I mean in all the other ways in which life is led.

If you are to play any part in the world, if you are to have great happiness, you must make up your mind that you are not going to shrink from risks, that you are going to face the fact that effort, and painful effort, will often be necessary; and you must count for your happiness, not on avoiding everything that is unpleasant, but of possessing in you the power to overcome and trample it under foot. If you have small, shallow souls, shallow souls and shallow hearts, I will not say you will be unhappy; you can obtain the bridge-club standards of happiness, and you can go through life without cares and without sorrows, and without conscious effort, in so far as your brains will enable you to do so; but you have richly deserved the contempt of everybody whose respect is worth having. On the other hand, you can make up your minds to lead your lives well and nobly, doing first of all your duty to yourself and to those immediately dependent upon you, the duty of father to son, of husband to wife, of wife to husband, of parents to children—to do those duties first, and then to do the duties that lie beyond them, the duty of joining with your fellows in common work toward a common end, in the effort to achieve in common something worth achieving for the sake of all. You can lead that kind of life—and it is the only kind of life worth leading, and the only kind of life worth living—you can lead it only on condition of making up your mind that you will not expect always to have an easy time, to escape care, to escape responsibility, to escape the burdens that inevitably must be carried by every man and every woman whose shoulders are broad enough to enable him or her to play a part in the world.

You have two duties to perform. In the first place, be able to pull your own weight; and then when you have done that, remember that that is only the beginning. We have a right to expect that, in addition to having worked for yourself so that you will not be a burden to any one else, in addition to your being able to take care of all those whom it is your duty to care for, your education has counted for little if you cannot, furthermore, do your part in helping the world move on.

We stand now well over the threshold of a century big with the fate of mankind. Many great problems confront us all over the civilized world, and nowhere do we face problems graver than those here in America. Ours is not an easy task. The continent is pretty well filled up, and our business is to make the best use of what we have received from our fathers, and leave it in better shape to our sons. Do not flatter yourselves that you can stand still, or that the nation can stand still. If you think you can stand still, you may be perfectly certain that you are going back. We as a nation will either go forward or backward; and whether we succeed or fail will depend more than anything else upon the kind of training that you and those like you receive in your own home and in institutions such as this, and upon the use that you make of that training.[1]

2. The Conditions of Success

There are two kinds of success. One is the very rare kind that comes to the man who has the power to do what no one else has the power to do. That is genius. I am not discussing what form that genius takes; whether it is the genius of a man who can write a poem that no one else can write, "The Ode on a Grecian Urn," for example, or "Helen, thy beauty is to me"; or of a man who can do one hundred yards in nine and three-fifths seconds. Such a man does what no one else can do. Only a very limited amount of the success of life comes to persons possessing genius. The average man who is successful—the average statesman, the average public servant, the average soldier, who wins what we call great success—is not a genius. He is a man who has merely the ordinary qualities that he shares with his fellows, but who has developed those ordinary qualities to a more than ordinary degree.

Take such a thing as hunting or any form of vigorous bodily exercise. Most men can ride hard if they choose. Almost any man can kill a lion if he will exercise a little resolution in training the qualities that will enable him to do it. [*Taking a tumbler from the table, Mr. Roosevelt held it up.*] Now it is a pretty easy thing to aim straight at an object about that size. Almost any one, if he practises with the rifle at all, can learn to hit that tumbler; and he can hit the lion all right if he learns to shoot as straight at its brain or heart as at the tumbler. He does not have to possess any extraordinary capacity, not a bit—all he has to do is to develop certain rather ordinary qualities, but develop them to such a degree that he will not get flustered, so that he will press the trigger steadily instead of jerking it—and then he will shoot at the lion as well as he will at that tumbler. It is a perfectly simple quality to develop. You don't need any

[1] *Works XIII,* pp. 578–81.

remarkable skill; all you need is to possess ordinary qualities, but to develop them to a more than ordinary degree.

It is just the same with the soldier. What is needed is that the man as soldier should develop certain qualities that have been known for thousands of years, but develop them to such a point that in an emergency he does, as a matter of course, what a great multitude of men can do but what a very large proportion of them don't do. And in making the appeal to the soldier, if you want to get out of him the stuff that is in him, you will have to use phrases which the intellectual gentlemen who do not fight will say are platitudes.

It is just so in public life. It is not genius, it is not extraordinary subtlety, or acuteness of intellect, that is important. The things that are important are the rather commonplace, the rather humdrum, virtues that in their sum are designated as character. If you have in public life men of good ability, not geniuses, but men of good abilities, with character—and, gentlemen, you must include as one of the most important elements of character common sense—if you possess such men, the government will go on very well.

I have spoken only of the great successes; but what I have said applies just as much to the success that is within the reach of almost every one of us. I think that any man who has had what is regarded in the world as a great success must realize that the element of chance has played a great part in it. Of course a man has to take advantage of his opportunities; but the opportunities have to come. If there is not the war, you don't get the great general; if there is not a great occasion, you don't get the great statesman; if Lincoln had lived in times of peace, no one would have known his name now. The great crisis must come, or no man has the chance to develop great qualities.

There are exceptional cases, of course, where there is a man who can do just one thing, such as a man who can play a dozen games of chess or juggle with four rows of figures at once—and as a rule he can do nothing else. A man of this type can do nothing unless in the one crisis for which his powers fit him. But normally the man who makes the great success when the emergency arises is the man who would have made a fair success in any event. I believe that the man who is really happy in a great position—in what we call a career—is the man who would also be happy and regard his life as successful if he had never been thrown into that position. If a man lives a decent life and does his work fairly and squarely so that those dependent on him and attached to him are better for his having lived, then he is a success, and he deserves to feel that he has done his duty and he deserves to be treated by those who have had greater success as nevertheless having shown the fundamental

297

qualities that entitle him to respect. We have in the United States an organization composed of the men who forty-five years ago fought to a finish the great Civil War. One thing that has always appealed to me in that organization is that all of the men admitted are on a perfect equality provided the records show that their duty was well done. Whether a man served as a lieutenant-general or an eighteen-year-old recruit, so long as he was able to serve for six months and did his duty in his appointed place, then he is called comrade and stands on an exact equality with the other men. The same principle should shape our associations in ordinary civil life.

I am not speaking cant to you. I remember once sitting at a table with six or eight other public officials and each was explaining how he regarded being in public life, how only the sternest sense of duty prevented him from resigning his office, and how the strain of working for a thankless constituency was telling upon him, and nothing but the fact that he felt he ought to sacrifice his comfort to the welfare of his country kept him in the arduous life of statesmanship. It went round the table until it came to my turn. This was during my first term of office as President of the United States. I said: "Now, gentlemen, I do not wish there to be any misunderstanding. I like my job, and I want to keep it for four years longer." I don't think any President ever enjoyed himself more than I did. Moreover, I don't think any ex-President ever enjoyed himself more. I have enjoyed my life and my work because I thoroughly believe that success—the real success—does not depend upon the position you hold, but upon how you carry yourself in that position. There is no man here to-day who has not the chance so to shape his life after he leaves this university that he shall have the right to feel, when his life ends, that he has made a real success of it; and his making a real success of it does not in the least depend upon the prominence of the position he holds. Gentlemen, I thank you, and I am glad I have violated the poet's hope and have preached to you.[2]

3. Service and Self-respect

Unless democracy is based on the principle of service by everybody who claims the enjoyment of any right, it is not true democracy at all. The man who refuses to render, or is ashamed to render, the necessary service is not fit to live in a democracy. And the man who demands from another a service which he himself would esteem it dishonorable or unbecoming to render is to that extent not a true democrat. No man has a right to demand a service which he does not regard as honorable to ren-

[2] *Ibid.*, pp. 574–7.

der; nor has he a right to demand it unless he pays for it in some way, *the payment to include respect for the man who renders it.* Democracy must mean mutuality of service rendered, and of respect for the service rendered.

A leading Russian revolutionist (who is, of course, like every true friend of freedom, an opponent of the Bolsheviki) recently came to this country from Vladivostock. He traversed the Siberian railway. The porter on his train refused to get him hot water or to black his boots; stating with true Bolshevistic logic that democracy meant that nobody must do anything for any one else and that anyhow his union would turn him out if he rendered such service.

Now, this Bolsheviki porter was foolish with a folly that can only be induced by prolonged and excessive indulgence in Bolshevism or some American analogue. But the root trouble in producing his folly was the fact that under the old system the men whose boots the porter blacked looked down on him for blacking them. Are we entirely free from this attitude in America? Until we are we may as well make up our minds that to just that extent we are providing for the growth of Bolshevism here. No man has a right to ask or accept any service unless under changed conditions he would feel that he could keep his entire self-respect while rendering it. Service which carries with it the slightest implication of social abasement should not be rendered.

For a number of years I lived on a ranch in the old-time cattle country; and I also visited at the house of a backwoods lumber-jack friend. In both places we lived under old-style American conditions. We all of us worked, and our social distinctions were essentially based on individual worth. We accepted as a matter of course that the difference in degree of service rendered ought at least roughly to correspond to the difference in reward. Each did most of the purely personal things for himself. But nobody thought of any necessary work as degrading.

I remember that once, when there was a lull in outdoor work, I endeavored to be useful in and around the house. I fed the pigs; and on an idle morning I blacked all the boots. Ordinarily our boots did not need blacking—most of them were not that kind. On this occasion I started, with an enthusiasm that outran my judgment, to black the dress boots of every one, of both sexes. I coated them with a thick, dull paste; only a few knobs became shiny; and the paste came off freely on what it touched. As a result I temporarily lost not merely the respect but even the affection of all the other inmates of the house. However, I did not lose caste because I had blacked the boots. I lost caste because I had blacked them badly. But I was allowed to continue feeding the pigs. The pigs were not so particular as the humans.

299

Now, there is no more reason for refusing to bring hot water or black boots or serve a dinner or make up a bed or cook or wash clothes (I have cooked and washed clothes often—but neither wisely nor well) than for refusing to shoe a horse, run a motor, brake a train, sell carpets, manage a bank, or run a farm. A few centuries back men of good lineage felt that they lost caste if they were in trade or finance—in some countries they feel so to this day. In most civilized lands, however, the feeling has disappeared, and it never occurs to any one to look down on any one else because he sells things. Just the same feeling should obtain, and as we grow more civilized will obtain, about all other kinds of service. This applies to domestic service. It is as entirely right to employ house-maids, cooks, and gardeners as to employ lawyers, bankers, and business men or cashiers, factory-hands, and stenographers. But only on condition that we show the same respect to the individuals in one case as in the other cases!

Ultimately I hope that this respect will show itself in the forms of address, in the courtesy titles used, as well as the consideration shown, and the personal liberty expected and accorded. I am not demanding an instant change—I believe in evolution rather than revolution. But I am sure the change is possible and desirable; and even although it would be foolish and undesirable to set up the entirely new standard immediately, I hope we can work toward it. One of the most charming gentlewomen I know, the wife of a man of rare cultivation, ability, and public achievement, lives on the top floor of a tenement-house in a Western city. The rooms are comfortably and daintily furnished—with an abundance of books. In this household the maid was introduced to me as Miss So-and-so; and this is the ideal. Of course it cannot be realized until there has been much education *on both sides*. But it should be the ideal. All relations between employer and employee should be based on mutuality of respect and consideration; arrogance met by insolence, or an alternation of arrogance and insolence, offers but a poor substitute.

Mutuality of respect and consideration, service and a reward corresponding as nearly as may be to the service—these make up the ideal of democracy.[3]

4. "On Sunday, go to church . . ."

For all those whose lives are led on a plane above the grimmest and barest struggle for existence church attendance and church work of some kind mean both the cultivation of the habit of feeling some responsibility

[3] *Works XIX*, pp. 338–40.

for others and the sense of braced moral strength which prevents a relaxation of one's own fiber. . . .

Therefore, on Sunday go to church. Yes—I know all the excuses. I know that one can worship the Creator and dedicate oneself to good living in a grove of trees, or by a running brook, or in one's own house, just as well as in church. But I also know that as a matter of cold fact the average man does *not* thus worship or thus dedicate himself. If he stays away from church he does not spend his time in good works or in lofty meditation. He looks over the colored supplement of the newspaper; he yawns; and he finally seeks relief from the mental vacuity of isolation by going where the combined mental vacuity of many partially relieves the mental vacuity of each particular individual. . . .

He may not hear a good sermon at church. But unless he is very unfortunate he will hear a sermon by a good man who, with his good wife, is engaged all the week long in a series of wearing and humdrum and important tasks for making hard lives a little easier; and both this man and this wife are in the vast majority of cases showing much self-denial and doing much for humble folks of whom few others think, and keeping up a brave show on narrow means. Surely the average man ought to sympathize with the work done by such a couple, and ought to help them; and he can't help them unless he is a reasonably regular church attendant. Otherwise he is an outsider, and is felt to be such, and the part he plays in useful church activities, in service by the church to its members and to the community at large, is only the part which an outsider can play. . . .

Even if he doesn't hear a good sermon, the probabilities are that he will listen to and take part in reading some beautiful passages from the Bible. And if he is not familiar with the Bible he has suffered a loss which he had better make all possible haste to correct. Moreover, he will probably take part in singing some good hymns. He will meet and nod to, or speak to, good, quiet neighbors.

If he does not think about himself too much he will benefit himself very much, especially as he begins to think chiefly of others. And he will come away feeling a little more charitably toward all the world—even toward those excessively foolish young men who regard churchgoing as a soft performance. . . .[4]

[4] *Ladies' Home Journal,* October, 1917.

nothing; and we shall do as little if we merely set the greed of envy against the greed of arrogance, and thereby destroy the material well-being of all of us. To turn this government either into government by a plutocracy or government by a mob would be to repeat on a larger scale the lamentable failures of the world that is dead.

We stand against all tyranny, by the few or by the many. We stand for the rule of the many in the interest of all of us, for the rule of the many in a spirit of courage, of common sense, of high purpose, above all in a spirit of kindly justice toward every man and every woman. We not merely admit, but insist, that there must be self-control on the part of the people, that they must keenly perceive their own duties as well as the rights of others; but we also insist that the people can do nothing unless they not merely have, but exercise to the full, their own rights. The worth of our great experiment depends upon its being in good faith an experiment—the first that has ever been tried—in true democracy on the scale of a continent, on a scale as vast as that of the mightiest empires of the Old World. Surely this is a noble ideal, an ideal for which it is worth while to strive, an ideal for which at need it is worth while to sacrifice much; for our ideal is the rule of all the people in a spirit of friendliest brotherhood toward each and every one of the people.[1]

2. "I dread having to plunge . . ."

To Henry Cabot Lodge

Christiania, May 5, 1910

Ugh! I do dread getting back to America, and having to plunge into this cauldron of politics. Our own party leaders did not realize that I was able to hold the Republican party in power only because I insisted on a steady advance, and dragged them along with me. Now the advance has been stopped and, whether we blame the people on the one side, or the leaders on the other, the fact remains that we are in a very uncomfortable position.

I do not attach any real importance to the seeming popularity which I for the moment enjoy. I don't see how it can work out for permanent good, and, as you know, I care nothing whatever for popularity, excepting as a means to an end. Of course I like to have the good-will and respect of those for whom I care, but wide popular acclaim, it seems to me, counts for almost nothing unless it can be turned to good tangible account, in the way of getting substantial advance along the lines of clean and wise

[1] *Works XVII*, pp. 170-1.

government. I have never cared in the least for the kind of popularity which Lafayette so thoroughly enjoyed, and which Jefferson enjoyed, popularity which the popular man basks in for and of itself, without reference to transmuting it into any positive achievement. I want to accomplish things. Now I don't for a moment believe that popularity of the kind that at the moment I seem to enjoy will avail when there is a tide of bitter popular feeling against a party or an organization. I may be mistaken, but this is my present view.[2]

3. "We have had a smashing defeat . . ."

To Arthur Hamilton Lee

Oyster Bay, November 11, 1910

We have had a smashing defeat. . . . In New York State we had to face as ugly a combination as can be imagined, consisting of Tammany Hall, Wall Street, and the professional intellectuals—not that the latter added much weight to the combination, but still they probably did count for a few thousand votes. In other words, it was corrupt politics at its worst, and the plutocracy at its worst, plus the "intellectuality" of the type of our friend the London *Nation* at its worst. . . .

I very earnestly hope that one result will follow, and that is the elimination of me as a possible candidate in 1912. . . . I know that your friendship does not depend in any way upon my success, but for Heaven's sake don't allow yourself to be misled into the belief that I am going on as a leader in politics. I do not see how such a thing is possible. At any rate, it is wildly improbable. For thirty years I have been active in political life. I have had a mighty good run for my money; I have worked hard and accomplished a certain amount; and now I am perfectly willing to step aside and see younger, or at least newer and more vigorous, men take up the task.[3]

4. *Nationalism and Democracy*

The true object of democracy should be to guarantee each man his rights, with the purpose that each man shall thereby be enabled better to do his duty. Government is a failure, no matter how well it preserves law and order, if it results only in securing to a few people an enormously disproportionate share of power and of material well-being, while the

[2] *Letters VII*, pp. 80–1.
[3] *Ibid.*, pp. 163–4.

conditions for the great mass of men are such as to forbid them achieving success by hard, honest, intelligent work. Similarly, democracy means failure if it merely substitutes a big privileged for a small privileged class, and if this big privileged class in its turn desires nothing more than selfish material enjoyment. The man who receives what he has not earned and does not earn, the man who does not render service in full for all that he has, is out of place in a democratic community; and he is equally out of place, whether he be a man living in idle luxury on millions which he has not earned or which he has won in ways that represent no service to the State; or whether he be a man living in idle poverty, enjoying the luxury of squalid sloth, content to exist on some form of charity, or, what is still worse, on what is in its nature the plunder of the industrious. Effortless ease ignobly enjoyed and the avoidance of serious work render a man equally unfit for citizenship in a republic, whether he be a multimillionaire or a tramp. The division between the worthy and the unworthy citizen must be drawn on conduct and character, and not on wealth or poverty. Arrogance and envy, the bitter scorn of the rich man for the poor man and the bitter hate of the poor man for the rich man, are merely the opposite sides of the same dark shield. . . .

The democracy, if it is to come to its own in this country, must set its face like steel against privilege and all the beneficiaries of privilege. It must war to cut out special privilege from our frame of government, and in doing so it must count upon the envenomed hostility, not only of the great industrial corporations and individuals who are the beneficiaries of privilege, but of their servants and adherents in the press and in public life.

Yet it is even more important that the people should be on their guard against themselves than it is that they should be on their guard against others. Each of us must hold his own against outsiders at times, but, after all, the chief dangers to each man dwell within that man's own heart and brain; and what is true of each of us individually is true of all of us in a mass. No man can do good work in the world for himself, for those whom he loves who are dependent upon him, or for the State at large, unless he has the great virtue of self-mastery, unless he can control his passions and appetites, and force head and hand to work according to the dictates of conscience. This is so obvious that to many people it will seem too obvious to need repetition. But, though obvious enough in theory, it is continually forgotten in practice; and the political leaders who address, not each man individually, but men in a mass, often forget to inculcate it even in theory. . . .

The greatness of our nation in the past has rested upon the fact that the people had power, and that they used it aright for great and worthy ends. Washington and Lincoln, each in the degree that his generation rendered possible, trusted to and believed in the people, steadfastly refused to represent anything save what was highest and best in the people, and by appealing to this highest and best brought it out and made it prominent. Each called upon his countrymen to lay down their lives for an ideal, and then called upon the survivors to perform the even harder task of leading their lives in such shape as to realize the ideal for which the dead men had died. Our aim, the aim of those of us who stand for true progress, for true Nationalism, for true democracy, is not only to give the people power, but, ourselves as part of the people, to try to see that the power is used aright, that it is used with wisdom, with courage, with self-restraint, and in a spirit of the broadest kindliness and charity toward all men. . . .

The Roman Republic fell, not because of the ambition of Cæsar or Augustus, but because it had already long ceased to be in any real sense a republic at all. When the sturdy Roman plebeian, who lived by his own labor, who voted without reward according to his own convictions, and who with his fellows formed in war the terrible Roman legion, had been changed into an idle creature who craved nothing in life save the gratification of a thirst for vapid excitement, who was fed by the state, and who directly or indirectly sold his vote to the highest bidder, then the end of the republic was at hand, and nothing could save it. The laws were the same as they had been, but the people behind the laws had changed, and so the laws counted for nothing.

We need good laws just as a carpenter needs good instruments. If he has no tools, the best carpenter alive cannot do good work. But the best tools will not make a good carpenter, any more than to give a coward a rifle will make him a good soldier. We wish to see the mass of our people move steadily upward to a higher social, industrial, and political level. To do this we wish to change the laws, and by this change to render it steadily easier for the right type of man, the right type of woman, to achieve better conditions. But unless the man and the woman are of the right type the laws can accomplish nothing. It rests within our own hands, it rests with us, the people of America, to determine our own fate; and character is the main factor in the determination. . . .

I believe that the average American citizen wishes nothing save what he can honestly obtain for himself by hard work and decent living. This is one reason why I so heartily believe in democracy. I believe in the future of the American people because I believe that fundamentally and at heart the average man and the average woman of America are sound; that, however deeply they may at times err, yet they have in them, fundamentally, the power of self-mastery, of self-control, the power to live their lives in accordance with a high and fine ideal, to do strict justice to others, and to insist upon their rights only as a vantage-point for the better performance of their duties.[4]

5. The 1912 Nomination

To Oscar King Davis[5]

Oyster Bay, May 31, 1911

As far as I can now see, no situation could arise which would make it possible for me to accept a nomination next year. However, it is academic, for I think we have taken steps to prevent all agitation on the subject. I have explained that every friend of mine will show his friendship by seeing that there is no movement started to have me nominated.

What an awful tangle things are in at Washington! I get almost as disgusted with most of the progressives as with the standpat crowd.[6]

To William E. Glasscock and Others[7]

New York, February 24, 1912

GENTLEMEN: I deeply appreciate your letter, and I realize to the full the heavy responsibility it puts upon me, expressing as it does the carefully considered convictions of the men elected by popular vote to stand as the heads of government in their several States.

I absolutely agree with you that this matter is not one to be decided with any reference to the personal preferences or interests of any man, but purely from the standpoint of the interests of the people as a whole. I will accept the nomination for President if it is tendered to me, and will adhere to this decision until the convention has expressed its preference.

One of the chief principles for which I have stood, and for which I now stand, and which I have always endeavored and always shall endeavor to reduce to action, is the genuine rule of the people, and therefore I hope that so far as possible the people may be given the chance, through direct primaries, to express their preference as to who shall be the nominee of the Republican Presidential Convention.[8]

[4] *Works XVII*, pp. 100–7.
[5] Journalist; secretary, Progressive National Committee; author of *Released for Publication*.
[6] *Letters VII*, pp. 273–4.
[7] These were seven governors who had petitioned Roosevelt to run for the Republican nomination.
[8] *Letters VII*, p. 511.

6. "Nothing has touched me more . . ."

To Paul A. Ewert[9]

Oyster Bay, July 5, 1912

Nothing has touched me more than the willingness of men in whom I earnestly believe to leave their official positions and come out in this fight. But in such a case I feel that the sacrifice ought not to be made unless the good that will be done outweighs the damage that will also be done. It is a good deal now as it was when I went to the war—I refused to take into my regiment any married man who was depending upon his own exertions for the livelihood of his wife and children, although I gladly took in married men who had an independent fortune so that his family would not suffer if he were killed. I did not feel that the emergency justified the sacrifice of the man's family. In the same way, just at present I do not feel that our cause is sufficiently bright to warrant me to have men like you . . . come out for me. Moreover, I am inclined to think that at present you can do better work for the public in office than you can by coming out for the cause.

Events shaped themselves so that I had no alternative except to lead, but I am under no illusion about it. It is a forlorn hope. The probabilities are against success. I have been careful to try to bring with me only the men of the crusading temperament and I have discouraged men from joining me if I felt that the damage done to their families, or to the public service was more than counterbalanced by the gain that would come to the cause. Probably all the men who are with me in this fight will suffer more or less because they are with me, and will gain nothing. Thank Heaven! I think I can conscientiously say that I myself will suffer most and gain least—otherwise I should be profoundly uncomfortable.

Now it is necessary that the fight should be made and, of course, there is some small chance of victory; but not enough for us to take into account. Under such circumstances a parallel of what I did in my regiment is complete! The men who come with me should be men who have little or nothing to lose and, unless they can render very great essential service to the cause by coming out for me, they ought not to do so at the cost of impairing their usefulness to the community in other positions.[10]

[9] A Justice Department agent working with the Five Civilized Tribes.
[10] *Letters VII*, pp. 571–2.

7. *The Meaning of Free Government*

When I say that I believe not only in the right of the people to rule, but in their duty to rule themselves and to refuse to submit to being ruled by others, I am not using a figure of speech, I am speaking of a vital issue which fundamentally affects our whole American life. I not merely admit but insist that in all government, and especially in popular government, there must be control; and, furthermore, that if control does not come from within it must come from without. Therefore it is essential that any people which engages in the difficult experiment of self-government should be able to practise self-control. There are peoples in the world which have proved by their lamentable experiences that they are not capable of this self-control; but I contend that the American people most emphatically are capable of it. I hold that in the long run, taken as a whole, our people can and will govern themselves a great deal better than any small set of men can govern them.

The attempt has recently been made to improve on Abraham Lincoln's statement that "this is a government of the people, for the people, by the people." As a substitute therefor it is proposed that this government shall hereafter be a government of the people, for the people, by a representative part of the people.

It is always a dangerous matter to try to improve on Lincoln when we deal with the rights and duties of the people, and this particular attempt at improvement is not a happy one. In substance it of course means nothing except that this is to be a government of the whole people by a part of the people. We have had such a government in various parts of this Union from time to time, and stripped of verbiage it simply means a government of the people by the bosses; a government of the whole people against instead of for the interest of the whole people by a part of the people which does the bidding of the holders of political and financial privilege.

Now, I want each of you to consider this governmental proposition from his own individual standpoint. Our contention is that just as each individual wishes, and ought to wish, to rule his own life for himself, so that all individuals taken together—that is, the people—must wish themselves to rule their collective life and not to be ruled by others. Each of us wants to lead his own life himself. . . .

This does not mean that none of us will make mistakes; on the contrary, each of us will sometimes make mistakes. You will make them. I will make them. But the mistakes I make will be my own and not somebody else's; and I will know that they are mistakes and will cure them

310

myself; whereas if somebody else was making them for me, maybe he and I would not agree as to what were mistakes and what were not, and in that case he could not cure them.

It is just the same way about the people as a whole. All of us, you and I, all of us together, want to rule ourselves, and we don't wish to have any body of outsiders rule us. That is what free government means. If people cannot rule themselves, then they are not fit for free government, and all talk about democracy is a sham.

And this is aside from the fact that in actual life here in the United States experience has shown that the effort to substitute for the genuine rule of the people something else always means the rule of privilege in some form or other, sometimes political privilege, sometimes financial privilege, often a mixture of both.

Whenever there is tyranny by the majority I shall certainly fight it. But the tyrannies from which we have been suffering in this country have, ninety-nine times out of a hundred, been tyrannies by a minority; that is, tyranny by privilege. Sometimes, as in the case of some public-utility franchise or other bit of grabbing by a few what belongs to the many, the tyranny is primarily commercial; at other times, it is primarily political. This, for instance, is true at the present day in those States where the people have been denied the right to vote at primaries in order to express their preferences for President.

In a government like ours, our representatives do not rule us in the sense that a monarchy or an aristocracy bears rule over the people. We, the people, rule ourselves, and what we really want from our representatives is that they shall manage the government for us along the lines we lay down, and shall do this with efficiency and in good faith. We welcome leadership and advice, of course, and we are content to let experts do the expert business to which we assign them without fussy interference from us. But the expert must understand that he is carrying out our general purpose and not substituting his own for it. The leader must understand that he leads us, that he guides us, by convincing us so that we will follow him or follow his direction. He must not get it into his head that it is his business to drive us or to rule us. His business is to manage the government for us. We rule ourselves, and we choose our representatives, not to rule us, but to manage the public business for us along the lines we have laid down and approved.

The men who disbelieve in the rule of the people, and who think that the people should be ruled by a part of them (for to call such a part "a representative part" is entirely meaningless), treat the Constitution as a strait-jacket for restraining an unruly patient—the people. We, on the contrary, treat the Constitution as an instrument designed to secure justice through giving full expression to the deliberate and well-thought-out judgment of the people. They are false friends of the people, and enemies of true constitutional government, who endeavor to twist the Constitution aside from this purpose.

We are engaged at the present day in a great struggle for social and industrial justice in this country, and our chief opponents in this struggle are the powers of pillage, the powers that profit by privilege at the expense of the rights of the plain people as a whole. I advocate genuine popular rule in nation, in State, in city, in county, as offering the best possible means for eliminating special privilege alike in politics and in business, and for getting a genuine equality of opportunity for every man to show the stuff there is in him. I do not demand equality of reward. There is wide inequality of service, and where this is the case it is but just that there should be inequality of reward, for it would be the rankest kind of injustice to reward the man who renders worthless service as well as we strive, however inadequately, to reward him who renders service that is literally priceless.

But I do ask that we endeavor so to shape our governmental policy as to bring about a measurable equality of opportunity for all men and all women so as to do justice to man and to woman, to big and to little, to rich and to poor.

I believe it is even more important for men to pay heed to their duties and to the rights of others than it is for them to pay heed to their own rights. But I believe also that they can only do their full duty when they enjoy fully their rights. I hold that we of this nation are false to our professions, false to the traditions handed down to us by the founders and the preservers of the Republic, if we do not make it in very truth a real republic, a democracy in fact as well as in name, a democracy where each man stands on his worth as a man and is judged as such; a democracy in which the people really rule themselves, where their representatives do not rule them but honestly and efficiently manage the government for them.

In our government we cannot permanently succeed unless the people really do rule. We have tried the other experiment. The present system means the rule of the powers of political and industrial privilege, and for that we propose to substitute the right of the people to rule themselves and their duty to rule so as to bring nearer the day when every man and every woman within the boundaries of this great land of ours shall have fair play, equal rights, shall receive and shall give justice, social and industrial, justice for every man, for every woman within our borders.[11]

[11] *Works XVII*, pp. 172–6.

312

8. The Stricken Standard-bearer[12]

It matters little about me but it matters all about the cause we fight for. If one soldier who happens to carry the flag is stricken, another will take it from his hands and carry it on. One after another the standard-bearers may be laid low, but the standard itself can never fall. You know that personally I did not want ever to be a candidate for office again. And you know that only the call that came to the men of the sixties made me answer it, in our day, as they did more nobly in their day. And now, as then, it is not important whether one leader lives or dies, it is important only that the cause shall live and win. Tell the people not to worry about me, for if I go down another will take my place. For always, the army is true. Always the cause is there, and it is the cause for which the people care, for it is the people's cause.[13]

9. The Fight Goes On

I wish to express my cordial agreement with the manly and proper statement of Mr. Bryan when, in arguing for a continuance of the discussion of the issues at stake in this contest, he said:

"The issues of this campaign should not be determined by the act of an assassin. Neither Colonel Roosevelt nor his friends could ask that the discussion should be turned away from the principles that are involved. If he is elected President, it should be because of what he has done in the past, and what he proposes to do hereafter."

I wish to point out, however, that neither I nor my friends have asked that the discussion be turned away from the principles that are involved; on the contrary, we emphatically demand that the discussion be carried on precisely as if I had not been shot. I shall be sorry if Mr. Wilson does not keep on the stump, and I feel that he owes it to himself and the American people to continue on the stump.

I wish to make one more comment on Mr. Bryan's statement. It is, of course, perfectly true that in voting for me or against me consideration must be paid to what I have done in the past and to what I propose to do. But it seems to me far more important that consideration should be paid to what the Progressive party proposes to do.

I cannot too strongly emphasize the fact, upon which Progressives insist,

---

[12] Statement sent by Mr. Roosevelt from his sickbed after his attempted assassination in Milwaukee, Wisc., to an audience in Louisville, Ky., October 16, 1912.

[13] *Works XVII*, p. 331.

that the welfare of any one man in this fight is wholly immaterial compared to the great and fundamental issues involved in the triumph of the principles for which our cause stands. If I had been killed the fight would have gone on exactly the same. . . . Hundreds of other men now on the stump are preaching the doctrines that I have been preaching, and stand for and represent just the same cause. They would have continued the fight in exactly the same way if I had been killed, and they are continuing it in just the same way now that I am for the moment laid up.

So far as my opponents are concerned, whatever could with truth and propriety have been said against me and my cause before I was shot can with equal truth and equal propriety be said against me, and it now should be so said; and the things that cannot be said now are merely the things that ought not to have been said before. This is not a contest about any man; it is a contest concerning principles.

If my broken rib heals fast enough to relieve my breathing, I shall hope to be able to make one or two speeches in the campaign. In any event, if I am not able to make them, the men I have mentioned and the hundreds like them will be stating our case right to the end of the campaign, and I trust our opponents will be stating their case also.[14]

10. The Purpose of the Progressive Party

Perhaps once in a generation, perhaps not so often, there comes a chance for the people of a country to play their part wisely and fearlessly in some great battle of the age-long warfare for human rights. To our fathers the chance came in the mighty days of Abraham Lincoln, of the man who thought and toiled and suffered for the people with a sad, patient, and kindly endeavor. To our forefathers the chance came in the troubled years that stretched from the time when the First Continental Congress gathered to the time when Washington was inaugurated as first President of the Republic. To us in our turn the chance has now come to stand for liberty and righteousness as in their day these dead men stood for liberty and righteousness. Our task is not as great as theirs. Yet it is well-nigh as important. Our task is to profit by the lessons of the past, and to check in time the evils that grow around us, lest our failure to do so may cause dreadful disaster to the people. We must not sit supine and helpless. We must not permit the brutal selfishness of arrogance and the brutal selfishness of envy, each to run unchecked its evil course. If we do so, then some day smouldering hatred will suddenly kindle into a consuming flame, and either we or our children will be called on to face a crisis as grim as any which this Republic has ever seen.

[14] *Ibid.*, pp. 332–3.

It is our business to show that nine-tenths of wisdom consists in being wise in time. Woe to our nation if we let matters drift, if in our industrial and political life we let an unchecked and utterly selfish individualistic materialism riot to its appointed end! That end would be wide-spread disaster, for it would mean that our people would be sundered by those dreadful lines of division which are drawn when the selfish greed of the *haves,* is set over against the selfish greed of the *have-nots.* There is but one way to prevent such a division, and that is to forestall it by the kind of a movement in which we are now engaged.

Our movement is one of resolute insistence upon the rights and full acknowledgment of the duties of every man and every women within this great land of ours. We war against the forces of evil, and the weapons we use are the weapons of right. We do not set greed against greed or hatred against hatred. Our creed is one that bids us to be just to all, to feel sympathy for all, and to strive for an understanding of the needs of all. Our purpose is to smite down wrong. But toward those who have done the wrong we feel only the kindliest charity that is compatible with causing the wrong to cease. We preach hatred to no man, and the spirit in which we work is as far removed from vindictiveness as from weakness. We are resolute to do away with the evil, and we intend to proceed with such wise and cautious sanity as will cause the very minimum of disturbance that is compatible with achieving our purpose.

Do not forget, friends, that we are not proposing to substitute law for character. We are merely proposing to buttress character by law. We fully recognize that, as has been true in the past, so it is true now, and ever will be true, the prime factor in each man's or woman's success must normally be that man's or that woman's own character—character, the sum of many qualities, but above all of the qualities of honesty, of courage, and of common sense. Nothing will avail a nation if there is not the right type of character among the average men and women, the plain people, the hard-working, decent-living, right-thinking people, who make up the great bulk of our citizenship. I know my countrymen; I know that they are of this type. But it is in civil life as it is in war. In war it is the man behind the gun that counts most, and yet he cannot do his work unless he has the right kind of gun. In civil life, in the every-day life of our nation, it is individual character which counts most; and yet the individual character cannot avail unless in addition thereto there lie ready to hand the social weapons which can be forged only by law and by public opinion operating through and operated upon by law.

Again, friends, do not forget that we are proposing no new principles. The doctrines we preach reach back to the Golden Rule and the Sermon on the Mount. They reach back to the commandments delivered at Sinai.

All that we are doing is to apply those doctrines in the shape necessary to make them available for meeting the living issues of our own day. We decline to be bound by the empty, little cut-and-dried formulas of bygone philosophies, useful once, perhaps, but useless now. Our purpose is to shackle greedy cunning as we shackle brutal force, and we are not to be diverted from this purpose by the appeal to the dead dogmas of a vanished past. We propose to lift the burdens from the lowly and the weary, from the poor and the oppressed. We propose to stand for the sacred rights of childhood and womanhood. Nay, more, we propose to see that manhood is not crushed out of the men who toil, by excessive hours of labor, by underpayment, by injustice and oppression. When this purpose can only be secured by the collective action of our people through their governmental agencies, we propose so to secure it. . . .

We are for liberty. But we are for the liberty of the oppressed, and not for the liberty of the oppressor to oppress the weak and to bind burdens on the shoulders of the heavy-laden. It is idle to ask us not to exercise the power of the government when only by the power of the government can we curb the greed that sits in high places, when only by the exercise of the government can we exalt the lowly and give heart to the humble and the downtrodden.

We care for facts and not for formulas. We care for deeds and not for words. We recognize no sacred right of oppression. We recognize no divine right to work injustice. We stand for the Constitution. We recognize that one of its most useful functions is the protection of property. But we will not consent to make of the Constitution a fetich for the protection of fossilized wrong. We call the attention of those who thus interpret it to the fact that, in that great instrument of justice, life and liberty are put on a full level with property, indeed, are enumerated ahead of it in the order of their importance. We stand for an upright judiciary. But where the judges claim the right to make our laws by finally interpreting them, by finally deciding whether or not we have the power to make them, we claim the right ourselves to exercise that power. We forbid any man, no matter what their official position may be, to usurp the right which is ours, the right which is the people's. We recognize in neither court nor Congress nor President, any divine right to override the will of the people expressed with due deliberation in orderly fashion and through the forms of law.

We Progressives hold that the words of the Declaration of Independence, as given effect to by Washington and as construed and applied by Abraham Lincoln, are to be accepted as real, and not as empty phrases. We believe that in very truth this is a government by the people themselves, that the Constitution is theirs, that the courts are theirs, that all the governmental agents and agencies are theirs. We believe that all true

316

leaders of the people must fearlessly stand for righteousness and honesty, must fearlessly tell the people what justice and honor demand. But we no less strongly insist that it is for the people themselves finally to decide all questions of pubic policy and to have their decision made effective.

In the platform formulated by the Progressive party we have set forth clearly and specifically our faith on every vital point at issue before this people. We have declared our position on the trusts and on the tariff, on the machinery for securing genuine popular government, on the method of meeting the needs of the farmer, of the business man, and of the man who toils with his hands, in the mine or on the railroad, in the factory or in the shop. There is not a promise we have made which cannot be kept. There is not a promise we have made that will not be kept. Our platform is a covenant with the people of the United States, and if we are given the power we will live up to that covenant in letter and in spirit.

We know that there are in life injustices which we are powerless to remedy. But we know also that there is much injustice which can be remedied, and this injustice we intend to remedy. We know that the long path leading upward toward the light cannot be traversed at once, or in a day, or in a year. But there are certain steps that can be taken at once. These we intend to take. Then, having taken these first steps, we shall see more clearly how to walk still further with a bolder stride. . . .

Our people work hard and faithfully. They do not wish to shirk their work. They must feel pride in the work for the work's sake. But there must be bread for the work. There must be a time for play when the men and women are young. When they grow old there must be the certainty of rest under conditions free from the haunting terror of utter poverty. We believe that no life is worth anything unless it is a life of labor and effort and endeavor. We believe in the joy that comes with work, for he who labors best is really happiest. We must shape conditions so that no one can own the spirit of the man who loves his task and gives the best there is in him to that task, and it matters not whether this man reaps and sows and wrests his livelihood from the rugged reluctance of the soil or whether with hand or brain he plays his part in the tremendous industrial activities of our great cities. We are striving to meet the needs of all these men, and to meet them in such fashion that all alike shall feel bound together in the bond of a common brotherhoood, where each works hard for himself and for those dearest to him, and yet feels that he must also think of his brother's rights because he is in very truth that brother's keeper.[15]

[15] *Ibid.*, pp. 334–40.

11. *"We fought the good fight . . ."*

To James Rudolph Garfield [16]

Oyster Bay, Nov. 8, 1912

DEAR JIM: We have fought the good fight, we have kept the faith, and we have nothing to regret. Probably we have put the ideal a little higher than we can expect the people as a whole to take offhand.[17]

12. *"The Progressive movement must . . . go forward . . ."*

To Arthur Hamilton Lee

Oyster Bay, Nov. 5, 1912

I am immensely pleased that you so clearly grasp just what we have been doing in this Progressive fight. It would be more accurate to say what we have been *trying* to do, for there is no use disguising the fact that the defeat at the polls is overwhelming. I had expected defeat, but I had expected that we would make a better showing. . . . But I suppose that I ought not to expect that in three months we could form a new Party that would do as well as we have actually done. We had all the money, all the newspapers and all the political machinery against us and, above all . . . the habit of thought of the immense mass of dull unimaginative men who simply vote according to the party symbol.

Whether the Progressive Party itself will disappear or not, I do not know; but the Progressive movement must and will go forward even though its progress is fitful. It is essential for this country that it should go forward.[18]

[16] Secretary of the Interior in Roosevelt's cabinet.
[17] *Works VII,* p. 637.
[18] *Ibid.,* p. 633.

Defender of the Faith

~~~~~~

The faith that Theodore Roosevelt preached during the years of the first World War was the faith he had preached as a budding public servant in the Eighteen Eighties and a rising political figure in the Nineties: undivided loyalty to American principles of life and government, courage to face the realities of international life, and readiness of body, mind and spirit to act where courage might lead. That meant, in terms of a world on fire, arms and ships and planes, a nation trained and disciplined, the will to resist the aggressor, the responsibility to assist the victim of aggression. Back of it all was character, the quality of the individual citizen. He summed it all up in the word "righteousness." "If there must be a choice between righteousness and peace," he said, "I choose righteousness."

~~~~~~

1. The Cataclysm

In this country we are both shocked and stunned by the awful cataclysm which has engulfed civilized Europe. By only a few men was the possibility of such a widespread and hideous disaster even admitted. Most persons, even after it occurred, felt as if it was unbelievable. They felt that in what it pleased enthusiasts to speak of as "this age of enlightenment" it was impossible that primal passion, working hand in hand with the most modern scientific organization, should loose upon the world these forces of dread destruction.

In the last week in July the men and women of the populous civilized countries of Europe were leading their usual ordered lives, busy and yet soft, lives carried on with comfort and luxury, with appliances for ease and pleasure such as never before were known, lives led in a routine which to most people seemed part of the natural order of things, something which could not be disturbed by shocks such as the world knew of old. A fortnight later hell yawned under the feet of these hard-working or pleasure-seeking men and women, and woe smote them as it smote the peoples we read of in the Old Testament or in the histories of the Middle Ages. Through the rents in our smiling surface of civilization the volcanic fires beneath gleamed red in the gloom.

What occurred in Europe is on a giant scale like the disaster to the *Titanic*. One moment the great ship was speeding across the ocean, equipped with every device for comfort, safety, and luxury. The men in her stoke-hold and steerage were more comfortable than the most luxurious travellers of a century ago. The people in her first-class cabins enjoyed every luxury that a luxurious city life could demand and were screened not only from danger but from the least discomfort or annoyance. Suddenly, in one awful and shattering moment, death smote the floating host, so busy with work and play. They were in that moment shot back through immeasurable ages. At one stroke they were hurled from a life of effortless ease back into elemental disaster; to disaster in which baseness showed naked, and heroism burned like a flame of light. . . .[1]

In the terrible whirlwind of war all the great nations of the world, save the United States and Italy, are facing the supreme test of their history. All of the pleasant and alluring but futile theories of the pacificists, all the theories enunciated in the peace congresses of the past twenty years, have vanished at the first sound of the drumming guns. The work of all the Hague conventions, and all the arbitration treaties, neutrality treaties, and peace treaties of the last twenty years has been swept before the gusts of war like withered leaves before a November storm. In this great crisis the stern and actual facts have shown that the fate of each nation depends not in the least upon any elevated international aspirations to which it has given expression in speech or treaty, but on practical preparation, on intensity of patriotism, on grim endurance, and on the possession of the fighting edge.[2]

2. *"To guard against any possible misconception . . ."*

To Bernhard Dernburg[3]

Oyster Bay, December 4, 1914

To guard against any possible misconception, let me put my own position concisely. I have a very hearty admiration for the German people. I am myself partly of German descent. I know no American citizens superior

---

[1] *Works XVIII,* pp. 3–4.
[2] *Ibid.,* pp. 183–4.
[3] Spokesman for the German government in New York in 1914.

to the American citizens of German descent. I immensely admire the efficiency of the German Empire, that is of the German people and government. I greatly wish that we in America would copy this efficiency, both military, industrial and social and we can only do that if we exercise the wise forethought and show the patriotism and the capacity for labor that Germany has exercised and shown. I understand entirely the great difficulties of Germany's position with France on one side and Russia on the other. But I do not and cannot accept and I never shall accept, the German theory of international morality as shown by Germany's action toward Belgium. What I say or do is of small moment; it is very possibly true that I represent only an inappreciable element of the American people; but I do represent a certain number of American citizens who emphatically believe in international morality, in international good faith, both on the part of the United States and on the part of other nations, and who no less emphatically believe that it is as wrong to show timidity and weakness as to show brutality and cynicism in international, no less than in private dealings.

Hitherto in this war Germany has on the whole been successful and it may be that you are right in your forecast that Germany will be victorious and will keep Belgium. If so, you will not have my sympathy and if I had the power you would not have my support. On the other hand, if you and the Austrians were beaten and if there was an attempt made to take, at the expense of Germany and Austria, the action which you so light-heartedly propose to take at the expense of Belgium, whatever I could do, by words, would be done on behalf of the Germans; and, if I had the power, I would, in such a case, exercise that power in your behalf. I would as greatly regret to see the German nation destroyed as I would to see France or England or Russia destroyed and if I had the power I would interfere as quickly to prevent one calamity as to prevent the other.

In short, my belief is that this nation should judge other nations each on its conduct; and that it should fearlessly and where possible effectively take action against wrongdoing; that it should prepare itself so as to make it unsafe for any other nation to do wrong to it; and that, in its turn, it should scrupulously do justice to every nation that acts rightly.[4]

To Raymond Robins[5]

Oyster Bay, N.Y., June 3, 1915

The present world war is in its essence one between militarism and democracy—and this although I . . . agree with you that Russia's siding

---

[4] *Letters VIII*, pp. 860–1.
[5] Chicago social worker, prominent in the Progressive Party.

at the moment with the cause of democracy, or at least of liberalism and freedom, *may* only be accidental and that in the not distant future we *may* have greatly to fear her—although I both hope and believe that Russia will be liberalized by the war. You are absolutely right when you say that Russia and Japan, with alien pasts, with alien institutions and alien ideals of world dominion by force of arms, *may* in the near future (although I hope and believe not) occupy a position of menace towards western civilization, with just one people to withstand their mastery; and that is our own nation with our ideals of democracy, of liberty under law, of social progress through peaceful industry, education and commerce and of uncorrupted Christianity—which Christianity after all must largely be the attempt to realize that noble verse of Micah, "What more doth the Lord require of thee than to do justly and to love mercy and to walk humbly with thy God?".

(This verse has always been a favorite of mine, because it embodies the Gospel of Works, with the necessary antidote in the last few words to that hard spiritual arrogance which is brought about by *mere* reliance on the Gospel of Works.)

I hope and believe that neither Russia nor Japan will ever occupy such a position; but it is of course possible that some day one or both of them may stand as Germany now stands, and menace civilization; and in such event we should be prepared to do just what we have so signally failed to do during the last ten months.[6]

3. Fear God and Take Your Own Part

Fear God; and take your own part! Fear God, in the true sense of the word, means love God, respect God, honor God; and all of this can only be done by loving our neighbor, treating him justly and mercifully, and in all ways endeavoring to protect him from injustice and cruelty; this obeying, as far as our human frailty will permit, the great and immutable law of righteousness.

We fear God when we do justice to and demand justice for the men within our own borders. We are false to the teachings of righteousness if we do not do such justice and demand such justice. We must do it to the weak, and we must do it to the strong. We do not fear God if we show mean envy and hatred of those who are better off than we are; and still less do we fear God if we show a base arrogance toward and selfish lack of consideration for those who are less well off. We must apply the same standard of conduct alike to man and to woman, to rich man and to poor man, to employer and employee. We must organize our social and indus-

[6] *Letters VIII*, p. 928.

trial life so as to secure a reasonable equality of opportunity for all men to show the stuff that is in them, and a reasonable division among those engaged in industrial work of the reward for that industrial work, a division which shall take into account all the qualities that contribute to the necessary success. We must demand honesty, justice, mercy, truthfulness, in our dealings with one another within our own borders. Outside of our own borders we must treat other nations as we would wish to be treated in return, judging each in any given crisis as we ourselves ought to be judged—that is, by our conduct in that crisis. If they do ill, we show that we fear God when we sternly bear testimony against them and oppose them in any way and to whatever extent the needs require. If they do well, we must not wrong them ourselves. Finally, if we are really devoted to a lofty ideal we must in so far as our strength permits aid them if they are wronged by others. When we sit idly by while Belgium is being overwhelmed, and rolling up our eyes prattle with unctuous self-righteousness about "the duty of neutrality," we show that we do not really fear God; on the contrary, we show an odious fear of the devil, and a mean readiness to serve him.

But in addition to fearing God, it is necessary that we should be able and ready to take our own part. The man who cannot take his own part is a nuisance in the community, a source of weakness, an encouragement to wrong-doers, and an added burden to the men who wish to do what is right. If he cannot take his own part, then somebody else has to take it for him; and this means that his weakness and cowardice and inefficiency place an added burden on some other man and make that other man's strength by just so much of less avail to the community as a whole. No man can take the part of anyone else unless he is able to take his own part. This is just as true of nations as of men. A nation that cannot take its own part is at times almost as fertile a source of mischief in the world at large as is a nation which does wrong to others, for its very existence puts a premium on such wrong-doing. Therefore, a nation must fit itself to defend its honor and interest against outside aggression; and this necessarily means that in a free democracy every man fit for citizenship must be trained so that he can do his full duty to the nation in war no less than in peace. . . .[7]

Fear God and take your own part! This is another way of saying that a nation must have power and will for self-sacrifice and also power and will for self-protection. There must be both unselfishness and self-expression, each to supplement the other, neither wholly good without the other. The nation must be willing to stand disinterestedly for a lofty ideal and yet it must also be able to insist that its own rights be heeded by others. Evil will come if it does not possess the will and the power for unselfish action on behalf of non-utilitarian ideals and also the will and the power for self-

[7] *Works XVIII,* pp. 199–200.

323

mastery, self-control, self-discipline. It must possess those high and stern qualities of soul which will enable it to conquer softness and weakness and timidity and train itself to subordinate momentary pleasure, momentary profit, momentary safety to the larger future.

There is not the slightest use of saying any of this unless we are willing and able to translate our speech into action. National unselfishness and self-sacrifice must be an affair of deeds. To utter lofty sentiments on the subject, to indulge in oratory about it, to write notes about it, and then when the occasion arises not to act in accordance with these sentiments, means moral degradation for the nation. Oratorical insincerity of this kind is nauseating to all honest men. Prolonged indulgence in this kind of emotional insincerity eats into the moral fibre of the people like a corrosive acid. . . .[8]

Let us be true to our democratic ideal, not by the utterance of cheap platitudes, not by windy oratory, but by living our lives in such manner as to show that democracy can be efficient in promoting the public welfare during periods of peace and efficient in securing national freedom in time of war. If a free government cannot organize and maintain armies and navies which can and will fight as well as those of an autocracy or a despotism, it will not survive. We must have a first-class navy and a first-class professional army. We must also secure universal and obligatory military training for all our young men. Our democracy must prove itself effective in making the people healthy, strong, and industrially productive, in securing justice, in inspiring intense patriotism, and in making every man and woman within our borders realize that if they are not willing at time of need to serve the nation against all comers in war, they are not fit to be citizens of the nation in time of peace. The democratic ideal must be that of subordinating chaos to order, of subordinating the individual to the community, of subordinating individual selfishness to collective self-sacrifice for a lofty ideal, of training every man to realize that no one is entitled to citizenship in a great free commonwealth unless he does his full duty to his neighbor, his full duty in his family life, and his full duty to the nation; and unless he is prepared to do this duty not only in time of peace but also in time of war. It is by no means necessary that a great nation should always stand at the heroic level. But no nation has the root of greatness in it unless in time of need it can rise to the heroic mood. . . .[9]

We are the citizens of a mighty Republic consecrated to the service of God above, through the service of man on this earth. We are the heirs of a great heritage bequeathed to us by statesmen who saw with the eyes of the seer and the prophet. We must not prove false to the memories of the nation's past. We must not prove false to the fathers from whose loins we

[8] *Ibid.,* p. 453.
[9] *Ibid.,* pp. 456–7.

sprang, and to their fathers, the stern men who dared greatly and risked all things that freedom should hold aloft an undimmed torch in this wide land. They held their worldly well-being as dust in the balance when weighed against their sense of high duty, their fealty to lofty ideals. Let us show ourselves worthy to be their sons. Let us care, as is right, for the things of the body; but let us show that we care even more for the things of the soul. Stout of heart, and pledged to the valor of righteousness, let us stand four-square to the winds of destiny, from whatever corner of the world they blow. Let us keep untarnished, unstained, the honor of the flag our fathers bore aloft in the teeth of the wildest storm, the flag that shall float above the solid files of a united people, a people sworn to the great cause of liberty and of justice, for themselves, and for all the sons and daughters of men.[10]

4. Americanism

There is no room in this country for hyphenated Americanism. When I refer to hyphenated Americans, I do not refer to naturalized Americans. Some of the very best Americans I have ever known were naturalized Americans, Americans born abroad. But a hyphenated American is not an American at all. This is just as true of the man who puts "native" before the hyphen as of the man who puts German or Irish or English or French before the hyphen. Americanism is a matter of the spirit and of the soul. Our allegiance must be purely to the United States. We must unsparingly condemn any man who holds any other allegiance. But if he is heartily and singly loyal to this Republic, then no matter where he was born, he is just as good an American as any one else.

The one absolutely certain way of bringing this nation to ruin, of preventing all possibility of its continuing to be a nation at all, would be to permit it to become a tangle of squabbling nationalities, an intricate knot of German-Americans, Irish-Americans, English-Americans, French-Americans, Scandinavian-Americans, or Italian-Americans, each preserving its separate nationality, each at heart feeling more sympathy with Europeans of that nationality than with the other citizens of the American Republic. The men who do not become Americans and nothing else are hyphenated Americans; and there ought to be no room for them in this country. The man who calls himself an American citizen and who yet shows by his actions that he is primarily the citizen of a foreign land, plays a thoroughly mischievous part in the life of our body politic. He has no place here; and the sooner he returns to the land to which he feels his real heart-allegiance, the better it will be for every good American. There is

[10] *Ibid.*, pp. 225–6.

no such thing as a hyphenated American who is a good American. The only man who is a good American is the man who is an American and nothing else.[11]

5. "Americanism means many things . . ."

To S. Stanwood Menken[12]

Oyster Bay, N.Y., January 10, 1917

Americanism means many things. It means equality of rights and therefore equality of duty and of obligation. It means service to our common country. It means loyalty to one flag, the flag of all of us. It means on the part of each of us respect for the rights of the rest of us. It means that all of us guarantee the rights of each of us. It means free education, genuinely representative government, freedom of speech and thought, quality before the law for all men, genuine political and religious freedom, and the democratizing of industry so as to give at least a measurable quality of opportunity for all, and so as to place before us, as our ideal in all industries where this ideal is possible of attainment, the system of co-operative ownership and management, in order that the tool users may, so far as possible, become the tool owners.

Everything is un-American that tends either to government by a plutocracy, or government by a mob. To divide along the lines of section or caste or creed is un-American. All privilege based on wealth, and all enmity to honest men merely because they are wealthy, are un-American—both of them equally so. Americanism means the virtues of courage, honor, justice, truth, sincerity, and hardihood—the virtues that made America. The things that will destroy America are prosperity-at-any-price, peace-at-any-price, safety-first instead of duty-first, the love of soft living, and the get-rich-quick theory of life.

Preparedness must be of the soul no less than of the body. We must keep lofty ideals steadily before us, and must train ourselves in practical fashion so that we may realize these ideals. Throughout our whole land we must have fundamental common purposes, to be achieved through education, through intelligent organization, and through the recognition of the great vital standards of life and living. We must make Americanism and Americanization mean the same thing to the native born and to the foreign born; to the men and to the women; to the rich and to the poor; to the employer and to the wage-worker. If we believe in American standards,

[11] *Ibid.*, pp. 392–3.
[12] New York lawyer and president of the National Security League.

we shall insist that all privileges springing from them be extended to immigrants, and that they in return accept these standards with whole-hearted and entire loyalty. Either we must stand absolutely by our ideals and conceptions of duty, or else we are against them. There is no middle course, and if we attempt to find one, we insure for ourselves defeat and disaster. . . .

Preparedness does not mean merely a man with a gun. It means that too; but it means a great deal more. It means that in this country we must secure conditions which will make the farmer and the workingman under-stand that it is in a special sense their country; that the work of prepared-ness is entered into for the defense of the country which belongs to them, to all of us, and the government of which is administered in their interest, in the interest of all of us. . . . Here in America we must do justice to the workers, or they will not feel that this is the country to which their devotion is due; and we must exact patriotic devotion to the flag from them, for if they fail to render it they are unfit to live in this country at all.

I appeal to all Americans to join in the common effort for the common good. Any man who holds back, and refuses to serve his country with wholehearted devotion, on the ground that enough has not been done for him, will do well to remember that any such holding back, or lukewarm-ness of patriotism, is itself an admission of inferiority, an admission of personal unfitness for citizenship in a democracy, and ought to deprive him of the rights of citizenship. As for the men of means, from whom we have the right to expect a special quality of leadership, let them remember that, as much has been given to them, so much will be expected of them, and that they have no moral right whatsoever to the enjoyment of the ease and the comforts of life beyond that their fellows enjoy, unless they render service beyond what their fellows render.

I advocate military preparedness not for the sake of war, but for the sake of safeguarding this nation against war, so long as that is possible, and of guaranteeing its honor and safety if war should nevertheless come. We hope ultimately the day will come on this earth when wars will cease. But at present the realization of that hope seems as far in the future as the realization of that other hope, that some day in the future all crime shall cease.[13]

6. *Warlike Power—the Prerequisite for the Preservation of Social Values*

In December last I was asked to address the American Sociological Con-gress on "the effect of war and militarism on social values." In sending my

[13] *Letters VIII*, pp. 1143–5.

answer I pointed out that infinitely the most important fact to remember in connection with the subject in question is that if an unscrupulous, warlike, and militaristic nation is not held in check by the warlike ability of a neighboring non-militaristic and well-behaved nation, then the latter will be spared the necessity of dealing with its own "moral and social values" because it won't be allowed to deal with anything. Until this fact is thoroughly recognized, and the duty of national preparedness by justice-loving nations explicitly acknowledged, there is very little use of solemnly debating such questions as the one which the sociological congress assigned me —which, in detail, was "How war and militarism affect such social values as the sense of the preciousness of human life; care for child welfare; the conservation of human resources; upper-class concern for the lot of the masses; interest in popular education; appreciation of truth-telling and truth-printing; respect for personality and regard for personal rights." It seems to me positively comic to fail to appreciate, with the example of Belgium before our eyes, that the real question which modern peace-loving nations have to face is not how the militaristic or warlike spirit within their own borders will affect these "values," but how failure on their part to be able to resist the militarism of an unscrupulous neighbor will affect them. Belgium had a very keen sense of the "preciousness of human life" and of "the need for the care of child welfare and the conservation of human resources," and there was much "concern" by the Belgian "upper classes for the lot of the masses," great "interest in popular education and appreciation of truth-telling and truth-printing and a high respect for personality and regard for personal rights." But all these "social values" existed in Belgium only up to the end of July, 1914. Not a vestige of them remained in 1915. To discuss them as regards present-day Belgium is sheer prattle, simply because on August 4, 1914, Belgium had not prepared her military strength so that she could put on her frontiers at least half a million thoroughly armed and trained men of fighting spirit. . . .

There are well meaning people, utterly incapable of learning any lesson taught by history, utterly incapable even of understanding aright what has gone on before their very eyes. There are plenty of politicians, by no means as well-meaning, who find it to their profit to pander to the desire common to most men to live softly and easily and avoid risk and effort. Timid and lazy men, men absorbed in money-getting, men absorbed in ease and luxury, and all soft and slothful people naturally hail with delight anybody who will give them high-sounding names behind which to cloak their unwillingness to run risks or to toil and endure. Emotional philanthropists to whom thinking is a distasteful form of mental exercise enthusiastically champion this attitude. The faults of all these men and women are of a highly non-militaristic and unwarlike type; and naturally they feel great satisfaction in condemning misdeeds which are incident to lives that they would themselves be wholly unable to lead without an amount of toil and effort that they are wholly unwilling to undergo. These men and women are delighted to pass resolutions in favor of anything with a lofty name, provided always that no demand is ever made upon them to pay with their bodies to even the smallest degree in order to give effect to these lofty sentiments. It is questionable whether in the long run they do not form a less desirable national type than is formed by the men who are guilty of the downright iniquities of life; for the latter at least have in them elements of strength which, if guided aright, could be used to good purpose. . . .

War like peace, is properly a means to an end—righteousness. Neither war nor peace is in itself righteous, and neither should be treated as of it-self the end to be aimed at. Righteousness is the end. Rightousness when triumphant brings peace; but peace may not bring righteousness. Whether war is right or wrong depends purely upon the purpose for which, and the spirit in which, it is waged. Here the analogy with what takes place in civil life is perfect. The exertion of force or violence by which one man masters another may be illustrated by the case of a black-hander who kidnaps a child; knocking down the nurse or guardian; and it may also be illustrated by the case of the guardian who by violence withstands and thwarts the black-hander in his efforts to kidnap the child, or by the case of the police-man who by force arrests the black-hander or white-slaver or whoever it is and takes his victim away from him. There are, of course, persons who believe that all force is immoral, that it is always immoral to resist wrong-doing by force. I have never taken much interest in the individuals who profess this kind of twisted morality; and I do not know the extent to which they practically apply it. But if they are right in their theory, then it is wrong for a man to endeavor by force to save his wife or sister or daughter from rape or other abuse, or to save his children from abduction and tor-ture. It is a waste of time to discuss with any man a position of such folly, wickedness, and poltroonery. But unless a man is willing to take this posi-tion, he cannot honestly condemn the use of force or violence in war—for the policeman who risks and perhaps loses or takes life in dealing with an anarchist or white-slaver or black-hander or burglar or highwayman must be justified or condemned on precisely the same principles which re-quire us to differentiate among wars and to condemn unstintedly certain nations in certain wars and equally without stint to praise other nations in certain other wars. . . .

The really essential things for men to remember, therefore, in connec-tion with war are, first, that neither war nor peace is immoral in itself, and, secondly, that in order to preserve the "social values" which were enumerated in the quotation with which I began this chapter it is absolutely essential to prevent the dominance in our country of the one form of militarism which is surely and completely fatal—that is, the military dominion of an alien enemy.

It is utterly impossible to appreciate social values at all or to discriminate between what is socially good and socially bad unless we appreciate the utterly different social values of different wars. The Greeks who triumphed at Marathon and Salamis did a work without which the world would have been deprived of the social value of Plato and Aristotle, of Æschylus, Herodotus, and Thucydides. The civilization of Europe, America, and Australia exists to-day at all only because of the victories of civilized man over the enemies of civilization, because of victories stretching through the centuries from the days of Miltiades and Themistocles to those of Charles Martel in the eighth century and those of John Sobieski in the seventeenth century. During the thousand years that included the careers of the Frankish soldier and the Polish king, the Christians of Asia and Africa proved unable to wage successful war with the Moslem conquerors; and in consequence Christianity practically vanished from the two continents; and to-day nobody can find in them any "social values" whatever, in the sense in which we use the words, so far as the sphere of Mohammedan influence and the decaying native Christian churches are concerned. There are such "social values" to-day in Europe, America, and Australia only because, during those thousand years, the Christians of Europe possessed the warlike power to do what the Christians of Asia and Africa had failed to do— that is, to beat back the Moslem invader.

The Sociological Society meets at Washington this year only because the man after whom the city was named was willing to go to war. If he and his associates had not gone to war, there would have been no possibility of discussing "social values" in the United States, for the excellent reason that there would have been no United States. . . .

No intelligent man desires war. But neither can any intelligent man who is willing to think fail to realize that we live in a great and free country only because our forefathers were willing to wage war rather than accept the peace that spells destruction. No nation can permanently retain any "social values" worth having unless it develops the warlike strength necessary for its own defense.[14]

[14] *Works XVIII*, pp. 227–34.

7. *"Masters of our own souls . . ."*

To Mrs. John G. Graham[15]

Oyster Bay, N.Y., March 5, 1915

I touch my hat to you, as the daughter and mother of brave men, and as braver than those men themselves. You have exactly expressed my idea. I loathe war. When I went to Cuba, I left my wife not yet recovered from the birth of her last baby. I left six children behind. In the night before each fight, I never dared to think of either my wife or children because it really tended to unman me. I doubt if there exists a more thoroughly domestic man than I am or one more devoted to the homely pleasant things of the life of the home. But I should be ashamed of my sons if they shirked war, just as I should be ashamed of my daughters if they shirked motherhood. You say that you have gone down to the edge of the grave to open the door of life to your children. You have exactly expressed it. I have seen my wife, for whom of course I care infinitely more than for myself, nearer to death in childbirth than ever I was on the battlefield. Surely if it would be wrong for her to shirk one danger, it would be infinitely worse for me, infinitely more cowardly and less excusable, if I shirked the other.

I remember John Mason Brown, formerly of your city, telling me that in 1861 he returned from a year's hunt in the Rockies to find that the Civil War had broken out. His father had served in the Mexican War and was dead. As soon as he came home, his mother brought him his father's sword, saying: "My son, this is your father's sword. I hope you will draw it under the flag for which your father fought; but draw it you must, for one side or the other." That woman, like you, my dear Mrs. Graham, and all the women of your stamp, represents the women whom I wish to see exercise a decisive influence in voting and in the political affairs of this country.

As a matter of fact, the present pacificist administration has fought one dreadful and foolish little war with Mexico, whereas during my seven and a half years of administration, not an American soldier or sailor was killed in action with any foreign power. Preparedness against war is the best means of averting war; but if it is impossible to avert war save at the cost of dishonor, then the women of your type and of the type of John Mason Brown's mother, and their sons, will face the dangers of battle, the dangers of war, just as these women faced the dangers of childbirth. It is our duty individually and as a nation to avoid all quarrels, to avoid every species

[15] From Louisville, Kentucky.

of brutality, of wrongdoing, of wanton offense, to try to inculcate gentleness and fair and upright dealing as between man and man, nation and nation; but it is also our duty to keep ourselves masters of our own souls and possessed of those stern virtues for the lack of which no softness of manners, no gentleness of nature and, above all, no soft and easy course of life, will in any way atone.[16]

8. *The Heroic Mood*[17]

I am deeply sensible of the honor conferred on me and of the good-will shown me by the gentlemen who have announced themselves as delegates to be elected in my interest in the Massachusetts presidential primary. Nevertheless I must request, and I now do request and insist, that my name be not brought into the Massachusetts primaries, and I emphatically decline to be a candidate in the primaries of that or of any other State. Months ago I formally notified the authorities of Nebraska, Minnesota, and Michigan to this effect.

I do not wish the nomination.

I am not in the least interested in the political fortunes either of myself or any other man.

I am interested in awakening my fellow countrymen to the need of facing unpleasant facts. I am interested in the triumph of the great principles for which with all my heart and soul I have striven and shall continue to strive.

I will not enter into any fight for the nomination and I will not permit any factional fight to be made in my behalf. Indeed, I will go further and say that it would be a mistake to nominate me unless the country has in its mood something of the heroic—unless it feels not only devotion to ideals but the purpose measurably to realize those ideals in action.

This is one of those rare times which come only at long intervals in a nation's history, where the action taken determines the basis of the life of the generations that follow. Such times were those from 1776 to 1789, in the days of Washington, and from 1858 to 1865, in the days of Lincoln.

It is for us of to-day to grapple with the tremendous national and international problems of our own hour in the spirit and with the ability shown by those who upheld the hands of Washington and Lincoln. . . .

We must clarify and define our policies, we must show that our belief in our governmental ideals is so real that we wish to make them count in the world at large and to make the necessary sacrifice in order that they

[16] *Letters VIII*, pp. 907–8.
[17] Statement given to the press at Port of Spain, Trinidad, British West Indies, March 9, 1916.

shall count. Surely we, of this great Republic, have a contribution to make to the cause of humanity and we cannot make it unless we first show that we can secure prosperity and fair dealing among our own men and women. I believe that in a crisis so grave it is impossible too greatly to magnify the needs of the country or too strongly to dwell on the necessity of minimizing and subordinating the desires of individuals.

The delegates who go to Chicago will have it in their power to determine the character of the administration which is to do or leave undone the mighty tasks of the next four years. That administration can do an incalculable amount to make or mar our country's future. The men chosen to decide such a question ought not to be politicians of the average type and parochial outlook; still less should they be politicians controlled by sinister influence from within or without. They should be the very best men that can be found in our country, whose one great mission should be to declare in unequivocal terms for a programme of clean-cut, straight-out, national Americanism, in deeds not less than in words, and in internal and international matters alike, and to choose as their candidate a man who will not merely stand for such a programme before election, but will resolutely and in good faith put it through if elected.

These men should be men of rugged independence, who possess the broadest sympathy with and understanding of the needs and desires of their fellows; their loyalty should be neither to classes nor to sections, but to the whole of the United States and to all the people that dwell therein. They should be controlled by no man and no interest and their own minds should be open.

June is a long way off. Many things may occur between now and then. It is utterly impossible to say now with any degree of certainty who should be nominated at Chicago. The crying, the vital need now is that the men who next June assemble at Chicago from the forty-eight States, and express the view of the entire country shall act with the sane and lofty devotion to the interest of our nation as a whole which was shown by the original Continental Congress. They should approach their task unhampered by any pledge except to bring to its accomplishment every ounce of courage, intelligence, and integrity they possess.[18]

[18] *Works XVII,* pp. 410–13.

9. "As long as I am in the prophet business . . ."

To Edwin A. Van Valkenburg[19]

Oyster Bay, April 21, 1918

Do you remember the thing I read aloud, intending to send it to the Kansas City *Star*? Probably by this time you know that they did not think it wise to publish it. I asked them to send it to you with that statement. I have seriously thought of asking them whether, in view of the fact they think some of my articles about Mr. Wilson and the war are too strong and in view of the further fact that these are the ones for which I most care, they would be willing when I write such an article to have me not send it to them but to send it direct to you (of course unpaid).

I appreciate to the full the reasons why they are reluctant to publish them and I am sure that they are correct in their judgment *as regards themselves*. On the other hand, as you know, *my* whole concern at this time is practically the same concern that Amos and Micah and Isaiah had for Jerusalem nearly three thousand years ago! In those days a prophet was very apt to get himself stoned. Nowadays he merely excites the ire of the persons who would otherwise read the magazines or newspapers in which his prophecies appear. But he hasn't any business to damage his magazine or newspaper.

I am not dead sure that the prophet business can be combined with keeping up circulation; and moreover I know that when a man with strong feelings and intense convictions reaches a certain age he is apt to get cater-cornered as regards the surrounding world and therefore his usefulness ceases, and I am quite prepared to feel that now that I am in my sixtieth year it would be to the interest of everybody that I should cease being a prophet and become that far pleasanter and more innocuous person, a sage. But as long as I am in the prophet business I wish to prophesy! [20]

10. Four Sons in the War

To Theodore Roosevelt, Jr.

Sagamore Hill, June 1st, 1918

I am not mistaken as to the feeling about you! In the same mail came a letter. . . . A stranger . . . writes that her cousin . . . is under you

[19] Editor, Philadelphia *North American;* prominent in Progressive Party.
[20] *Letters VIII*, p. 1312.

and . . . says: "My major is the best man I ever met . . . utterly fearless and the most amazing and astounding energy I have ever seen . . . he is as big a man as his father who happens to be Theodore Roosevelt. There isn't a man or an officer in this outfit who wouldn't start to take a message to Berlin tonight if he asked it." . . .

Kermit transferred to our army as Captain of artillery. . . . He has received the British War Cross for gallantry in action, in command of a light armored motor battery; he is to report to Pershing; and I suppose will be immediately sent to the front. . . . Poor Quentin has had the hardest luck; and it does not seem as tho the War Department would let Flora go across. I am very, very proud of all four of you, and of Dick;* and you have done best of all.

I absolutely agree with you about having Kermit in our army; it is a load off my mind to have him transferred. The last five years have made me bitterly conscious of the shortcomings of our national character; but we Roosevelts are Americans, and can never think of being anything else, and wouldn't be anything else for any consideration on the face of the earth; a man with our way of looking at things can no more change his country than he can change his mother; and it is the business of each of us to play the part of a good American and try to make things as much better as possible.

This means, at the moment, to try to speed up the war; to back the army to the limit; and to support or criticize every public official precisely according to whether he does or does not efficiently support the war and the army. The smug complacency and the boasting and lying of many of our highest public officials have been intolerable. I have been holding these officials to sharp account; and, for the very reason that the Administration loathes me, I can flail them into a shambling and reluctant acceleration of speed. . . . Talking is a pretty poor business at such a time as this; but it is all I am permitted to do—and I do it.

I have just finished a week's trip to Ohio, Iowa, Wisconsin and Michigan. Whenever possible—and it was generally possible—I had a staunch American of German blood introduce me; I preached the straightest kind of doctrine on Americanism and on putting the war through, by hard, downright fighting, by the use of millions of men in the fighting line, with ample number of guns and airplanes; and I was cheered to the echo. Our people are waking up. Wisconsin accepted the anti-German pro-War doctrine with enthusiasm. . . .

Did I tell you that Peter Dunne met me the other day, grinned, and remarked: "Well! the first thing you know your four sons will put the name of Roosevelt on the map!" They have done it! And if I *had* to

* Richard Derby, husband of Ethel Roosevelt.

choose, I would rather have had you four stand at Armageddon even than stand there myself. You, personally, are now in the position of greatest danger; but when the trumpets sound for Armageddon only those win the undying honor and glory who stand where the danger is sorest.

Sagamore Hill, July 7th, 1918.

The reputation you have made for yourself is extraordinary; and close behind you come your three brothers. I cannot begin to tell you how proud I am of you. . . . John King, the Connecticut National Committeeman, has just written me that in Washington the Congressmen feel that what my four sons have done makes *me* a person of consequence! It is the sober truth that for the last year my strongest title to the regard of my fellow countrymen has lain in the gallantry and efficiency of you four boys. And Dick stands alongside you.[21]

Sagamore Hill, July 21st, 1918.

After three days of uncertainty yesterday afternoon it was definitely announced that Quentin had been killed and not captured. . . .

Flora[22] is utterly heartbroken, of course. She is young, and time will mercifully heal her sorrow; but she has had her golden dream and it has proved only a dream. If only she could have married Quentin! Thank Heaven, you other boys have wives and children.

The fine gallantry of Quentin's death has stirred our whole people; I have never known such widespread expressions—in editorials, in speeches, in articles—of pride and sorrow and admiration.

I need hardly tell you that Mother has borne herself with the dauntless courage she always shows in hours of great trial. We have both, of course, gone about our business as usual. I kept my engagements to speak to the Saratoga Republican convention and to receive Harry Davison and the Japanese Red Cross mission. . . .

Well, no four boys in the country—nor in any other country—have made such a record as you four have made. And Dick, too, and Eleanor[23] almost more than all. It is very bitter to me that all of you, the young, should be facing death while I sit in ease and safety;[24] I don't think I could bear it if I couldn't look back twenty years and know that in a far

---

[21] Unpublished letters in the possession of Mrs. Theodore Roosevelt, Jr.

[22] Flora Whitney was engaged to Quentin Roosevelt.

[23] Eleanor Alexander, wife of Theodore Roosevelt, Jr.

[24] Mr. Roosevelt offered to raise two divisions of "outdoor men," beyond draft age—285,000 men, in fact, clamored to serve under him. Congress authorized the formation of the divisions but President Wilson refused his permission.

less dangerous but somewhat similar matter I did the same kind of thing myself.[25]

Sagamore Hill, July 24th, 1918

Well, Quentin will take his place with young Shaw and young Lowell of the Civil War; and the "fighting Roosevelts" will stand beside the "fighting McCooks." . . . Hadley of Yale wrote me . . . quoting the great line of Napier's about the English officer at the storming of Badajos: "None died that night with greater glory; yet many died and there was great glory"! Just at the time the papers came containing the full accounts of your wound and success and leadership and proud gallantry; and I got Napier and read the whole account of the storming of Badajos to Mother and Alice and Ethel; it was one of the great feats of valor of the ages; and yet already our four boys had shown that they had the right to stand on the honor roll beside the bravest in that or any other battle of recorded history.[26]

To Belle Willard Roosevelt[27]

Dark Harbor, Maine, August 11, 1918

It is no use pretending that Quentin's death is not very terrible. It is most so for poor Flora who is staying here with Ethel, as we are. But it is almost as hard for Mother. They have both been very brave. There is nothing to comfort Flora at the moment; but she is young. . . . As for Mother, her heart will ache for Quentin until she dies. I would not for all the world have had him fail fearlessly to do his duty, and to tread his allotted path, high of heart, even altho it led to the gates of death. But it is useless for me to pretend that it is not very bitter to see that good, gallant, tender-hearted boy, leave life at its crest, when it held Flora, and such happiness, and certainly an honorable and perhaps a distinguished career.

Evidently Archie is crippled, at least for many months to come, and I wish he would come home. Hitherto the rascal has refused. I wouldn't suggest it if he could render any service with the army, but to spend months of pain and idleness in Paris, instead of at least being with his wife and baby and his mother, doesn't seem worth while.

Ted has apparently recovered from the gassing, and will soon recover from the bullet wounds in his leg; I am so glad he is with Eleanor. I don't

[25] Unpublished letters in the possession of Mrs. Theodore Roosevelt, Jr.
[26] *Ibid.*
[27] Wife of Kermit Roosevelt.

yet know just what Kermit is doing, for I have had no letter from him since he got to France.[28]

Oyster Bay, N.Y., Aug. 13, 1918.

When we reached here we found Quentin's last letters; he was at the fighting front, very proud and happy—and singularly modest, with all his pride, and his pleasure at showing his metal. Of course that was a wonderful company of men, flying in the swift battle planes—not the ordinary observation or bombing planes—at the front; they were bound together in the close ties of men who knew that most of them are to die, and who face their fate high of heart and with a gallant defiance; and Quentin wrote that he would not for any consideration have been anywhere else. Two days before he was killed he was with Eleanor in Paris; and she was so proud of him, and took him round as the young hero. He had his crowded hour of glorious life.[29]

To Georges Clemenceau[30]

Oyster Bay, N.Y., July 25, 1918

It is a very sad thing to see the young die when the old, who are doing nothing, as I am doing nothing, are left alive. Therefore it is very bitter to me that I was not allowed to face the danger with my sons. But whatever may be their fate, I am glad and proud that my sons have done their part in this mighty war against despotism and barbarism. Of my four boys, Quentin, as you know, has been killed, and two of the other three wounded and all three of these have been decorated for gallantry and efficiency in action.

Thank Heaven, it begins to look as if at last Germany had spent her strength, and I thank Heaven also that we now have at least a few hundred thousand Americans to fight beside the French.[31]

11. The Great Adventure

Only those are fit to live who do not fear to die; and none are fit to die who have shrunk from the joy of life and the duty of life. Both life and death are parts of the same Great Adventure. Never yet was worthy adventure worthily carried through by the man who put his personal safety first. Never yet was a country worth living in unless its sons and daugh-

[28] *Letters VIII*, pp. 1359–60.
[29] *Ibid.*, pp. 1360–1.
[30] Leading French political leader; subsequently Premier of France.
[31] *Letters VIII*, pp. 1354–5.

ters were of that stern stuff which bade them die for it at need; and never yet was a country worth dying for unless its sons and daughters thought of life not as something concerned only with the selfish evanescence of the individual, but as a link in the great chain of creation and causation, so that each person is seen in his true relations as an essential part of the whole, whose life must be made to serve the larger and continuing life of the whole. Therefore it is that the man who is not willing to die, and the woman who is not willing to send her man to die, in a war for a great cause, are not worthy to live. Therefore it is that the man and woman who in peace-time fear or ignore the primary and vital duties and the high happiness of family life, who dare not beget and bear and rear the life that is to last when they are in their graves, have broken the chain of creation, and have shown that they are unfit for companionship with the souls ready for the Great Adventure. . . .

With all my heart I believe in the joy of living; but those who achieve it do not seek it as an end in itself, but as a seized and prized incident of hard work well done and of risk and danger never wantonly courted, but never shirked when duty commands that they be faced. And those who have earned joy, but are rewarded only with sorrow, must learn the stern comfort dear to great souls, the comfort that springs from the knowledge taught in times of iron that the law of worthy living is not fulfilled by pleasure, but by service, and by sacrifice when only thereby can service be rendered.

No nation can be great unless its sons and daughters have in them the quality to rise level to the needs of heroic days. Yet this heroic quality is but the apex of a pyramid of which the broad foundations must solidly rest on the performance of duties so ordinary that to impatient minds they seem commonplace. No army was ever great unless its soldiers possessed the fighting edge. But the finest natural fighting edge is utterly useless unless the soldiers and the junior officers have been through months, and the officers of higher command and the general staff through years, of hard, weary, intensive training. So likewise the citizenship of any country is worthless unless in a crisis it shows the spirit of the two million Americans who in this mighty war have eagerly come forward to serve under the Banner of the Stars, afloat and ashore, and of the other millions who would now be beside them overseas if the chance had been given them; and yet such spirit will in the long run avail nothing unless in the years of peace the average man and average woman of the duty-performing type realize that the highest of all duties, the one essential duty, is the duty of perpetuating the family life, based on the mutual love and respect of the one man and the one woman, and on their purpose to rear the healthy and fine-souled children whose coming into life means that the family and, therefore, the nation shall continue in life and shall not end in a sterile death.

Woe to those who invite a sterile death; a death not for them only, but for the race; the death which is insured by a life of sterile selfishness.

But honor, highest honor, to those who fearlessly face death for a good cause; no life is so honorable or so fruitful as such a death. Unless men are willing to fight and die for great ideals, including love of country, ideals will vanish, and the world will become one huge sty of materialism. And unless the women of ideals bring forth the men who are ready thus to live and die, the world of the future will be filled by the spawn of the unfit. Alone of human beings the good and wise mother stands on a plane of equal honor with the bravest soldier; for she has gladly gone down to the brink of the chasm of darkness to bring back the children in whose hands rests the future of the years. But the mother, and far more the father who flinch from the vital task earn the scorn visited on the soldier who flinches in battle. And the nation should by action mark its attitude alike toward the fighter in war and toward the child-bearer in peace and war. The vital need of the nation is that its men and women of the future shall be the sons and daughters of the soldiers of the present. Excuse no man from going to war because he is married; but put all unmarried men above a fixed age at the hardest and most dangerous tasks; and provide amply for the children of soldiers, so as to give their wives the assurance of material safety.

In such a matter one can only speak in general terms. At this moment there are hundreds of thousands of gallant men eating out their hearts because the privilege of facing death in battle is denied them. So there are innumerable women and men whose undeserved misfortune it is that they have no children or but one child. These soldiers denied the perilous honor they seek, these men and women heart-hungry for the children of their longing dreams, are as worthy of honor as the men who are warriors in fact, as the women whose children are of flesh and blood. If the only son who is killed at the front has no brother because his parents coldly dreaded to play their part in the Great Adventure of Life, then our sorrow is not for them, but solely for the son who himself dared the Great Adventure of Death. If, however, he is the only son because the Unseen Powers denied others to the love of his father and mother, then we mourn doubly with them because their darling went up to the sword of Azrael, because he drank the dark drink proffered by the Death Angel.

In America to-day all our people are summoned to service and sacrifice. Pride is the portion only of those who know bitter sorrow or the foreboding of bitter sorrow. But all of us who give service, and stand ready for sacrifice, are the torch-bearers. We run with the torches until we fall, content if we can then pass them to the hands of other runners. The torches whose flame is brightest are borne by the gallant men at the front, and by the gallant women whose husbands and lovers, whose sons and brothers are at the front. These men are high of soul, as they face their fate on the shell-shattered earth, or in the skies above or in the waters beneath; and no less high of soul are the women with torn hearts and shining eyes; the girls whose boy-lovers have been struck down in their golden morning, and the mothers and wives to whom word has been brought that henceforth they must walk in the shadow.

These are the torch-bearers; these are they who have dared the Great Adventure.[32]

12. "I cannot be with you . . ."

To Richard M. Hurd[33]

Oyster Bay, N.Y., January 3, 1919

I cannot be with you and so all I can do is to wish you Godspeed.[34] There must be no sagging back in the fight for Americanism merely because the war is over. There are plenty of persons who have already made the assertion that they believe the American people have a short memory and that they intend to revive all the foreign associations which most directly interfere with the complete Americanization of our people. Our principle in this matter should be absolutely simple. In the first place, we should insist that if the immigrant who comes here does in good faith become an American and assimilates himself to us, he shall be treated on an exact equality with everyone else, for it is an outrage to discriminate against any such man because of creed, or birthplace, or origin. But this is predicated upon the man's becoming in very fact an American and nothing but an American. If he tries to keep segregated with men of his own origin and separated from the rest of America, then he isn't doing his part as an American. There can be no divided allegiance here. Any man who says he is an American but something else also, isn't an American at all. We have room for but one flag, the American flag, and this excludes the red flag which symbolizes all wars against liberty and civilization, just as much as it excludes any foreign flag of a nation to which

---

[32] *Works XIX*, pp. 243–7.

[33] President, American Defense Society.

[34] This letter was read by a representative of the American Defense Society to the audience at an all-American benefit concert held at the Hippodrome in New York on January 5, 1919. The papers reported it next morning as "Colonel Roosevelt's last message to the American people."

we are hostile. We have room for but one language here and that is the English language, for we intend to see that the crucible turns our people out as Americans, of American nationality, and not as dwellers in a polyglot boarding-house; and we have room for but one soul loyalty, and that loyalty is to the American people.[35]

[35] *Letters VIII,* p. 1422.

DATE DUE

FE 21 '63	April 29,66	
AP 5 '63	May 13, 86	
	May 27, 86	
DE 10 '63	MAY 2 6 '66	
FEB 1 2 '65		
MY 10 '65		
DE 28 '65		
JA 17 '66		
FEB 2 1 '68		
MAR 6 '68		
MAR 1 8 '68		
APR 2 '68		
'APR 1 3 '69		
JAN 2 5 '70		
MAY 1 84		
MAY 1 3 1984		
APR 1 '86		
April 15, 86		